Fodor's

ESSENTIAL CROATIA

WELCOME TO CROATIA

Croatia's splendors extend from the deep-blue waters of the Adriatic coastline to the waterfall-laced mountains of the Dinaric Alps and throughout its medieval towns. From Dubrovnik's walled city where baroque buildings are surrounded by centuries-old forts to the lively islands of Brač and Hvar, this Central European country is an exciting blend of glamour and tradition. Croatia's vibrant, historic cities, sprawling vineyards, gorgeous beaches, and thousand-plus islands give travelers plenty of places to dance, sip wine, sail, and soak up the sunshine.

TOP REASONS TO GO

★ **History:** Dubrovnik's walled Old Town, Split's Diocletian palace.

★ **Cool Cities:** Zagreb's museums and café culture, Rovinj's old city charm.

★ **Beaches:** From secluded hideaways to ocean-side party spots, each beach is unique.

★ **Natural Parks:** Plitvice Lakes, Brijuni Islands, Mljet.

★ **Wine:** From Istria to Korčula, vineyards and wineries abound.

★ **Sailing:** Southern Dalmatia's dramatic coastline is paradise for boating enthusiasts.

12 TOP EXPERIENCES

Croatia offers terrific experiences that should be on every traveler's list. Here are Fodor's top picks for a memorable trip.

1 Dubrovnik

Few sights in Croatia are as impressive or popular as this medieval wonder of a city. With its ancient walls and bell towers set high above the blue waters of the Adriatic, Dubrovnik commands a spectacular location. *(Ch. 8)*

2 Sailing

A coastline studded with stunning islands, emerald inlets, unspoiled beaches, and lively towns makes the country a paradise for avid boating enthusiasts. *(Ch. 1)*

3 Diocletian's Palace, Split

The city's main attraction, the Roman emperor Diocletian's summer palace, dates to the 3rd century AD. The walls of this spectacular site surround the old town. *(Ch. 7)*

4 Hvar Town

The seaside town of Hvar is the country's nightlife capital and a favorite destination of yachting revelers and nature enthusiasts alike. *(Ch. 7)*

5 Seafood

Croatians believe in simple yet high-quality cooking. Many restaurants serve delicious fresh seafood, and sometimes you can pick a fish to be cooked right off the platter. *(Ch. 7)*

6 National Parks

Parks protect some of Croatia's abundant natural wonders. Plitvice National Park, one of the most spectacular, has 16 magnificent lakes connected by cascades. *(Ch. 2)*

7 Museums in Zagreb

Two of the country's best museums are in Zagreb, the charming capital set in the interior: the Museum of Contemporary Art and the Museum of Broken Relationships. *(Ch. 2)*

8 Wine

Vineyards produce excellent wines, many from Istrian villages like Motovun. Sometimes touted as "the new Tuscany," Istria is known for its white Malvazija and red Teran. *(Ch. 4)*

9 Café Culture

Coffee drinking is a favorite national pastime. Do it the local way: linger at a café, unwind, and make that cappuccino or espresso last for at least an hour. *(Ch. 2)*

10 Beaches

Lovely beaches abound in Croatia, but Zlatni Rat, a spit of land on Brač Island, is particularly stunning with its white sand, lush pine groves, and intensely blue water. *(Ch. 7)*

11 Biking

Exploring towns and the countryside by bike is both fun and smart. Village streets aren't always easy to navigate on foot, and rural roads have scenic views. *(Ch. 4)*

12 Picturesque towns

It's hard to imagine a city with a more romantic and relaxing setting than quaint Rovinj, with its gentle sea breezes, limestone alleys, and colorful architecture. *(Ch. 4)*

CONTENTS

CONTENTS

MAPS

ABOUT THIS GUIDE

Fodor's Recommendations

Everything in this guide is worth doing—we don't cover what isn't—but exceptional sights, hotels, and restaurants are recognized with additional accolades. Fodor's Choice★ indicates our top recommendations. Care to nominate a new place? Visit Fodors.com/contact-us.

Trip Costs

We list prices wherever possible to help you budget well. Hotel and restaurant price categories from **$** to **$$$$** are noted alongside each recommendation. For hotels, we include the lowest cost of a standard double room in high season. For restaurants, we cite the average price of a main course at dinner or, if dinner isn't served, at lunch. For attractions, we always list adult admission fees; discounts are usually available for children, students, and senior citizens.

Hotels

Our local writers vet every hotel to recommend the best overnights in each price category, from budget to expensive. Unless otherwise specified, you can expect private bath, phone, and TV in your room. Hotel reviews have been shortened. For full information, visit Fodors.com.

Top Picks
- ★ Fodor's Choice

Listings
- Address
- Branch address
- Telephone
- Fax
- Website
- E-mail
- Admission fee
- Open/closed times
- Subway
- Directions or Map coordinates

Hotels & Restaurants
- Hotel
- Number of rooms
- Meal plans
- Restaurant
- Reservations
- Dress code
- No credit cards
- Price

Other
- See also
- Take note
- Golf facilities

Restaurants

Unless we state otherwise, restaurants are open for lunch and dinner daily. We mention dress code only when there's a specific requirement and reservations only when they're essential or not accepted. To make restaurant reservations, visit Fodors.com.

Credit Cards

The hotels and restaurants in this guide typically accept credit cards. If not, we'll say so.

EUGENE FODOR

Hungarian-born Eugene Fodor (1905–91) began his travel career as an interpreter on a French cruise ship. The experience inspired him to write *On the Continent* (1936), the first guidebook to receive annual updates and discuss a country's way of life as well as its sights. Fodor later joined the U.S. Army and worked for the OSS in World War II. After the war, he kept up his intelligence work while expanding his guidebook series. During the Cold War, many guides were written by fellow agents who understood the value of insider information. Today's guides continue Fodor's legacy by providing travelers with timely coverage, insider tips, and cultural context.

EXPERIENCE CROATIA

WHAT'S WHERE

1 Zagreb. Croatia's interior capital is a charming, well-kept city that evokes a distant Habsburg past and features a pretty Upper Town. That said, Zagreb does fall short of Vienna or Prague in terms of stature and architecture. Good roads lead to the coast: Plitvice National Park—a spectacular series of 16 cascading lakes nestled in a wild forest—is about halfway to Zadar.

2 Slavonia. The country's largest and least-visited region offers charming Panonian villages and quiet rural life. Come if you want to get away from the hordes of tourists and experience traditional local food and arts fairs.

3 Istria. The distinct Roman and Venetian influences blend into a vibrant café scene and authentic culinary delights. Croatia's western peninsula is well situated, with the western coast as the highlight and beautiful hilltops and vineyards inland.

4 Kvarner. Protected by mountain ranges on three sides, Kvarner enjoys a particularly mild climate. Opatija, the best-known destination, offers a whiff of the faded aristocratic grandeur of the Habsburgs and acts as a portal to the postindustrial Rijeka and the green Kvarner islands.

5 Northern Dalmatia. Zadar doesn't rival Split or Dubrovnik for ancient ruins, but it is surrounded by four beautiful national parks and offers good museums, some excellent restaurants, and the impressive Church of St. Donatus.

6 Split and Central Dalmatia. Split boasts good transport connections and its main attraction: the Diocletian's palace, which dominates the Old Town. You're also in a great position to set out island hopping, be it to Vis, Brač, or Hvar, a haven for partiers and yachting revelers.

7 Southern Dalmatia. Few cities in the world impress as Dubrovnik does, with its ancient walls and towers perched above the deep blue waters of the Adriatic. If you need to escape, strike out for Korčula, Marco Polo's birthplace, or the quiet Mljet Island.

8 Montenegro. An independent country since 2006, tiny Montenegro lies on the Adriatic coast and is bordered by Croatia, Bosnia-Herzegovina, Serbia, Kosovo, and Albania. Although its name means "black mountain," the main draw is its beautiful coastline.

NEED TO KNOW

AT A GLANCE

Capital: Zagreb

Population: 4,284,889

Currency: Kuna (Kn)

Money: ATMs are common, and cash preferred at cheaper places

Language: Croatian

Country Code: 385

Emergencies: 112

Driving: On the right

Electricity: 200v/50 cycles; electrical plugs have two round prongs

Time: Six hours ahead of New York

Documents: Up to 90 days with valid passport; Schengen rules apply

Mobile Phones: GSM (900 and 1800 bands)

Major Mobile Companies: T-Mobile, Vipnet, Tele2

WEBSITES

Croatia: 🌐 *www.croatia.hr*

Dubrovnik: 🌐 *www.tzdubrovnik.hr*

Hvar Town: 🌐 *www.tzhvar.hr*

GETTING AROUND

✈ **Air Travel:** The major airports are Zagreb, Dubrovnik, and Split.

Boat Travel: Frequent ferries link Split to Hvar, and a (rather slow) twice-weekly coastal ferry runs between Split and Dubrovnik.

Car Travel: You might rent a car to drive down the coast from Split to Dubrovnik or to explore the interior of the island of Hvar, but in Split and Dubrovnik themselves, a car is unnecessary.

Train Travel: Daily trains link Zagreb with Split, but there is no rail service south of Split to Dubrovnik.

PLAN YOUR BUDGET

	HOTEL ROOM	MEAL	ATTRACTIONS
Low Budget	€100	60 Kn	War Photo Limited, Dubrovnik, 60 Kn.
Mid Budget	€160	150 Kn	City Walls, Dubrovnik, 90 Kn.
High Budget	€400	240 Kn	Dubrovnik Summer Festival ticket, 150 Kn–350 Kn

WAYS TO SAVE

Eat lunch picnic-style. Shop for fresh bread, cheese, and seasonal fruit, and eat by the sea.

Book a rental apartment. Dalmatia has plenty of comfortable self-catering apartments, offering more space and a kitchen, which are cheaper than hotels.

Use public transport. Bus travel between Dubrovnik and Split is easier than driving. Hvar has good bus service.

Night of the Museums. On the last Friday in January, more than 100 Croatian museums and galleries offer free entry from 6 pm to 1 am.

PLAN YOUR TIME

Hassle Factor	Medium. There are no nonstop flights from the United States to Croatia, but in summer numerous airlines offer air connections via Europe to Dubrovnik and Split.
3 days	You can visit both Dubrovnik and Split for a brief taste of what Dalmatia has to offer.
1 week	Combine the magnificent coastal cities of Dubrovnik and Split with a few days' chilling out on the island of Hvar.
2 weeks	You have time both to move around and to see the highlights, including several days in both Dubrovnik and Split, plus excursions to the islands, most notably Hvar, and adventure sports such as sailing, scuba diving, and sea kayaking.

WHEN TO GO

High Season: July through August is the most expensive and popular time to visit Dalmatia. August is especially crowded. The weather is hot and sunny, ideal for the beach.

Low Season: Winter offers the least appealing weather, though it's the best time for hotel deals and seeing Dalmatia without the tourists. However, some hotels and many restaurants close completely, and museums have restricted opening hours.

Value Season: May through June and September through October offer warm, sunny weather, though you should be prepared for occasional rain—at times torrential—as the seasons change in May and October. As it's not too hot or crowded, these months are ideal for sightseeing. Hotel prices tend to be more reasonable and restaurants less busy.

BIG EVENTS

February: Dubrovnik's Carnival week culminates with a masked ball before Lent.

July/August: Dubrovnik Summer Festival sees world-renowned musicians and actors performing at open-air venues in the Old Town. 🌐 www.dubrovnik-festival.hr

July/August: The Split Summer Festival brings opera, classical music, dance, and theater. 🌐 www.splitsko-ljeto.hr

August: The Hvar Half Marathon draws competitors on a run from Stari Grad (Old Town) to Hvar Town. 🌐 www.hvarmarathon.com

READ THIS

- ***Black Lamb and Grey Falcon,*** Rebecca West. A journey through pre-WWII Yugoslavia.
- ***Croatia: A Nation Forged by War,*** Marcus Tanner. How Croatia won its independence.
- ***Café Europa:*** *Life after Communism*, Slavenka Drakulić. Yugoslavia after the fall of communism.

WATCH THIS

- ***Game of Thrones.*** Filming locations in both Dubrovnik and Split.
- ***Casanova.*** This BBC miniseries was partly filmed in Dubrovnik.
- ***Bridget's Sexiest Beaches.*** The Travel Channel series (Season 1, Ep. 2) visited Dubrovnik and Hvar.

EAT THIS

- ***Salata od hobotnice:*** a flavorful octopus salad
- ***Crni rižot:*** black risotto, made from cuttlefish ink
- ***Škampi na buzaru:*** shrimps sautéed with olive oil, garlic, and white wine
- ***Pršut:*** Dalmatian smoked, dried ham, similar to Italian prosciutto
- ***Pašticada:*** beef stewed in wine and prunes, served with gnocchi
- ***Palačinke:*** crepes, filled with walnut cream, chocolate, or apricot jam

CROATIA TODAY

After centuries of being a part of larger political entities, Croatia's quarter century of independence has been anything but steady. Coming out of the blocks into a messy civil war, Croatia very swiftly traveled the long and winding road from a war zone to one of Europe's must-see travel destinations.

Politics and economy aside, Croatian territory encompasses some of the most stunning locations on the Mediterranean. From the truffle-bearing forests of Istria to the stunning limestone cities of Dalmatia, Croatia is hands-down a singularly beautiful country. As little as five years ago, it still stood out as the "best buy" spot on the Mediterranean, with history, sights, service, and safety at reasonable rates. But with the migrant crisis that affected Turkey, Greece, and Italy, Croatia has seen an unprecedented tourist boom in the last three years. A rapid expansion in hotel units has been coupled by a significant increase in prices, making the country part ways with its budget-friendly reputation. That said, it has hardly caught up with top Italian and French destinations.

Communist Turned Elitist Goes Commercial

The stunning coast was always there. Different rulers treated it differently, and to this date it is clearly visible in the architecture, ranging from Roman to Venetian and Napoleonic, Habsburg, Italian, and finally communist. The communist government of Yugoslavia built numerous simple, working-class hotels in the 1960s and '70s. Yugoslavia is no more, but the buildings remain. In the 1990s many of them housed refugees from the war. Hotels became dilapidated, and tourism was pushed back decades.

It took surprisingly little for the country to rebound, attract investors, and completely remodel the socialist hotels. They're still a bit of an eyesore on the outside, but inside are all necessary amenities, which increasingly flirt with luxury. The older hotels, most of them from the Habsburg era, as well as the ones built after Croatia's independence, are generally on the high end and can compete with luxury hotels anywhere on the continent. In a short time, Croatia has stepped up and entered the ring with the European tourism heavyweights.

On the downside, the continued increase in visitors is also leading to a potential trap: the untouched coast gives way to large resorts, overcrowded beaches, and traffic issues. Ironically, the success of the national tourist board's former slogan, "The Mediterranean as It Once Was," has made itself obsolete.

Open Borders and Economic Woes

Unlike the booming tourist industry, the rest of the country's economy has had two and a half very rough decades and looks toward the future with a pessimistic eye. The transition period from communism to capitalism was marked by a lack of transparency and by controversy on the highest levels, leaving the young country industrially handicapped as it entered the third millennium. Consequently, more focus was placed on developing tourism as an industry, a move that has proven successful, but only really offering work stability for six months a year, neglecting the question of long-term economic growth and demographic recovery.

The long-awaited accession into the European Union in 2013 opened the door for a freer movement of capital and people. Considerable capital entered the country, but people, especially young Croats seeking a more secure future, left for places like Germany and Ireland.

Safe and Sporty

Despite its standards not yet being on par with Western Europe, Croatia is still a remarkably safe country with one of the lowest violent crime rates in Europe. Social frustration is more often vented on the roads, with some Croatian drivers choosing to obey few rules or even common sense. Even experienced drivers should be cautious while navigating the narrow local roads, as many local drivers always seem to be in a hurry and angry about something.

The one place where there is little anger, however, is undoubtedly in the domain of sports. Croatians are very passionate about sports and, for a country of just 4.8 million, extremely successful, too. If visiting during a major international competition like the Olympic Games or the World Cup, you will have a chance to spend your evening at one of the many cafés where locals and tourists gather to watch games and share in the excitement. The game, mind you, is just the beginning of the night: a fruitful platform for recollections of times and successes past.

In Tune

If there is one thing that a visitor to Croatia should not miss in the summer months, it would be a concert or a music festival. From house to Wagner, from pop to jazz, Zagreb and the coast have it all covered. There are big music festivals and concerts that attract thousands of Croatians and foreigners alike, but there are also countless small-scale gigs that resound with the Croatians' appreciation of eclectic music.

The thriving music scene partly compensates for the mostly uninspiring theatrical events and fine arts exhibitions, of which there is ample quantity but considerably less quality. Bigger cities like Zagreb, Split, or Dubrovnik will occasionally host memorable international events. Additionally, visitors will find a satisfactory number of film festivals in Croatia, most of them carrying an interesting blend of non-mainstream international films.

The New Generation

Few differences are as apparent as the schism in customer service and attitude between the generation that grew up in communist Yugoslavia and the younger generation that has been exposed to Western influences and education. Perhaps the most pragmatic difference is of linguistic nature: older people will be more likely to speak German, Italian, or even Russian, while younger ones inexorably lean toward English, which they speak very well.

Despite the steep increase in tourism numbers, customer service is not universally understood around Croatia, and there are still places, especially in Dalmatia, where you will wait for 10 or more minutes before the waiter notices you, or worse, your hosts decides to share their views of U.S. politics without having been asked to do so. Thankfully, such instances are few and far between, but if they do occur, try to smile and not let the unpleasantness affect the amazing holiday that Croatia can offer.

QUINTESSENTIAL CROATIA

Dalmatian Summer

For many Croatians, summer holidays mean Dalmatia. Every family has its favorite spot on the coast and people fondly remember their blissful childhood holidays here. Tales of Dingač or Plavac wine, *paski sir* (sheep cheese from the island of Pag), and fresh sea bass enjoyed in a simple seaside restaurant feature heavily in the national memory. Whether a holiday means a wooded campsite in a national park, a sandy beach on Brač, or a small pension on Losinj, summer holidays begin and end for Croatians on their own splendid coast. Roads, accommodations, and ferry travel along the coast have improved over the years, turning Dalmatia into an international tourist destination. After you've relaxed for a week or more, soaking up the sun Dalmatian-style, you'll ask the same question the Croatians do: why go anywhere else?

Rakija

Get one or two Croatians together, and somebody's bound to introduce *rakija,* a distilled herbal or fruit spirit that makes up an important part of Croatian culture. All across the country, business deals are sealed, friendships are cemented, and journeys are begun to the clink of a few shot glasses of the fiery schnapps. Croatians often brew rakija themselves at home, using everything from plums and pears to herbs and juniper berries. In the countryside you can often find roadside stands selling the family blend with pride. Rakija is also enjoyed in Slovenia, where it often begins a meal as an aperitif. If you're game to order one on your travels in the region, start first with the sweeter, fruitier brews (blueberry is a good choice), and then work your way up to the somewhat digestive herbals.

If you want to get a sense of contemporary Croatian culture, and indulge in some of its pleasures, start by familiarizing yourself with the rituals of daily life. These are a few highlights—things you can take part in with relative ease.

Naturism

There's a long history of naturism here and Croatia has been one of the most progressive in pioneering the nude resort. Naturist campsites, beaches, and even sailing charters abound in certain parts of the coast (mainly Istria), and hundreds of thousands come here each year to enjoy some fun in the sun *au naturel*. Naturism in Croatia goes back to before World War II, when a leading Viennese naturist developed a beach on the island of Rab. Since then, a thriving culture has taken root, mainly among European enthusiasts. A glossy brochure published by the Croatian National Tourist Board lists 14 naturist "camps" and "villages" and about as many officially designated "free naturist beaches" on the country's Adriatic coast. Croatians themselves don't seem to make up the bulk of the clientele at naturist resorts, but they graciously make visitors welcome.

Face to Face

Generally speaking, Croatians make for good hosts who are eager to help and show you around. This is true for people who don't work in tourism but are happy to be asked a question, dust off their English, and share their opinions of the places you should see. Feel free to give your smartphone a day off and ask for directions the old-fashioned way. There is just one thing, though: personal space is significantly smaller in Croatia than it is the United States. Croatians stand a mere foot from each other as they communicate, often giving out the impression that they are all discussing matters of utmost delicacy. It might feel like you're being crowded but don't be taken aback—it's the local communication culture.

GREAT ITINERARIES

WESTERN CROATIA IN A WEEK: ZAGREB, ISTRIA, AND KVARNER

Zagreb makes an excellent starting point if your trip is meant to cover western Croatia in a week. You'll get the mountains and the seaside, city and countryside, and a first-class Roman ruin. This itinerary is best done by car, but it can be done (perhaps a bit more slowly) by train and bus.

Day 1: Zagreb

Zagreb is a compact city that begs to be explored on foot. Begin at the massive Ban Jelačić Square and check out the statue of Ban Josip Jelačić, hero of Croatian resistance to the Austro-Hungarian empire. It's an imposing figure on an imposing square. From here walk to the funicular and head to the Gornji grad (Upper Town). Stroll around the castle area and visit the Croatian Historical Museum. You'll get a glimpse of Croatia's recent history, including the controversial nationalism of the 1990s. From here, head back down to the Lower Town and check out Ilica, Zagreb's modern high street. Spend the night here.

Day 2: Plitvice Lakes

The next morning head south toward the coast, getting off the highway in Karlovac in the direction of Plitvice National Park. Plitvice is a naturally occurring water world, with 19 crystal-clear pools and connectted by cascades and waterfalls connecting. A UNESCO World Heritage Site, this is one of Croatia's biggest tourist sites and has been for years, so the park is well protected and organized. Consider getting a map and exploring the lakes, which cover about 300 square km (186½ square miles) on your own. The park is well marked, but the guided tours take you only to the highlights. Relax in the evening when the all tour buses have gone home and spend the night at a hotel in one of the nearby towns of Mukinje or Jezerce. Both are a nice walking distance from the park.

Day 3: Rab Island

The drive to Rab Island from Plitvice involves heading down the country's biggest mountain, Velebit, to the eastern Kvarner coast. Catch a ferry to Rab, one of the bay's most beautiful islands. The northeastern side of the island is mostly barren but the southwestern side is covered by one of the last oak forests of the Mediterranean. Once there, take in the sights of the medieval stone town of Rab, renowned for its history, coast, and Mediterranean herbs. Also take the opportunity to visit one of Croatia's top wineries, where you can also spend the night. If you still have the energy, take a ferry from Rab to the island of Krk and enjoy the cliff-top town of Valbiska, home of the Zlahtina white wine.

Day 4: Rijeka and Opatija

Take the ferry from Rab or the bridge from Krk and head out to Opatija, briefly stopping in the city of Rijeka for a stroll down the pedestrian zone Korzo. Once you see the palm trees lining the streets of Opatija, you'll see this is a place for winding down, Habsburg-style. Choose one of the atmospheric, turn-of-the-century hotels for a little slice of nostalgia and settle in with a good book. Should you visit in winter, you'll find the weather downright Mediterranean. Take time to stroll along a part of the 12-km-long (7½-mile-long) promenade that zigzags along the sea. If you get antsy for more seaside diversity, plan instead to leave Opatija and catch the Istrian side ferry

to the islands of Cres and Lošinj. The islands—with their attractive Venetian town squares—have a different character altogether.

Day 5: Pula

From Opatija or Lošinj head south or west, respectively, to Pula and spend a part of the day exploring the incredible Roman amphitheater. This is one of the best-preserved sites in the Roman world. After walking about the Roman forum and amphitheater, as well as Napoleon's fortress on the top of the hill, take a boat to the Brijuni Islands for the afternoon and see the zoo and tropical gardens that Tito designed. Drive the short distance to Rovinj for the night.

Day 6: Rovinj and Poreč

Wake up to the beautiful limestone architecture of Rovinj before exploring the Venetian houses and Church of St. Euphemia in the morning. From there, stop off at one of the many fine wineries en route to Poreč, another Roman-meets-Venetian-meets-Habsburg seaside gem. Check out the St. Euphrasius basilica, one of the most important remnants of Byzantine art on the Adriatic. Spend the night at any of the fine hotels.

TIPS

- This itinerary is well served by bus, although that may take more time than driving yourself.
- The main highway connecting Zagreb to Istria, the A6, is well maintained and offers beautiful views of Gorski Kotar. Toll can be paid in cash or by card.
- Since Plitvice is on the main highway from Zagreb to Zadar, consider seeing the park on a weekday, when traffic is lighter.
- The closest ferry crossing from Opatija to Cres and Lošinj is at Brestova in Istria. If you plan to take your car in the height of summer, count on a wait. In winter it is much less crowded.

Day 7: Motovun and Zagreb

Head back to Zagreb via the Istrian interior. Drive east toward Pazin, stopping in the medieval hill towns of Motovun or Grožnjan for lunch and breathtaking views. These medieval villages are in the heart of truffle country, so keep your eyes open for some fresh goods to bring home. Continue northeast toward Zagreb on A6, possibly stopping at the mountain town of Fužine for the famous cherry strudel with views of Lake Bajer.

GREAT ITINERARIES

ISLAND HOPPING AND NATIONAL PARKS: CENTRAL AND NORTHERN DALMATIA

Well connected to the rest of the country, Central and Northern Dalmatia have a lot to offer, even beyond the staple cities of Split and Zadar. Plan for a combination of car and boat travel, and try to schedule the car trips on weekdays. The roads can get busy during weekends, peaking on Saturday, especially if you get on the A1 highway. Avoid taking the car to the islands to circumvent both intimidating ferry lines and scarily narrow island roads. Both Split and Zadar have international airports, so you can start this itinerary from either one.

Day 1: Split

Arrive in Split and head to a hotel (which you booked months ago) or take one of the many private rooms available around town. Spend this first day getting your bearings and exploring the Meštrović Gallery and the Archaeological Museum, two of the city's best museums, before dedicating at least half a day to Diocletian's Palace. Sit in the open peristyle and admire the imperial quarters, the Cathedral of St. Domnius, and the Egyptian black sphinx before supper and a good night's sleep.

Days 2 and 3: Island Hopping

Take one of the ferries or catamarans from Split to Brač, Hvar, or Vis, and spend the night in an island paradise. This is the heart of Dalmatia, after all, and these islands are the stuff of glossy tourist brochures. Book your accommodations in advance, or try to book a private room through an agency in Split. In summer, ferries, hydrofoils, and catamarans operate regularly to the islands. Rent a bike or scooter once you've landed and tour the back roads, where you can find uncrowded coves and beaches. Remember, Hvar also has some of the finest Dalmatian wineries, not to mention the glitzy nightlife.

Day 4: Kornati National Park

Take a ferry back to Split and from there make your way down the stunning coastline to Vodice, stopping off at Primošten and Šibenik for sights and food along the way. At Vodice, board one of the many boats heading out for day trips to Kornati national park, the largest archipelago in the Adriatic with over 100 privately owned islands. This bare and beautiful archipelago's bone-white-to-ochre colors are in striking contrast the shockingly blue sea. If possible, take a boat that will drop you off at Zadar on the way back. Alternatively, drive from Vodice to Zadar to spend the night.

Days 5 and 6: Zadar and Paklenica National Park

Zadar has fast emerged into one of the top Croatian tourist destinations and not without reason. The beautiful peninsula on which the medieval city center was built hides many remarkable architectural, cultural, and gastronomic feats. Zadar's Old Town is bustling and beautiful, with marble pedestrian streets, Roman ruins, medieval churches, palaces, museums, achives, and libraries. Be sure to visit the St. Donatus church, a massive cylindrical structure that is one of the largest early Byzantine churches in Croatia. Don't miss the sea organ and the Greeting to Sun. Take a drive or a bus to neighboring Nin and see the former seat of the Dalmatian royal family as well as a quaint little salt museum.

The following day, venture out to Paklenica National Park, an imposing canyon in

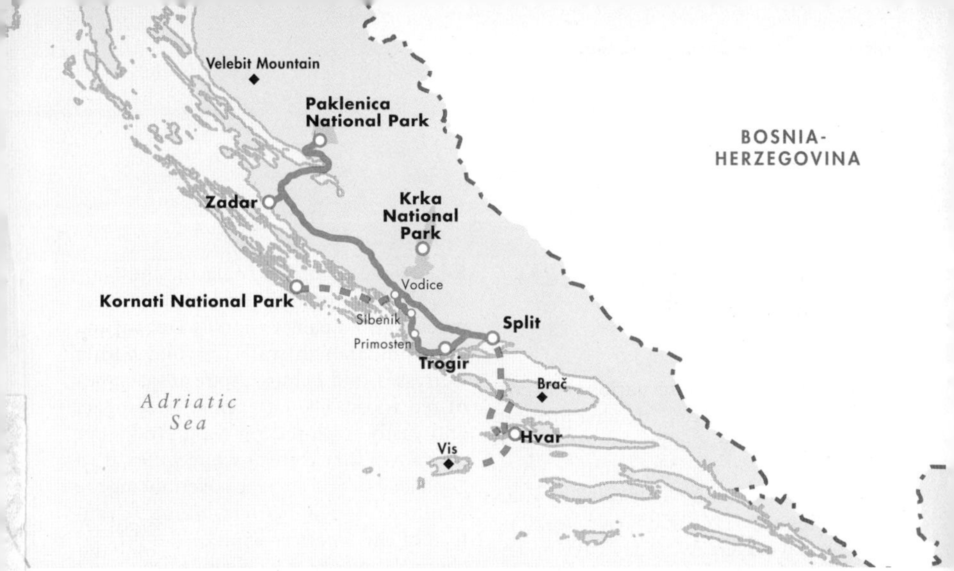

Velebit Mountain. This rugged limestone offers some great hiking and the ultimate challenge for cliff climbers. Also check out the old A-bomb shelter that Marshal Tito had built in the 1950s in case Stalin got a little too aggressive.

Day 7: Krka National Park, Trogir, and Split

Head back toward Split and stop along the way at Krka National Park. The Krka River cuts a path through a gorge shaded by limestone cliffs and dense forest, tumbling down toward the sea in a series of beautiful pools and waterfalls. The river's estuary challenges Plitvice Lakes for cascading water and amazing turquoise waterfalls. Be sure to wear at least sneakers and, in the summer months, a bathing suit as it is hard to say no to the lure of this pristine river. From there it is an easy drive to Split via Trogir, a UNESCO World Heritage Site. This small island is a pristinely preserved medieval town that's attached to the mainland with one bridge. The town's jewel is the powerful Cathedral of St. Lawrence, a superb example of Romanesque architecture.

TIPS

- Don't take a car to the islands. Ferry reservations for cars must be made well in advance, and you won't need one once you arrive.
- As you get closer to Velebit Mountain, expect the chances of summer showers to grow, so bring an umbrella or, better, a waterproof jacket.

GREAT ITINERARIES

DUBROVNIK, SOUTHERN DALMATIA, AND MONTENEGRO

Dubrovnik has an international airport that is well connected to all European hubs during the summer season. It is extremely popular in the summer, so be warned: you won't be sightseeing by yourself in August. Try to start your weeklong trip on a weekday (Monday to Monday, for example) instead of the weekend, so that your weekend is spent on a quiet island instead of in bustling Budva or Dubrovnik.

Days 1 and 2: Dubrovnik

If arriving by sea or air, you'll see one of the prettiest fortified cities in the world, and you are very likely to immediately fall in love with it. From this view, you can tell why Dubrovnik (formerly Ragusa) was once master of all of Dalmatia. Choose a hotel slightly outside the city walls, as the crowds flock there daily in high season. Have lunch in one of the many fish restaurants near the fish market and enjoy some Dalmatian wine. Save the sightseeing for the late afternoon, when the cruise-ship day-trippers have departed. Stroll along the *placa* in the early evening with the locals, stopping along the way for some Italian-style ice cream.

Day 3: The Pelješac Peninsula and Korčula

Pelješac Peninsula is home to Croatia's best red wine–growing region, Dingač. Do not miss the opportunity to travel down the windy roads via Mali Ston (renowned for its oysters) and stopping off at the family-owned wineries producing varietals like Plavac Mali or Pošip. At the town of Orebić catch a short ferry ride to Korčula, a treasure trove of Gothic and Renaissance churches, palaces, and piazzas, all built from fine local stone. It's very much like a small version of Dubrovnik, with similar high walls, circular corner fortresses, and a church spire among a sea of red roofs. The city center is compact and easily explored on foot. And since it's known for excellent white wines, it's a good idea to find a terrace overlooking the hundreds of windsurfers taking advantage of the *maestral* wind in the Pelješki channel, and order a delicious fish dinner with a glass of white. Check out the local sword dance, the Moreška. Either spend a night at a local hotel or apartment or head back to Dubrovnik to your hotel.

Day 4: Perast, Montenegro

Travel by bus or hire a car and drive from Dubrovnik down the coast to the sparkling Bay of Kotor in Montenegro. Plan on spending your first night in the tiny waterfront village of Perast, which is best known for a pair of tiny islets, each topped with a church. See the Roman mosaics at Risan and stay at one of the town's charming boutique hotels.

Day 5: Kotor, Montenegro

Continue on to the UNESCO World Heritage town of Kotor, which sits on Europe's most southerly fjord. Spend the day exploring its churches, markets, and wandering the Old Town's labyrinth of winding cobbled streets. Have lunch in one of the splendid marble piazzas. Don't miss hiking up to St. Johns Fortress, following the medieval walls for breathtaking views.

Day 6: Sveti Stefan, Montenegro

The stunning Sveti Stefan is known as the jewel of the Montenegrin coastline. It's a tiny island with several dozen limestone cottages and a small church, all of which are protected by 600-year-old defensive

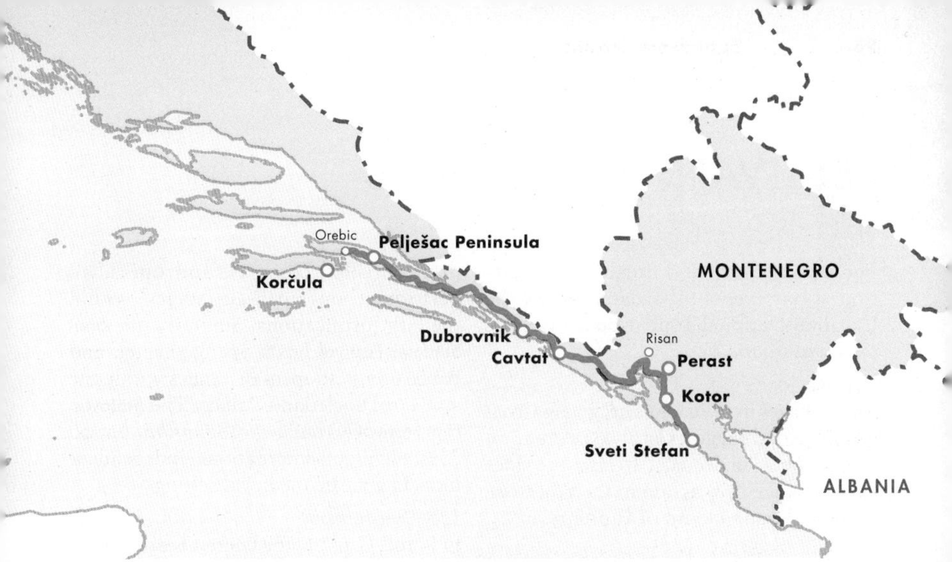

walls. The island is connected to the mainland by a narrow causeway. It was once a fishing village and it's now a exclusive resort of luxury suites run by the Aman hotel group. A night's stay is the perfect end to this itinerary.

Day 7: Cavtat

Day 7 will most likely be a travel day, no matter if you travel by car, plane, or ferry. Have one last seafood lunch at the town Cavtat, taking the time to visit the mausoleum by Croatia's prime sculptor Ivan Meštrović, buy a bottle of Dalmatian wine to take home, and vow to come back next year.

> **TIPS**
>
> ■ Don't take a car to Korčula. Ferry reservations for cars must be made well in advance. Once you're there, it's easy enough to get around by bus or rented scooter.
>
> ■ Be wary of *soba* (room) offers. Although many are legitimate, there are unscrupulous vendors out there hard at work in high season. And always have a map ready to mark the location to make sure you aren't out in the sticks.

FESTIVALS AND EVENTS

For exact dates and further information about events in Croatia, check the Croatian National Tourist Board website (🌐 *www.croatia.hr*).

February

Rijeka stages its own **Karneval,** giving Croatia the second-biggest Carnival celebration in Europe after Venice. It also provides Croatia some fiery action in the otherwise bleak and rainy month of February.

April

Zagreb, Croatia's capital, hosts a **Biennale,** an international festival of contemporary music. It's attended by the heavy hitters of the classical world as well as groundbreaking pioneers.

June

Lavender Festival on the island of Hvar takes place toward the end of June and features the best that this polyvalent herb has to offer. From oils and ornaments to cakes and lavender bread, this is a sure shot for lovers of Mediterranean herbs.

July

The Roman Arena in Pula makes Istria a stunning venue for the five-day **Pula Film Festival.** Around the same time, the five-day **International Folklore Festival** in Zagreb attracts folklore groups from Eastern Europe and beyond, staging music and dance in traditional costume.

July and August

Practically every island and city up and down the Dalmatian coast has some kind of music festival in July and August, most taking place in a pretty church or palazzo on the Old Town square. Check with local tourist offices once you arrive for what's going on that week. Croatia's largest and most prestigious cultural event, the **Dubrovnik Summer Festival** (🌐 *www.dubrovnik-festival.hr*), draws international artists and musicians and features drama, ballet, concerts, and opera, all performed on open-air stages within the city fortifications. Similarly, the **Split Summer Festival** hosts opera, theater, and dance events at open-air venues within the walls of Diocletian's Palace. The **Motovun Film Festival** (🌐 *www.motovunfilmfestival.com*) highlights international independent films in a rustic medieval setting.

July–September

In Poreč, Croatia, the **Concert Season** in the Basilica of St. Euphrasius features eminent musicians from Croatia and abroad, with sacral and secular music from all periods played inside the magnificent 6th-century basilica.

September

The **Epidaurus Festival** brings a variety of concerts, mostly classical and jazz, as well as an excellent selection of hands-on workshops to the town of Cavtat, just south of Dubrovnik toward the Montenegrin border.

September and October

The **Varaždin Baroque Evenings** see eminent soloists and orchestras from Croatia and abroad perform Baroque music recitals in the city's most beautiful churches.

November

In Zagorje, Croatia, **Martinje (St. Martin's Day),** which is November 11, sees the blessing of the season's new wine, accompanied by a hearty goose feast and endless toasts.

Nearby Slovenia, too, celebrates **St. Martin's Day** on November 11, which sees festivities throughout the country, culminating with the traditional blessing of the season's young wine.

KIDS AND FAMILIES

Croatia could very well be the most kid-friendly country on the Mediterranean. It is not so much the programs that make it suitable to bring the little ones along, but the sheer unspoiled beauty of nature. Whether you are pursuing history, nature, food, or sports, the kids can be easily incorporated into the trip and, what is more, have a fun learning experience.

Where to Stay. Resorts are not to be found everywhere in Croatia. Western Istria, island Krk, Zadar, and Dubrovnik offer the most options, luring travelers with great deals for kids staying in the same room. Always be sure to ask for children's discounts, which will typically vary according to your children's ages. Private accommodation, or self-catering apartments, is on the rise in Croatia both in terms of quantity and quality. These are ideally suited for families as they can fit the whole entourage at only a fraction of what the hotel would cost and you are also free to cook your own food (and, regrettably, do your own dishes). If booking online, make sure to read the reviews of previous guests, as pictures can often be deceiving and descriptions incomplete. Finally, Croatia is also dotted with very attractive campsites along the Adriatic, which is especially appealing for parents who don't mind their children getting a little dusty every now and again. Campsite accommodations range from tents to elitist bungalows with all modern amenities.

Outdoor Activities. Croatia was not designed for staying indoors, especially in the eyes of children. The crystal-clear Adriatic is an instant magnet for almost any little one, but make sure to pack a pair of rubber sandals for them—most of the coast is rocky, and sea urchins, too, enjoy the clear shallow waters. There are a number of sailing schools along the coast and snorkeling is never bad due to the water's clarity. Most of the coast immediately transforms into mountains, particularly lush toward the west, which offers great hiking opportunities. All Croatian national parks are also great places to spend a day with the offspring, and they do offer discounts for families. Most importantly, Croatia is very safe, and it is not at all uncommon to see children playing by themselves at playgrounds while the parents catch a breath of sea air or a glass of cool wine. Do be aware, however, that kids' clubs or cafés are in short supply, so make sure to have a plan of action for the occasional rainy day.

Sports Camps. It is well known that, when it comes to sports, Croatia punches above its weight. All those accolades have to come from somewhere and there are indeed many sports camps for children and youth that visitors can join, provided that you plan and research in advance. From the national pastimes like soccer, basketball, and water polo to individual sports like tennis, cliff climbing, and sailing, there are many options that will occupy (and exhaust) the energy bombs while the parents take a breather.

Culture and History. Over the past years, there has been a strong push toward making museums and historic buildings, well, less boring for the children. In addition to free or symbolic entrance, many museums now offer interactive programs in which the younger visitors get to participate as opposed to just observing. The trick, if it is a trick, has worked quite well thus far.

FLAVORS OF CROATIA

Throughout history, Croatia has served as the crossroads between Western Europe and Asia, and this shows in cultural facets and especially the food, which reflects Italian, Hungarian, and Turkish culinary influences. You can still dine in old-school eateries that offer traditional renditions of favorite dishes, but the recent tourism boom has also brought a new generation of chefs in Zagreb and the bigger cities along the coast; they get creative with fresh ingredients and serve up noteworthy hybrids of old and new.

Adriatic Sea Food

You needn't look too hard for good fish restaurants along the coast. Indeed, with all the bays, coves and islands, the Croatian side of the Adriatic serves as a plentiful source of fish, both wild and farmed. The two most common choices are the dorade and sea bass, traditionally served with a delectable side of Dalmatian-style *blitva,* chard cooked with potatoes and olive oil. The same side is also recommended with grilled squid, and it is not uncommon to find scampi and lobster on the menu. Tuna lovers will not be disappointed: in addition to wild-caught tuna, the country now has two large farms to aid the supply. Finally, the more adventurous should try what the locals refer to as "blue fish" (sardines, anchovies, mackerel, or sprat), which are rich in omega-3s and are often eaten whole with lemon, olive oil, and the omnipresent bread.

Cured Meats and Cheese

Most summertime dinners begin with a platter of starters. The centerpiece will typically be *pršut* (prosciutto) and cheese. Add some olives, spicy peppers, and pork or tuna fish paste, and you're off to a good start. Prosciutto is very popular along the coast: Dalmatians cure it longer and with more spices than the Istrians, but both are indubitably worth a try. In Zagreb and Slavonia, you are more likely to come across *kulen,* a richly flavored pork sausage cut in thin slices. The meat would not be complete without the other member of the delightfully comestible tandem: cheese. And while the choices are many, people commonly agree that the sheep cheese from the island of Pag takes home the gold medal. The island offers limited pasture areas mostly by the sea, and the grass receives a liberal salty sprinkling carried by the north east wind off the Adriatic. Saltier grass makes saltier milk and this, in turn, provides gourmets with an excellent, inherently salty cheese.

Lamb and Veal

Croatians' love for veal and lamb has lasted centuries, and one favorite dish is *janje* (lamb) or *tele* (calf) cooked under an iron bell called a *peka*. The bell is buried under a pile of hot coals so that the meat (together with potatoes, carrots, rosemary, sage, and other Mediterranean herbs) stews slowly in its own juice until it falls off the bone. Peka is mostly found in Dalmatia but is also a menu staple along the old Lika magistrala road connecting Zagreb to Zadar via Plitvice lakes. Pair peka with Plavac Mali wine and finish with *šljivovica,* a plum-based grappa.

Truffles and Homemade Pasta

The rolling hills of inland Istria are home to highly prized truffles. The black truffle season conveniently peaks at the same time as the tourist season, from May until October, so it's relatively easy (if not inexpensive) to find this rare mushroom on the menus of Istrian restaurants. The white truffle, on the other hand, grows in the winter months and may be harder to come by. The secretive, flavorful truffles are rooted out in forests by specially trained dogs or pigs and incorporated a variety of dishes. To keep the experience truly local though, order truffle sauce on homemade fuži or *pljukanci* pasta and wash it down with a glass of Malvasia, Istria's staple white wine.

Spoon-Friendly Entrees

Croatia's cuisine differs significantly from one part of the country to another, but you will seldom find a restaurant that does not offer at least one dish, outside of regular broths, that is best eaten by spoon. In Istria you will feast on the *maneštra,* the backbone of which are beans, corn, and olive oil, though the stew will also typically include potatoes, sausages, and sauerkraut during the winter. In Lika and Dalmatia, ask for *pasulj,* a bean-dominated thick stew loved by the locals, or *pašticada,* the Dalmatian signature beef dish cooked in red wine sauce. Finally, when in Slavonia, do not miss the fish *paprikash.* This stew joins the classic Hungarian preparation with the fish from Danube's tributaries. The meal can be cooked using trout, pike, catfish—or all of the above—together with onions, paprika, peppers, and white wine.

Wine

Croatia's wine-making renaissance continues with many France-, Napa Valley–, or Italy-educated winemakers returning to make the best of some truly exceptional terroirs. Croatian wine is quite difficult to find at international wine shops, which is all the more reason to delve into these craftily revisited local vintages during your stay. The four main wine-growing regions are Istria, renowned for the Malvasia white and Teran red; Dalmatia, the home of some excellent reds like Plavac Mali and Vranac; Zagorje, which produces small quantities of very crisp dessert wines and Rieslings; and Eastern Slavonia, with its millennia-long tradition of producing the Graševina white varietal. The best producers are well represented in better restaurants, and there is an upsurge in specialized wine bars and tasting tours.

Jasenka Piljač's book, *Zinfandel: A Croatian-American Wine Story* (🌐 *www.crozinfandel.com*) chronicles her work as a part of the Meredith Zinquest team who searched for origins of the Zinfindel grape in Croatia and includes in-depth information about Croatia's viticultural past, present, and future.

WINES OF CROATIA

A wine renaissance is occurring in Croatia today. The early 20th century was bad for the wine business—phylloxera, war, crippling economic policies, all of which ravaged wineries here and led to the mass emigration of many vintners to the United States, New Zealand, Australia, South Africa, and South America. Taking their knowledge of vine cultivation and wine production with them, they left Croatia's vineyards virtually deserted.

More recently, the 1990–95 war for Croatian independence nearly wiped out what remained of the viticulture. It appears, however, that the land itself cannot forget its heritage. Blessed with unique geography that's ideal for wine, Croatia currently hosts more than 100 indigenous grapes—second only to Italy. The country's wines are once again finding a special place in the hearts of oenophiles everywhere. The Mediterranean landscape is particularly suited to *Vitis vinifera L* (the cultivated grapevine), a hearty and prolific yet temperamental plant that requires precise combinations of climate, geography, and soil to flourish. In Croatia, with her numerous, diverse microclimates, the grape has had the necessary conditions to proliferate.

Wine-Making and Its Deep Roots

The Delmati, an Illyrian tribe, were the first to cultivate the vine in modern-day Croatia, as early as the 11th century BC. When the Romans invaded the Dalmatian Coast in the 3rd century BC, they discovered an entire wine industry. The Greeks, who'd been sharing the region with the Illyrians, had not failed to exploit *Vitis sylvestris* (the wild grapevine), which was plentiful there, merging it with the strains of the cultivated vines they brought from their own country. The conquering Roman soldiers also brought new varietals with them as a way of expanding their culture; the vine itself was a symbol of their power.

By the 9th century, Croatian princes had a cup bearer as part of their court staff. When Venice subjugated much of Dalmatia and Istria in the 14th century, the planting of new vineyards was restricted to the areas around Split. It was in this period that noble families, after building their vineyards, built fortresses in the middle of their estates for protection, perhaps anticipating the destruction of the coming Venetian-Turkish wars. By the time the Habsburgs had ousted the Ottomans, the Austrians were already well on their way to introducing new varietals to the area, capitalizing on the superior wine-producing capacity of their newly acquired resources.

Modern developments in cloning techniques and the use of industrial machinery brought wine-making in Croatia to the economic position it occupies today, where 10% of the population derives income from the industry.

The Napa Valley Connection

Croatia has had some world-class help in reestablishing its wine-making industry. Miljenko "Mike" Grgić of Napa Valley fame is at the forefront of the race to realize the potential of Croatia's indigenous varietals. Feeling stifled by the communist government, Grgić left for California in 1954 and became renowned as a winemaker when his 1973 Chateau Montelena Chardonnay won a blind tasting in Paris. Afterward, the top-quality wine market opened its mind and wallet to wines from all over the world. Mr. Grgić then established Grgich Hills Cellar in Napa Valley, and it is now one of California's most respected producers.

Grgić Vina. When Croatia won its independence in 1995, Croatian-born Mike Grgić went back from Napa Valley to establish Grgić Vina in a tiny town of some 100 residents on the Pelješac Peninsula in Southern Dalmatia, the home of the Dingač terroir. Croatia's first international winery surprised everyone by turning a profit within two years (5–10 years is typical). The winery produces high-end boutique wines: a flavorful, fruity white from the indigenous Pošip; and a ruby-red, from the hearty Plavac Mali, the "little blue" grape that is widely considered the highest-quality Croatian varietal, closely related to Zinfandel. These bottles range between $20 and $50 a bottle. Grgić hopes to support the local wine communes by using their grapes as well. ✉ *Trstenik 78, Trstenik* ☎ *020/748–090 from Croatia* 🌐 *www.grgich.com.*

Regions and Wineries

Croatia is split into two main wine-growing regions: the arid continental part and the coastal region, much of which shares the same latitude as Bordeaux, Provence, Tuscany, and Oregon. The continental region produces 90% of the country's whites, the coastal almost 70% of the reds. There are 12 subregions in Croatia, the most important of which are **Central and Southern Dalmatia,** where the hearty Plavac Mali flourishes on the Pelješac Peninsula; **Middle Dalmatia,** where the famous Babić grape is grown near Primošten; and the **Northern Coastal Belt,** which includes the islands of Cres, Lošinj, Rab, Pag, and Krk. These are breathtaking regions, as is **Istria,** known for its Malvasia Istriana (white) and Teran (red). The region of **Međimurje,** situated in continental Croatia along the Slovenian and Hungarian border, also has some fine wineries specializing in white wines made from Graševina grapes, better known as Welschriesling, as well as Tramina, Chardonnay, and Sauvignon Blanc.

The Zinquest: Finding Zinfandel in Croatia

Much excitement has been generated around California's ubiquitous Zinfandel grape, whose origin had long been guessed at, but that remained shrouded in mystery. In 1998 Professor Carole Meredith of the University of California at Davis, a renowned grapevine geneticist who had previously uncovered the origins of Chardonnay, Cabernet Sauvignon, and Petit Syrah, began a similar search for Zinfandel's origin. The exciting four-year project, which entailed the collection of leaf samples from indigenous varieties of southern Dalmatia, DNA fingerprinting analyses of samples' cultivars, and comparisons with Zinfandel cuttings from California, shed new light on the origins of the state's most popular grape.

In the spring of 1998, Professor Meredith collected leaf samples from 148 individual Plavac Mali vines in Southern Dalmatia, including Hvar, Pelješac, and Korčula. Although the initial search gave no positive matches with Zinfandel, the expeditions that followed led the team of scientists to an old vineyard in Kaštel Novi, where a few additional "suspects" were discovered. The DNA analyses performed at Davis confirmed that a wine locally known as Crljenak Kaštelanski—completely forgotten and virtually eradicated from Dalmatian vineyards—is the long-sought Croatian corollary of Zinfandel.

SAILING AND CRUISING IN CROATIA

The Croatian Adriatic has more than 2,000 km (1,242 miles) of mainland coast, with more than 1,000 islands and islets (67 of which are inhabited). The islands run parallel to and close to the mainland coast, which means easy island hopping in protected waters.

Besides the picturesque coastal towns, Croatia has three national parks on the sea: Brijuni National Park (a cluster of 14 small green islands just off Istria), Kornati National Park (an archipelago of 89 arid, rocky islands, off North Dalmatia), and Mljet National Park (a large fertile island, in South Dalmatia). In addition, Krka National Park (a spectacular series of waterfalls in a canyon in Central Dalmatia), can even be approached by sailboat, if you sail up the Šibenik Channel as far as Skradin.

Sailing

A holiday aboard a sailboat is now an affordable alternative to a land-bound vacation. In fact, it is the ultimate way to explore Croatia's stunningly beautiful mainland coast and islands. And, surprisingly, a week aboard a sailing boat can be cheaper than staying in a mid-range hotel.

If you are already an experienced sailor, you can charter a so-called bareboat yacht, meaning that you rent just the boat and sail independently. By Croatian law, at least one of the crew needs to have an internationally recognized sailing license, plus a radio certificate (available from all port authorities).

If you have never sailed before, or have little experience, then you will need a skipper. Generally skippers do more than just guide the boat: most are from the region and, therefore, know the local waters and weather conditions, the history and culture, the protected coves for putting down anchor, the local gastronomic hideouts, and the best diving spots.

The third option is sailing in a flotilla. A flotilla is a group of yachts, with people of mixed levels of sailing experience, led by a qualified expert.

A typical one-week sailing itinerary in Central Dalmatia could run as follows. Day 1: Set sail from Split to Maslinica on the island of Šolta. Day 2: Maslinica to Vis Town on the island of Vis. Day 3: Sail around the island, from Vis Town to Komiža, calling at Biševo en route. Day 4: Komiža to Hvar Town on the island of Hvar. Day 5: Hvar Town to Bol on the island of Brač. Day 6: Bol to Milna on the island of Brač. Day 7: Early morning departure from Milna to Split.

Charter Companies

On the Croatian Adriatic there are more than 140 charter companies operating tens of thousands of boats of all sizes, making this one of the busiest charter areas in Europe. As a rough guide to prices, in summer 2017 high season, Sail Croatia offered an eight-berth Beneteau Cyclades 43 sailing boat for €3,600 per week, though this price does not include food, fuel, or mooring fees.

The season runs from May through October, with the best winds for sailing in May and June. Demand and prices peak in July and August, when you can expect calmer sea and less wind, making conditions ideal for motorboats but less fun for true sailors. During peak season, charter rentals generally begin at 5 pm Saturday and end at 9 am the following Saturday.

ZAGREB AND ENVIRONS

Updated by Sierra Christianson and Ivan Verunica

Zagreb has emerged as a tourist destination in recent years, and much of its success has to do with the country's spectacular Adriatic coast—beautiful medieval towns, crystal clear azure waters, and, of course, well-developed tourist resorts. It's all too easy, however, to overlook the fact that much of the country's natural beauty and cultural heritage is rooted in places well inland from the sea. Unless you arrive overland from Slovenia—by boat from Italy, or by one of the few air routes that deliver you straight to the coast—chances are that your first encounter with Croatia will be Zagreb, an eminently strollable capital city of attractive parks, squares, and museums.

Instead of hightailing it to Dalmatia or Istria, stay a few days to explore the capital's historic center and pastoral environs. You'll be in for a pleasant surprise and will go home with a fuller, more satisfying appreciation of what this alluring country is all about. With its historic center on the northern bank of the Sava River, Zagreb has the walkability of Prague with the added bonus that the streetcars have to yield to pedestrians. Spacious, inviting public spaces, grand Austro-Hungarian architecture, and a rich array of churches and museums will lure you down small side streets.

ORIENTATION AND PLANNING

With the exception of the vast plains of Slavonia that stretch to the east *(Chapter 3)*, the rest of the inland region, with Zagreb as its approximate center, can be divided into two parts: north and south. To the north is the hilly, castle-rich Zagorje region; the smaller, often-overlooked and yet likewise appealing Međimurje region; and, just a tram and bus ride from the city center, the hiking trails and ski slopes of Sljeme. To the south is the relatively busy route to the coast that includes Karlovac, an important regional center, as well as Croatia's most visited national park, Plitvice Lakes; and a second route along the less traveled banks of the Sava River to Lonjsko Polje, known for its natural beauty, a 16th-century fortress, and historical reminders of Croatia's role in World War II.

2

GREAT ITINERARIES

To explore Croatia's interior, begin with Zagreb and work your way outward from there. If you have just a day or two, stick to the capital, but the more time you have beyond that, the more you will want to explore. If you're headed to the coast anyway, you'll pass by Plitvice Lakes National Park; keep that natural wonder on your radar for a daytime visit at the very least.

IF YOU HAVE 3 DAYS

Stick to **Zagreb**, with a side trip to its immediate environs. As compact as it is, compared with other regional capitals such as Budapest, Croatia's capital nonetheless invites long strolls and more than a fleeting look into at least a few of its museums and parks. This alone can take three days; but you can probably cover most key sights without feeling rushed in two days, leaving a bit of time to spare for a half-day excursion to the charming village of **Samobor**, for example, or to the scenic hills of Sljeme north of the capital. Renting a car will allow you to cover more of the castles and towns of the **Medvednica hills** and the Zagorje region, but even if you have only one full day at your disposal, you can take in a couple of these nearby sites by bus.

IF YOU HAVE 5 DAYS

Start as above, devoting at least two or, better yet, two and a half days to Zagreb, with a half-day excursion to the Medvednica hills on the third day. Visit a castle or two in the Zagorje, such as the recently renovated **Veliki Tabor**, on the fourth day, and spend the night either in the nearby countryside or else in the ancient town of **Varaždin** before making your way back for a fond farewell to Zagreb on the fifth.

IF YOU HAVE 7 DAYS

Do all of the above, but take in both a castle in the Zagorje and an afternoon and evening in Varaždin; throw in a one-night visit to **Plitvice Lakes National Park**, with a daytime stopover to visit the Old Town center of Karlovac on the way. This one-week option will work well if, for example, you wish to spend the second (or first) week on the Adriatic coast.

PLANNING

WHEN TO GO

Although Zagreb and environs are well worth a visit at any time of year, the capital really comes alive in spring and summer, which essentially means anytime between April and late September. Since summer is coastal vacation time for so many, July and August are considered low season in the capital, meaning that the city is much less crowded and more economical than the coast.

GETTING HERE AND AROUND

AIR TRAVEL

Zagreb International Airport (ZAG) is actually located in the city of Velika Gorica, 17 km (10 miles) southeast of Zagreb.

There are no direct flights between the United States and Zagreb, but Croatia Airlines and several major European carriers fly to Zagreb from Amsterdam, Brussels, Frankfurt, Munich, London, Paris, Vienna,

TOP REASONS TO GO TO ZAGREB

Walkable cities: With lovely parks, squares, museums, and churches, hoofing it in Croatia's compact capital is an unforgettable experience. If your feet fail, you can always jump on a convenient tram.

Sparkling waterfalls: Plitvice Lakes National Park, a UNESCO World Heritage site, is Croatia's most visited park, with 16 crystal-clear turquoise lakes connected by waterfalls and cascades.

Forests and fortresses: Zagorje's forested hills north of Zagreb are ornamented with some lovely fortresses, built to ward off centuries of onslaughts by various foes.

Baroque beauty: Varaždin is the most harmonious and beautifully preserved Baroque town in this corner of the continent.

Unique cuisine: Here you get the best of both worlds: top-notch seafood *and* Central European meaty, spicy fare. And best of all, prices are fairly reasonable even at the top restaurants.

Moscow, Rome, and other cities. Croatia Airlines operates at least two flights daily to Split (45 minutes) and three flights daily to Dubrovnik (55 minutes). In summertime there are also flights to Lisbon (2 hours, 25 minutes), Barcelona (2 hours, 10 minutes), Tel Aviv (3 hours, 15 minutes), and other cities.

A regular shuttle bus runs from the airport to the main bus station every 30 minutes from 7 am to 8 pm, and from the main bus station to the airport from 4:30 am to 8:30 pm. A one-way ticket costs 30 Kn, and daily return ticket costs 40 Kn. The trip takes 30 minutes. By taxi, expect to pay 150 Kn to 200 Kn to make the same journey; the trip will be slightly faster, about 20 minutes.

Airport Contacts **Zagreb International Airport** (*Zagreb Pleso Airport*). ✉ *Rudolfa Fizira 1, Velika Gorica* ☎ *01/456–2222 general info, 060/320–320 within Croatia, +3851/456–2170 outside Croatia* 🌐 *www.zagreb-airport.hr.*

Airport Transfer Contacts **Airport bus** (*Pleso prijevoz*). ✉ *Pleso prijevoz, Avenija Marina Držića 4, Zagreb* ☎ *01/633–1982* 🌐 *www.plesoprijevoz.hr.*

BUS TRAVEL

Frequent regular coach service to destinations all over mainland Croatia departs from the capital. The traveling time is 6 hours from Zagreb to Split and 10½ hours from Zagreb to Dubrovnik. There are also daily international bus lines to Slovenia (Ljubljana), Hungary (Barcs and Nagykanisza), Serbia (Belgrade), Austria (Graz), Germany (Munich, Stuttgart, Frankfurt, Dortmund, Cologne, and Düsseldorf), and Switzerland (Zurich). Timetable information is available from the main bus station, a 20-minute walk from the center.

About 30 buses run daily between Zagreb and Karlovac in just under an hour and for a one-way fare of around 45 Kn.

Samobor is a 50-minute bus ride from Zagreb; buses between Zagreb and Samobor run every 30 minutes or so weekdays, roughly every hour on weekends; the fare is around 30 Kn each way, and Samobor's small bus station is about 100 yards north of the main square.

There are daily direct buses to Plitvice Lakes National Park. Some buses between Zagreb and Split will stop at both entrances to Plitvice Lakes National Park; the fare is around 95 Kn one-way between Zagreb and Plitvice.

A small handful of buses go daily from Zagreb to Sisak and then continue on narrow, two-lane roads to the charming village of Čigoć.

Contacts Varaždin Bus Station. ✉ *Zrinskih i Frankopana BB, Varaždin* ☎ *042/407–888.* **Zagreb Bus Station.** ✉ *Avenija Marina Držića 4, Zagreb* ☎ *060/313–333* 🌐 *www.akz.hr.*

BUS AND TRAM TRAVEL WITHIN ZAGREB

An extensive network of city buses and trams—almost exclusively trams within the town center—run 24 hours a day, with less frequent night service starting at approximately 11:30 pm and lasting until 4 am. Tickets cost 10 Kn for a day-service ride and 15 Kn for a night-service ride. A full-day ticket (30 Kn), available at some kiosks, is valid until 4 am the next morning. As an alternative, you can buy the Zagreb Card for 90 Kn; this covers public transport within the city limits for three days and offers substantial discounts at various museums and other cultural venues. After you board the bus or tram, you must validate your ticket with a time stamp (little yellow machines located only in the first and last cars of each tram); tickets are good for 1½ hours and are transferable in the same direction. If you are caught without a valid ticket, you will be fined 250 Kn, payable on the spot.

Contact ZET (*Zagreb Transport Authority*). ✉ *Ozaljska 105* ☎ *060/100–001* 🌐 *www.zet.hr.*

CAR TRAVEL

Prices vary, and you will probably pay less if you rent from a local company that's not part of an international chain; it's best to shop around. You can find economy cars (e.g., Seat Ibiza or Volkswagen Polo) from 350 Kn per day, compact cars (e.g., Volkswagen Golf or Hyundai) from 450 Kn per day, intermediate cars (e.g., Skoda Octavia) from 720 Kn per day, or standard cars (e.g., Audi A4) from 850 Kn per day. If you can't drive a stick shift, beware: automatic transmission is rarely available on smaller cars. These prices include unlimited mileage, CDW (collision damage waiver) and TP (theft protection), but not PAI (personal accident insurance). If you drive one-way (say, from Zagreb to Dubrovnik), there is an additional drop-off charge, but it depends on the type of car and the number of days you are renting. While staying in the capital you are better off without a car, but if you wish to visit the nearby hills of Zagorje, or go farther afield to the Međimurje region, a vehicle is helpful unless you want to take a bus to a different attraction each day.

TAXI TRAVEL

You can find taxi ranks in front of the bus and train stations, near the main square of Ban Jelačić, and in front of the larger hotels. Several companies are now available: Radio Taxi Zagreb, Taxi Zagreb 3628,

Eko Taxi and Taxi Cammeo. It is also possible to order a taxi. All drivers are bound by law to run a meter—but this doesn't necessarily mean they will unless you ask—and the price can vary from 8.80 Kn for flagfall and from 4.90 Kn per km. Most companies have the same prices for day and night riding, as well as for rides on Sundays and holidays. Most companies do not charge for luggage.

Contacts **Eko Taxi.** ✉ *Vodovodna 20a, Zagreb* ☎ *01/889–2012* 🌐 *www.ekotaxi.hr.* **Radio Taxi.** ✉ *Ulica Božidara Magovca 55* ☎ *600/800–800,* 🌐 *www.radio-taksi-zagreb.hr.* **Taxi Cammeo.** ✉ *Radnička cesta 27, Zagreb* ☎ *01/1212* 🌐 *www.taxi-cammeo.hr* 🌐 *www.taxi-cammeo.hr.*

TRAIN TRAVEL

Zagreb's main train station lies in Donji grad, a 10-minute walk south from the main square of Ban Jelačić. There are daily international trains to and from Budapest (Hungary), Belgrade (Serbia), Munich (Germany), Vienna (Austria), and Venice (Italy). From Zagreb there are six trains daily to Split in Dalmatia (6–8 hours) and three trains daily to Rijeka in Kvarner (3½–4½ hours). The easiest way to get to Varaždin from Zagreb is by rail, with some 15 trains daily. Travel time is about 2½ hours and costs 65 Kn each way. About 15 trains run daily between Zagreb and Karlovac (with a similar number of buses), in just under an hour for a one-way fare of 36 Kn. If you don't have wheels, your best bet to reach Sisak is by rail for 34 Kn, with 15 trains daily from Zagreb that take about an hour.

Contacts **Hrvatske željeznice** (*Croatia Railways*). ✉ *Trg kralja Tomislava 12, Donji Grad* ☎ *060/333–444 info* 🌐 *www.hzpp.hr.* **Karlovac Train Station.** ✉ *Vilima Reinera 3, Karlovac* ☎ *060/333–444 info, 060/646–244 info.* **Varaždin Train Station.** ✉ *Kolodvorska 17, Varaždin* ☎ *060/333–444.* **Zagreb Train Station.** ✉ *Trg kralja Tomislava 12, Donji Grad* ☎ *060/333–444* 🌐 *www.hznet.hr.*

TOURS

The tourist information centers inside the Zagreb train station and on the main square (Trg bana Jelačića 11) organize amusing and informative guided tours of the city.

Hop on Hop off Zagreb. Zagreb's open-top buses operate along two routes (red and green) throughout the city. The red line (1-hour tour) operates within the narrow city center with six stops along the route. The green line (1½-hour tour) includes the best known green oases of Zagreb with seven stops along the route. Tickets are valid for an entire day, which is plenty of time to see most of Zagreb's most famous landmarks. This service is provided by the Zagreb Electric Tram Company (ZET) in cooperation with the Zagreb Tourist Board. The departure point is from Bakačeva Street on Kaptol. The red line departs at 10, noon, 2, and 4; the green line departs at noon and 3. The 24-hour ticket costs 70 Kn for adults and 35 Kn for children under 18. You can purchase tickets from the driver or at the ZET office, Petrićeva 4, from 8 am to 9 pm Monday through Friday and from 8 am to 3:50 pm on Saturday. ✉ *Zagreb* ☎ *060/100–001* 🌐 *www.zet.hr.*

Ibus. Every day of the week the Ibus travel agency offers combination bus-and-walking guided tours of the city center for 165 Kn a person (minimum four people); call a day in advance to reserve. It also provides tours of attractions farther afield, including Veliki Tabor, Trakošćan and Varaždin, and Plitvice Lakes National Park. ✉ *Tkalčićeva 7/1, Gornji Grad* ☎ *01/369–4333, 01/364–8633* 🌐 *www.ibus.hr.*

Segway CityTour. For a state-of-the-art experience, you can try the Segway CityTour from mid-April through mid-October. The 50-minute "Basic Ride" costs 250 Kn per person and the 130-minute "All Around Tour" costs 500 Kn per person. They also offer themed tours such as Sensual Zagreb, Zagreb Talks, Zagreb by Bike, Secret Zagreb Walks, and a Night Tour of Gornji Grad called the "Secret of Grič." Tours meet in front of the Hotel Esplanade at Mihanovićeva 1. ☎ *01/456–6055* 🌐 *www.segway.hr.*

ABOUT THE RESTAURANTS

Although there are seafood restaurants in Zagreb and large towns like Varaždin, this inland region is better known for roasted meats accompanied by heavy side dishes such as *zagorski štrukli* (baked cheese dumplings). For dessert, walnut-, jam-, and sweet cheese-filled *palačinke* (crepes) are on nearly every menu. Balkan-style grilled meats such as *ćevapčići* (well-seasoned sausage links, often served with raw onions) are popular, and lower in price than more elaborate main courses. The influence of Slavonia to the east and Hungary to the north is evident in the form of paprika-rich dishes, whether *fiš paprikaš* (made from fish and also called *riblji paprikaš*) or various goulashes. Some restaurants, particularly in Zagreb, and especially those owned and operated by folks from Dalmatia, do excel in fresh seafood straight from the Adriatic. But when it comes to fish, you are likely to find more freshwater options such as carp, pike, and pike-perch. Many restaurants serve pasta and pizza as budget alternatives, but there is not as much Italian-style fare here as there is on the coast. If you head to Varaždin or a smaller town, prices will drop somewhat, though not dramatically. Last but not least, note that some restaurants close for two to four weeks between late July and August, when everybody heads to the coast for vacation.

ABOUT THE HOTELS

It's a fact of life that Zagreb doesn't get the same sort of tourist traffic as the coast, so the region's major hotels have gone to great lengths since the end of the Yugoslav war to cater to business travelers. Although this trend has yielded a spate of impressive renovations (some still ongoing or planned as of this writing), it has also driven prices up considerably. Rates of €100 or (much) more for a double room are not uncommon in central Zagreb's largest hotels, though a 10- to 20-minute walk or short tram ride from downtown will bring you to comfortable, modern pensions for considerably less. You have to go to smaller towns or to the countryside to get cheaper options, though some private rooms and agritourism-style accommodations are quite affordable. Regardless of the price range, Croatian hotels often count two single beds pushed together as a double bed. If it's important to you, be sure to ask if they have rooms with a double mattress.

Hotel reviews have been shortened. For full information, visit Fodors.com.

WHAT IT COSTS IN EUROS (€) AND CROATIAN KUNA (KN)

	$	$$	$$$	$$$$
Restaurants	under 50 Kn	50 Kn–120 Kn	121 Kn–250 Kn	over 250 Kn
	under €8	€8–€20	€21–€40	over €40
Hotels	under 450 Kn	450 Kn–900 Kn	901 Kn–1,500 Kn	over 1,500 Kn
	under €60	€60–€120	€121–€200	over €200

Restaurant prices are the average cost of a main course at dinner or, if dinner is not served, at lunch. Hotel prices are the lowest cost of a standard double room in high season.

VISITOR INFORMATION

Zagreb's main tourist information center is right on the main square, Trg bana Jelačića. It's open weekdays 8:30 am to 9 pm, weekends 9 to 6 (summer working hours). A smaller office in the train station is open weekdays 9 to 9 and weekends noon to 8:30.

Contacts Croatian National Tourist Board. ✉ *Iblerov trg 10/IV, Zagreb* ☎ *01/469–9300* 🌐 *croatia.hr.* **Plitvice Lakes National Park Tourist Information.** ✉ *Entrance No. 1 to NP Plitvička Jezera, Velika Poljana* ☎ *053/776–798 Tourist Board office* 🌐 *www.tzplitvice.hr.* **Samobor Tourist Information.** ✉ *Trg Krajla Tomislava 5, Samobor* ☎ *01/336–004* 🌐 *www.tz-samobor.hr.* **Varaždin Tourist Information.** ✉ *Ivana Padovca 3, Varaždin* ☎ *042/210–987* 🌐 *www.tourism-varazdin.hr.* **Zagreb Tourist Information.** ✉ *Trg bana Josipa Jelačića, Donji Grad* ☎ *01/481–4051, 01/481–4052, 01/481–4054* 🌐 *www.zagreb-touristinfo.hr.*

ZAGREB

The capital of Croatia, Zagreb has a population of roughly 1 million and is situated at the extreme edge of the Pannonian Plain, between the north bank of the Sava River and the southern slopes of Mt. Medvednica. Its early years are shrouded in mystery, though there are indications of a Neolithic settlement on this site. The Romans are said to have established a municipality of sorts that was destroyed around AD 600, when Croatian tribes moved in.

Like so many other notable European cities, Zagreb started out as a strategic crossroads along an international river route, which was followed much later by north–south and east–west passages by road and rail. For much of its history the city also served as a bastion on a defensive frontier, pounded for half a millennium by thundering hordes of invaders, among them Hungarians, Mongols, and Turks.

From the late Middle Ages until the 19th century, Zagreb was composed of two adjoining but separate towns on the high ground (Gornji grad): one town was secular, the other expressly religious. In 1242 the secular town, named Gradec (Fortress), was burned to the ground in a wave of destruction by the Tartars, after which it locked itself up behind protective walls and towers. It is from this time that the real Zagreb (meaning Behind the Hill) began to evolve; it was accorded the status of a free royal city in the same year by the Hungarian-Croatian king Bela IV. In the 15th century the ecclesiastical center, named Kaptol (Chapter House), also enclosed itself in defensive walls in response to the threat of a Turkish invasion.

When Zagreb became the capital of Croatia in 1557, the country's parliament began meeting alternately in Gradec and at the Bishop's Palace in Kaptol. When Kaptol and Gradec were finally put under a single city administration in 1850, urban development accelerated. The railway reached Zagreb in 1862, linking the city to Vienna, Trieste, and the Adriatic. It was at this time that Donji grad (Lower Town) came into being. Lying between Gornji grad and the main train station, it was designed to accommodate new public buildings—the National Theater, the university, and various museums. Built in grandiose style and interspersed by wide, tree-lined boulevards, parks, and gardens, it makes a fitting monument to the Habsburg era.

The Tito years brought a period of increasing industrialization coupled with urban expansion, as the new high-rise residential suburb of Novi Zagreb was constructed south of the Sava. In 1991 the city escaped the war of independence relatively unscathed, except for an attempted rocket attack on the Croatian Parliament building in Gradec. Zagreb did, however, suffer severe economic hardship as the country's industries collapsed, post-communist corruption set in, and an influx of refugees—mainly from Bosnia and Herzegovina—arrived in search of a better life.

Since 2000 public morale has picked up considerably: trendy street cafés are thriving, numerous smart new stores have opened, and the public gardens are once again carefully tended. However, underlying this apparent affluence, unemployment remains a lingering problem. That said, unlike in Budapest, the much larger capital of neighboring Hungary, obvious signs of economic distress—such as panhandlers and homeless people—are relatively rare, and the casual observer will probably notice a general atmosphere of prosperity (fueled in part by coastal tourism). Croatia's accession to the European Union in July 2013 holds the promise of continued economic vitality.

GETTING HERE AND AROUND

After arriving in this regional hub city by any one of numerous flights from Germany (Frankfurt, Munich), United Kingdom (London), France (Paris), Austria (Vienna), Hungary (Budapest), or elsewhere, the best way to get into the city is by taxi or the economical airport shuttle. The best way to get around the city is by the efficient tram system, for which you can buy multiuse and all-day tourist cards online and at many hotels and hostels.

EXPLORING

The city is clearly divided into two distinct districts: **Gornji grad** (Upper Town) and **Donji grad** (Lower Town). While hilltop Gornji grad is made up of winding cobbled streets and terra-cotta rooftops sheltering beneath the cathedral and the Croatian Parliament building, Donji grad is where you'll find the city's most important 19th-century cultural institutions, including the National Theater, the university, and a number of museums—all in an organized grid.

GORNJI GRAD (UPPER TOWN)

The romantic hilltop area of Gornji grad dates back to medieval times, and is undoubtedly the loveliest part of Zagreb.

TOP ATTRACTIONS

Fodor's Choice ★ **Crkva svetog Marka** (*St. Mark's Church*). The original building was erected in the 13th century and was once the parish church of Gradec. The Baroque bell tower was added in the 17th century, while the steeply pitched roof—decorated in brilliant, multicolored tiles arranged to depict the coats of arms of Zagreb on the right and the Kingdom of Croatia, Dalmatia, and Slavonia on the left—was added during reconstruction in the 19th century. It underwent another reconstruction in the first half of the 20th century. At that time, renowned painter Jozo Kljakovic painted its walls, while the altar was decorated with works of famous sculptor Ivan Mestrovic. ✉ *Trg Svetog Marka 5, Gornji Grad* ☎ *01/485–1611* 🎫 *Free.*

Dolac (*Market*). Farmers from the surrounding countryside set up their stalls here daily, though the market is at its busiest on Friday and Saturday mornings. On the upper level, fresh fruit and vegetables are displayed on an open-air piazza under the protective shade of oversized umbrellas with a distinctive red color, known as *Sestinski kisobrani* because much smaller versions form part of the traditional garb of Sestine, a village just north of Zagreb. Dairy products and meats are sold in an indoor market below. ✉ *Tržnica, Dolac 9, Gornji Grad* 🌐 *www.trznice-zg.hr.*

Fodor's Choice ★ **Museum of Broken Relationships.** Opened in 2010, this museum displays objects connected to love stories that didn't work out. The entire exhibition is made up of personal belongings donated by people from around the world who endured a failed relationship, and each exhibit is accompanied by a brief text, explaining the connection between the object and the relationship. Subtly illustrating the tragicomedy that is love, it is now one of Zagreb's most visited museums, and its collection has toured numerous locations in Asia, Africa, the U.S., and Europe. ✉ *Ćirilometodska 2, Gornji Grad* ☎ *01/485–1021* 🌐 *www.brokenships.com* 🎫 *25 Kn.*

Museum of Contemporary Art (*Muzej suvremene umjetnosti*). This long-awaited museum displays works created since 1950 by Croatian and foreign artists. It's well worth a visit for anyone interested in modern art—the vast collection includes paintings, sculptures, graphic design, films, and videos. It lies outside the city center. To get here, take Tram 6 from the Trg bana Jelačića (east direction); journey time is approximately 30 minutes. ✉ *Avenija Dubrovnik 17, Novi Zagreb* ☎ *01/605–2700* 🌐 *www.msu.hr* 🎫 *30 Kn.*

Muzej grada Zagreba (*Zagreb City Museum*). Well worth a visit for anyone interested in urban design, this museum traces the city's most important historical, economic, political, social, and cultural events from medieval times to the present day. Exhibits include detailed scale models of how the city has evolved, as well as sections devoted to the old trade guilds, domestic life, and sacred art. ✉ *Opatička 20, Gornji*

Grad ☎ *01/485–1361, 01/485–1362* 🌐 *www.mgz.hr* 🎫 *30 Kn* ⏲ *Closed public holidays.*

WORTH NOTING

Crkva svete Katarine (*St. Catherine's Church*). Built for the Jesuit order between 1620 and 1632, this church is the most beautiful Baroque church in Zagreb. It is a one-nave church with six side chapels and a shrine. The vaults and the walls are decorated with pink and white stucco from 1732 as well as 18th-century illusionist paintings. The altars are the work of Francesco Robba and 17th-century Croatian artists. The church was thoroughly reconstructed after the 1880 earthquake, based on the design of Hermann Bolle. ✉ *Katarinin trg BB, Gornji Grad* ☎ *01/485–1950* 🎫 *Free.*

Hrvatski muzej naivne umjetnosti (*Croatian Museum of Native Art*). This unusual school of painting dates back to the 1930s, and the museum features more than 1,600 works of untutored peasant artists, primarily from the village of Hlebine in Koprivnica Križevci County. Canvases by the highly esteemed Ivan Generalić dominate here, though there are also paintings, drawings, sculptures, and prints by other noted members of the movement, plus a section devoted to foreigners working along similar lines. ✉ *Sv. Ćirila i Metoda 3, Gornji Grad* ☎ *01/485–1911* 🌐 *www.hmnu.org* 🎫 *20 Kn* ⏲ *Closed Mon. and public holidays.*

Kamenita Vrata (*Stone Gate*). The original 13th-century city walls had four gates, of which only Kamenita Vrata remains. Deep inside the dark passageway, locals stop to pray before a small shrine adorned with flickering candles. In 1731 a devastating fire consumed all the wooden elements of the gate, except for a painting of the Virgin and Child, which was found in the ashes, remarkably undamaged. Kamenita Vrata has since become a pilgrimage site, as can be seen from the numerous stone plaques reading *Hvala Majko Bozja* (Thank you, Mother of God). ✉ *Kamenita Vrata, Gornji Grad* 🌐 *www.zagreb-touristinfo.hr.*

OFF THE BEATEN PATH

Mirogoj Cemetery. A satisfying if somber little outing can be had by catching Bus 106 or 226 on Kaptol, in front of the Zagreb Cathedral, and riding it about 10 minutes to the fifth stop, Arkade. Designed by architect Herman Bollé and opened in 1872, Zagreb's most celebrated cemetery is set on a hillside north of downtown and features an imposing entrance: a long, massive brick wall topped by a row of striking green cupolas. Just behind this is the black-marble grave of Franjo Tuđjman, the man who served as Croatia's first president after the nation declared its independence from the former Yugoslavia. This lovely parklike cemetery, marked by paths lined with towering horse chestnut trees and by more black marble graves than you can count, is the final resting place for those of many creeds, from Roman Catholic and Serbian Orthodox to Jewish and Muslim. ✉ *Aleja Hermanna Bollea 27* 🌐 *www.gradskagroblja.hr.*

Kula Lotrščak (*Lotrščak Tower*). Formerly the entrance to the fortified medieval Gradec, Kula Lotrščak now houses a multilevel gallery with occasional exhibits of contemporary art. Each day at noon a small cannon is fired from the top of the tower in memory of the times when it was used to warn of the possibility of an Ottoman attack.

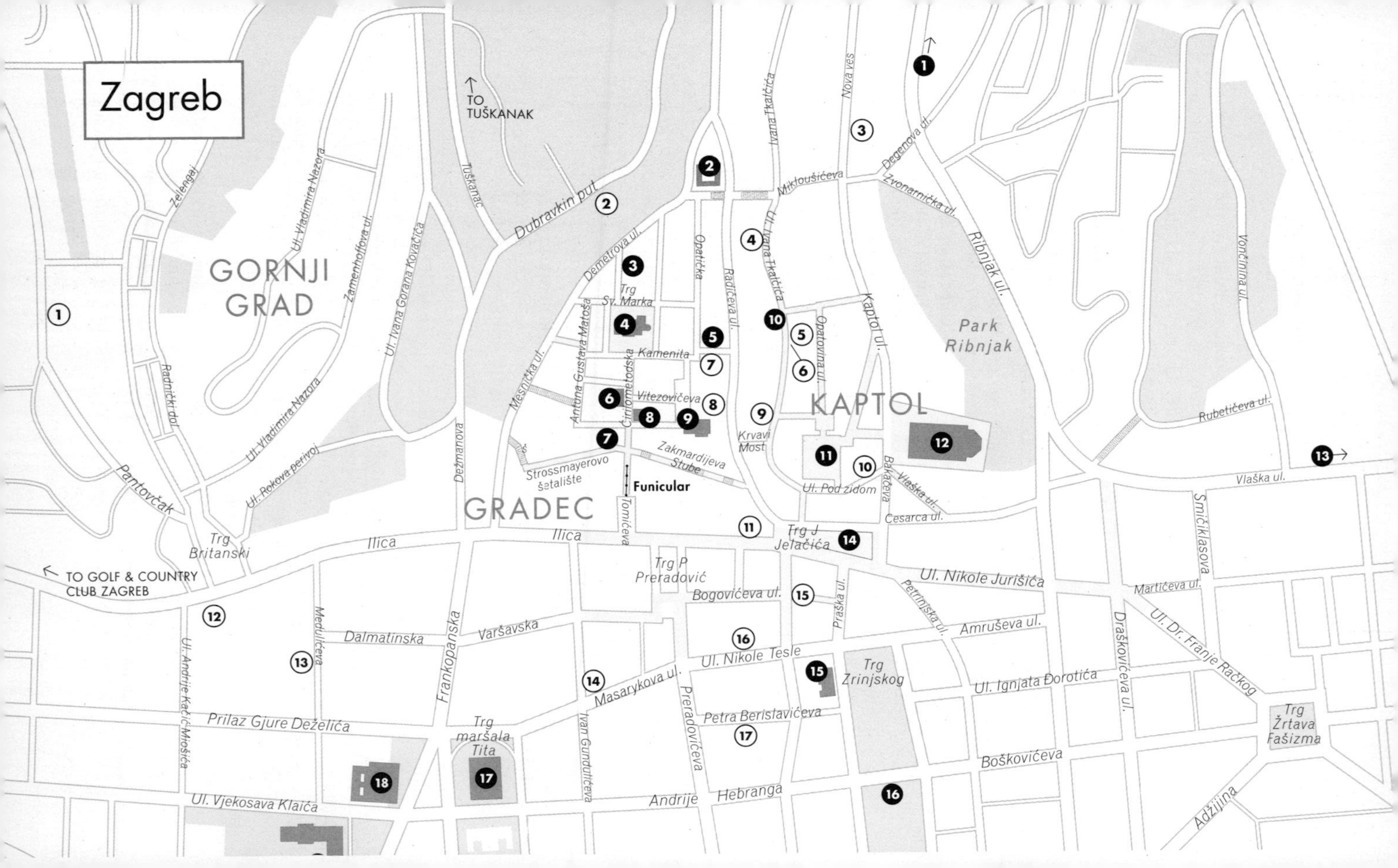
Zagreb
TO TUŠKANAK
GORNJI GRAD
GRADEC
KAPTOL
Park Ribnjak
TO GOLF & COUNTRY CLUB ZAGREB
Funicular
Zelengaj
Ul. Vladimira Nazora
Zamenhoffova ul.
Ul. Ivana Gorana Kovačića
Tuškanac
Dubravkin put
Radnički dol
Ul. Rokova perivoj
Pantovčak
Trg Britanski
Ilica
Dežmanova
Mesnička ul.
Demetrova ul.
Trg Sv. Marka
Antuna Gustava Matoša
Ćirilometodska
Kamenita
Vitezovićeva
Opatička
Radićeva ul.
Zakmardijeva Stube
Strossmayerovo šetalište
Tomićeva
Krvavi Most
Ul. Ivana Tkalčića
Ivana Tkalčića
Nova ves
Degenova ul.
Miklouišićeva
Zvonarnička ul.
Opatovina ul.
Kaptol ul.
Ribnjak ul.
Vončinina ul.
Rubetićeva ul.
Vlaška ul.
Ul. Pod zidom
Bakačeva
Cesarca ul.
Trg J Jelačića
Trg P Preradović
Bogovićeva ul.
Praška ul.
Petrinjska ul.
Ul. Nikole Jurišića
Martićeva ul.
Smičiklasova
Draškovićeva ul.
Ul. Dr. Franje Račkog
Trg Žrtava Fašizma
Adžijina
Amruševa ul.
Ul. Nikole Tesle
Trg Zrinjskog
Ul. Ignjata Đorotića
Boškovićeva
Andrije Hebranga
Petra Berislavićeva
Preradovićeva
Masarykova ul.
Ivan Gundulićeva
Varšavska
Dalmatinska
Frankopanska
Medulićeva
Trg maršala Tita
Prilaz Gjure Deželića
Ul. Andrije Kačić Miošića
Ul. Vjekosava Klaića

Exploring

- Arheološki muzej **15**
- Botanički vrt **20**
- Crkva svete Katarine **9**
- Crkva svetog Marka **4**
- Dolac **11**
- Hrvatski muzej naivene umjetnosti **6**
- Hrvatski narodno kazolište **17**
- Kamenita Vrata **5**
- Kula Lotrščak **7**
- Maksimir Park **13**
- Meštrovič Atelier **3**
- Mirogoj Cemetery **1**
- Museum of Broken Relationships **8**
- Museum of Contemporary Art **21**
- Muzej grada Zagreba **2**
- Muzej Mimara **19**
- Muzej za umjetnost i obrt **18**
- Strossmayerova galerija starih majstora **16**
- Tkalčićeva Street **10**
- Trg bana Jelačića **14**
- Zagrebačka katedrala ... **12**

Restaurants

- Agava **5**
- Amélie **17**
- Baltazar **3**
- Bio-bistro Zrno **13**
- Boban **15**
- Caffe Galerija Lav **8**
- The Cookie Factory Café **9**
- Dubravkin put **2**
- Ivek i Marek **4**
- Pivnica Medvedgrad **18**
- Pod Zidom **10**
- Rocket Burger **6**
- Sherry's Wine & Bites **12**
- Takenoko **14**
- Teneo Coffee Box **25**
- Trilogija-Vino i kuhinja **7**
- Vinodol **16**
- Zinfandel's Restaurant .. **21**

Hotels

- Best Western Premier Hotel Astoria ... **22**
- Esplanade Zagreb **20**
- Hotel Dubrovnik **24**
- Hotel Jägerhorn **11**
- Hotel President Pantovcak **1**
- Sheraton Zagreb **23**
- The Westin Zagreb **19**

You can climb the tower partway, via a spiral wooden staircase, for a look into the gallery rooms (which occupy several floors), or you can ascend all the way to the observation deck for splendid views of Zagreb and environs. ✉ *Strossmayerovo šetalište, Gornji Grad* ☎ *01/485–1926* 🌐 *www.galerijaklovic.hr* 🎫 *Observation deck 20 Kn; gallery free.*

> **CITY VIEWS**
>
> For sublime views east toward the Old Town, with its three prominent church steeples and many red-tile rooftops (including more than a few satellite dishes), stroll through the open wrought-iron gate just to the right of St. Catherine's Church. You'll find yourself on a spacious concrete plaza where you can take in the scene and then catch a flight of steps down past a lively café-bar toward Ilica.

Meštrović Atelier. This 17th-century building, with its interior courtyard, served as home and studio to Ivan Meštrović from 1922 until his emigration to the United States in 1942. The building was extensively remodeled according to plans devised by the artist and was turned into a memorial museum with a permanent exhibition of his sculptures and drawings after his death in 1962. (There is a larger collection of his works in the Meštrović Gallery in Split.) ✉ *Mletačka 8, Gornji Grad* ☎ *01/485–1123, 01/485–1124* 🌐 *www.mdc.hr* 🎫 *20 Kn* ⊗ *Mon., Public Holiday.*

Fodor's Choice ★ **Tkalčićeva Street.** This street was once a channel forming the boundary between Kaptol and Gradec, then known as Potok (the brook). Today, it is a charming, well-maintained pedestrian zone lined with 19th-century town houses, many of which have been converted into popular café-bars at street level—attracting a huge cross section of Croatian and international youth from morning until late at night. ✉ *Tkalčićeva, Gornji Grad.*

Trg bana Jelačića (*Ban Jelačić Square*). Buildings lining the square date from 1827 onward and include several fine examples of Viennese Secessionist architecture. The centerpiece is an equestrian statue of Ban Jelačić, the first Croatian viceroy, erected in 1866. Originally facing north toward Hungary, against which Jelačić waged war as a commander in the Austrian Imperial Army, the statue was dismantled after World War II by the communist government, only to be reinstalled in 1990, this time facing south. The square features the Manduševac fountain located to the east. ✉ *Between Ilica to the west, Praška to the south, and Jurišićeva to the east, Gornji Grad.*

Fodor's Choice ★ **Zagrebačka katedrala** (*The Cathedral of Assumption of the Blessed Virgin Mary and Saint Stephen and Saint Ladislaus*). Dedicated to the Assumption of Mary and to the kings Saint Stephen and Saint Ladislaus, the Zagreb Cathedral was built on the site of a former 12th-century cathedral destroyed by the Tartars in 1242. The present structure was constructed between the 13th and 16th centuries. The striking neo-Gothic facade was added by architect Herman Bollé following the earthquake of 1880, its twin steeples being the identifying feature of the city's skyline. Behind the impressive main altar are crypts of Zagreb's archbishops and of Croatian national heroes. The interior is imposing and inspires silent reflection. Don't neglect the north wall, which bears an inscription of the Ten Commandments in 12th-century Glagolithic script. ✉ *Kaptol 31, Gornji Grad* ☎ *01/481–4727* 🌐 *www.zg-nadbiskupija.hr* 🎫 *Free.*

NEED A BREAK

Pingvin Sandwich Bar. If you are looking for a quick and inexpensive lunch, consider the Pingvin Sandwich Bar, groundbreaking for being the first in the city. This popular stand, just a few minutes' walk from Trg bana Jelačića, offers things like grilled chicken sandwiches or veggie burgers. Ordering is simple: not only do most clerks speak English, but there are also user-friendly pictures and English translations. ✉ ***Nikole Tesle 7, Donji Grad*** ☎ ***01/481-1446.***

WHY HIKE WHEN YOU CAN RIDE?

If you're walking along Ilica from the main square, you might wonder about the best route up the hill to Lotrščak Tower and beyond to St. Mark's Church. Well, you can save yourself the steep hike up by catching the funicular, which runs six times an hour, 6:30 am to 10 pm, from short Tomićeva ulica (just off Ilica) just a few hundred yards up the hillside. The cost is 4 Kn; you can buy the ticket when you board.

DONJI GRAD (LOWER TOWN)

Donji grad came into being during the late 19th century. The urban plan, which follows a grid pattern, was drawn up by Milan Lenuci and combines a succession of squares and parks laid out in a "U" shape (known as the Green Horseshoe), all overlooked by the city's main public buildings and cultural institutions.

TOP ATTRACTIONS

Arheološki muzej (*Archaeological Museum*). Museum exhibits focus on prehistoric times to the Tartar invasion. Pride of place is given to the Vučedol Dove, a three-legged ceramic vessel in the form of a bird, dating back to the 4th millennium BC, and a piece of linen bearing the longest known text in ancient Etruscan writing. The courtyard features a collection of stone relics from Roman times. ✉ *Trg Nikole Šubića Zrinskog 19, Donji Grad* ☎ *01/487–3000, 01/487–3101* 🌐 *www.amz.hr* 🎫 *30 Kn* ⏲ *Mon and Public Holidays.*

Botanički vrt (*Botanical Garden*). Founded in 1889 as research grounds for the Faculty of Biology at Zagreb University, the garden includes an arboretum with English-style landscaping, a small artificial lake, and an ornamental Japanese bridge. ✉ *Marulićev trg 9a, Donji Grad* ☎ *01/489-8060* 🌐 *hirc.botanic.hr/vrt/home.htm* 🎫 *Free.*

Strossmayerova galerija starih majstora (*Strossmayer Gallery of Old Masters*). Now under the custody of the Croatian Academy of Sciences and Arts, this impressive gallery was founded in 1884 by Bishop Strossmayer and later expanded to include many private donations. Works by Venetian Renaissance and Baroque artists such as Bellini and Carpaccio predominate, but there are also masterpieces by Dutch painters Brueghel and Van Dyck, as well as a delightful Mary Magdalene by El Greco. ✉ *Trg Nikole Šubića Zrinskog 11, Donji Grad* ☎ *01/489–5111* 🌐 *www.mdc.hr* 🎫 *30 Kn* ⏲ *Closed Mon.*

WORTH NOTING

Hrvatsko narodno kazalište (*Croatian National Theater*). The building dates from 1895, designed by the Viennese firm Hellmer and Fellner as part of the preparations for a state visit by Emperor Franz Josef. In front of the theater, set deep in a round concrete basin, is Meštrović's little, eerily lifelike sculpture *Zdenac Života* (*Fountain of Life*), from 1912, which depicts four naked couples writhing uncomfortably in each other's arms around a small pool of water while one lone, likewise naked gentleman stares meditatively into the pool. The only way to see the impressive, stately interior of the theater is to attend a performance. ✉ *Trg maršala Tita 15, Donji Grad* ☎ *01/488–8418* 🌐 *www.hnk.hr.*

Muzej Mimara (*Mimara Museum*). In a huge gray building that's dull compared to some of those nearby, this vast private collection, including paintings, sculptures, ceramics, textiles, and rugs, was donated by Ante Topić Mimara (1898–1987), a Croatian who spent many years abroad where he made his fortune, supposedly as a merchant. On display are canvases attributed to such old masters as Raphael, Rembrandt, and Rubens, as well as more modern works by the likes of Manet, Degas, and Renoir, and ancient artifacts including Egyptian glassware and Chinese porcelain. ✉ *Rooseveltov trg 5, Donji Grad* ☎ *01/482–8100, 01/482–6079* 🌐 *www.mimara.hr* 🎫 *40 Kn.*

Muzej za umjetnost i obrt (*Museum of Arts and Crafts*). Designed in 1888 by Herman Bollé, the architect responsible for the Zagreb Cathedral facade, this pleasant museum traces the development of the applied arts from the Baroque period to the 20th century. Exhibits are displayed in chronological order, and although furniture design predominates, there are also sections devoted to sacred art, clocks, and clothing. ✉ *Trg maršala Tita 10, Donji Grad* ☎ *01/488–2111* 🌐 *www.muo.hr* 🎫 *30 Kn.*

OFF THE BEATEN PATH

Maksimir Park. For a peaceful stroll in southeastern Europe's oldest landscaped, English-style park, hop on a tram and go visit Maksimir Park. A short ride east of the center of Zagreb (10 minutes on Tram 11 or 12 from Trg bana Jelačića or 15 minutes on Tram 4 or 7 from the train station), this 44½-acre expanse of vine-covered forests and several artificial lakes was a groundbreaker when it opened back in 1794. After getting off the tram, you walk forward a bit and enter on the left, through a prominent gate opposite the city's main soccer stadium, aptly named Stadion Maksimir. A long, wide promenade flanked by benches leads from here to Bellevue Pavilion (1843), perched atop a small hill and featuring a café. Be sure to check out the Echo Pavilion (Paviljon jeka), built in the late 19th century in honor of the Greek nymph Echo. Stand in the middle and you can hear the whispers of anyone standing within the pavilion, as if they were right next to you. To your right along the way are some small lakes and, beyond, the city's modest zoo, **Zoološki vrt Zagreb,** where admission is 30 Kn; it's open daily from 9 to 8 (last tickets sold at 6:30). To your left is a playground.

WHERE TO EAT

For budget fare, leave the main square, Trg bana Jelačića, and go up the steps toward Dolac (the main market). Halfway up the steps on your right is a row of bistros where you can get everything from *bureks* (a savory cheese- or meat-filled pastry) to simple pizzas to Balkan-style grilled meats for around half what you'd pay at a modestly priced restaurant. And do remember, though Zagreb is not exactly overflowing with budget sandwich shops, traditional bakeries have long fulfilled that role for locals; at such places, which are on practically every street corner, you can pick up a burek for as little as 10 Kn a piece.

SUMMER BREAK

If you're in town between late July and the third week of August, don't be surprised to find many restaurants closed for two to four weeks while the staff are off at the coast, as is much of Zagreb.

GORNJI GRAD (UPPER TOWN)

$$ MEDITERRANEAN

Agava. Worth the steep walk up a flight of steps, in warm weather you can enjoy your meal sitting on wooden terrace overlooking the street, or else bask in the homey elegance of the inside space, with its wood-beamed ceiling, parquet floor, and rattan furnishings. Large windows let you gaze out onto the pedestrian thoroughfare below. **Known for:** people watching on the terrace; continental dishes; good value. *Average main: 120 Kn* *Tkalčićeva 39, Gornji Grad* *01/482–9826* *www.restaurant-agava.hr.*

$$$$ MEDITERRANEAN

Baltazar. Nestled in a courtyard lying 10 minutes' walk uphill beyond the cathedral, just beyond Pizzeria 2, Baltazar is best known for classic Balkan dishes such as *ražnjići* (pork on the spit), *čevapčići* (spiced ground-meat kebabs), and *zapečeni grah* (oven-baked beans). The interior is elegant, albeit slightly smoky, and the spacious courtyard has leaf-shaded seating. **Known for:** large Balkan platters; local wine list; expansive garden. *Average main: 300 Kn* *Nova ves 4, Gornji Grad* *01/466–6999, 01/466–6824* *www.baltazar.hr.*

$ CAFÉ Fodor's Choice ★

Caffe Galerija Lav. Don't let the casual café fare fool you; this place is anything but standard. Located just up the hill (first right) from Kamenita Vrata, it is a perfect place to take a load off after the alpine climb into Gornji Grad, before heading on to seeing the parliament, Museum of Broken Relationships, and Crkva Svetog Marka. **Known for:** art collection; black and white modern decor; stone terrace. *Average main: 35 Kn* *Opaticka 2, Gornji Grad* *01/492–2108* *No credit cards.*

$$ JAPANESE

Takenoko. Don't be deterred by the tiny English-language translations on the menu outside; inside, the menu of this utterly chic, sparkling restaurant is completely readable. You can choose between sushi, both traditional Japanese rolls and American-style varieties; teriyaki; wok dishes; and specialties such as carrot and tofu soup or sea bass in jalapeño-wasabi sauce. **Known for:** upscale vibe; extensive drink list; best sushi in town. *Average main: 90 Kn* *Nova Ves 17, Gornji Grad* *01/486–0530* *www.takenoko.hr.*

$$ MEDITERRANEAN

Trilogija-Vino i kuhinja. In Gornji grad close to Kamenita Vrata, this quaint, unpretentious restaurant offers superb food, an excellent wine list, and friendly professional staff. The menu changes frequently depending on the seasons and what's fresh at the morning market, but you can expect creative dishes such as shrimp risotto with wild asparagus, tuna steak with green polenta, as well as a hearty steak sandwich. **Known for:** creative tapas; events; wine list. *$ Average main: 100 Kn ✉ Kamenita 5, Gornji Grad ☎ 01/485–1394 🌐 www.entrilogija.weebly.com.*

DONJI GRAD (LOWER TOWN)

$ CAFÉ Fodor's Choice ★

Amélie. For a cake and coffee experience that the French namesake of this cute little café would be proud of, pop into Amélie just down the hill from the Zagreb Cathedral. The wooden tables and cozy white interior give the place a charming, even slightly rustic feel, and the surprisingly varied selection of delectable cakes and pies will release all your caloric inhibitions. **Known for:** homemade everything; unique cakes; quiches. *$ Average main: 30 Kn ✉ Vlaska 6, Donji Grad ☎ 01/558–3360 🌐 www.slasticeamelie.com.*

$$ VEGETARIAN

Bio-bistro Zrno. If you want to strengthen the body and nourish the spirit with seasonal, organic fresh fruits and vegetables, walk a few blocks west from the main square to Bio-bistro Zrno, which offers fresh vegetables, tofu, seitan, warm sourdough bread, organic coffee, wine, tea, juice, smoothies, and shakes. All ingredients are delivered each day directly from Croatia's first organic farm of the same name. **Known for:** vegan dishes; local produce; cheerful environment. *$ Average main: 75 Kn ✉ Medulićeva 2, Donji Grad ☎ 01/484–7540 🌐 www.zrnobiobistro.hr.*

$$ ITALIAN

Boban. Just down the street from the Hotel Dubrovnik, Boban is not only a street-level bar but also a restaurant in the large vaulted cellar space below (with a stylish dining room at street level and several tables outside for dining, chilling with a glass of Croatian wine, and people-watching). Specializing in pasta dishes, it is extremely popular with locals, so be prepared to line up for a table, since reservations are not accepted. **Known for:** popularity with locals; posh bar; hearty meals. *$ Average main: 90 Kn ✉ Gajeva 9, Donji Grad ☎ 01/481–1549 🌐 www.boban.hr.*

$ CAFÉ Fodor's Choice ★

The Cookie Factory Café. Think of your favorite bakery, ice cream parlor, and basic café rolled into one, and that's the Cookie Factory. With its bright white interior, its walls gaily decorated with quirky graffiti, and its extensive selection of cookies, brownies, and cakes hard to find on this side of the Atlantic, you'll simply have to stop here for a little while. **Known for:** brownies; charming atmosphere; quick bites. *$ Average main: 30 Kn ✉ Tkalčićeva 21, Donji Grad ☎ 099/494–9400 🌐 www.cookiefactory.hr ▭ No credit cards.*

$$$ SEAFOOD Fodor's Choice ★

Dubravkin put. Nestled in a verdant dale in Tuškanac Park, a 15-minute walk from the center in a low-rise building that might be mistaken for a ranch-style house, this prestigious fish restaurant specializes in creative Mediterranean fare, with the house favorites including *buzara* (stew prepared with shellfish and scampi and/or fish) and sea bass fillets in saffron and scampi sauce, as well as appetizers like avocado with scampi, not to mention a few meat delicacies. The dining room is light and airy, with candlelit tables, a wooden floor, palmlike little trees, and colorful abstract art. **Known for:** location inside the park; excellent seafood; high-end service. $ *Average main: 150 Kn* ✉ *Dubravkin put 2* ☎ *01/483–4975* 🌐 *www.dubravkin-put.com* ⏲ *Closed Sun., all of August.*

$$ EASTERN EUROPEAN ✕ **Ivek i Marek.** Celebrated for its delectable cakes made with whole wheat and unrefined brown sugar, Ivica i Marica also serves traditional Croatian pastas, likewise using whole wheat, as well as hearty meat dishes. Try the tofu-stuffed pepper, homemade ravioli stuffed with spinach and cheese, or Zagorje specialties including *štrukli* (baked pastry filled with cheese). **Known for:** Croatian pasta; costumed waitstaff; folk atmosphere. $ *Average main: 85 Kn* ✉ *Tkalčićeva 70* ☎ *01/481–7321* 🌐 *www.ivicaimarica.com.*

$$ EASTERN EUROPEAN ✕ **Pivnica Medvedgrad.** Best known for its excellent beers brewed on the premises, all of the four Pivnica Medvedgrad locations serve up generous portions of roast meats, goulash, and beans and sausage, accompanied by a range of salads. Ilica, the cavernous beer hall—replete with long wooden tables, high leather-backed chairs, and wood-beamed ceilings—is about a 10-minute walk west from the main square. **Known for:** local brews; hearty meals; beer-hall ambience. $ *Average main: 65 Kn* ✉ *Ilica 49, Donji Grad* ☎ *01/484–6922* 🌐 *www.pivnica-medvedgrad.hr.*

$$ EASTERN EUROPEAN Fodor's Choice ★ ✕ **Pod Zidom.** Wedged between the cathedral and the Dolac farmer's market, jazzy bistro Pod Zidom offers a creative take on traditional Croatian dishes, making the most of fresh ingredients at its doorstep. The chef is renowned for his beef cheek with celery and goat cheese sauce, cooked for 12 hours before making it to your plate. **Known for:** brunch with live music; fresh organic meat; excellent selection of Croatian wines. $ *Average main: 90 Kn* ✉ *Pod Zidom 5* ☎ *099/325–3600.*

$$ AMERICAN ✕ **Rocket Burger.** This may well be the only place in Zagreb, if not the entire country, where you can get a relatively authentic American breakfast. Though the establishment itself projects a limited dinner vibe, as it is forced to occupy a small closet-space of wire-rimmed tables and squat bar stools offering no room for a proper spread, the menu does the job quite nicely. **Known for:** American specialties; large breakfasts; late-night eats. $ *Average main: 60 Kn* ✉ *Tkalčićeva 44, Donji Grad.*

$ EUROPEAN ✕ **Sherry's Wine & Bites.** Nestled on a terrace across from the British Square and just a few steps from Ilica Street, this funky bar pulls patrons in with its large selection of Croatian and foreign wines, as well as exceptional bites such as pancetta bruschetta, seaweed and microgreens salad, and mini *sarmas* (oblong balls of mixed meat wrapped in sauerkraut) until as late as midnight. The lively atmosphere is greatly enhanced with live music. **Known for:** live music; popular evening venue; creative small plates. $ *Average main: 45 Kn* ✉ *Ilica 73 (in the yard)* ☎ *01/400–8150.*

$ CAFÉ ✕ **Teneo Coffee Box.** Situated in a quiet, residential area of Zagreb, just three steps from the Tresnjevacki trg stop on Tram 12 and less than 10 minutes' walk from the Hotel Panorama, this 129-square-foot cafe full of hot, cold, and iced-coffee and tea options makes most other Zagreb cafés seem bland by comparison. Caramel Latte, White Chocolate Mocha and dozens of other concoctions are on offer; be sure to try the aptly named Tiger Chai, whose delicate spices will tingle your palate. **Known for:** variety of coffees; home roast; coffee workshops. $ *Average main: 15 Kn* ✉ *Trešnjevački Trg 2, Donji Grad* ☎ *095/868–0604* 🌐 *www.facebook.com/teneocoffee* ▭ *No credit cards.*

$$ EASTERN EUROPEAN Fodor's Choice ★ **Vinodol.** A few blocks southwest of the main square, the Vinodol is an elegant spot locals flock to when they hanker for traditional meaty fare such as veal and lamb, pork with plum sauce, or, for starters, *zagorska juha* (Zagorje-style potato soup with ham and mushrooms). Enjoy all this in a spacious, shaded courtyard or inside under brick-vaulted ceilings and amid low lighting that contrive to give you an elegant, wine-cellar sensation even though you're not in a cellar at all. **Known for:** meaty fare; large semi-outdoor garden; local hangout. *Average main: 120 Kn* ✉ *Nikole Tesle 10, Donji Grad* ☎ *01/481–1427* 🌐 *www.vinodol-zg.hr.*

$$$$ EUROPEAN **Zinfandel's Restaurant.** Just inside the Esplanade Hotel lies one of Zagreb's most elegant dining destinations known for its formal yet comfortable atmosphere and its history as a stop on the Orient Express. Order from the tasting menu, where wines are carefully selected by a sommelier to perfectly complement each dish. **Known for:** tasting menu; stunning views from Oleander Terrace; caters to dietary restrictions. *Average main: 500 Kn* ✉ *Mihanoviceva 1* ☎ *01/456–6644* 🌐 *www.zinfandels.hr.*

WHERE TO STAY

Zagreb offers a good choice of large, expensive hotels geared to the needs of business travelers. This may be in part because tourists tend to frequent the coast, whereas the corporate crowd sticks to the city. However, for summertime vacationers who choose to check out the capital, this is good news: since so much of the country and indeed Europe are on the coast, Zagreb's "low season," when rates are lowest at many hotels, is from early July through late August. Since 2000, several of the capital's major hotels have come under new ownership and been given complete makeovers, guaranteed to appeal to those seeking mid- to upper-range accommodations.

DONJI GRAD (LOWER TOWN)

$$ HOTEL **Best Western Premier Hotel Astoria.** Less than five minutes by foot from the train station and 10 minutes from downtown, the hotel offers bright, modern rooms with the silky bedspreads and partly marble bathrooms that meet the requirements of its Premier category. **Pros:** goodl ocation on a quiet side street midway between train station and main square; luxurious bathrooms with excellent amenities; top-notch 24-hour business center; free parking for guests. **Cons:** smallish rooms; no health facilities or pool. *Rooms from: 800 Kn* ✉ *Petrinjska 71* ☎ *01/480–8900* 🌐 *www.hotelastoria.hr* *100 rooms* *Breakfast.*

$$$ HOTEL Fodor's Choice ★ **Esplanade Zagreb.** This beautiful hotel, diagonally across from the train station, was built in 1925 for travelers on the original *Orient Express.* Louis Armstrong, Elizabeth Taylor, Charles Lindbergh, Orson Welles, Woody Allen, Queen Elizabeth II, and Richard Nixon all stayed here, among other famous names, many of whom left photos for the celebrity wall downstairs. **Pros:** unmitigated luxury; right by the train station; great fitness center. **Cons:** pricey and formal (i.e., not a place to shuffle around in your cut-offs); smallish lobby. *Rooms from: 1,500 Kn* ✉ *Mihanovićeva 1, Donji Grad* ☎ *01/456–6666* 🌐 *www.esplanade.hr* *208 rooms.*

$$ HOTEL **Hotel Dubrovnik.** Claiming the most central location in the city, just off Trg bana Jelačića, Hotel Dubrovnik has been popular with business travelers and tourists since opening back in 1929. **Pros:** right off the main square; numerous amenities; recently renovated. **Cons:** lacking character. *Rooms from: 700 Kn* ✉ *Gajeva 1, Donji Grad* ☎ *01/486–3555* *www.hotel-dubrovnik.hr* *222 rooms* *Breakfast.*

$$ HOTEL **Hotel Jägerhorn.** Located at the far end of a shop-filled courtyard off Zagreb's busiest shopping street and just a minute's walk from Ban Jelačić Square, this charming little hotel is the oldest in Zagreb (but fully updated) and a perfect base for exploring the city. **Pros:** central location; updated rooms; excellent breakfast. **Cons:** small, so often fully booked. *Rooms from: 900 Kn* ✉ *Ilica 14, Donji Grad* ☎ *01/483–3877* *www.hotel-jagerhorn.hr* *18 rooms* *Breakfast.*

$$$ HOTEL FAMILY **Hotel President Pantovcak.** About a 20-minute walk from the city center and set in a quiet residential neighborhood, this stylish boutique hotel has a mix of antique furnishings, contemporary art, and floor-to-ceiling windows that flood with light year round and are open in summer months. **Pros:** lovely garden; bottomless champagne breakfast; friendly staff. **Cons:** a walk to the city center; no pool. *Rooms from: 1,000 Kn* ✉ *Pantovchak 52* ☎ *01/488–1480* *www.president-zagreb.com* *10* *Breakfast.*

$$ HOTEL **Sheraton Zagreb.** Located on a small side street in a somewhat nondescript part of town but only a 20-minute walk from the city center, the Sheraton Zagreb's high standards make this modern, six-story hotel a relative bargain. **Pros:** top-notch facilities and services; modern rooms; quality dining options. **Cons:** 20-minute walk from the main square; not exactly cozy. *Rooms from: 900 Kn* ✉ *Kneza Borne 2, Donji Grad* ☎ *01/455–9107* *www.hotel-sheratonzagreb.com* *335 rooms* *Breakfast.*

$$ HOTEL Fodor's Choice ★ **The Westin Zagreb.** After a complete renovation in 2005, this colossal 17-story modern structure between the Mimara Museum and the Botanical Garden—previously the Opera Zagreb—still looks homely on the outside, but on the inside it's a sparkling five-star affair. **Pros:** big, comfy rooms; top-notch luxury; excellent amenities and services; superb dining options. **Cons:** 15 minutes from main square. *Rooms from: 850 Kn* ✉ *Izidora Kršnjavoga 1, Donji Grad* ☎ *01/489–2000* *www.hotelwestinzagreb.com/hr* *349 rooms* *Breakfast.*

NIGHTLIFE AND PERFORMING ARTS

Climbing full-steam-ahead out of the economic depression caused by the war, Zagreb now has a lively entertainment scene. Bars, clubs, and cinemas are predominantly frequented by the city's student population, whereas the concert hall and theater remain the domain of the older generation. For information about what's on, pick up a free copy of the monthly *Events and Performances*, published by the city tourist board.

NIGHTLIFE

GORNJI GRAD (UPPER TOWN)

Swanky Monkey Garden. A trendy vintage bar housed in an industrial space (a former dry cleaning factory) with exposed brick and lofty ceilings, Swanky Monkey Garden also has outdoor seating on a beautiful terrace covered in lights. ✉ *Ilica 50* ☎ *01/400–4248* *www.swanky-hostel.com.*

DONJI GRAD (LOWER TOWN)

Alcatraz. With a lively combination of Zagreb locals and tourists, great drinks on the cheaper side, and good music, this location is the best bar in the city center for an authentic "Zagreb feel." ✉ *Preradoviceva Uliva 12* ☎ *91/531–3703* 🌐 *www.alcatraz.pondi.hr.*

Bulldog. This popular split-level café-cum-wine-bar and bistro has a summer terrace. At night it becomes a club where you can enjoy soul, rock, blues, and jazz performers. ✉ *Bogovićeva 6, Donji Grad* ☎ *01/400–2072* 🌐 *www.bulldog-pub-zagreb.com.*

Gallery. Gallery's prime setting on the shore of Lake Jarun, known as the "Zagreb Sea," consistent party-driving music, and dapper yet approachable crowd makes it a go-to spot for a night out to remember in Zagreb. If you're in need of a dance break, their beautiful terrace looking out over the lake is there to give you a chance to cool down and chat. Gallery is over 2 miles from the city center, so rather than chance your luck, you should call ahead to get on the guest list—especially if you wish to reserve a table. ✉ *Aleja Matije Ljubeka 33* ☎ *91/531–3703* 🌐 *www.gallery.hr.*

PERFORMING ARTS

ARTS FESTIVALS

Promenade Concerts. For the best of concerts in the park, keep your eye out for the free Promenade Concerts by Croatian chamber orchestras, brass bands, and choirs, held every Saturday from 11 am to 1 pm from around mid-June to mid-August at the music pavilion set amid the lovely plane trees and fountains of Zrinjevac Park, on trg Nikole Šubića Zrinskog. Adding color to this series are 19th-century-costume contests and displays, an antiques market, a play area and programs for children, rides in horse-drawn carriages, and even souvenir stands. Sunday from 11 to noon is reserved for the legendary Wing Orchestra of Zagreb Electric Tram, which performs waltzes, marches, evergreens, and patriotic songs. If you are in the Upper Town on Saturday or Sunday between 10 and noon, you will enjoy the streets filled with the romantic sound of street musicians. If you want to visit Maksimir Park, Sunday would be the perfect day; waltzes, polkas, chansons, and arias from operettas fill the air there between 10:30 and 12:30. 🌐 *www.zagreb-touristinfo.hr.*

Fodor's Choice ★ **Summer on Stross - Strossmartre.** Embark on a journey toward the Strossmayer Promenade, next to the Lotrščak Tower and you will see one of the best Zagreb entertainment projects. Strossmartre brings you a bit of the Parisian spirit—lots of concerts, exhibitions, art workshops, and great wine and beer offers for more than 100 days, from the end of May until the beginning of September. And don't forget to come to the Half New Year's Party on June 30. ✉ *Strossmayerovo šetalište* 🌐 *www.ljetonastrosu.com.*

World Theatre Festival. For one week in mid-September, the World Theatre Festival brings to Zagreb theater companies from all over Europe—if not exactly the world—for one or more performances each evening at various theatrical venues about town. ☎ *01/487–4562* 🌐 *www.zagreb-theatrefestival.hr.*

FILM

Cineplexx. Cineplexx is Croatia's first multiplex cinema, in the Centar Kaptol shopping complex, wedged in a serene, parklike atmosphere a 10-minute walk north of the cathedral. Head first along Kaptol and then along Nova Ves. Most foreign films (including those from the United States) are shown in their original language with Croatian subtitles. ✉ *Nova Ves 17, Gornji Grad* ☎ *01/563–3888* 🌐 *www.cineplexx.hr.*

SHOPPING

Although Zagreb may not be a shopping mecca, a walk down the bustling Ilica or other nearby streets will take you past plenty of stores brimming with the latest fashions. Frankopanska particularly is turning into something of a fashion avenue, with labels like Lacoste, Cacharel, and others. Don't pass up the chance to stroll through the beautiful Oktogon shopping arcade, with its long, spacious yellow hall, elaborate wrought-iron gates at each end, and lovely glass ceilings from 1901. The arcade connects Ilica 5 with Trg Petra Preradovića and offers more than a few high-class shops along the way. In the center of the arcade you'll find the elegant Croata, with its wide selection of silk scarves, men's dress shirts, and, suitably for the birthplace of the cravat, countless variations on the classical necktie.

THE ZAGREB CARD

Sold in 26 venues around town, including several major hotels, The Zagreb Card offers unlimited travel on public transport in Zagreb and discounts of up to 50% at more than 30 museums and galleries, as well as discounts at the zoo, on parking and car rental, and 20% discounts at many shops, restaurants, theaters, and concert halls. Considering the cost of similar cards in other European capitals, this is truly a bargain. It's valid for 24 or 72 hours (from the date and time stamped on the card) and costs 60 or 90 Kn.

GORNJI GRAD (UPPER TOWN)

SHOPPING CENTERS AND MARKETS

Fodor's Choice ★ **Dolac open-air market.** For an authentic Croatian shopping experience, visit the Dolac open-air market, where besides fresh fruit and vegetables there are also a number of arts-and-crafts stalls. It's open weekdays 7 to 3 and weekends until 2. ✉ *Tržnica Dolac, Dolac 9* 🌐 *www.trznice-zg.hr.*

Importanne Centar. It's easy to miss downtown's largest shopping mall, the Importanne Centar, since it's completely underground and not well marked on the street level. Look for the escalators leading down, and once you're inside, good luck finding your way back out. There's a 24-hour parking garage here as well. ✉ *Trg Ante Starčevića 7* ☎ *01/467–7076* 🌐 *www.importanne.hr.*

WINE

Fodor's Choice ★ **Vinoteka Bornstein.** Housed in a tastefully arranged, vaulted brick cellar, Vinoteka Bornstein stocks a wide range of quality Croatian wines, olive oils, and truffle products. ✉ *Kaptol 19, Gornji Grad* ☎ *01/481–2361* 🌐 *www.bornstein.hr.*

DONJI GRAD (LOWER TOWN)

CLOTHING

Croata. Ties may not be the most original of gifts, but they are uniquely Croatian. During the 17th century, Croatian mercenaries who fought in France sported narrow, silk neck scarfs, which soon became known to the French as *cravat* (from the Croatian *hrvat*). At Croata you can buy "original Croatian ties" in presentation boxes, accompanied by a brief history of the tie. There, you can also find tasteful gifts for ladies, including scarves, shawls, and accessories. ✉ *Ilica 5, within the Oktogon arcade, Donji Grad* ☎ *01/481–2726* 🌐 *www.croata.hr.*

FOODSTUFFS

Natura Croatica. All manner of Croatian delicacies that use only natural ingredients are offered here from brandies and liqueurs to jams, olive oils, cheeses, truffles, soaps, wild-game jerkies, and pâtés. ✉ *Preradovićeva 8, Donji Grad* ☎ *01/485–5076* 🌐 *www.naturacroatica.com.*

Story of Salt. In search of a gift that will capture the pure sun and breeze of the Adriatic? Try visiting this brand-new gift shop–museum run by the Solana Nin Saltworks, a major sea salt manufacturer based near Zadar on the coast. Here you can buy the "salt flower" (*cvjet soli*), affectionately called the "caviar of salt" for its unique flavor and composition. Spend several minutes taking in the images and implements that pay tribute to the sea salt industry; the mini-museum features several implements from traditional (and modern) salt manufacturing, including salt rakes, transport wagons, and a wooden packing unit. ✉ *Gajeva 8, Donji Grad* ☎ *01/487–6765* 🌐 *www.solananin.hr.*

SPORTS AND THE OUTDOORS

GOLF

Golf & Country Club Zagreb. In addition to the gently challenging 18-hole course and a 9-hole executive course, the Golf & Country Club Zagreb—which opened as the capital's first golf course in 1995—has a driving range (30 Kn for 50 balls) with 40 grass bays, a 12-bay covered area in the event of bad weather, fitness facilities, and a restaurant. ✉ *Jadranska avenija 6* ✥ *Follow the sign for Karlovac at the roundabout near the Zagreb Fair. Turn right at the second light, pass the hospital on your left, and continue for about 1 km (½ mile).* ☎ *01/653–1177* 🌐 *www.gcczagreb.hr* 🎫 *Greens fees 130 Kn, additional 50 Kn for daily ticket* 🏌 *18 holes, 9-hole executive course, 7002 yards, par 72.*

WATER SPORTS

You don't have to go all the way to the Adriatic to find a beach. Zagreb's pride and joy, Lake Jarun, is not terribly natural-looking but is apparently a quite clean body of water in the middle of an urban oasis located 4 km (2½ miles) from the center. Here you will find beaches (equipped with showers, sanitary facilities, and changing stalls); a children's pool; canoe, paddle-boat, bicycle, and rollerblade rentals; a jogging track; mini-golf and table tennis; restaurants, cafés, bars, and dance clubs including the ultrahip Aquarius. A long peninsula actually creates two lakes: *malo jezero* (small lake) and *veliko jezero* (large lake). The clear, spring-fed water is carefully regulated to maintain its quality. Though you can walk here from the train station in less than an hour, you can also take Tram 17 from Trg bana Jelačića 15 stops east (direction: Prečko) or Tram 5 from the bus station 17 stops (direction: Prečko). After 11 pm there's service every 40 minutes.

EXCURSIONS NORTH OF ZAGREB

A favorite excursion to the outskirts of Zagreb is to the heights of Sljeme and its observatory. And then there is the peaceful spa town of Stubičke Toplice and, a bit farther to the northeast, the Catholic pilgrimage site of Marija Bistrica. Farther to the north, beyond the Medvednica Hills, lies a pastoral region known as Zagorje. The scenery is calm and enchanting: redbrick villages, such as Kumrovec, are animated with ducks and chickens, and the hillsides are inlaid with vineyards and orchards. Medieval hilltop castles, including Veliki Tabor and Dvor Trakošćan, survey the surrounding valleys. To the northeast of Zagreb is the charming Baroque town of Varaždin. Although Sljeme and Stubičke Toplice are reasonably easy to get to from the capital by bus, having a car at your disposal for a day or two will give you a chance to cover more ground efficiently (e.g., without having to return to Zagreb to board yet another bus).

SLJEME

5 km (3 miles) north of Zagreb by tram and bus.

A favorite excursion on the outskirts of Zagreb is to the heights of Sljeme, the peak of Mt. Medvednica at 3,363 feet.

GETTING HERE AND AROUND

You can reach Sljeme by taking Tram 14 (direction: Mihaljevac) all the way to the terminal stop, where you should change to the bus, which goes to Sljeme (Tomislavov dom).

EXPLORING

Fodor's Choice ★ **Sljeme.** Sljeme is an ideal place for picnicking, but you may wish to save your appetite for dinner at one of the excellent restaurants on the road home. On the southwest flank of the summit of Mt. Medvednica is a reconstructed fortress called **Medvedgrad.** The original was built in the 13th century by Bishop Filip of Zagreb, and after a succession of distinguished owners over the next two centuries it was destroyed in an earthquake in 1590. You can wander around the outside (for free) and take in great views of Zagreb. It's a one-hour trek to the fortress from the cable car, or you can reach it more directly by taking Bus 102 from Britanski trg in central Zagreb (just off Ilica, a 20-minute walk west of Trg bana Josipa Jelačića) to the "Blue Church" in Šestine, and then hiking some 40 minutes uphill from there. Take trail No. 12, which is off the paved road past the church cemetery. ✉ *Sljeme* 🌐 *www.sljeme.hr*.

WHERE TO EAT

$$ EASTERN EUROPEAN ✕ **Stari Puntijar.** On the road between Zagreb and Sljeme, Stari Puntijar is renowned for game and traditional 19th-century Zagreb dishes such as *podolac* (ox medallions in cream and saffron), *orehnjača*

Excursions from Zagreb
HUNGARY
SLOVENIA
BOSNIA-HERZEGOVINA
Štrigova
Mursko Središće
The Međimurje
Mura
Ormož
Čakovec
Varaždin
Drava
Trakošćan
Veliki Tabor
Krapina
A2
Koprivnica
Bilo gora
Kumrovec
A4
Tuheljske Toplice
Križevci
Marija Bistrica
Stubičke Toplice
Medvednica Nature Park
Vrbovec
Bjelovar
Medvedgrad
Sljeme
Zaprešić
28
Sesvete
Dugo Selo
Samobor
ZAGREB
Žumberak-Samoborko Nature Park
Ivanić-Grad
Velika Gorića
26
E71
A1
31
Lonjsko polje Nature Park
36
Kupa
Karlovac
Sisak
Lonja
Petrinja
Sava
Duga Resa
Čigoč
A6
Dobra
Vrbovsko
6
Glina
30
Vojnić
Topusko
Korana
Jasenovac
Ogulin
Hrvatska Kostajnica
Dubica
Slunj
Plaški
Dvor
Una
Brinje
Nacionalni park Plitvička jezera
Plitvice
Otočac
Plitvička Ljeskovac
Korenica
0
20 miles
0
20 kilometers

(walnut loaf), and *makovnjača* (poppy-seed cake). The wine list is excellent, and the interior design is marked by trophies, hunting weapons, old paintings, and big chandeliers. **Known for:** game dishes; old-world vibe; connected to museum hotel. $ *Average main: 80 Kn* ✉ *Gračanska cesta 65, Medvešcak* ☎ *01/467–5600* 🌐 *www.hotelpuntijar.com.*

2

STUBIČKE TOPLICE

37 km (23 miles) north of Zagreb.

Established in 1805 on the foundations of a Roman-era thermal bath and expanded into a full-fledged complex in 1930, this peaceful spa at the northern edge of the Medvednica hills is where the capital's residents go to soak away those nerves and ailments in temperatures ranging from 113°F to 149°F (45°C to 65°C).

MARIJA BISTRICA

17 km (11 miles) east of Stubičke Toplice, 40 km (25 miles) northeast of Zagreb.

Other than its famous pilgrimage site, there's not much of interest in Marija Bistrica. Definitely do this as a day trip, unless you want to spend a night in nearby Stubičke Toplice.

Hodočasnička Crkva Majke Božje Bistričke (*Pilgrimage Church of St. Mary of Bistrica*). Croatia's preeminent religious pilgrimage site is home to the Blessed Virgin of Bistrica, a black, wooden, 15th-century Gothic statue of the Holy Mother associated with miraculous powers (having survived not only the Turkish invasion but a subsequent fire) and set in the main altar. The church, which was proclaimed a Croatian shrine by the nation's parliament in 1715, was rebuilt in neo-Renaissance style in the late 19th century by Hermann Bollé, who also designed the Zagreb Cathedral; the shrine complex adjacent to the church was enlarged in time for a 1998 visit by Pope John Paul II, who was in town to beatify Alojzije Stepinac, who became Archbishop of Zagreb in 1937 but was jailed and later placed under house arrest in Tito-led postwar Yugoslavia. Behind the church is a huge amphitheater that was built for the pope's visit, and from there you can climb up Kalvarija (Calvary Hill) to the stations of the cross, ornamented with sculptures by Croatian artists. ✉ *Župni ured, Trg pape Ivana Pavla II 32, Marija Bistrica* ☎ *049/469–156* 🌐 *www.svetiste-mbb.hr* 🎟 *Free.*

KUMROVEC

40 km (25 miles) northwest of Zagreb.

The former Yugoslavia's late president Josip Broz Tito was born here in 1892, and his childhood home has been turned into a small memorial museum. In the courtyard of his birthplace stands an imposing bronze likeness of him by Antun Augustinčić.

FAMILY Fodor's Choice ★ **Kumrovec Staro selo** (*Kumrovec Old Village*). The old quarter of Kumrovec is an open-air museum with beautifully restored thatched cottages and wooden farm buildings, orchards, and a stream giving a lifelike reconstruction of 19th-century rural life. On weekends craftsmen, including a blacksmith, a candlemaker, and others, demonstrate their skills. ✉ *Kumrovec BB* ☎ *049/225–830* 🌐 *www.mss.mhz.hr* 🎫 *20 Kn.*

VELIKI TABOR

15 km (9 miles) north of Kumrovec.

On a lofty hilltop stands the massive fortress of Veliki Tabor. The main pentagonal core of the building dates back to the 12th century, whereas the side towers were added in the 15th century as protection against the Turks.

GETTING HERE AND AROUND

Nine buses daily will get you here from Zagreb's main bus station in 2½ hours for 69 Kn one-way; but after getting off you have a 3-km (2-mile) walk still ahead of you. Hence, as is true more generally of site-hopping in the Zagorje region, a rental car may come in handy.

Fodor's Choice ★ **Veliki Tabor.** Don't miss wandering around the interior of the impressive Veliki Tabor. The colonnaded galleries of the interior cast sublime shadows in moonlight. To reach it, you really need to rent a car and make it part of a half-day tour of rural Zagorje. ✉ *Košnički Hum 1, Desinic* ☎ *049/374–970* 🌐 *www.veliki-tabor.hr/en* 🎫 *20 Kn.*

WHERE TO EAT

$$ EASTERN EUROPEAN ✕ **Grešna Gorica.** Visiting this rustic tavern is like stepping into a friend's home. That said, your friend's home is unlikely to have a stuffed fawn and a pair of *kuna* (martens), the national currency's namesake, on the wall. (The use of kuna dates back from when the fur of this large, weasel-like creature was in fact a currency.) All produce used here is supplied by local farmers, and the menu features typical Zagorje dishes, including *zagorski štrukli* (baked pastry filled with cheese) and *pura s mlincima* (turkey with savory pastries). **Known for:** typical Zagorje dishes; regional štrukli; views onto Veliki Tabor fortress. $ *Average main: 70 Kn* ✉ *Veliki Tabor, Desinic* ☎ *049/343–001* 🌐 *www.gresna-gorica.com* 💳 *No credit cards.*

WHERE TO STAY

$$ HOTEL Fodor's Choice ★ **Dvorac Bežanec.** A lovely old manor house, just a 15-minute drive east of Veliki Tabor, offers spacious rooms with period furniture and breakfast, too, for under €100 a night. **Pros:** historic charm; period decor and Croatian artwork; reasonable rate. **Cons:** far from major tourist areas and towns. $ *Rooms from: 700 Kn* ✉ *Valentinovo 55, Pregrada* ☎ *049/376–800, 098/230–343* 🌐 *www.hotel-dvorac-bezanec.hr* 🛏 *20 rooms, 5 suites* 🍴 *No meals.*

KRAPINA

20 km (12½ miles) east of Veliki Tabor, 66 km (41 miles) north of Zagreb.

Zagorje's quaint administrative and cultural center is on the tourism radar screen primarily as the home of *krapinski pračovjek* (Krapina Neanderthal)—no, not the town's one male inhabitant but a Neanderthal of a sort, whose bones were discovered on a hillside a short walk from the town center in 1899, in what was a settlement of these early humanlike creatures 30,000 to 40,000 years ago. Indeed, this may be one of the few places in the world today where you can meet up with a family of such hominids and even a fearsome bear in the woods—that is, with life-size statues of Neanderthals going about their daily business (wielding clubs, throwing rocks, tending fire), at the spot where the discovery was made.

Fodor's Choice ★ **Kraneamus Krapina Neanderthal Museum** (*Muzej krapinskih neandertalaca*). The new Krapina Neanderthal Museum is located near the world-famous site of the Krapina Neanderthals "Hušnjakovo," and its architecture evokes the habitat of the prehistoric man. Displays at the museum provide insight into who these early Neanderthals were and how they lived, and more broadly into the region's geology and history. ✉ *Šetalište Vilibalda Sluge BB* ☎ *049/371–491* 🌐 *www.mkn.mhz.hr* 🎫 *50 Kn.*

TRAKOŠĆAN

41 km (25½ miles) west of Varaždin, 36 km (22½ miles) northeast of Veliki Tabor.

Perched resplendently several hundred feet above the parking lot where the tour buses come and go, the romantic white hilltop Dvor Trakošćan is set amid beautifully landscaped grounds, overlooking a lovely lake circled by a hiking trail.

Fodor's Choice ★ **Dvor Trakošćan** (*Trakošćan Castle*). Croatia's most visited castle took on its present neo-Gothic appearance during the mid-19th century, compliments of Juraj VI Drašković, whose family had already owned the castle for some 300 years and would go on to live there until 1944 (there has been a building here since the 14th century). The inside is as spectacular as the outside, with the wood-paneled rooms—a Baroque room, a rococo room, a neoclassical room, and so on—filled with period furnishings and family portraits, giving you some idea of how the wealthy local aristocracy once lived. A restaurant, café, and souvenir shop occupy an uninspiring, Ministry of Culture–owned building at the foot of the hill. ✉ *5 km (3 miles) northwest of the village of Bednja, Trakošćan 1, Bednja* ☎ *042/796–281, 042/796–422* 🌐 *www.trakoscan.hr* 🎫 *30 Kn.*

VARAŽDIN

70 km (48 miles) northeast of Zagreb.

Situated on a plain just south of the River Drava, Varaždin (pop. 50,000) is the most beautifully preserved Baroque town in this corner of the continent. A vibrant commercial and cultural center, still basking in the glow of its heyday in the 18th century, Varaždin is richly adorned by extraordinary churches and the palaces of the aristocratic families that once lived here. It was Croatia's capital from 1756 until a devastating fire in 1776 prompted a move to Zagreb. First mentioned under the name Garestin in a document by the Hungarian-Croatian king Bela III from 1181, it was declared a free royal town by King Andrew II of Hungary's Arpad dynasty in 1209 and went on to become an important economic, social, administrative, and military center. Near the heart of the city, in a park surrounded by grassy ramparts, the well-preserved castle is the main attraction. A short walk from the castle, on the outskirts of town, is one of Europe's loveliest cemeteries, with immense hedges trimmed and shaped around ornate memorials. Note that Varaždin's main churches are open only around an hour before and after mass, which is generally held several times daily, more often on weekends; the tourist information office can help you contact individual churches to arrange a look inside at other times.

GETTING HERE AND AROUND

After arriving in this charming city by bus from Zagreb, the best thing to do is to walk straight to the historical downtown, which will serve as your base for sightseeing and café-visiting.

EXPLORING

TOP ATTRACTIONS

Franjevačka crkva (*Franciscan Church*). Consecrated in 1650 on the site of a medieval predecessor, the pale yellow Franjevačka crkva has the highest tower in Varaždin, at almost 180 feet. In front is a statue of 10th-century Croatian bishop Grgur Ninski, a replica of the original, which is in Split; another such replica can be seen in Nin. ✉ *Franjevački trg 8* ☎ *042/213–166.*

Gradska vijećnica (*City Hall*). This imposing landmark, one of Europe's oldest city halls, has been the seat of Varaždin's public administration since December 14, 1523. It was completely restored after the great fire of 1776. From May through October you can stop by on a Saturday morning between 11 and noon to watch the changing of the guard called Purgari, a 250-year-old tradition that lives on. ✉ *Trg kralja Tomislava 1* ☎ *042/210–987* 🌐 *www.varazdin.hr.*

Fodor's Choice ★ **Gradsko groblje** (*Town Cemetery*). Built in 1773 and thoroughly relandscaped in 1905 by Hermann Haller, a self-taught landscape architect who revolutionized traditional notions of what graveyards should look like, Varaždin's Gradsko groblje is as pleasant a place for a restful stroll as it may be, when the time comes, to be laid to rest in. Replete with flower beds and rows of tall cedars and linden trees flanking ornate memorials and laid out in geometric patterns, the cemetery sublimely manifests Haller's conviction that each plot should be a "serene, hidden

CLOSE UP

Varaždin's Guitar Great

Although the global economic crisis forced Vladimir Šimunov Proskurnjak, Varaždin's most famous string instrument maker, to close his workshop on Krančevićeva 5, his legacy lives on. It's not by chance that he specialized in guitars. This particular instrument holds a special place in the hearts of the classical-music lovers of Varaždin. Indeed, there was a time when the guitar was among the most popular instruments in Croatia and elsewhere in Europe and earned the respect of the great music critics of the day. That time, in Croatia, peaked in the first half of the 19th century. The nation's greatest guitarist of the era, and one of the continent's best, was Varaždin's own Ivan Padovec. Born in 1800, Ivan was often ill as a child and extremely nearsighted. To make matters worse, at the age of 10 he was left half blind when a stone thrown at him by another boy hit his left eye. Since his physical limitations meant he could not become a priest, as his parents had hoped, Padovec trained to become a teacher. However, he chose quite another path.

By the age of 19 Ivan Padovec had not only taught himself to play the guitar, he was able to support himself by giving lessons to friends. Before long he decided to devote his life to music. Within five years, Padovec had a reputation not only as a virtuoso guitarist but also as a talented composer. By 1827 he was giving concerts from Zagreb and Varaždin to Zadar, Rijeka, and Trieste, and before long he'd earned the respect of even the court in Vienna. While living in the Austrian capital from 1829 to 1837, Padovec gave concerts throughout Europe, though weakening eyesight eventually forced a return to his native Varaždin. After a concert in Zagreb in 1840, one critic wrote, "[Padovec] showed that even on such an instrument it was possible to play tenderly and skillfully, thus surpassing everyone else." In addition to writing more than 200 compositions, he authored an influential book on guitar instruction and invented a 10-string guitar. Completely blind by 1848, Padovec retreated to his sister's house in Varaždin, unable to compose or teach. In 1871 he gave his final performance at the city theater. A life of music reaped little financial compensation for Padovec, and he died in poverty on November 4, 1873. Appropriately, Varaždin's tourist office is located in the house where he was born, at Ivana Padovca 3.

place only hinting at its true purpose, with no clue as to whether its occupant is rich or poor, since all are tended equally, surrounded by every kind of flower…producing perfect harmony for the visitor." Haller himself, who ran the cemetery from 1905 to 1946, is buried here in a rather conspicuous mausoleum. You can reach the cemetery by walking about 10 minutes east of the castle along Hallerova aleja. ✉ *Hallerova aleja* ☎ *042/210–987* 🌐 *www.tourism-varazdin.hr/en.*

Palača Varaždinske županije (*Varaždin County Hall*). Palača Varaždinske županije rivals City Hall (on nearby Trg kralja Tomislava) in terms of sheer visual appeal, even if it is more than two centuries younger, what with its flamingo-pink facade and its location right across from the Franciscan Church. Opened in 1772, it boasted a late-Baroque pediment for four years only, until the fire of 1776 did away with that, and saw it bestowed with a triangular, neoclassical one. ✉ *Franjevački trg* ☎ *042/210–987* 🌐 *www.tourism-varazdin.hr/en.*

Fodor's Choice ★ **Stari grad** (*Castle*). Today a historical museum, Varaždin's main attraction is the massive Stari grad, which assumed its present form in the 16th century as a state-of-the-art defense fortification against the Turks, complete with moats, dikes, and bastions with low, round defense towers connected by galleries with openings for firearms. In the ensuing centuries it was often reconstructed by the families that owned it; for more than three centuries, until its 1925 purchase by the city, it belonged to the Erdödy clan. From the 12th century up until 1925, the castle served as the seat of the county prefect. You enter through the 16th-century tower gatehouse, which has a wooden drawbridge, to arrive in the internal courtyard with three levels of arcaded galleries. Indoors, there's an extensive display of antique furniture, with pieces laid out in chronological order and each room representing a specific period. Even if you don't go inside, do take a stroll around the perimeter, along a path that takes you between the outer wall and a ditch that used to be the moat. ✉ *Strossmayerovo Šetalište 7* ☎ *042/658–754* ✉ *muzej@gmv.hr* 🌐 *www.gmv.hr/en* 🎫 *12 Kn* ⏱ *Closed Mon. and public holidays.*

WORTH NOTING

NEED A BREAK

Food market. For a bite of Varaždin's specialty bakery product, a *klipić* (a salted, finger-shape bread), stop by one of the bakeries at the city's open-air food market, which is open Monday through Saturday from 7 am to 2 pm. ✉ *Gradska tržnica, Augusta Šenoe 12* ☎ *042/320–956* 🌐 *www.varazdinskiplac.hr.*

FAMILY **Entomološka zbirka** (*Entomological Collection*). Housed in the Herzer Palace, the Entomološka zbirka museum has a fascinating presentation of some 50,000 different insect specimens. ✉ *Franjevački trg 6/I* ☎ *042/658–754* 🌐 *www.gmv.hr* 🎫 *25 Kn* ⏱ *Closed Mon.*

Galerija starih i novih majstora (*Gallery of Old and Modern Masters*). Housed in the striking, 18th-century rococo Palača Sermage (Sermage Palace)—characterized by cinnamon-colored, black-framed geometric medallions decorating its facade and an impressive wrought-iron terrace—this gallery has a rich array of traditional paintings by Croatian and other European artists. ✉ *Trg Miljenka Stančića 3* ☎ *042/658–754* 🌐 *www.gmv.hr* 🎫 *25 Kn.*

Lisakova kula (*Lisak Tower*). The 16th-century Lisakova kula is the only part of Varaždin's northern town wall that has been preserved. The wall formed part of the onetime city fortress, but most of it was razed in the early 19th century. Unfortunately, you can't enter the tower. ✉ *Trg bana Jelačića* 🌐 *www.varazdin-online.com.*

Uršulinska crkva Rođenja Isusovog (*Ursuline Church of the Birth of Christ*). The Uršulinska crkva Rođenja Isusovog, a single-nave, pale-pink Baroque church with a particularly colorful, late-Baroque altar, was consecrated in 1712 by the Ursuline sisters, who came to Varaždin from Bratislava nine years earlier at the invitation of the Drašković family. Its charming, strikingly slender tower was added in 1726. ✉ *Uršulinska 3* 🌐 *www.ursulinke.hr.*

Župna crkva Sv. Nikole (*Parish Church of St. Nicholas*). Consecrated to Varaždin's patron saint in 1761 on the site of an older church, the Župna crkva Sv. Nikole is a Baroque structure that is more attractive on the outside than the inside. Note the false yet imposing white columns in the facade; the red-tiled, conical steeple; and the sculpture at the foot of the steeple of a firefighting St. Florian pouring a bucket of water onto a church, presumably an allusion to the fire that devastated Varaždin in 1776. ✉ *Trg slobode 11* 🌐 *www.zupa-sv-nikole-varazdin.hr.*

WHERE TO EAT

$$ EUROPEAN FAMILY

✕ **Palatin Restoran & Caffe Bar.** Set in the heart of Varaždin city, Palatin Restoran & Caffe Bar is a peaceful spot for a delicious meal of traditional Croatian dishes such as Istrian steak with truffles and venison medallions in "Lukarski" sauce. There is also a wide variety of vegan and vegetarian options to suit all diners. **Known for:** traditional Croatian dishes; complex flavors; Palatin cake. 💲 *Average main: 60 Kn* ✉ *Ulica Brace Radic 1, Zagreb* ☎ *54/239–8300* 🌐 *www.palatin.hr* ▭ *No credit cards.*

WHERE TO STAY

Hotel options were limited in Varaždin until 2006—with just one large hotel, the characterless Hotel Turist, and a couple of pension-style accommodations. But that changed in 2007 with the opening of the Hotel Istra.

$$ HOTEL

Hotel Istra. Varaždin's one and only centrally located accommodation, the Istra has 11 simply furnished but sleek rooms with small windows that don't offer much of a view. **Pros:** near attractions, shops, and restaurants; all rooms have bathtubs. **Cons:** hallways are hot in warm weather; small windows; few frills. 💲 *Rooms from: €120* ✉ *Ivana Kukuljevića 6* ☎ *042/659–659* 🌐 *www.istra-hotel.hr/* *11 rooms* 🍽 *Breakfast.*

$ B&B/INN

Pansion Garestin. A short walk from the town center, this small hotel has 13 simply furnished rooms, with ochre carpeting, sturdy if scratched desks, and small windows under a pitched roof. **Pros:** reasonably priced; comfy basic rooms; pleasant outdoor dining terrace. **Cons:** small bathrooms; few frills; no Internet access. 💲 *Rooms from: €55* ✉ *Zagrebačka 34* ☎ *042/214–314* 🌐 *www.gastrocom-ugostiteljstvo.com/en/restorani/garestin-restaurant-and-b-b.html* *13 rooms* 🍽 *Breakfast.*

$$ B&B/INN

Pansion Maltar. A short walk from the town center, this small guesthouse has clean, no-frills, but spacious rooms that are quite acceptable for a short stay. **Pros:** good value; friendly service; a five-minute walk to the town center. **Cons:** smoky café; modest decor. 💲 *Rooms from: €65* ✉ *Franca prešerna 1* ☎ *042/311–100, 042/311–521* 🌐 *www.maltar.hr* *28 rooms* 🍽 *Breakfast.*

NIGHTLIFE AND PERFORMING ARTS

Advent in Varaždin. Throughout the month of December, the town celebrates Advent in Varaždin, when the streets and squares come alive with the Christmas spirit. Ornaments and sweets are on sale, there's outdoor skating, and, yes, Santa Claus wanders about handing out gifts to kids. 🌐 *www.tourism-varazdin.hr.*

Aquamarin. Aquamarin is one of several bustling cafés on or near Trg kralja Tomislava, the site of City Hall. Trg Miljenka Stančića, by the tourist office, is another good place to sit back at one of the cafés and enjoy some drinks. ✉ *Gajeva 1* ☎ *042/311–868.*

Rock Art Café. For a beer or two between walls adorned with pictures of famous revolutionaries from Elvis to Che Guevara, not to mention glass-encased electric guitars, stop by the Rock Art Café, which has frequent live-music evenings September through April. ✉ *Petra Preradovića 24* ☎ *042/321–123.*

Špancirfest. For 10 days in late August, the Špancirfest (translated in tourist brochures as "Street Walkers' Festival") occupies various squares in the center of town. It features a colorful array of free, open-air theatrical and acrobatic performances, live music from classical to rock, traditional and modern dance, arts-and-crafts exhibits, and more. 🌐 *www.spancirfest.com.*

Fodor's Choice ★ **Varaždin Baroque Evenings.** For three weeks from mid-September to early October, the Varaždin Baroque Evenings take the form of classical-music concerts in various churches, palaces, and other venues throughout town. This is one of the most important cultural events in northern Croatia. ✉ *A. Cesarca 1* ☎ *042/212–907* 🌐 *www.vbv.hr.*

ČAKOVEC AND THE MEĐIMURJE

15 km (9½ miles) northeast of Varaždin.

At the northernmost tip of Croatia, between the Drava River to the south and the Mura River to the north, the Međimurje region looks small on the map, but it possesses a distinctive character that makes it ripe for at least a day's worth of exploration. Long off the radar screens of Croatia-bound visitors, the Međimurje is also one of the country's newest up-and-coming inland tourist destinations: its largest town, Čakovec, is the most important cultural center between Varaždin and Hungary and Slovenia to the north (many Zagreb–Budapest trains stop there). Its many small villages are the home of rich wine-making and embroidery traditions, and there is even a locally cherished spa town, Toplice Sveti Martin, to the very north close to the Mura River. Back in the 13th century, Count Dimitrius Chaky, court magistrate of the Croatian-Hungarian king Bela IV, had a wooden defense tower erected in the central part of the Međimurje that eventually became known as Chaktornya (Chak's Tower). It was around this tower and other nearby fortifications that Čakovec saw a period of economic and cultural development under the influential Zrinski family, from the mid-16th century to the late 17th century. After a failed rebellion by the Zrinskis and the Frankopans against the Viennese court, the Viennese imperial army plundered the tower for building materials, and the last Zrinski died in 1691. A disastrous earthquake in 1738 saw the old, Gothic architecture give way to the Baroque. Međimurje's last feudal proprietors were the Feštetić counts, who lived here from 1791 to 1923—a period during which the region came under the administrative control of Hungary, then Croatia, then Hungary once again (until 1918). Toward the close of the 19th century the region was linked inextricably to the railroad network of the Austro-Hungarian Empire, setting the stage for intense economic development.

GETTING HERE AND AROUND

After arriving by bus from Zagreb, walk directly to the city center and begin experiencing the history all around you.

EXPLORING

TOP ATTRACTIONS

Župna crkva sv. Nikole Biskupa i franjevački samostan (*Parish Church of St. Nicolas Bishop and the Franciscan Monastery*). Čakovec's key ecclesiastical landmark was built between 1707 and 1728 on the site of a wooden monastery that burned down in 1699. The bell tower was added in the 1750s. Inside is a late-Baroque altar decorated with elaborate statues; on the outside is a facade from the turn of the 20th century (when Hungary ruled the region), with reliefs of several great Hungarian kings from ages past. ✉ *Franjevački trg 1, Cakovec* ☎ *040/312–806* 🌐 *www.ofm.hr/zupa_cakovec.*

WORTH NOTING

Stari grad Zrinskih (*Zrinski Castle*). Set in the middle of a large, shaded park right beside the main square is Čakovec's key landmark, the massive four-story Stari grad Zrinskih. Built over the course of a century from around 1550 by Nikola Šubic Zrinski, in an Italian-Renaissance style, it was the Zrinski family nest until the late 17th century. The fortress's foremost present-day attraction, the **Muzej Međimurja** (Museum of Međimurje), can be reached through the courtyard. Though it receives too few visitors to have regular opening hours, a staff member will be happy to let you in; just climb the steps to the hallway of offices on the second floor to find someone. If you kindly overlook the lack of English-language text, you will be treated on this floor to an intriguing, life-size look at a year in the life of a peasant family, from season to season as you proceed through the rooms. Move up a floor for a chronological display of the region's history, from the Stone Age to the recent past. Also on this floor are individual rooms dedicated to the Zrinski family (this one does have English text); lovely period furniture; displays of printing machinery; an old pharmacy; a fascinating collection of 19th- and 20th-century bric-a-brac; and, last but not least, a three-room gallery of impressive modern art by various painters. ✉ *Trg Republike 5, Cakovec* ☎ *01/313–499* 🌐 *www.mmc.hr* 🎫 *20 Kn.*

Trgovački Kasino (*Commercial Casino*). Čakovec's main square, Trg Republike, is a mostly bland, modern affair—with the striking exception of Trgovački Kasino. Odd that the key gathering place of the town's early-20th-century rising bourgeois class should have survived the communist era intact, but here it has stood since 1903, wearing its Hungarian art nouveau style very much on its sleeve: red brick interspersed with a white stucco background, squares and circles across the bottom, curved lines formed by the brickwork working their way to the top. Back in its heyday, this was much more than a casino in the gambling sense of the word: in addition to a card room and a game parlor, it housed a ladies' salon, a reading room, and a dance hall. It was mostly a trade-union headquarters in the post–World War II era—and so it is today, rendering the inside off-limits to the public. Just off the main square, by the way, is Trg kralja Tomislava, the town's one and only major pedestrian shopping street. ✉ *Trg Republike, Cakovec* 🌐 *www.tourism-cakovec.hr.*

OFF THE BEATEN PATH

Štrigova. Disregard the unfortunately translated sign outside one of Međimurje's most important ecclesiastical landmarks: "Saint Jerome's Church is a zero category monument of culture." In this case the "zero" means "top," for this church (plus a well-developed local wine industry) is what guarantees the otherwise sleepy, out-of-the-way village of Štrigova a place on the tourism map. In a bucolic hilly setting near the Slovenian border, 15 km (9½ miles) northwest of Čakovec, Štrigova is indeed best known for **Crkva Sv. Jeronima** and as the largest producer of Međimurje wines. Whether you arrive by bus (45-minute runs from Čakovec daily) or car, the first thing you are likely to notice is the striking yellow-and-white double steeple of the church, which is perched sublimely on a hillside just above the village center. Completed in 1749 on the site of a 15th-century chapel that was destroyed in the region's 1738 earthquake, the church is dedicated to the village's most famous son: St. Jerome (340–420), known for translating the Bible from Greek and Hebrew into Latin. Note the painting of a bearded St. Jerome on the facade, framed by two little windows made to look like red hearts. The church is most famous, actually, for its lovely wall and ceiling frescoes by the famous Baroque artist, Ivan Ranger the Baptist (1700–1753). The main steeple was completed only in 1761, and the church also has two smaller steeples. The church is usually closed, but you can call the local parish to arrange a look inside. While you can get to Štrigova easily enough by one of several daily buses from Čakovec, it's good to have a car if you want to drop by the smaller village of Železna Gora, some 5 km (3 miles) south of Štrigova, along a country road to Čakovec. Travel just 2½ km (1½ miles) south of the center of Železna Gora, and you will find the best restaurant in these parts, **Restoran Dvorac Terbotz.** ✉ *Štrigova* ☎ *040/851–325* 🌐 *www.strigova.info.*

WHERE TO EAT

$$ EASTERN EUROPEAN FAMILY

✕ **Restoran Dvorac Terbotz.** In the village of Železna Gora some 5 km (3 miles) south of Štrigova, along a country road to Čakovec, stands the best restaurant in these parts where you can dine on everything from poultry to pork to wild game to seafood, in a lovely country house with wood-beamed ceilings. A spacious terrace overlooks the area's sweeping vineyards, and on a breezy day you'll hear the clackety-clack of the windmill just outside. **Known for:** vineyard setting; unique flavors of Međimurje; locally sourced ingredients. $ *Average main: 70 Kn* ✉ *Železna Gora 113, Štrigova* ☎ *040/857–444* 🌐 *www.terbotz.hr* ⏲ *Closed Mon.*

WHERE TO STAY

You can stay in Varaždin and venture into Međimurje for a day trip, but Čakovec does have a couple of decent lodging options, one of which is a short walk from the main square.

$$ HOTEL **Rooms Aurora.** A short walk from both the bus station and the main square, this uninspiring modern building has a light-filled interior, whose simply furnished rooms have dark blue carpeting, pinkish walls, and a sofa and coffee table in each. **Pros:** close to the bus station and the main square; large common areas and breakfast room; reasonable rates. **Cons:** small windows; along a bland, busy road; few frills. *Rooms from: 480 Kn* ✉ *Franje Punčeca 2, Cakovec* ☎ *040/310–700* *9 rooms* *Breakfast.*

EXCURSIONS SOUTH OF ZAGREB

SAMOBOR

20 km (12½ miles) west of Zagreb.

That Samobor has been one of the capital's top weekend haunts since before the turn of the 20th century without really being on the way to anything else in Croatia testifies to its abundant cultural and natural charms. Close to the Slovenian border, this picturesque medieval town on the eastern slopes of the lushly forested Samoborsko gorje was chartered by the Hungarian-Croatian king Bela IV in 1242. The town and environs are popular with hikers, with trails leading into the hillside right from the center of town. Perched in those hills, just 30 minutes from town on foot, are the ruins of a 13th-century castle, which ennoble the main square from their sublime heights. And what would a visit to Samobor be without a stroll along Gradna, the peaceful stream that runs through town?

After an energetic hike, you may wish to fortify yourself with a glass of locally made *bermet,* a vermouth-like drink whose secret recipe was apparently brought here by French forces during their occupation from 1809 to 1813.

GETTING HERE AND AROUND

Take a 45-minute bus ride from the central bus station in Zagreb or travel for about 30 minutes by rental car to this charming getaway town where you can while away half a day leisurely strolling along the river and cobblestone streets and soak in the atmosphere from yesteryear.

EXPLORING

WORTH NOTING

Museum Marton. May 2003 saw Croatia's first private museum open in a quiet street just above Trg kralja Tomislava. Museum Marton was created to house a private collection of furniture, paintings, glass- and metalware, porcelain, and clocks previously on loan to the Zagreb Museum of Arts & Crafts. ✉ *Jurjevska 7* ☎ *01/336–4160, 01/483–8700* 🌐 *www.muzej-marton.hr* *10 Kn.*

Samobor Museum. Located in a lovely streamside park by the square, the Samobor Museum tells the story of the town's past. ✉ *Livadićeva 7* ☎ *01/336–1014* 🌐 *www.samobor.hr/muzej* 🎫 *8 Kn* 🕒 *Closed Mon.*

Samoborski fašnik. By far Samobor's most famous event, its carnival draws many thousands of visitors to town for several days beginning the weekend before Lent to catch the dazzling sight of its parades, featuring floats and masked revelers. ✉ *Trg kralja Tomislava 5* ☎ *01/336–0044* 🌐 *www.fasnik.com.*

Trg kralja Tomislava. The rectangular main square is called Trg kralja Tomislava. Its largely Baroque look is positively lovely, all the more so because some building facades show art nouveau influences. In particular, the pharmacy building at No. 11 has two angels presiding, appropriately, on top. Also overlooking the square is a 17th-century parish church. ✉ *Samobor* 🌐 *www.samobor.hr.*

NEED A BREAK

U prolazu. If you need a dose of sugar to perk you up, try some *samoborska kremšnita*, a mouthwatering block of vanilla custard between layers of flaky pastry served warm that can be tasted at its best at this otherwise small and smoky café. ✉ ***Trg kralja Tomislava 5*** ☎ ***01/336–6420*** 🌐 ***www.tz-samobor.hr.***

WHERE TO EAT

$$ EASTERN EUROPEAN FAMILY

Pri staroj vuri. Small yet ever so cozy, its walls decorated with old clocks (whence its name, in Croatian) and paintings by noted Croatian artists, this lovely old villa a few minutes' walk from the main square is the best place in town to try such meaty fare as *teleća koljenica* (knuckle of veal) and *češnjovke* (smoked sausage cooked in sour cabbage). Unfortunately, the latter is available only late in the year, after the hogs are butchered and the sausage smoked. **Known for:** hearty dishes; Croatian art; surrounded by green space. $ *Average main: 70 Kn* ✉ *Giznik 2* ☎ *01/336–0548* 🌐 *www.staravura.pondi.hr.*

WHERE TO STAY

$$ HOTELHOTEL

Hotel Livadic. If you want to spend more than a half-day in Samobor, you could do much worse than this elegant and pleasant hotel right on the main square. **Pros:** centrally located; redolent of history. **Cons:** rooms vary in size; downstairs café is smoky; few frills. $ *Rooms from: €62* ✉ *Trg kralja Tomislava 1* ☎ *01/336–5850* 🌐 *www.hotel-livadic.hr* *21 rooms* 🍽 *Breakfast.*

KARLOVAC

40 km (25 miles) southwest of Zagreb.

Many tourists taste the beer, but few stop by for a taste of the city. Karlovac is much more than home to one of Croatia's most popular brews, Karlovačko. Founded by the Austrians in 1579 as a fortress intended to ward off the Turks, Karlovac is today that big dot on the map between Zagreb and the coast. Visitors to the country, more often than not, simply pass it by, but anyone intrigued by the question of how a onetime fortress—still much in evidence—can develop into an urban center will want to stop here for at least a half-day and, perhaps, spend a night on the way to or from the coast. Once you pass through the city's industrial-looking suburbs, there is an inviting historical center awaiting you, one rendered more romantic because it is wedged between two of Croatia's most important rivers, the Kupa and the Korana. The city's Renaissance-era urban nucleus is popularly known as the Zvijezda (Star), since its military planners were moved to shape it as a six-pointed star—evidenced in the surrounding moat, which is today a pleasant, if sunken, green space that is even home to a basketball court. Eventually, this center's military nature gave way to civilian life, and it took on the Baroque look more visible today. Though the town walls were razed in the 19th century, their shape is still discernible.

GETTING HERE AND AROUND

By far the best way to come here is by bus from Zagreb; it is along the route of countless buses from the capital. Once there, the best thing is to make a pedestrian beeline to the historical center.

EXPLORING

Trg bana Josipa Jelačića. At the center of this old part of town, which you access over any of several bridges over the moat, is the main square, Trg bana Josipa Jelačića, one side of which, alas, features a great big empty building with some missing windows. At the center of this otherwise largely barren square is an old well dating to 1869; long filled in, it is ornamented with allegorical imagery. ✉ *Karlovac* 🌐 *karlovac-touristinfo.hr.*

WHERE TO EAT

$$$ EUROPEAN Fodor's Choice ★

✕ **Bistro Kastel.** Climb the stone stairs onto the spacious terrace or dine inside the softly lit 13th-century manor, one of the most impressive examples of feudal architecture in Croatia. Kastel's offerings reflect its geographic location, representing both the Adriatic Sea and the continental plains with delicious detail. **Known for:** beautiful castle setting; views of the town; craft beers and good wines. 💲 *Average main: 160 Kn* ✉ *Dubovac Castle, Zagrad gaj 5* ☎ *091/253–3470.*

$$ SEAFOOD FAMILY

✕ **Ribarska kuća Mirna.** Off on its own, overlooking the quietly flowing Korana River on the edge of the town center, this restaurant, which has a terrace for outdoor dining, makes the best of the view. The seafood here—whether squid, octopus, sea bass, or freshwater varieties such as carp, pike-perch, catfish, pike, or trout—is abundant and excellent. **Known for:** fixed-price lunch menu; seafood; local wine list. 💲 *Average main: 75 Kn* ✉ *Rakovačko šetalište BB* ☎ *047/654–172* 🌐 *www.ribarska-kuca-mirna.com.*

WHERE TO STAY

$$$ HOTEL

🏨 **Hotel Korana Srakovčić.** Deep within a tree-shaded park a few minutes' walk from the Old Town, this luxury hotel overlooks a peaceful stretch of its namesake, the Korana River. **Pros:** luxurious, spacious rooms; tranquil park setting; excellent amenities. **Cons:** 25-minute walk from the town center; pricey; caters to business travelers. 💲 *Rooms from: €130* ✉ *Perivoj Josipa Vrbanića 8* ☎ *047/609–090* 🌐 *www.hotelkorana.hr* 🛏 *19 rooms* 🍽 *Breakfast.*

CLOSE UP

Bloody Easter

It's called "Bloody Easter" for a good reason. Sunday, April 2, 1991, has gone down in Croatian history as the day Croatia suffered its first casualties—and its first fatality—in its war of independence from the former Yugoslavia. And the unlikely setting was none other than one of Europe's most visited natural wonders, Plitvice Lakes National Park.

Two days earlier, Croatian Ministry of Interior commando units—under the direction of General Josip Lucić, later to become head of the Croatian Armed Forces—were dispatched to Plitvice to restore order after the region had been occupied by Serbs led by Milan Martić, who aimed to annex the park to Serbian Krajina. The commandos were ambushed en route, near the group of hotels at Entrance 2, and one member of the team, Josip Jović, was killed and seven of his comrades were wounded. As recorded in the annals of Croatian history, nine of the "terrorists" were arrested, and order was restored. For a time.

The region, which had long been home to many Serbs, was occupied by Serb forces for the next four years. The national park became a military encampment, and soldiers threatened to blow up the fragile travertine dams separating the lakes. UNESCO sent missions to prevent war from wreaking such havoc on a natural wonder. In the end, with the exception of the park's red-deer population, which fell dramatically during the occupation—the park's natural beauty pulled through intact. Only the human infrastructure was damaged, including the hotels. By 1999, four years after Croatian forces reoccupied the park and painstakingly cleared the area of mines, the last of the three hotels reopened, and the park was back in business.

Today a memorial in the park—behind the bus stop at Entrance 2 on the southbound side of the road—marks the life and death of Josip Jović, the first fatality in what was to be a long and bloody war.

NACIONALNI PARK PLITVIČKA JEZERA

135 km (84 miles) southwest of Zagreb.

Triple America's five Great Lakes, shrink them each to manageable size (i.e., 536 acres in all), give them a good cleaning until they look virtually blue, envelop them in lush green forest with steep hillsides and cliffs all around, and link not just two but all of them with a pint-size Niagara Falls. The result? Nacionalni park Plitvička jezera, a UNESCO World Heritage Site and Croatia's top inland natural wonder.

GETTING HERE AND AROUND

The park is on the route of numerous cross-country buses starting from the coast (Zadar, Dubrovnik, Split) or from the capital, Zagreb. After arriving at the park, your feet are the only things you need to work your way around the wonders of this natural miracle.

Fodor's Choice ★ **Nacionalni park Plitvička jezera** (*Plitvice Lakes National Park*). The park is right on the main highway (E71) from Zagreb to Split, and it's certainly worth the three-hour trip from the capital. This 8,000-acre park is home to 16 beautiful emerald lakes connected by a series of cascading waterfalls, stretching 8 km (5 miles) through a valley flanked by high, forested hills home to deer, bears, wolves, and wild boar. Thousands of years of sedimentation of calcium, magnesium carbonate, algae, and moss have yielded the natural barriers between the lakes, and since the process is ongoing, new barriers, curtains, stalactites, channels, and cascades are constantly forming and the existing ones changing. The deposited sedimentation, or tufa, also coats the beds and edges of the lakes, creating their sparkling, azure look. Today a series of wooden bridges and waterside paths leads through the park. The only downside: as lovely as it is, all of Europe and a lot of Asia want to see it, so the trails can get crowded from June through September. That said, there's no litter along the way—a testament either to respectful visitors or to a conscientious park staff or to both. No camping, no bushwhacking, no picking plants—and no swimming! This is a place to look, to spend a day or two, but not to touch. It is, however, well worth the 180 Kn summertime entrance fee. There are three entrances just off the main road about an hour's walk apart, creatively named Entrance 1, Entrance 2, and auxiliary Entrance Flora. The park's pricey hotels are near Entrance 2, the first entrance you'll encounter if arriving by bus from the coast. However, Entrance 1—the first entrance if you arrive from Zagreb—is typically the start of most one-day excursions, if only because it's within a 20-minute walk of Veliki slap, the 256-foot-high waterfall. Hiking the entire loop that winds its way around the lakes takes six to eight hours, but there are other hikes, ranging from two to four hours. All involve a combination of hiking and being ferried across the larger of the park's lakes by national park service boats.

There are cafés near both entrances, but avoid them for anything but coffee, as the sandwiches and strudels leave much to be desired. Instead, buy some of the huge, heavenly strudels sold by locals at nearby stands, where great big blocks of cheese are also on sale. **■ TIP→ At the boat landing near Entrance 2, you can rent gorgeous wooden rowboats for 50 Kn per hour.** ✉ *Plitvicka Jezera* ☎ *053/751–014, 053/751–015* 🌐 *www.np-plitvicka-jezera.hr* 🎫 *July–Aug., 180 Kn; Apr.–June and Sept.–Oct., 110 Kn; Nov.–Mar., 55 Kn.*

WHERE TO EAT

Although there's a restaurant near the hotels at Entrance 2, it has the same uninspiring look and feel as the hotels, and few people flock to it. You're much better off heading over to the excellent restaurant at Entrance 1—unless of course the food store near Entrance 2 provides you enough in the way of staples to fuel your hikes.

$$ EASTERN EUROPEAN FAMILY

✕ **Restoran Lička Kuća.** With unadorned log walls, wood-beam ceilings, white-curtained windows, lively Croatian folk music playing, and an open kitchen with an open hearth, this is exactly what a restaurant in a great national park should be. Fill up on hearty *lička juha* (a creamy soup of lamb, vegetables, and eggs), followed by boiled lamb with vegetables, suckling pig, or a "peasant platter" (a wide array of meats—from beef to turkey, pork chops to sausage and bacon). **Known for:** proximity to national park; sausages and veal; hearty fare. $ *Average main: 85 Kn* ✉ *Rastovača BB, Across entrance 1, Plitvicka Jezera* ☎ *053/751–023.*

WHERE TO STAY

None of the park's state-run, communist-era hotels is much to write home about—and they were damaged extensively by Serb forces during the early 1990s. However, the main advantage of staying in a park hotel is that you'll be right in the center of all the hiking action. The hotels are particularly convenient if you arrive without your own car.

As an alternative, there are lots of private rooms in the immediate vicinity, where doubles go for around 240 Kn, a bargain compared to the hotels. We recommend checking out the tiny village of Mukinje, about a 15-minute hike south of Entrance 2. A bit farther south is the village of Jezerce, which also has rooms. (Note that the bus does not stop at either Mukinje or Jezerce, but it's a pleasant walk to both.) You can also get a private room in the rather faceless, one-road village of Rastovača, just off the main road a few hundred yards north of Entrance 1 (where the bus stops). Practically every one of the village's newish-looking houses has rooms for rent, and they're generally bright, clean, and modern.

A bit farther afield, the village of Rakovica, 12 km (7½ miles) north of the park, usually has more vacancies in high season and is a good option if you have a car. The tourist office in Rakovica (☎ *047/784–450*) can help with bookings. Last but not least, bear in mind that there's no place to store your bags in the park during the day if you arrive by bus and plan to head on to the coast or to Zagreb later in the day—so unless you're ready to cart your bags for hours along the park's steep trails or are traveling light, plan on an overnight stay.

$$ HOTEL **Hotel Jezero.** Yards away from two other, lower-priced, fewer-frills hotels (the Plitvice and the Bellevue), this long, three-story wood-paneled building looks almost like a U.S.-style motel. The rooms are simply furnished and a bit worn, but clean, and offer cheap plastic chairs on the unappealing terraces (not all rooms have terraces). **Pros:** centrally located; the best of the park's three hotel options; decent array of services and amenities. **Cons:** slightly worn rooms; pricey for what it is; filled with tourists. *$ Rooms from: €115 ✉ Nacionalni park Plitvička jezera, near Entrance 2, Plitvicka Jezera ☎ 053/751–500 🌐 www.np-plitvicka-jezera.hr/en 229 rooms 🍽 Breakfast.*

EXCURSIONS IN LONJSKO POLJE

An excursion southeast of Zagreb to the Lonjsko polje region along the Sava River will bring you to an area that is rarely seen by most visitors. Along Croatia's extensive border with Bosnia and Herzegovina are two sights of pronounced historical interest, and one—Lonjsko polje Nature Park—holds special appeal to lovers of big birds, along with plenty of pretty wooden architecture in and around the sleepy villages along the way.

SISAK

75 km (47 miles) southeast of Zagreb via the Autocesta Expressway.

The unassuming little town of Sisak was the site of one of the more important battles in Croatia's history.

Knightly Tournament. On a weekend in early June, locals celebrate their victory over the Turks with an annual Knightly Tournament. A whole lot of folks in medieval garb will entertain you with archery and equestrian contests, not to mention balloon rides, souvenirs, and plenty of food and drink. Check with the Sisak tourist-information office for details on this free event. 🌐 *www.sisakturist.com.*

Sisak Fortress. A bit to the south of the town center—3 km (2 miles) to be exact, where the rivers Kupa and Sava meet—stands the once-mighty Sisak Fortress (built 1544–50), with one prominent bastion at each point of its famously triangular form and a hugely significant past. It was here, on June 22, 1593, that the Habsburgs, in the company of Croats and Slovenes, pulled off a monumental victory over the fearsome Ottoman Turks, a triumph that figured prominently in halting the Turks' advance toward Zagreb and farther into Western Europe. ✉ *Sisak* 🌐 *www.sisakturist.com/.*

ČIGOĆ

28 km (17½ miles) southeast of Sisak.

The charming village of Čigoć is officially known as the "European Village of Storks" because it draws so many of the migrating birds each spring, and a testament is its annual Stork Festival in late June. Several hundred of the birds while away much of the summer here before embarking on their long journey to southern Africa. That said, people live here, too, evidenced by the wooden, thatched-roof houses that are likewise a sight to behold.

Fodor's Choice ★ **Čigoč and Lonjsko polje Nature Park.** The Čigoč Information Center, in a traditional house of posavina oak, is situated on the main road that runs through the village center. It is the top regional source for all you need to know about storks, the Stork Festival, and last but not least, Lonjsko polje Nature Park. It's open daily 8–4, and park maps are available for purchase. The admission in the Nature Park is 40 Kn. Be sure to find out about the park's educational programs or attractive boat trips, in case you're interested. ✉ *Čigoč 26* ☎ *044/715–115, 098/222–085 (ask for Davor Anzil)* 🌐 *www.pp-lonjsko-polje.hr.*

JASENOVAC

35 km (22 miles) southeast of Čigoć.

Located where the Sava takes on the task of tracing Croatia's long east–west border with Bosnia and Herzegovina until taking a turn into Serbia more than 150 km (94 miles) away, Jasenovac is the site of Croatia's most notorious World War II labor camps. Current estimates are that somewhere between 56,000 and 97,000 people—mostly Serbs, it is believed, along with Jews, Gypsies, and Croatian antifascists—perished at this string of five camps on the banks of the Sava River between 1941 and 1945 from exhaustion, illness, cold weather, and murder.

As a contrast to the labor-camp memorial, Jasenovac is also home to the headquarters of the beautiful Lonjsko Polje Nature Park. One of the largest floodplains in the Danubian basin, this unique ecological and cultural landscape of 20,506 acres along the Sava River was accorded park status in 1990 and is included on UNESCO's roster of World Heritage sites. It has numerous rare and endangered plant and animal species, from white-tailed eagles and saker falcons to otters and the Danube salmon—as well as storks, which are as easy to come by as in Čigoć. Its 4,858 acres of pastureland is also home to Croatia's highest concentration of indigenous breeds of livestock. Traditional village architecture—in particular, houses made of posavina oak—further contributes to the region's appeal. The park office provides park maps and other information on where to go and what to see; and, yes, it issues park entrance passes (40 Kn). The easiest way to access the park is by car: while driving from Zagreb, exit the motorway at Popovača and take the road to the right through the villages of Potok and Stružec toward Sisak.

Fodor's Choice ★ **Lonjsko polje Nature Park.** As a happier contrast to its labor-camp memorial, Jasenovac is home to the headquarters of Lonjsko Polje Nature Park. ✉ *Krapje 16, Krapje* ☎ *044/672–080, 044/611–190* 🌐 *www.pp-lonjsko-polje.hr* 🎟 *40 Kn.*

Memorial Museum Jasenovac. Although the camp was razed after the war, a memorial park was eventually established at the site, along with a museum featuring photographs and other documentation of what happened. ✉ *Braće Radić 147* ☎ *044/672–319* 🌐 *www.jusp-jasenovac.hr* 🎟 *Free.*

CROATIA OSI HOTEL
Allianz
OTAC DOMOVINE
dr. Ante Starčević
BIPA

3

SLAVONIA

Updated by Andrea Macdonald

Somewhere beyond the sea, there is a region called Slavonia. And it's a place you didn't think still existed in Europe. There is no coastline here, which has always meant fewer tourists. What it offers instead is something increasingly rare: unspoiled culture and undiscovered treasures. There are art galleries in Osijek, centuries-old wine cellars in Ilok, Baroque towns, natural parks, hot springs and rural festivals. As the breadbasket of Croatia, it has miles of cornfields, vineyards, and, in the right season, towering sunflowers in bloom. There are even sandy beaches along the Danube. One thing is certain: Slavonia will not stay undiscovered for long. But for now, it's all yours. Welcome to the green heart of Croatia.

One of the four historical regions of Croatia, the sweeping agricultural plain of Slavonia has been inhabited since ancient times, when the Romans had a settlement called Mursa on the outskirts of present-day Osijek. Though its flatness is broken in places—by the Papuk Hills in the center and around the celebrated wine region of Ilok in the east—the region's largely lowland terrain has been inhabited and traversed through the ages by more ethnicities than practically any other region of Croatia: Croats, Serbs, Hungarians, Germans, Ottomans, and others have all left their mark on its culture. First settled by Slavic tribes in the 7th century and later an integral part of the Hungarian-Croat kingdom, Slavonia experienced a major change of culture with Sultan Suleiman the Magnificent's march toward Hungary and Austria in 1526. For almost 150 years much of the region became an Ottoman stronghold. Osijek and Požega flourished not as part of Christian Europe, but rather as full-fledged, mosque-filled Turkish towns. The Turkish retreat in the late 17th century ushered in an era of Austrian influence, with Osijek, now with a vastly different look, the region's economic, administrative, and cultural capital.

Long a vital transport route, particularly between Zagreb and Belgrade, Slavonia was badly affected during the war in the 1990s and has spent the past couple of decades recovering. Despite some remaining hurdles, much of Slavonia today looks and feels almost as rejuvenated as the rest of Croatia. The region's sleepy towns and rural surroundings—from cornfields to forest-covered hills—have a distinctive low-key charm that can only be called Slavonian.

TOP REASONS TO GO TO SLAVONIA

Charming towns: Strolling around Osijek, Slavonia's largest town, packs a lot of charm into a compact space, from attractive churches and parks to Tvrđa, the Old Town redolent of ages past.

Bird-watching: Head out with your binoculars to serenely beautiful Kopački Rit Nature Park, one of the last great wetlands on the continent.

Tradition: Discover a land lost in time in the unspoiled Baranja region, which, with its charming inns, extraordinary restaurants and emphasis on agritourism, manages to somehow feel up-and-coming.

Rebirth: The Baroque town of Vukovar is a testament to the destruction wrought by the Yugoslav war and to the quiet strength of Croatia's rejuvenation.

Wine country: Cruise the wine roads of Slavonia, visiting 600-year-old cellars in Ilok, or the region around Kutjevo that the Romans nicknamed "Golden Valley."

ORIENTATION AND PLANNING

GETTING ORIENTED

Occupying the northeastern section of Croatia, Slavonia is wedged in between Serbia to the east, Hungary to the north, and Bosnia to the south.

PLANNING

WHEN TO GO

Slavonia can be swelteringly hot in summer which is considered the low season, when many establishments close because everyone, including the locals, have fled to the coast. You may want to save this region for spring or early fall, which are conveniently the same months when hundreds of thousands of birds gather at the Kopački Rit Nature Park. Late August and September are harvest season, when there are plenty of local festivals throughout the region; it's a great time to visit a winery or farmhouse and maybe even lend a hand. It gets cold and snowy in Slavonia in winter, but there are traditional Christmas markets, winter festivals, and local mulled wine to keep you warm.

GETTING HERE AND AROUND

AIR TRAVEL

There are direct flights from Zagreb, Dubrovnik, Rijeka, Pula and Split to Osijek with Croatia Airlines.

Contacts Osijek Airport. ✉ *Vukovarska ulica 67, Klisa, Osijek* ☎ *031/284–611* 🌐 *www.osijek-airport.hr.*

BUS TRAVEL

Public transport in Slavonia is, to put it mildly, difficult. It is infrequent, particularly on weekends and holidays. Come summer, when kids aren't traveling to school, many routes are cancelled entirely. If you must use public transport, the bus is more reliable than the train. There are around six buses daily travelling between Zagreb and Osijek (4 hours, 125 Kn), several daily buses making the 45-minute trip to Vukovar, or to Đakovo an hour away for around 30 Kn.

Contacts Đakovo Bus Station. ✉ *Splitska BB, Đakovo* ☎ *060/353–353.* **Osijek Bus Station.** ✉ *Bartula Kašića 70, Osijek* ☎ *060/353–353.* **Vukovar Bus Station.** ✉ *Ulica Kardinala Alojzija Stepinca 3, Vukovar* ☎ *060/337–799.*

CAR RENTALS

Having wheels will make your life a whole lot easier, particularly if you want to travel on weekends, or visit wineries, parks or small towns that are not served by public transport. If starting your trip in Zagreb, you might consider taking a train or bus to Osijek and then renting a car here for a day or two.

Uni Rent. ✉ *Osijek Downtown, Reisnerova 70, Osijek* ☎ *031/205–058* 🌐 *www.uni-rent.net.*

TRAIN TRAVEL

Due to funding cuts, train services have been reduced in recent years and many stations have fallen into disrepair. Traveling between Zagreb and Osijek is quick and comfortable; venturing further afield is a different story. Fortunately, the train and bus stations are usually next to each other, so you can easily figure out which option best suits your schedule (or use a combination of the two). The most reliable source for train scheduling information is, strangely enough, the German website 🌐 *bahn.de.* Once you actually get onto the train, the experience is quite whimsical; it cuts right through the heart of Slavonia, giving you a real sense of the sweeping vistas of Croatia's breadbasket. Six trains run daily between Zagreb and Osijek (around 110 Kn one-way), one of these being an three-hour express run; most take four to five hours.

Contacts Osijek Train Station. ✉ *Trg Lavoslava Ružičke 2, Osijek* ☎ *060/333–444.*

TOUR COMPANIES

Boho Travel Art. This boutique travel company organizes day trips and activities in various locations around Slavonia, including bike tours, craft-beer tasting, and photo safaris. They create tailor-made itineraries for their clients, so contact them directly to make a plan. ☎ *021/863–471* 🌐 *bohotravelart.com.*

Tureta Travel. This Zagreb-based boutique travel agency runs custom-made private tours around Slavonia and Baranja. They can organize everything based on the client's personal preferences, from transport to accommodation to wine tasting, and they specialize in local, off-the-beaten-track experiences. If you don't have your own transport but want to explore the region, these guys should be your first call. ☎ *095/252–1992* 🌐 *www.tureta-travel.com.*

ABOUT THE RESTAURANTS

There aren't many Slavonian restaurants, as locals generally prefer to dine at home, then go out for coffee or ice cream, which explains the many trendy café-bars. Apart from Osijek, where you'll be spoiled for choice, your best bet is often hotels or wineries. There you can sample hearty, spicy and delicious Slavonian cuisine. Cabbage and cottage cheese are common side dishes, and with paprika-rich Hungary not far away, you'll often see dishes characterized by an unmistakable, bright-red zest. Meat is a key part of the dining picture; regular menu staples include *čobanac,* a stew made with game meat, bathed in paprika sauce and usually served with spaetzle; chicken paprikash; and, last but not least, *kulen* (spicy, air-dried sausage). Slavonia also counts river fish among its staples—namely, carp, pike, catfish, and pike-perch. One of the must-try menu items is the spicy-hot, paprika-flavored fish stew known as *riblji paprikaš* or *fiš paprikaš,* usually served in a bowl big enough for two. Of course no trip to Slavonia would be complete without local wine. Slavonia is the largest wine-producing region in the country and locals will tell you the only difference between their vineyards and the best wineries in France and Italy—with whom it shares the renowned 45th parallel, considered ideal for wine-growing—is centuries of marketing. The region is best-known for its whites: look for varieties such as *Graševina,* known elsewhere as Welschriesling, and Traminac, a type of Gewürztraminer. Red wine lovers should try the delicious *frankovka.* A tour of a winery here, including several tastings and often a platter of local meats and cheeses, generally costs 40 Kn–75 Kn and should be organized in advance. Hearty meals, delicious wine, and extremely affordable prices all add up to one certainty: you are going to eat and drink far too much in Slavonia, and you'll love it.

ABOUT THE HOTELS

In most Slavonian towns—apart from Osijek, which offers a nice selection of hotels plus a few smaller, pension-style accommodations—your sleeping choices are quite limited. The few luxury hotels are expensive by Slavonian standards, and compared to other parts of Croatia there are relatively few private rooms or apartments. But fear not: rural tourism is blossoming. If you're happy to stay slightly out of the center, there is a wealth of wonderful accommodations options, from converted farmhouses to horse stables to wineries, where you can enjoy the countryside, taste homemade products, and even get your hands dirty helping out at harvest time. *Hotel reviews have been shortened. For full information, visit Fodors.com.*

WHAT IT COSTS IN EUROS (€) AND CROATIAN KUNA (KN)

	$	$$	$$$	$$$$
Restaurants	under 35 Kn	35 Kn–60 Kn	61 Kn–80 Kn	over 80 Kn
	under €5	€5–€8	€9–€10	over €10
Hotels	under 925 Kn	925 Kn–1,300 Kn	1,301 Kn–1,650 Kn	over 1,650 Kn
	under €121	€121–€170	€171–€216	over €216

Restaurant prices are the average cost of a main course at dinner or, if dinner is not served, at lunch. Hotel prices are the lowest cost of a standard double room in high season.

VISITOR INFORMATION

The websites of the tourist boards responsible for **Osijek-Baranja County** (🌐 *www.tzosbarzup.hr*) and **Vukovar-Srijem County** (🌐 *www.tzvsz.hr*) have information on towns within the regions.

Contacts **Đakovo Tourist Information.** ✉ *Kralja Tomislava 3, Đakovo* ☎ *031/812–319* 🌐 *www.tz-djakovo.hr.* **Daruvar Tourist Information.** ✉ *Trg. Kralja Tomislava 12, Daruvar* ☎ *043/331–382* 🌐 *www.visitdaruvar.hr.* **Ilok Tourist Information.** ✉ *Trg. Sv. Ivana Kapistrana 5, Ilok* ☎ *032/590–020, 032/592–966* 🌐 *www.turizamilok.hr.* **Osijek Tourist Information.** ✉ *Županijska 2, Osijek* ☎ *031/203–755* 🌐 *www.tzosijek.hr.* **Vukovar Tourist Information.** ✉ *J. J. Strossmayera 15, Vukovar* ☎ *032/442–889* 🌐 *turizamvukovar.hr.*

OSIJEK

280 km (175 miles) east of Zagreb.

If there was ever a time to visit Osijek, it's now. Far from where sea-spirited tourists typically tread—and surrounded on all sides by cornfields—Osijek, Croatia's fourth-largest city and the capital of Slavonia, is an often overlooked treasure trove of cultural and architectural attractions. But it is quietly emerging as one of the most interesting cities in the country. Croatia's first craft beer bar is here, as is one of the best restaurants in the region, and it's the gateway to the famous Slavonian wine roads. There are music and BMX festivals, weekly parties in the main square, miles of tree-lined streets and bike lanes, beach bars along the river and no less than 17 parks. It rests on the south bank of the Drava River, which runs the length of the city and is the favorite recreational area for locals; you'll see them biking, rollerblading, walking dogs or sitting at one of the many riverside terraces for a coffee. It's a fascinating place for intrepid travellers to discover what a real Croatian city is like.

GETTING HERE AND AROUND

As Slavonia's main city, Osijek is also the easiest place to get to and from, so if you don't have a car you should base yourself here and take day trips to the more far-flung areas. There are regular buses and trains from Osijek to Zagreb (4 hours) and other destinations around the region. Although it is certainly possible to walk everywhere, hopping aboard one of the trams that wind their way around the city will save you time. To get between Gornji grad and Tvrđa, take Tram No. 1; to get between the train station and Gornji grad, it's Tram No. 2. Osijek also has miles of bike lanes, particularly along the river; bikes can be rented from Guesthouse Maksimilian.

EXPLORING

By the mid-12th century, Osijek was a prosperous market town in the Hungarian-Croatian kingdom, occupying the area of present-day **Tvrđa** (Citadel). After more than 150 years of Ottoman occupation in the 16th and 17th centuries, it was a flowering Turkish town. At 11 am on September 26, 1687, that era ended with the flight of the last Turkish soldier. (As a continuing legacy of this watershed event, the church bells

Slavonia
SLOVENIA
HUNGARY
SERBIA
BOSNIA-HERZEGOVINA
Mursko Središće
Čakovec
Mura
Varaždin
Lepoglava
Krapina
Koprivnica
Drava
Danube
Križevci
Bilo gora
Zabok
Medvednica Nature Park
Vrbovec
Bjelovar
Kurija Janković
Virovitica
ZAGREB
Samobor
Žumberak-Samoborko Nature Park
Ivanić-Grad
Čazma
Česma
Velika Gorica
Garešnica
Daruvar
Slatina
Donji Miholjac
Beli Manastir
Zmajevac
Batina Monument
Karanac
The Baranja Region
Belišće
Valpovo
Kopački Rit Nature Park
Bizovac
Erdutski Vinogradi
Aljmaš
Čepin
Tenja
Osijek
see detail map
Borovo
Vukovar
Vučedol Culture Museum
Spomen Dom Ovčara
Vinkovci
Ilok
Županja
Đakovo
Slavonski Brod
The Golden Valley
Papuk Nature Park
Krauthaker
Kutjevo
Našice
Vuka
Požega
Nova Gradiœka
Pakrac
Lipik
Novska
Okučani
Kutina
Sisak
Lonjsko polje
Sava
Petrinja
Hrvatska Kostajnica
Dubica
Glina
Dvor
Karlovac
Kupa
Duga Resa
Korana
Plitvice Lakes National Park
0
20 miles
0
20 kilometers

GREAT ITINERARIES

IF YOU HAVE 3 DAYS

Spend your first day exploring **Osijek**. On the second day, get an early start to nearby **Kopački Rit Nature Park** for a morning boat trip and a bit of bird-watching. Spend the afternoon driving around Baranja, checking out the small villages and popping into a winery or two. Stay in **Karanac** where you can bike ride through the fields and have dinner at one of the region's best restaurants. On the third day, drive to **Vukovar** for a full day of sightseeing. If you want to take your time, stay the night; otherwise, keep driving all the way to **Ilok** to finish your trip at one of the town's renowned wineries.

IF YOU HAVE 5 DAYS

Spend your first three days as above. On the fourth morning, drive to Đakovo for the afternoon to see its red cathedral and white horses before carrying on to **Kutjevo** for your final two nights. On the fifth day, go for a hike in Papuk Nature Park in the morning, then spend your final afternoon wine-tasting in the Golden Valley.

of Osijek undertake a celebratory ringing every Friday at 11 am.) Osijek henceforth became a military garrison under the Austrians, who turned it into a walled fortress in the late 17th century. The **Gornji grad** (Upper Town) was developed by the Austrians during this period; today it's the city's commercial and administrative center. You can see beautiful Baroque architecture along Europska Avenija, which stretches between the two parts of the city.

TOP ATTRACTIONS

Fodor's Choice ★ **Konkatedrala Sv. Petra i Pavla** (*Co-cathedral of Saints Peter and Paul*). This majestic single-nave church is the highlight of Osijek's downtown skyline. At 292 feet, its redbrick, neo-Gothic steeple is the second-highest structure in Croatia. Built between 1894 and 1898 on the initiative of the famous Đakovo-based bishop Josip Juraj Strossmayer, it has five altars and the walls are painted with colorful frescoes. ✉ *Trg Pape Ivana Pavla II, Gornji Grad* ☎ *031/310–020* 🌐 *www.svpetaripavao.hr.*

Muzej Likovnih Umjetnosti (*Museum of Fine Arts*). Europska Avenija is the broad avenue that connects the new and old towns. It is lined with late-19th- and early-20th-century neoclassical and art nouveau houses built as private residences, complete with gardens and cast-iron railings. One of those mansions, formerly belonging to a prominent attorney, is now the home of the Museum of Fine Arts, with a focus on Croatian and Slavonian artists and a permanent collection of paintings, sculpture, and graphic arts from the 18th century to now. It is well worth a visit, particularly to check out its temporary exhibitions on the ground floor. ✉ *Europska avenija 9, Gornji Grad* ☎ *031/251–280* 🌐 *www.mlu.hr* 🎟 *15 Kn.*

FAMILY **Perivoj Krajla Tomislava** (*King Tomislav Gardens*). With 17 around town, Osijek is known as a city of parks, and this is one of the nicest. The King Tomislav Gardens is a spacious, forested oasis that was laid out in the 18th century for the Austrian officers to take a breather from life

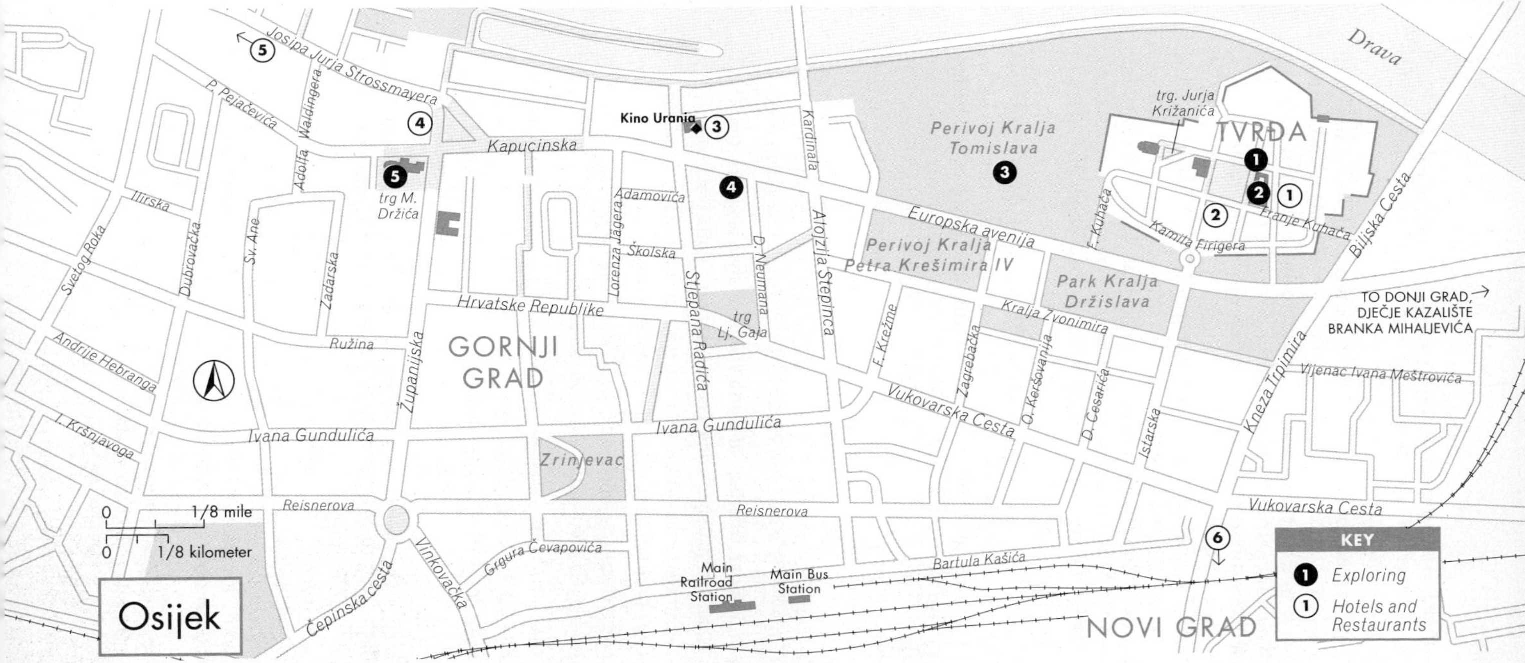

Exploring

Konkatedrala Sv. Petra i Pavla **5**

Muzej Likovnih Umjetnosti **4**

Muzej Slavonije **2**

Perivoj Krajla Tomislava **3**

Tvrda **1**

Restaurants

Kod Ruže **2**

Kompa **4**

Lumiere **3**

Muzej Okusa **6**

Hotels

Guesthouse Maksimilian ... **1**

Hotel Waldinger **5**

in the citadel. It separates historic Tvrđa from Gornji grad, the more bustling, commercial heart of town. The park is home to playgrounds and a tennis club. ✉ *2 Europska avenija.*

Fodor's Choice ★ **Tvrđa.** This walled fortress has a history dating back to the mid-12th century when the site was a market town in the Hungarian-Croatian kingdom. It was later occupied by the Ottomans, and finally became a fortified military garrison under the Austrians in the 17th century. It has one of the best-preserved ensembles of Baroque buildings in Croatia, with old barracks, churches, and monasteries. Facing the Drava River, the Water Gate, once known by the Latin appellation Porta Aquatica, is the only remaining gate in the original fortress wall, most of which was razed in the 1920s. Today Tvrđa is a somewhat sleepy old town, but you'll find the Museum of Slavonia here, some of the best restaurants, bars, and nightlife in Osijek, plus Guesthouse Maksimilian. ✉ *Tvrda.*

WORTH NOTING

Muzej Slavonije (*Museum of Slavonia*). One of the largest and oldest museums in Croatia, the Museum of Slavonia encompasses two buildings on Tvrđa's Holy Trinity Square. The renovated city guardhouse has an impressive range of artifacts from Slavonia through the ages, from the neolithic Starčevo culture through to Celtic and Roman times. The magistrate building, the oldest public building in Osijek and once used as the city hall, has myriad objects on display concerning the region's folklore, culture, and natural history; everything from stuffed animals and old coins to pottery and swords. ✉ *Trg Sv. Trojstva 6, Tvrda* ☎ *031/250–730* 🌐 *www.mso.hr* 🎟 *15 Kn* ⏲ *Closed Sun. and Mon.*

NEED A BREAK

Kavana Waldinger. Offering old-world Viennese-style elegance, the Kavana Waldinger is Osijek's finest café. Part of the Hotel Waldinger family—which also includes the trendier, more stylish Gold by Waldinger café across the street—it is a wonderful place to relax over a cocktail, coffee, or spectacularly indulgent cake. ✉ *Hotel Waldinger, Županijska 8, Gornji Grad* ☎ *031/250–450* 🌐 *www.waldinger.hr.*

WHERE TO EAT

$$$ EASTERN EUROPEAN

✕ **Kod Ruže.** Kod Ruže seems to have all the trappings you'd expect from a typical Slavonian restaurant but with a modern touch; heavy furniture, faded old photos, and embroidered hand towels—all very antique chic. The menu gives traditional dishes a creative bent: river fish on skewers and uniquely flavored stews. **Known for:** fiš paprikaš; fun traditional atmosphere; live music on weekends. $ *Average main: 80 Kn* ✉ *Kuhačeva 25a, Tvrda* ☎ *031/206–066* 🌐 *www.omnia-osijek.hr/krcma-kod-ruze.*

$$ EASTERN EUROPEAN Fodor's Choice ★

✕ **Kompa.** On the bank of the Drava, just across the river from the Osijek zoo, Kompa takes traditional dishes to another level. Their homemade sausages are perfectly spicy, the *koljenica* (pig's knuckle) is a firm favorite, and if you are around on a Sunday or holiday, join the locals for a big feast of *teleće pečenje* (roast veal). **Known for:** riverside location; unique range of traditional food; sunset views. $ *Average* *main: 60 Kn ✉ Splavarska 1, Gornji Grad ☎ 031/375–755 🌐 www.restorankompa.hr.*

$$$$ ITALIAN
Lumiere. Under the glow of the Kino Urania sits Lumiere restaurant, a bright light in a city full of traditional restaurants. The menu is Italian-inspired, with a wide range of pasta, steaks and seafood, and a great wine list. **Known for:** sophisticated ambience; Italian-inspired cuisine; romantic terrace. *$ Average main: 120 Kn ✉ Šetaliste Kardinala Franje Šepera 8, Gornji Grad ☎ 031/201–088 🌐 www.lumiere.com.*

$$$ EASTERN EUROPEAN Fodor's Choice ★
Muzej Okusa. This grand, stylish restaurant (which means Museum of Taste) was voted Best in Slavonia five months after it opened. Enjoy sophisticated risotto, fine ribeye steak, and top quality fish, all prepared with pride and at local prices. **Known for:** classiest restaurant in town; top-quality food and wine; beautifully refurbished building. *$ Average main: 80 Kn ✉ Martina Divalta 4, Gornji Grad ☎ 095/543–3050 🌐 www.muzej-okusa.com.*

WHERE TO STAY

$ B&B/INN Fodor's Choice ★
Guesthouse Maksimilian. Art, history, culture, and comfort come together in this 14-room guesthouse in Tvrđa, a one-of-a-kind accommodation option in Osijek. **Pros:** beautifully decorated guest rooms; friendly and personal service; excursions of the region can be arranged. **Cons:** rooms can be noisy. *$ Rooms from: 330 Kn ✉ Franjevačka 12, Tvrda ☎ 031/497–567 🌐 maksimilian.hr ⇨ 14 rooms 🍽 Breakfast.*

$$ HOTEL Fodor's Choice ★
Hotel Waldinger. Located in a 19th-century art nouveau building on one of central Osijek's main thoroughfares, the Waldinger—named after famous local painter Adolf Waldinger—offers luxury on a cozy scale with a period look and feel. **Pros:** parking included; lavish breakfast; old-world luxury. **Cons:** pricey (for Slavonia); rooms on top floor have smallish windows. *$ Rooms from: 950 Kn ✉ Županijska 8, Gornji Grad ☎ 031/250–450 🌐 www.waldinger.hr ⇨ 15 rooms, 1 suite 🍽 Breakfast.*

NIGHTLIFE AND PERFORMING ARTS

NIGHTLIFE

Osijek has a large student population so its bars and cafés are full day and night with people drinking coffee, eating ice cream, or enjoying a local Osječko.

American Bar Dollar. Located in the Upper Town, across the street from the tourist information center, is a hot spot that serves burgers, ribs, and craft beers in a space with kitschy, vintage Americana decor. It's a fun place to hang out with the local cool kids. *✉ Županijska 5, Gornji Grad ☎ 031/284–625 🌐 americanbardollar.com.*

Gajba. The first craft-beer bar in Croatia, this tiny establishment in the Upper Town is a great place to try Croatian and international craft brews. The staff are serious beer aficionados who also organize the very popular Osijek Craft Beer Festival. *✉ Sunčana 3, Gornji Grad 🌐 www.gajba.hr.*

St. Patrick's Pub. The main square in Tvrđa is lined with café-bars and terraces, distinguishable only by their different-colored umbrellas. St. Patrick's Pub, a paean to all things Irish, was the pioneer, and still one of the most popular. ✉ *South side of Trg Svetog Trojstva, Franje Kuhača 15, Tvrda* ☎ *031/205–202.*

Trica. The promenade along the city harbor (Zimska Luka) is lined with inviting café-bars and really comes alive on summer weekends with live music across the outdoor terraces. A great option is Trica, a popular student hangout on a side street with a lively soundtrack and quirky decor; it stretches over three rooms on split levels, with a few tables in the lovely garden out back. ✉ *Lučki prilaz 2, Gornji Grad* ☎ *031/778–414.*

PERFORMING ARTS

Hrvatsko Narodno Kazalište (*Croatian National Theater*). The Croatian National Theatre is Osijek's venue for a broad array of Croatian and international plays. The building that has housed the theater since 1907 is an imposing ochre structure whose Venetian-Moorish style renders it the most striking of a string of classical facades along Županijska ulica. ✉ *Županijska 9, Gornji Grad* ☎ *031/220–700* 🌐 *www.hnk-osijek.hr.*

Kino Urania (*Urania Cinema*). This historic art nouveau cinema, which screened its first films back in 1912, was designed by famed Osijek architect Viktor Axmann. Movie fans will love the old-school charm, particularly the vintage posters on the walls. Films are in English with subtitles. ✉ *V. Hengla 1, Gornji Grad* ☎ *031/205–507* 🌐 *www.kinematografi-osijek.hr.*

SHOPPING

There are two big shopping malls in Osijek: Portanova and the Avenue Mall; a bus runs from the center to both of them. There are also independent boutiques in Gornji grad, particularly along bustling Županijska.

NEED A BREAK

The Kavana. A great place for your afternoon coffee break is on the terrace of The Kavana, right in the shadow of the Cathedral. It's a stylish café with revolving art installations, designer furniture from Istanbul, and the bragging rights of being the only café in town that serves Lavazza coffee. ✉ ***Županijska 2, Gornji Grad*** ☎ ***091/752–5523.***

Fodor's Choice ★ **Osijek Antiques Market.** If you're lucky enough to visit Osijek on the first Saturday of the month, head to the Osijek Antiques Market in Tvrđa's main square, where more than 100 antiques dealers from Croatia and beyond sell everything from porcelain to furniture to weapons. The market typically lasts from 9 am to 2 pm. ✉ *Trg. Svetog Trojstva, Tvrda.*

THE BARANJA REGION

314 km (195 miles) east of Zagreb.

The unspoiled Baranja region, whose name means "Mother of Wine" in Hungarian, is located in the northeast of Croatia on the borders of Hungary and Serbia. It begins on the other side of the Drava River from

Osijek, but seems a world away from city life. It is full of farmhouses and quaint villages with only a few thousand residents at most. Life is lived around the Danube, in vineyards and fertile fields, and near the swamps of Kopački Rit. There are fish-stew cook-offs, harvest festivals, labyrinths of flowers, wine, goulash, and everything is sprinkled with paprika; just one aspect of the strong Hungarian influence here.

Though the area seems old-fashioned, its best days are hardly behind it; with the travel trends toward agritourism and local experiences, this is a region on the rise and embracing the fact that its traditional ways might just be the way of the future. The best village to spend the evening is Karanac, full of traditional, long Pannonian houses and two of the best restaurants in Slavonia. The entire region is quite compact, but it is tricky to get around Baranja by public transport. Arrange a tour if you don't have a car.

EXPLORING

Batina Monument. High on a hill above the border where Croatia meets Hungary and Serbia is this striking WWII monument, dedicated to the 2,000 members of the Red Army who died in the Battle of Batina. It was built in 1946, three years after the battle, by Croatian sculptor Antun Augustinčić. The monument itself, topped by a 89-foot-high obelisk, is quite impressive, but the views of the Danube, forests, and three countries below are the best part of the visit.

Erdutski Vinogradi. The village of Erdut, with a medieval castle overlooking the Danube, is just 37 km (23 miles) east of Osijek. The Erdut Agreement, which brought a peaceful resolution to the war in 1995 in Eastern Croatia, was signed here. There are several wineries to visit around the village, including Erdutski Vinogradi, which dates from 1450 and has produced wine since 1730. There are lovely views from the winery, which is also home to one of the quirkiest sights in the Croatian wine world: a barrel made of 150-year-old Slavonian oak that holds 75,000 liters of Graševina. ■ **TIP→ An interesting stopover near Erdut is the tiny village of Aljmaš; every August 15, tens of thousands of people from nearby villages, even as far as Serbia, make their way on foot to a shrine in this typically sleepy town to celebrate the Feast Day of the Assumption of Mary.** ✉ *Trg Branka Hercega 1, Erdut* ☎ *031/596–555* 🌐 *erdutski-vinogradi.hr.*

Fodor's Choice ★ **Josić Winery.** One of the best wineries in the country also has easily the best restaurant in Slavonia. The progressive Josić winery in the settlement of Zmajevac is a must-visit. Located on a narrow street lined by other wineries, it's the biggest of the small wineries in the region and a local favorite. The restaurant is candlelit and romantic, the ambience welcoming, and the menu is next-level. Those craving a glass of red wine will be happy to learn that Josić is known for its experimental cuvée of Merlot, Cabernet Sauvignon, and Shiraz. Call ahead to arrange a free tour of the cellars and wine tasting. ✉ *Planina 194, Zmajevac* ☎ *031/734–410* 🌐 *www.josic.hr.*

Fodor's Choice ★ **Kopački Rit Nature Park.** One of the most popular sites in the region, Kopački Rit Nature Park is one of the largest remaining wetlands along the Danube and a place of serene beauty. Embracing more than

SLAMA ART FESTIVAL

While strolling around Osijek, you might start to notice unusual sculptures on roundabouts, in the middle of gardens and fields, and possibly even near your hotel. They might be in the shape of a bird, a bike, maybe even a high-heeled shoe, and they all have one thing in common: they're made of straw. One of the most unique rural festivals in the country, Slama is a multiday "Land Art" festival held every summer in a field somewhere in Slavonia. It began in 2006, when seven local artists set out to explore the possibilities of their region's most abundant natural material, the way coastal Croatians use their famous white stone. An ancient harvest ritual in the area involved building monuments out of straw and setting them on fire, believing it would grant fertility to the soil for the following year, so they gave it a try. Since then, the sculptures have grown bigger and more complex, and the festival itself has grown to attract artists from around Croatia and beyond, plus thousands of festival goers who come to enjoy the traditional food, music, even sports competitions such as bale throwing. And like any good party in a field, it all ends with a bonfire, as the sculptures are burned to the ground. Information can be tricky to find; check the tourism website of Baranja for up-to-date details.

74,100 acres immediately north of the Drava, 10 km (6 miles) northeast of Osijek, the park is covered with immense reed beds, willow, poplar, and oak forests, and crisscrossed by ridges, ponds, shallow lakes, and marshes. More than 300 bird species, hundreds of varieties of plants, and dozens of species of butterflies, mammals, and fish live here, and it is also a breeding area for numerous endangered species, including the white-tailed sea eagle, the black stork, and the European otter. Egrets, herons, and cormorants are abundant, as are red deer, roe deer, and wild boar.

The best times of year to visit are during spring and autumn bird migrations, when there are often several hundred thousand birds in the park. There is an information office at the entrance in Kopač. A boardwalk leads to the landing where boat excursions set out daily into the marshy heart of the park, along a channel to Kopačevo Jezero, the largest lake.

There are different guided tours available, but the best is the Beaver's Trail, which includes entrance into the park and boardwalk, plus a small boat tour through the wetlands (1 hour). The best time to do the Beaver's Trail is during the morning when bird-spotting is best.

Getting to Kopački Rit from Osijek is simple if you have a car—just follow the signs once you're in Bilje. If you go by bus, get off in Bilje and follow the signs on foot for some 4 km (2½ miles) along rural roads to the entrance of the park, or ride a bike from Osijek. ✉ *Information Center near Kopačevo, Kopacevo* ☎ *031/445–445* 🌐 *www.pp-kopacki-rit.hr* 🎫 *120 Kn for Beaver's Trail.*

3

WHERE TO EAT

$$$ EASTERN EUROPEAN Fodor's Choice ★ **Baranjska Kuća.** Considered one of the best restaurants in Slavonia, Baranjska Kuća doubles as an impressive outdoor ethnographic museum, complete with a model street and houses showing what life in rural Baranja was once like. It's a great place to try typical Slavonian dishes such as čobanac and beans cooked in clay pots, or more unusual dishes such as snails in nettle sauce. **Known for:** traditional Slavonian food; ethnographic museum; some unusual dishes. *Average main: 70 Kn* ✉ *Kolodvorska 99* ☎ *031/720–180* 🌐 *www.baranjska-kuca.com.*

WHERE TO STAY

$ B&B/INN Fodor's Choice ★ **Ivica i Marica.** The most welcoming and unique place to stay in Baranja is this beautifully restored, working farmhouse in the tiny village of Karanac. **Pros:** large outdoor area; excellent breakfast of local and homemade products; beautifully decorated rooms. **Cons:** difficult to reach by public transport; not many amenities within walking distance. *Rooms from: 450 Kn* ✉ *Ive Lole Ribara 8A* ☎ *091/137–3793* 🌐 *www.ivica-marica.com* *25 rooms* *Breakfast.*

SHOPPING

Asztalos Kermaik. Located in a renovated steam mill from 1911 and run by artist Daniel Asztalos, this quirky little ceramics shop sells lovely, original items, like spice pots, beer mugs, wine glasses, and olive-oil bottles, and offers pottery workshops if you want to create your own keepsake. Find it in the settlement of Suza on the road between Karanac and Batina. ✉ *Maršala Tita 96* ☎ *098/945–5990* *Weekends 9–6; call for appointment any other time.*

VUKOVAR

35 km (22 miles) southeast of Osijek.

There's no doubt that a visit to Vukovar hurts. As you visit the sights, the story of what happened here will slowly unfold, made even sadder by the glimpses of what a beautiful, cultural city this once was. It's a place that holds a tender spot in the hearts of most Croatians, and it will earn a spot in yours, too. But today, it is as much the scene of urban renewal as it is of destruction, and this is a perfect time to visit, as Vukovar begins to recover from its painful past and strives to regain its former vitality.

In 1991, Vukovar was a prosperous city. Located at the confluence of the Danube and Vuka rivers, it had a lovely ensemble of Baroque architecture, fine museums, and many restaurants. It was named after the ancient Vučedol culture that inhabited a site 5 km (3 miles) downstream from the present-day city some 5,000 years ago. The area was later the site of a Roman settlement, and by the 11th century a community existed at the town's present location; this settlement became the seat of Vukovo County in the 13th century. After Turkish rule (1526–1687), almost all of Vukovar and environs was bought by the counts of Eltz, a

German family that strongly influenced the development of the town for the next two centuries and whose palace is home to the town museum.

When Yugoslavia started to break apart in 1991 and Croatia declared independence, the JNA (Yugoslav People's Army) and Serb militias began seizing control of areas with a large Serbian population. Vukovar, which at the time had a mixed population of 47% Croatians and 37% Serbians, was steadfastly claimed by both sides. A battle for the city ensued; it was up to lightly armed soldiers of the newly created Croatian National Guard, as well as 1,100 civilian volunteers, to defend it. During the 87-day siege, 12,000 shells and rockets were launched daily in the fiercest European battle since World War II. Those who had not fled Vukovar in the beginning became trapped inside, taking refuge in Cold War–era bomb shelters. On the 18th of November, the defenders of the city, running out of ammunition, numbers, and strength, could hold on no longer and Vukovar fell. The once-lovely city was reduced to rubble. More than 30,000 Croatian residents were deported, thousands were killed, and thousands more are still reported as missing. Several military and political officials have since been indicted and jailed for war crimes, including those involved in the notorious Vukovar hospital massacre.

In 1998, Vukovar was peacefully reintegrated into Croatia, and on the surface it has come back to life. Ten years ago it would have been unfathomable that a visit here could involve anything other than war, but today, besides the many poignant war memorials and sites around town, there are plenty of other ways to pass your time. There are new modern shopping malls and cinemas, the Eltz Castle and the Franciscan Monastery have been rebuilt, and the ultramodern Vučedol Culture Museum is the first step in a planned archaeological park. Vukovar is a stop along the Danube bike path network, attracting cycling groups each summer, and its proximity to Ilok has made it a stop on many wine tours. The center is once again full of busy cafés and bustling markets, and there is even a six-day Vukovar Film Festival in August, featuring films also shown at the Cannes or Berlin Film Festivals.

Yet the memories are never far away. Next to brand-new structures are the burnt-out frames of old buildings. Walls are still pockmarked, houses remain empty, and many of the city's main sights take on deeper significance due to the destruction wrought upon them. The population is now half of what it was pre-war, and although it is mixed, the two ethnic communities remain divided. There is hope in the air, but it's usually not long before a conversation with a local will, inevitably, turn to the past.

In a poignant reminder, one cannot help but notice a steady, somber stream of pedestrian traffic to one of Vukovar's most conspicuous sites: a tall, simple white cross situated at the tip of a narrow causeway overlooking the Danube, with inscriptions in both Cyrillic and Roman letters, honoring victims on both sides. Vukovar is a living war museum.

GETTING HERE AND AROUND

Around five trains and buses make the daily 45-minute journey from Osijek to Vukovar, several of them continuing onward to Ilok farther south. Regular buses and trains also travel between Zagreb and Vukovar, stopping in Vinkovci along the way.

The main sights in Vukovar are spread out over an 8-km (5-mile) stretch from one end of the city to the other, starting with the Hospital Museum and ending at the Vučedol Culture Museum on the road to Ilok. If you have a car it is best to use it for sightseeing; parking is easy to find around the city. If you aren't driving, ask the Tourist Information for assistance—they can arrange a guide to accompany you to the main sights outside of the center. If you are planning to visit both the Vučedol Culture Museum and the Vukovar Town Museum, it is worth buying the Vuseum Pass (60 Kn), which will save you money on both of the entrance fees and includes a walking tour app. Ask at either of the museums or the tourist information center.

EXPLORING

TOP ATTRACTIONS

Fodor's Choice ★ **Gradski Muzej Vukovar** (*Vukovar Town Museum*). The 18th-century palace Dvorac Eltz has housed the Gradski Muzej Vukovar since 1969. During the siege of Vukovar, the palace was severely damaged and the collection was moved to a Zagreb museum for safekeeping. After decades of reconstruction, the entire museum and all 2,000 of its pieces are once again open for viewing, a positive sign that Vukovar is back in business. Founded in 1946, the museum was originally housed in an old school and then a post office before the palace became its home. It has an excellent range of local archaeological artifacts, from the Vučedol culture that flourished around 3000 BC right up to the siege of Vukovar. ✉ *Županijska 2* ☎ *032/441–270* *40 Kn (or free with Vuseum Pass)* ⏲ *Closed Mon.*

Fodor's Choice ★ **Mjesto Sjećanja–Vukovar Bolnica** (*Place of Memory—Vukovar Hospital*). You'll want to bring a steady set of nerves with you to this site. During the siege of Vukovar, the top four floors of the hospital were destroyed by consistent bombing, despite being designated an official safe zone; still, staff continued to work in the basement and bomb shelter, helping civilians and soldiers, operating even without running water. After Vukovar fell in 1991, and despite an agreement that the hospital must be safely evacuated, more than 200 people were removed from the hospital by a Serbian militia and brought to Ovčara farm, where they were beaten, tortured, and eventually executed. Others were sent to prisons or to refugee camps. Today, the structure has been rebuilt and functions as a regular hospital again, but the areas used during that time have been converted into a chilling multimedia museum-memorial. Opening hours are very sporadic, but in theory it is open from 8 am to 1 pm. Reach the memorial through the main gate of the hospital (under the Bolnica sign); ask at the small guard station on your right if it's open. You'll then find the memorial down the ramp to the right; the entrance is marked by a giant red cross, full of holes. ✉ *Županijska 35* 🌐 *www.ob-vukovar.hr* ⏲ *Closed weekends and afternoons.*

Fodor's Choice ★ **Spomen Dom Ovčara** (*Ovčara Memorial*). On November 20–21, 1991, more than 200 soldiers and civilians were brought from the hospital to this former agricultural hangar, 4 km (2½ miles) outside the city and surrounded by fields of crops, by a Serbian militia. They were beaten, tortured, and eventually executed at another site 1 km (½ mile) away. The mass grave was exhumed in 1996, and 194 bodies were identified; among the dead were men ranging from 16 to 77 years old, one woman, a prominent radio journalist, and a French volunteer. Ovčara Memorial is a somber, powerful site; it respectfully pays homage to the victims as well as conveys the horror that took place here. To get to the site, follow signs along the road to Ilok for 6 km (4 miles) past the Memorial Cemetery of Homeland War Victims, the largest mass grave in Europe since WWII—eventually turning right and driving another 4 km (2½ miles) down a country road. If you don't have wheels, check with the tourist information center about your transportation options. ✉ *Ovčara* ☎ *032/512–345* 🎫 *5 Kn.*

WORTH NOTING

FAMILY **Ada.** Vukovar locals live their lives on the banks of the Danube, and when it gets hot outside, they hop right into it! Ada is the name of a sandy beach on Vukovar Island, in the middle of the river where locals go to swim, play volleyball, and suntan. There is a café on the island, but not many other facilities. It is a fun retreat, 10 minutes from the city, and can be reached by boats that leave regularly from near the Hotel Lav and Vrske restaurant. A return ticket costs 10 Kn. ✉ *Island of Vukovar.*

Franjevački Samostan i Župa Sv. Filipa i Jakova (*Franciscan Monastery & Church of Sts. Philip and James*). High on a hill southeast of the town center you'll find Vukovar's main ecclesiastical attraction, and one of the largest in Croatia. Construction on the Baroque monastery began in 1723, and it held one of the richest and most valuable libraries in the country, as well as prominent paintings and gold and silver vessels. Both have been restored to their former glory after being ravaged in the war. ✉ *Samostanska 5* ☎ *032/441–381* ⏲ *Closed Sun.*

NEED A BREAK

Antique Caffe Bar. This classy café in the center of Vukovar has a breezy backyard that makes a perfect retreat on a hot summer day. Come for a coffee or try one of their pelinkovac liqueurs (a bitter liqueur based on wormwood). ✉ ***Dr. Franje Tudmana 8*** ☎ ***099/426–0915.***

Vučedol Culture Museum. Located 6 km (3.7 miles) from the center of Vukovar on the road to Ilok is the impressive Vučedol Culture Museum, a modern marvel celebrating the ancient Vučedol culture that once flourished in the vicinity. Exhibitions include the oldest Indo-European calendar, skulls demonstrating sacrificial practices, and the pit where the famous Vučedol Dove was discovered. Opened in 2015, this fascinating museum, spread across 19 rooms and built on a slope so that it almost seems part of the landscape, is the first step in a planned archaeological park. If this is the last sight you visit on your way out of town you're left with a very encouraging sense of the city's future. ✉ *Archaeological Site Vučedol* ☎ *032/373–930* 🌐 *www.vucedol.hr* 🎫 *40 Kn (free with Vuseum Pass)* ⏲ *Closed Mon.*

Water Tower. Visible from everywhere in Vukovar is its most famous symbol: the water tower. Rising 150 feet into the air, the imposing, red-brick structure once had a restaurant at the top with lovely views over the river and surrounding vineyards. Its sheer size made it a frequent target during the siege; it was hit with artillery more than 600 times. But it is still standing, with gaping holes on all sides, and although renovation is underway to restore the interior, the facade will remain that way as a constant reminder and a testament to the strength of the city. ✉ *1 Ulica Velika Skela.*

WHERE TO EAT

$$ EASTERN EUROPEAN ✕ **Dunavska Golubica.** With a sprawling terrace overlooking the Danube, this large restored restaurant has an old-fashioned fireplace as its centerpiece and pictures of old Vukovar on the walls. It specializes in river fish like everywhere else in town but also does a nice meat platter and delicious "complex salads" with chicken or smoked fish, which make great lunch options. **Known for:** riverside location; reliable traditional food; good salads. [$] *Average main: 60 Kn* ✉ *Dunavska šetnica 1* ☎ *032/445–434.*

$$ PIZZA ✕ **Stari Toranj.** This cozy family restaurant with a small patio and pleasant, down-to-earth staff is a local favorite. They serve up reliably good pizza and traditional meals. **Known for:** pizza; cozy space; local vibe. [$] *Average main: 50 Kn* ✉ *Trg Republike Hrvatske* ☎ *099/732–1255* 🌐 *www.restoran-stari-toranj.com.hr.*

WHERE TO STAY

$ HOTEL **Hotel Lav.** A sparkling white building with a glass front, Hotel Lav is the only luxury hotel in Vukovar. **Pros:** the only luxury hotel in town; centrally located. **Cons:** expensive by Slavonian standards; no pool. [$] *Rooms from: €110* ✉ *J. J. Strossmayera 18* ☎ *032/445–100* 🌐 *www.hotel-lav.hr* *47 rooms* *Breakfast.*

$ HOTEL Fodor's Choice ★ **Rooms Biser Dunava.** Halfway between a boutique hotel and a private apartment, this peaceful property is run by a friendly young local named Davor in the family home that he renovated himself. **Pros:** small, intimate hotel; swimming pool on-site; friendly staff. **Cons:** outside the center of Vukovar; breakfast costs extra; not everyone is into a shared kitchen. [$] *Rooms from: 250 Kn* ✉ *Osječka 11* ☎ *092/271–7082* 🌐 *www.biserdunava.com* *6 rooms.*

ILOK

37 km (22 miles) southeast of Vukovar, 74 km (45 miles) southeast of Osijek

Perched high on the western slopes of the Fruška Gora hills above the Danube and built around a medieval fortress, Ilok, Croatia's easternmost town, is one of the loveliest in Slavonia (although it is technically in the region of Syrmia, as the locals will proudly tell you). It's a great place to spend a couple of days visiting local wineries, hanging out beside the Danube, and taking day trips into Vukovar or even Serbia just across the border; on a clear day, you can see all the way across the Vojvodina plain to Novi Sad just 30 km (18 miles) away.

Ilok has been inhabited since the Neolithic era, but its golden age came in the 15th century under the Iločki family, particularly Nicholas of Ilok, the Ban of Croatia and King of Bosnia. He built a fortification on a plateau overlooking the river and a castle within, turning Ilok into a fortified royal residence, and began the first construction of wine cellars. The last member of the Iločki family died in 1524; two years later, Ilok was occupied by the Ottomans, under whose rule it remained until 1697. There are still the remains of a hammam and a Turkish grave in the Old Town from this period. After defeating the Turks, the Habsburgs gave Ilok to the aristocratic Odescalchi family from Italy as thanks for their assistance in the Ottoman wars, and they quickly set about rebuilding the town, particularly the castle, in Baroque style. They developed the wine cellars below the castle, and began production of the celebrated Traminac wine. Besides Stari Podrum (Old Cellar), there are now a dozen other vineyards around town producing many varieties of wine, particularly Graševina and Traminac. All can be visited by appointment.

Ilok became part of Yugoslavia in 1918. At the beginning of the war in 1991, it was rapidly surrounded and occupied by Serb forces, sparing it the drawn-out devastation suffered by nearby Vukovar. Ilok was integrated into the Republic of Serb Krajina, and not reintegrated into Croatia until 1998.

Ilok is composed of two parts: the upper half is where the feudal families lived and where today you'll find the cities' historical sights and the remains of the fortified walls, and the lower half where traditionally the townsfolk lived and worked, and where you'll find sandy beaches along the Danube.

GETTING HERE AND AROUND

There are frequent buses between Vukovar and Ilok (45 minutes, 35 Kn), many of which start or finish in Osijek; the bus will let you off in the center of the lower town. Ilok is best explored by foot as most of the main sites, hotels, and wineries are around the center of town. If you plan to visit a winery out of town, contact them or the helpful folks at the tourist information center and someone will usually come to pick you up.

EXPLORING

TOP ATTRACTIONS

Fodor's Choice ★ **Muzej Grada Iloka** (*Town Museum of Ilok*). This impressive collection takes you through the ages of Ilok, from the Ottoman era to the Austrian Empire, the wars of the 20th century, and right up to a modern art gallery. There are particularly interesting exhibits on the region's Jewish population pre-1945, relics from a 19th-century pharmacy, and an ethnological section on the top floor focusing on Ilok's large Slovak population. The museum is housed in the Odescalchi Castle, an imposing fortified structure overlooking the Danube, which was built on the foundations of the 15th-century castle of Nicholas of Ilok. Legend says that Suleiman the Magnificent once slept in this castle. The rooms themselves are exquisitely designed with period pieces, even mood music, in keeping with their original function, such as the hunting room and the drawing room. ✉ *Šetalište o Mladena Barbarića 5* ☎ *032/827–410* 🌐 *www.mgi.hr* 🎟 *20 Kn* ⏱ *Closed Sun. and Mon.*

Fodor's Choice ★ **Stari Podrum** (*Old Cellar*). A wine cellar, restaurant, hotel, and history lesson all rolled into one, Stari Podrum is a must-see when visiting Ilok. It is located next door to the Odescalchi Castle; in fact, the incredibly atmospheric cellars, stretching 100 meters long, stretch underneath it. The Odescalchi family began producing high-class wines here in the 18th century, including the celebrated Traminac, which was served at the coronation of Queen Elizabeth II. A private tour will take you through the cool cellars, past Slavonian oak barrels, to the prestigious archive wines and old bottles, full of dust and cobwebs, that were hidden behind a wall for protection during the Homeland War. You can try all of the wines produced here, and buy souvenir bottles at very reasonable prices. The on-site restaurant serves delicious Slavonian dishes, including freshwater fish paprikash with homemade noodles; you can eat inside surrounded by traditional embroidery and heavy wooden furniture, or outdoors in the sunny central courtyard. Accommodation can also be arranged in one of 18 on-site rooms. ✉ *4 Šetalište O. M. Barbarića* ☎ *032/590–088* 🌐 *www.ilocki-podrumi.hr.*

WORTH NOTING

Župa Sv. Ivana Kapistrana (*Church of St. John of Capistrano*). This Franciscan church and monastery overlooking the Danube, first constructed in 1349, holds the remains of St. John of Capistrano, a Franciscan friar and Catholic priest. In 1456, at age 70, he led a successful battle against the Ottomans, which earned him the nickname "Soldier Priest." He died three months later in Ilok of the bubonic plague but was said to have performed miracles even on his deathbed. The church—which also holds the remains of Nicholas and Lawrence of Ilok, both of whom made expansions to the monastery complex during their reign—was given a 20th-century neo-Gothic face-lift by Herman Bollé, the same architect who helped design the Cathedrals in Đakovo and Zagreb, as well as Zagreb's Mirogoj Cemetery. The tourist information center is next door; if the church is closed, contact them to arrange a visit. ✉ *Trg Sv. Ivana Kapistrana 3.*

WHERE TO STAY

The best restaurants are found in the main hotels around town, so planning a visit to each of them for either lunch, wine-tasting, or dinner makes for a nice tour of Ilok.

$ HOTEL FAMILY **Hotel Dunav.** Located right on the riverbank, this upscale family-run hotel makes a great base for exploring both parts of the town. **Pros:** riverside location; excellent restaurant. **Cons:** feels slightly empty in low season; distance from wineries. [$] *Rooms from: €65* ✉ *Julija Benešića 62* ☎ *032/596–500* 🌐 *www.hoteldunavilok.com* 🛏 *16 rooms* 🍽 *Breakfast.*

$ HOTEL **Principovac Country Estate.** Located 1½ km (1 mile) from Ilok in the Baroque summer house of the Odescalchi family, this is an elegant retreat amid miles of rolling vineyards. **Pros:** beautifully designed premises; romantic escape; great for walking, biking, tennis, or golf. **Cons:** far from civilization; no public transport. *Rooms from: 610 Kn ✉ Principovac 1 ☎ 032/593–114 6 rooms Breakfast.*

$ HOTEL **Villa Iva.** This peaceful boutique hotel and restaurant is located in the lower part of Ilok, at the base of the steps leading up to the Old Town. **Pros:** nicely decorated rooms; on-site wine cellar and restaurant. **Cons:** not in Old Town; far from main sights. *Rooms from: 330 Kn ✉ S. Radića 23 ☎ 032/591–011 🌐 villa-iva-ilok.com 13 rooms Breakfast.*

ĐAKOVO

38 km (24 miles) southeast of Osijek.

Đakovo is a peaceful little town, where the din of bicycles and the dribbling of basketballs on a Sunday afternoon outdo the roar of cars. The relatively bustling pedestrian main street is Ivana Pavla II, whose far end has a little parish church that was built rather cleverly from a former 16th-century mosque, one of the few remaining structures left in Slavonia from 150 years of Ottoman rule. The best time to be in town is the last weekend in September, during the annual Đakovački Vezovi (Đakovo Embroidery Festival), which sees a folklore show replete with traditional embroidered costumes, folk dancing, and folk singing, an array of song-and-dance performances, and an all-around party atmosphere—even a show by the famous Lipizzaner horses.

GETTING HERE AND AROUND

You can get to Đakovo from Osijek in about 40 minutes by one of several daily trains or buses for roughly 35 Kn one-way. The Đakovo train station is 1 km (½ mile) east of the center, at the opposite end of Kralja Tomislava, while the bus station is near the center of town.

EXPLORING

Đakovačka Katedrala (*Đakovo Cathedral*). Đakovo's centerpiece is its majestic, redbrick neo-Gothic cathedral, which towers above the city and is a stunning first sight as you arrive into town. Commissioned by the Bishop of Đakovo, Josip Juraj Strossmayer (1815–1905), and consecrated in 1882 after two decades of construction, the cathedral was called the "most beautiful church between Venice and Constantinople" by Pope John XXIII. *✉ Trg Strossmayera.*

FAMILY **Lipizzan State Stud Farm.** The history of the Đakovo stud farm dates back to 1506, when one of the bishops kept 90 Arabic horses there. But perhaps the year that really put it on the map was 1972, when Queen Elizabeth II saw the famous Đakovo four-horse team perform at the opening ceremony of the Olympics and insisted on paying them a visit. The story goes that there was no paved road outside the stud farm at the time; by the time the queen arrived to take a carriage ride, one had been built. There are two locations in Đakovo where the prized white Lipizzaners are trained and bred; the Stallion Stable in the center of Đakovo, where a musical show is also held twice per month and plans are in place to build a museum; and Ivandvor, 6 km (4 miles) away, a pasture where the mares and offspring are kept in a peaceful, rural setting. It is possible to visit both farms to catch a glimpse of the horses and their stables, and a carriage ride through town can also be arranged. ✉ *Augusta Šenoe 45* ☎ *031/822–535* 🌐 *www.ergela-djakovo.hr* 🎫 *Guided tour of stud farm 30 Kn.*

WHERE TO EAT

$$ PIZZA ✕ **Mon Ami.** Located in a big redbrick building around the corner from the Cathedral, this dark, publike restaurant specializes in grilled meat and pizza cooked in a giant wood oven. **Known for:** grilled meat; slavonian breakfast. $ *Average main: 50 Kn* ✉ *L. Botića 12* ☎ *031/821–477.*

$$$ EASTERN EUROPEAN Fodor's Choice ★ ✕ **Sokak.** One of the best places to find traditional Slavonian food in Đakovo, Sokak not only offers the chance to try local specialties such as Slavonian soup or veal *peka* (cooked under the bell—order in advance), it also gives you a glimpse at what a traditional Slavonian neighborhood used to look like. The restaurant was built to resemble the two sides of a street, one half symbolizing the side where the wealthy people owned houses, the other half where the rural workers lived. **Known for:** traditional Slavonian food. $ *Average main: 70 Kn* ✉ *Augusta Šenoe 40* ☎ *031/820–332.*

WHERE TO STAY

$ HOTEL **Hotel Đakovo.** With cheerful rooms, a big restaurant specializing in Slavonian food and wine, and a game room perfect for kids, this is your best hotel option in town. **Pros:** friendly service; on-site restaurant; spacious rooms. **Cons:** far from town and public transport; heavily focused on wedding parties. $ *Rooms from: 470 Kn* ✉ *N.Tesle 52* ☎ *031/840–570* 🌐 *www.hotel-djakovo.hr* *25 rooms* *Breakfast.*

THE GOLDEN VALLEY

150 km (94 miles) southeast of Zagreb, 96 km (60 miles) southwest of Osijek.

In the center of a fertile, vineyard-rich valley in Požega-Slavonia County (one of the smallest in Croatia), lies the area that the ancient Romans knew as "Vallis Aurea," or the Golden Valley. Going against Slavonia's reputation as one big, flat agricultural plain, this area is mountainous, with forested hills covered by the vineyards of more than 30 private wineries. It is a wonderful place to base yourself for a couple of days to sample great wine, local gastronomy and explore nearby Papuk Nature Park.

The administrative and cultural center of the area is Požega (pop. 21,000). Požega was first mentioned in historical documents in 1227, but not much remains of that early era of local history. During the

150-year-long period of Ottoman rule that began in 1537, Požega became central Slavonia's most important administrative and military center. By the 19th century Požega's cultural dynamism had earned it a reputation as the "Athens of Slavonia," and in 1847 it became the first city to officially adopt the Croatian language. Today it is one of the prettiest towns in central Slavonia.

Just 23 km (14 miles) northeast of Požega is a small town called Kutjevo. With a history of wine making that dates back to the 13th century, if there is any town where all of life is dedicated to viticulture, it is here. Nearly all 2,500 residents make a living from wine, and even the main square is named Trg Graševine after Slavonia's signature white wine, Graševina (known elsewhere as Welschriesling); indeed, this is an excellent place to try it as 80% of total Graševina production is here.

GETTING HERE AND AROUND

As with all of Slavonia's interior, reaching the Golden Valley is easiest by car. There are buses and trains from Osijek to Požega (three hours, 100 Kn), and only a couple of buses per day to Kutjevo from there.

EXPLORING

TOP ATTRACTIONS

Fodor's Choice ★ **Krauthaker.** A smaller winery you won't want to miss is Krauthaker, one of the first private wine producers to emerge after the fall of communism. It dates back to 1992 and produces 24 different varieties, including an award-winning Chardonnay. The location is lovely, with a terrace overlooking the town, a small pond and quaint bridge, and colorfully painted wine barrels scattered around the premises. ✉ *Ivana Jambrovića 6, Kutjevo* ☎ *034/315–000* 🌐 *www.krauthaker.hr* 🎫 *40 Kn wine cellar tour and tasting* ⏲ *By appointment.*

Kutjevačko Vinogorje. There are 30 different wineries to choose from around Kutjevo; the biggest, and oldest, is Kutjevačko Vinogorje. The story of this winery is the story of the Kutjevo itself; its cellars date back to 1232 (though the guides will tell you Romans were producing wine here long before that), when the town was founded by Cistercian Monks from Hungary. Over the years, it passed into the hands of Ottomans, Jesuits, Habsburgs, and private families, and the stories of each of these eras and the influence they left on Kutjevo are etched chronologically onto the Slavonian oak barrels in the cellar. Ask your guide about the legend of Maria Theresa Habsburg and her dalliances on the circular stone table (where wine tastings are done). ✉ *Kralja Tomislava 1, Kutjevo* ☎ *034/255–002* 🌐 *www.kutjevo.com* 🎫 *30 Kn wine cellar tour and tasting* ⏲ *By appointment.*

OFF THE BEATEN PATH

Daruvar. The ancient Romans called this town Aquae Balissae (very strong springs) and they certainly knew a good spa site when they saw one. On the forested slopes of the Papuk Hills, just west of Papuk National Park, Daruvar makes a lovely stopover en route to Kutjevo or the park. Thermal Aqua Park Aquae Balissae and the thermal pools located within Daruvarske Toplice, a hotel and rehabilitation complex, are both open to visitors. The present-day face of Daruvar's center, including an imposing two-story Baroque manor house, took shape from 1760 to 1777 within the estate of Count Antun Jankovič. Daruvar and some nearby villages carry the unusual distinction of being home to Croatia's largest population of ethnic Czechs; they originally came over at the behest of Count Jankovič, who wanted to populate his new town. Many here still speak their native tongue and observe Czech customs, so it is not surprising that Daruvar produces Staročeško pivo Old Bohemian Beer, which is based on an old Czech recipe. You can visit the brewery and taste their original beer and the new 5th Element craft beers. Contact the very helpful tourist information office to arrange a visit to the main sites around town. ✉ *Daruvar* ☎ *043/623–623.*

Fodor's Choice ★ **Papuk Nature Park.** Home to the largest mountain in Slavonia (953 miles), this was the first geopark in Croatia to be recognized by UNESCO for its geological, biological and cultural diversity. Within its 336 square kilometers (129 square miles) are beech, oak, and fir forests, fresh rivers, the beautiful Jankovac Forest Park, and the large and inviting Orahovica lake. There are hiking and biking trails and guided tours can be arranged. There are also archaeological sites from the Sopot and Starčevačka cultures (5500–3500 BC) as well as **Ružica Grad,** an abandoned medieval castle that was built in the 15th century during Hungarian rule. It can be reached by hiking 15 minutes uphill from Lake Orahovica; it's very much worth the effort if you're looking for a bit of solitude. The visitors center is located in Velika, but the lakes and Ružica Grad can be reached in a half hour from Kutjevo. ✉ *Papuk Nature Park* 🌐 *pp-papuk.hr* 🎫 *25 Kn.*

Požega. Požega is one of the prettiest cities in central Slavonia and worth visiting for an afternoon. The striking **Holy Trinity Square** has a 19th-century Franciscan Monastery to one side and the massive Bishop's Palace at the other end. There is a plague column (built in memory of the nearly 800 citizens who died from the plague of 1739) in the middle of the square; an inscription explains that the pillar was sculpted by one Gabriel Granici at a cost of 2,000 eggs and 300 forints. He didn't eat the eggs or give them to his relatives. They were used to cement the pillar's marble sand. Tucked away in the corner of the main square is the **City Museum,** whose collection ranges from regional ethnography, history, art, and archaeology, from prehistoric times to the present day. ✉ *Požega* 🌐 *www.visit-pozega.com.*

OFF THE BEATEN PATH

Kurija Janković. If you're traveling between Hungary and Slavonia, an interesting place to stop for the night is the Kurija Janković Hotel, the lovingly restored former holiday home of the Janković family, who had a huge influence over the entire region. **Pros:** elegant and spacious rooms; great buffet breakfast with local products; friendly service. **Cons:** isolated location; lack of other amenities nearby. $ *Rooms from: €50* ✉ *Kapela Dvor 22* ☎ *033/639–767* 🌐 *www.kurija-jankovic.com* 🛏 *18 rooms* 🍽 *Breakfast.*

WHERE TO STAY

$ B&B/INN Fodor's Choice ★ **Sontacchi Boutique Winery Hotel.** The only hotel in Kutjevo, but the only place you'd have wanted to stay anyway; the young Sontaki brothers, Anton and Kruno, will take care of everything you need, from arranging tastings at local wineries (including their own), to preparing organic dinner on their homemade BBQ (which you'll be grateful for, as there are few restaurants in the area). **Pros:** excellent full breakfast with local, organic products; great mix of boutique hotel and family-run B&B; walking distance to main sights around Kutjevo. **Cons:** some rooms are expensive by Slavonian standards; hard to reach by public transport; not many amenities nearby. *Rooms from: €45* ✉ *Trg Grasevine 4* ☎ *099/512–2312* 🌐 *www.sontacchi-vinarija.hr* *5 rooms* *Breakfast.*

4

ISTRIA

Updated by Vera Brljevic and Frank Galparsoro

Explore a remarkable 1,900-year-old Roman amphitheater in Pula. Visit Poreč and Rovinj, Croatia's two most popular seaside resorts, with Venetian-style campanili, loggias, and reliefs. Discover a thousand years of rich Istrian history in hilltop fortresses, early Christian churches, Byzantine mosaics, and Baroque palaces, and treat your taste buds to two local specialties: white and black truffles (a series of festivals is dedicated to them) and wine (crisp, fruity white Istarska Malvazija and light, harmonious red Teran).

The word conjures something magical as it rolls off the tongue: *Istria.* Beyond sounding poetic, however, the name of this region of Croatia is derived from the name of the Illyrian people who occupied the area well before the Romans first arrived in the 3rd century BC—namely, the Istrians, whose chief architectural legacy comprised numerous hilltop fortresses. In the northwest corner of Croatia bordering Slovenia, the triangular-shape Istrian peninsula looks rather like a bunch of grapes—a happy coincidence, given its strong viticultural heritage.

Much of Europe's history has passed through Istria for more than a thousand years, not least the history associated with three great civilizations—the Roman, the Germanic, and the Slavic. Centuries of Venetian rule later reinforced by years of Italian occupation between the world wars have left a sizable Italian minority here, and Italian influence is apparent in the architecture, the cuisine, and the local dialect. Here, even the effects of the concrete-box style of communist-era architecture seem relatively minimal compared to the overall sense of a much deeper past suggested by the rich mix of architectural styles—from a whole array of well-preserved Roman ruins to Romanesque basilicas; from breathtakingly well-preserved medieval towns, towers, and town walls to Baroque palaces and Austro-Hungarian fortifications.

The region's principal city and port, Pula, is on the tip of the peninsula and is best known for its remarkably preserved 1,900-year-old Roman amphitheater and Forum as well as the Triumphal Arch of the Sergians. Close by, the beautifully nurtured island retreat of Brijuni National Park can be visited in a day. Towns along the west coast have an unmistakable Venetian flavor left by more than 500 years of Venetian occupation. Poreč and Rovinj, Croatia's two most popular seaside resorts, are both endowed with graceful campanili and reliefs of the winged lion of St. Mark, patron saint of Venice. The effects of package tourism have long encroached—to varying degrees—on the outskirts of various towns, most notably Poreč among Istria's largest coastal destinations. Rovinj, though likewise brimming with tourists in high season, retains more of its ravishing historic beauty and redolence than almost any other town on the Adriatic. A side trip to the romantic hill towns of Motovun and

Grožnjan will prove unforgettable, whether as a brief excursion from the sea in the warmer months or as a more substantial autumn journey. This inland area is particularly rich in truffles and mushrooms, and from mid-September to late October these local delicacies are celebrated with a series of gastronomic festivals.

ORIENTATION AND PLANNING

GETTING ORIENTED

Located in the Northern Adriatic region of Croatia, Istria is the country's largest peninsula, facing the Venetian lagoon to the west and Kvarner Bay to the southeast. Reaching Istria is easy: many large European cities are less than a five-hour drive away. Pula is a seasonal airport, and airports in Venice, Trieste, and Zagreb are all within a three-hour drive.

PLANNING

WHEN TO GO

If you are partial to sun and the idea of swimming in the warm, blue-green waters of the Adriatic, and you don't mind crowds and a bit of extra expense, by all means visit Istria in summer. Otherwise, this tourism-trampled region might be best saved for spring or fall (the water stays warm well into September), when you might save as much as 15% to 20% on lodging. The season in Istria for many restaurants and bars is Easter through the first week in November. You won't find much going on at all in January.

GETTING HERE AND AROUND

AIR TRAVEL

Croatia Airlines operates flights to Pula from Zagreb from April through October. Ryanair has service to Pula from London Stansted (two times a week) and from Trieste, Italy (four times a week). Jet2.com flies from Leeds, Manchester, Edinburgh, and London Stansted to Pula from May until late September.

Contacts Croatia Airlines. ✉ *Pula Airport, Valtursko polje 210, Ližnjan, Pula* ☎ *052/218–909* 🌐 *www.croatiaairlines.com.* **Jet2.com.** 🌐 *www.jet2.com.* **Ryanair.** 🌐 *www.ryanair.com.*

BOAT AND FERRY TRAVEL

From May to October, Venezia Lines runs a catamaran service from Venice to Rovinj, Pula, and Poreč. Tickets are available online.

Contacts Venezia Lines. ✉ *Zagrebačka 7, Poreč* ☎ *052/422–896* 🌐 *www.venezialines.com.*

BUS TRAVEL

There are domestic connections all over mainland Croatia to and from Pula, Poreč, and Rovinj, and local services between these towns and smaller inland destinations such as Motovun and Vodnjan. International buses offer daily connections to Italy (Trieste) and Slovenia (Ljubljana, Koper, Piran, and Portorož). Bus stations in Pula, Rovinj, and Poreč, are

GREAT ITINERARIES

IF YOU HAVE 3 DAYS

There is so much to see in Istria that three days is a must, though it may seem like a rush if that's all the time you have. Start in Pula, if you are coming from Zagreb; if from the north (Slovenia or Italy), start with Rovinj instead. Either way, do visit Rovinj. If you are interested in Istria's ecclesiastical heritage, you may want to prioritize Poreč over Pula; if Roman ruins are more your thing, by all means focus on Pula, whose architecture also gives you more of a sense of Istria's Austro-Hungarian past. On the first day, start off in **Pula.** Visit the Arena and at least take a stroll to the Forum. Plan to spend the night here. A short drive or bus ride toward the Verudela or Stoja resort area gets you to eminently swimmable, if rocky, stretches of shoreline. The next morning, head off to **Rovinj.** Visit the 18th-century Baroque Crkva Sv. Eufemije, and just revel in strolling about the most beautiful town on the Istrian coast. On the third day, spend some more time in or around Rovinj, whether strolling the Old Town or taking a dip in the sea. If you're up to it—particularly if you have a car—move on to **Poreč** to see the Eufrazijeva Basilica.

IF YOU HAVE 5 DAYS

Spend your first day as above, but consider adding an excursion from Pula to **Vodnjan** or **Brijuni National Park,** depending on whether you're more interested in Vodnjan's countryside, medieval atmosphere, mummies, and food, or in Brijuni's natural splendors and luxurious, seaside ambience. Move on to **Rovinj** by the evening of Day 2 or the morning of Day 3, spending at least a full day or more there. On Day 4, it's on to **Poreč.** Perhaps go inland and spend the night in **Motovun.** On Day 5, if you're driving, take a look at **Grožnjan** as well before heading back. If you're getting around by bus, it's time to head back to a major town on the coast. Indeed, why not spend a few more hours in Rovinj or Pula before bidding adieu to Istria?

IF YOU HAVE 7 DAYS

Spend your first five days as above, but be sure to supplement your time in Rovinj, Pula, and Poreč with a lunch in **Labin,** on the east coast of Istria. If you're driving from Zagreb, do it on the way to the more important towns; if you're driving through the countryside that takes you through both **Motovun** and **Grožnjan,** spend a night in or near Motovun. Before going inland, you may want to pay a visit to Vrsar and the Limski kanal or, instead, Baredine Cave. If you have a car, you can do so as you go inland or on your way back to the coast; if traveling by bus, you can get to these places most easily on a group excursion from Poreč or Rovinj. You may want to visit **Novigrad,** too, especially if you're driving, but save Umag for a 10-day trip. Spend Day 6 in Grožnjan then go back to Poreč or, better yet, Rovinj for the night. On Day 7, proceed to **Pula,** with a stop in **Labin** if you haven't been there yet and will be going farther east. Perhaps spend your final night in Labin as well.

TOP REASONS TO GO TO ISTRIA

Roman ruins: Take a walk through the Roman area in Pula, where you will find one of the world's biggest and best-preserved amphitheaters (in fact, the sixth-largest in the world).

Fresh seafood: Have dinner at one of Rovinj's elegant restaurants (Barba Danilo and Monte are among the city's finest dining establishments).

Medieval hill towns: A scenic drive through the medieval towns of Grožnjan and Motovun in the hilly interior is not to be missed; these are villages that time seems to have forgotten. Indulge in a wine or olive-oil tasting at Kabola, Cuj, or Chiavalon estates.

Ancient churches: Enjoy a tour of the amazing 6th-century Byzantine mosaics at St. Euphrasius Basilica in Poreč; St. Euphrasius is one of the best-preserved early Christian churches in Europe.

Delicious gelato: As in Italy, gelato is available everywhere in dozens of flavors all over Istria. Grab a cone and enjoy the early evening passeggiata, just like a local.

run by one bus company, Autotrans. Additionally in summer, Flixbus, a Germany-based company offering low-cost bus travel throughout Europe, connects Istrian coastal towns with Germany (Munich), Italy (Venice, Padua, Brescia, Milano), and Austria (Villach, Vienna, Graz). Timetables are available at all bus stations. However, as elsewhere in Croatia, the sheer number of different companies offering bus service out of each station can be confusing; it's best to confirm at the information window what you might find posted on the wall.

Contacts **Autotrans.** ☎ *060/300-800.* **Flixbus.** 🌐 *www.flixbus.com.*

Information **Poreč Bus Station.** ✉ *Karla Huguesa 2, Poreč* ☎ *060/333–111.* **Pula Bus Station.** ✉ *Trg I. Istarske brigade 1, Pula.* **Rovinj Bus Station.** ✉ *Trg na Lokvi 6, Rovinj* ☎ *060/333–111.*

CAR TRAVEL

While visiting Pula, Rovinj, and Poreč a car may be more of a hindrance than an asset: all three towns are served by good bus connections, and having your own vehicle only causes parking problems. The best way to see the Istrian interior, however, is by car. The "sight" to see is the countryside itself and the small villages that dot it, so renting a car even for a day will give you much more satisfaction than trying to arrange a bus trip to one or another hill town. (And bus connections to the interior are infrequent.) If you are traveling from Zagreb, you can, of course, rent there, but major agencies have offices in Pula. Other towns along the coast all have one or more local agencies that generally offer better rates than the major chains without sacrificing quality of service; however, they may be less equipped than the major chains and have fewer cars on offer. (Some, such as Vetura, also rent bicycles, e-bicycles, and scooters [i.e., mopeds].) Lastly, bear in mind that finding an available car on short notice in midsummer can be tricky regardless of the agency involved.

Contacts Europcar. ✉ *Pula Airport, Valtursko polje 210, Pula* ☎ *098/475–346* 🌐 *www.europcar.com.* **GoAdria Agency.** ✉ *Mirna 2, Novigrad* ☎ *052/555–555.* **Greenway Travel.** ☎ *095/558–000* 🌐 *www.greenway-travel.net.* **Interauto.** ✉ *Trgovačka 19, Umag* ☎ *052/743–111* 🌐 *www.inter-auto.hr.* **Oryx Rovinj.** ✉ *Šetalište Vjeća Europe BB, Rovinj* ☎ *052/814–259* 🌐 *www.oryx-rent.hr.* **Vetura.** ✉ *Trg Joakima Rakovca 2, Poreč* ☎ *052/434–700* 🌐 *www.vetura-rentacar.com.* **Vetura.** ✉ *Pula Airport, Valtursko polje 210, Pula* ☎ *091/494–9627, 052/550–900* 🌐 *www.vetura-rentacar.com.* **Vetura.** ✉ *Šetalište Vjeća Europe BB, Rovinj* ☎ *052/815–209, 091/730–4408* 🌐 *www.vetura-rentacar.com.*

TRAIN TRAVEL

Istria is not well connected to the rest of Croatia by rail. To get to Zagreb or Split, you need to transit through Rijeka, partly by bus.

Contact Pula Train Station. ✉ *Kolodvorska 5, Pula* ☎ *052/541–982, 060/333–444 from Croatia.*

TOUR COMPANIES

Self-guided cycling tours of Istria can be arranged by Fiore Tours, a Poreč-based cycling outfit. They also arrange gourmet tours, including wine-tasting tours of Istria.

Fiore Tours. This Poreč-based agency specializing in cycling tourism offers self-guided cycling holidays to Istria. The eight-day tour starts in Poreč and leads you through the Istrian countryside and the coast. Daily distances range from 47 km to 70 km (30 to 43 miles). Fiore tours arranges all accommodation, luggage transfers, and provides you with an itinerary. ✉ *Mate Vlašića 6, Poreč* ☎ *052/431–397* 🌐 *www.fiore.hr* 🎫 *From €570.*

TRAVEL AGENCIES

Kompas Travel can arrange daily excursions to Venice or Plitvice, as well as tours to inland Istria or Postojna Cave in Slovenia from either Poreč or Rovinj. Excursions Delfin arranges tours to the Limski kanal, as do several other local companies and independent operators who happen to own boats and post flyers about their towns.

Information Excursions Delfin. ✉ *Zagrebačka 5, Rovinj* ☎ *091/514–2169* 🌐 *www.excursion-delfin.com.* **Kompas Travel.** ✉ *M. Vlašića 20, Poreč* ☎ *052/451–100* 🌐 *www.kompas-travel.com.*

4

ABOUT THE RESTAURANTS

Food in Istria is more sophisticated and varied than in the rest of Croatia. Culinary tourism is one of the region's biggest draws, and you will get (for a price) a markedly better meal here than elsewhere in the country. The quaysides and old town squares have a plethora of touristy restaurants, and many new exceptional places have opened in recent years, helping to set the standard for the country's gastronomical identity. Istrian food today means fresh and simple seafood dishes, locally made *fuži* (egg noodles), elegant truffle sauces and flavors, and earthy *pršut* (air-dried local ham), alongside the familiar Italian staples of pizza and pasta. Seafood is usually grilled, baked in sea salt, or served *crudo* (raw) with a dash of local olive oil. Truffles are the superstars of the interior villages and work their way onto autumn menus in pastas, game dishes, and on beds of homemade polenta. Keep your eyes peeled for traditional favorites like *supa,* a brew of red wine, sugar, olive oil, pepper, and warm, toasted bread; and *maneštra,* an Istrian bean soup, both popular in winter. All these gourmet aspirations mean that dining in Istria can be costly relative to much of inland Croatia. Average prices for main courses start at 50 Kn for pasta and pizza, and move up to 80 Kn, or even twice that, for seafood (much of which is priced by the kilogram) and certain beef dishes. For a quick and cheap, albeit greasy, lunch, you can buy a *burek* (a curd-cheese- or meat-filled pastry) in a bakery for around 12 Kn.

ABOUT THE HOTELS

In Istria, as in most other reaches of the Croatian coast, it's basically a question of whether to stay at the big, impersonal resorts on the beach, with a full range of services and activities available, or at smaller, boutique, sometimes family-run hotels. Either way it's imperative to book ahead, as most places—big and small—book up fast for the summer months. Bear in mind that some smaller hotels and pensions impose a surcharge—usually 20%—for stays of fewer than three nights in high season, since they cater primarily to tourists who stay a week or two. Hotels listed here are geared toward the traveler who is looking to stay fewer than seven nights in the same city. *Hotel reviews have been shortened. For full information, visit Fodors.com.*

VILLA RENTALS

Villa rentals are popular in Istria, where many properties—from one-bedroom apartments to houses for 16—offer a high standard of accommodation. The medieval villages of the hilly interior are scenic and offer sweeping (and almost uninterrupted) views of vineyards and olive groves. Hunkering down in a stone farmhouse and exploring the rest of the peninsula from there is certainly a leisurely way to appreciate Istria. Istria is still not nearly as crowded as other parts of Europe, so you won't have to share your view with the hordes.

WHAT IT COSTS IN EUROS (€) AND CROATIAN KUNA (KN)

	$	$$	$$$	$$$$
Restaurants	under 35 Kn	35 Kn–60 Kn	61 Kn–80 Kn	over 80 Kn
	under €5	€5–€8	€9–€10	over €10
Hotels	under 925 Kn	925 Kn–1,300 Kn	1,301 Kn–1,650 Kn	over 1,650 Kn
	under €121	€121–€170	€171–€216	over €216

Restaurant prices are the average cost of a main course at dinner or, if dinner is not served, at lunch. Hotel prices are the lowest cost of a standard double room in high season.

VISITOR INFORMATION

Although the official tourist offices listed here can provide you with every bit of information imaginable, they generally leave the booking of rooms and excursions to private tourist agencies and hotels.

Contacts Fažana Tourist Information. ✉ *Titova riva 2, Fažana* ☎ *052/383-727* 🌐 *www.infofazana.hr.* **Grožnjan Tourist Information.** ✉ *Umberta Gorjana 12, Grožnjan* ☎ *052/776-131, 052/776-064* 🌐 *www.tz-groznjan.hr.* **Istria Tourist Board.** ☎ *052/880-088* 🌐 *www.istra.hr.* **Labin & Rabac Tourist Information.** ✉ *A. Negri 20, Labin* ☎ *052/855-560 main office, 052/852-399 info point* 🌐 *www.rabac-labin.com.* **Novigrad Tourist Information.** ✉ *Mandrač 29a, Novigrad* ☎ *052/757-075* 🌐 *www.coloursofistria.com.* **Poreč Tourist Information.** ✉ *Zagrebačka 9, Poreč* ☎ *052/451-293* 🌐 *www.myporec.com.* **Pula Tourist Information.** ✉ *Forum 3, Pula* ☎ *052/219-197* 🌐 *www.pulainfo.hr.* **Rovinj Tourist Information.** ✉ *Obala Pina Budičina 12, Rovinj* ☎ *052/811-566* 🌐 *www.tzgrovinj.hr.* **Umag Tourist Information.** ✉ *Trgovačka 6, Umag* ☎ *052/741-363* 🌐 *www.coloursofistria.com.* **Vodnjan Tourist Information.** ✉ *Narodni trg 10, Vodnjan* ☎ *052/511-700* 🌐 *www.vodnjandignano.com.*

PULA

270 km (168 miles) southwest of Zagreb.

Today an industrial port town and Istria's chief administrative center (pop. 58,000), as well as a major tourist destination, Pula became a Roman colony in the 1st century BC. This came about a century after the decisive defeat by the Romans, in 177 BC, of the nearby Histrian stronghold of Nesactium, prompting the Histrian king Epulon to plunge a sword into his chest lest he fall into the hands of the victors, who indeed conquered all of Istria. Remains from Pula's ancient past have survived up to the present day: as you drive in on the coastal route toward its choice setting on a bay near the southern tip of the Istrian peninsula, the monumental Roman amphitheater blocks out the sky on your left. Under Venetian rule (1331–1797), Pula was architecturally neglected, even substantially dismantled. Many structures from the Roman era were pulled down, and stones and columns were carted off across the sea to Italy to be used for new buildings there. Pula's second great period of development took place in the late 19th century, under the Habsburgs, when it served as the chief base for the Imperial Austro-Hungarian Navy. Today it's as much working city as tourist town, where Roman ruins and Austro-Hungarian architecture serve as backdrop for the bustle of everyday life amid a bit of communist-era soot and socialist realism, too. James Joyce lived here for a short time, in 1904–05, before fleeing what he dismissed as a cultural backwater for Trieste. What's more, there are some outstanding restaurants and a number of pleasant family-run hotels, not to mention the nearby resort area of Verudela, where seaside tourism thrives in all its soothing, sunny sameness.

GETTING HERE AND AROUND

Pula is Istria's main entry point, home to the only regional airport for commercial flights located 9 km (5½ miles) from the town center. There is a shuttle bus from the airport to Pula's main bus station (located downtown), but also to the resort areas of Verudela, Medulin, and Puntižela. The best way to get around Pula is on foot. However, buses run every 20 minutes to half an hour depending on the line.

EXPLORING

Pula's compact commercial and administrative center is on a small, semicircular protrusion of land in the Puljski Zaljev (Bay of Pula), which faces west into the Adriatic. Several ringlike streets radiate inward from the port, culminating in the small, fortress-capped hill at the center of this semicircle. Most of the cultural and historical sites are along this web of streets to the south, west, and north of the hill, with the huge Roman amphitheater on the northeastern fringes of this zone (accessible via Giardini and then Istarska ulica, on the landward side of the hill, a couple of blocks in from the bay); the bus station is another few minutes' walk from there. Meanwhile, a long walk (or a short drive) south of the city center are suburbs that culminate with the Verudela and Stoja peninsulas, home to bustling tourist resorts, beaches, and some excellent restaurants.

TOP ATTRACTIONS

Fodor's Choice ★ **Arena** (*Roman Amphitheater*). Designed to accommodate 23,000 spectators, Pula's arena is the sixth-largest building of its type in the world (after the Colosseum in Rome and similar arenas in Verona, Catania, Capua, and Arles). Construction was completed in the 1st

Exploring
Aquarium Pula .. **8**
Arena **1**
Floor mosaic **6**
Forum **7**
Kaštel **3**
Katedrala uznesenja Blazene Djevice Marije .. **9**
Roman Theater . **2**
Slavoluk Sergijevaca **5**
Sveta Srca Gallery **4**

Restaurants
Alla Becaccia ... **1**
Batelina **5**
Farabuto **6**
Jupiter **3**
Vodnjaka Pula .. **8**

Hotels
D&A Center Apartments **4**
Hotel Amfiteatar **2**
Hotel Park Plaza Histria **7**

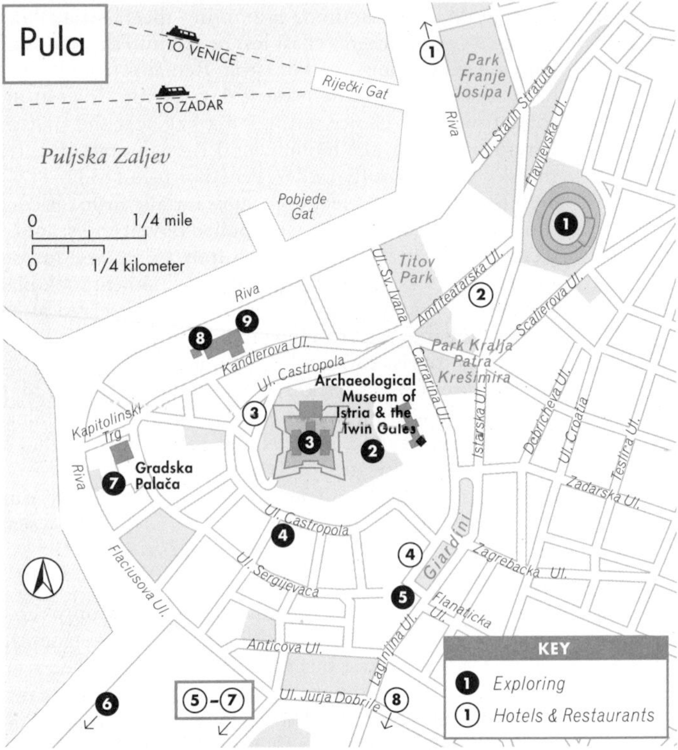

century AD under the reign of Emperor Vespasian, and the Romans staged gladiator games here until such bloodthirsty sports were forbidden during the 5th century. It has remained more or less intact, except for the original tiers of stone seats and numerous columns that were hauled away for other buildings. Today it is used for summer concerts (by musicians including Sting, James Brown, and Jose Carreras), opera performances, and the annual film festival in mid-July. The underground halls house a museum with large wooden oil presses and amphorae. ✉ *Flavijevska ulica BB* ☎ *052/219–028* 🌐 *www.ami-pula.hr* 🎫 *50 Kn.*

Forum. Still Pula's most important public meeting place after 2,000 years, the ancient Roman forum is today a spacious paved piazza ringed with cafés. There were once three temples here, of which only one remains. Next to it stands the **Gradska Palača** (Town Hall), which was erected during the 13th century using part of the Roman temple as the back wall. The Renaissance arcade was added later. The perfectly preserved Augustov Hram (Temple of Augustus), the Forum's only remaining temple, was built between 2 BC and AD 14 on the north side of the square. ✉ *Forum* 🌐 *www.ami-pula.hr* 🎫 *Forum free, Augustov Hram 10 Kn* ⏲ *Closed Nov.–Apr.*

NEED A BREAK

Café Galerija Cvajner. Stop at the chic but unpretentious Café Galerija Cvajner for morning coffee or an evening aperitif. Inside, contemporary art and minimalist furniture play off frescoes uncovered during restoration, and outdoor tables offer great views onto the Forum square. ✉ ***Forum 2*** ☎ ***052/216–502.***

Kaštel (*Fortress*). Whether from the cathedral or elsewhere along Kandlerova ulica, a walk up the hill will lead you within minutes to the 17th-century Venetian fortress, the Kaštel, that towers over Pula's city center and houses the **Historical and Maritime Museum of Istria.** Though the museum has a somewhat lackluster collection, including scale-model ships as well as Habsburg-era relics, it does carry the value-added benefit of allowing you to wander around its ramparts. **■TIP→ Simply walking around its perimeter ensures fine views of the city's shipyard below and, if you look to the north, the steeple of Vodnjan's church 12 km (7½ miles) away.** ✉ *Gradinski uspon 6* ☎ *052/211–566* 🌐 *www.ppmi.hr* 🎫 *20 Kn.*

Slavoluk Sergijevaca (*Triumphal Arch of the Sergians*). Built by the Sergi family in 29 BC as a monument to three relatives who were great warriors, this striking monument features elaborate reliefs that inspired even Michelangelo to draw the arch during a 16th-century visit to Pula. The surrounding city gate and walls were removed in the 19th century to allow the city's expansion beyond the Old Town. Locals call it *Zlatna vrata*, or Golden Gate. ✉ *Between Giardini and Sergijevaca ulica.*

WORTH NOTING

FAMILY **Aquarium Pula.** On the ground floor of the onetime Austro-Hungarian fortress in the resort complex of Verudela, a few kilometers from the city center, the aquarium also serves as a sea-turtle rescue center. Its 35 pools offer a colorful look at hundreds of sea creatures from the Adriatic's underwater world, and include a touch pool with sea stars, sea urchin, crab, and sea squirt. **■TIP→ Climb to the roof of the fort for great vistas over Pula.** ✉ *Verudela BB* ☎ *052/381–402* 🌐 *www.aquarium.hr* 🎫 *75 Kn.*

Floor mosaic. The central scene of this large and lovely mosaic—which otherwise features geometric patterns and plants aplenty—is of the punishment of Dirce, who, according to Greek legend, lies under the enraged bull to whose horns she is about to be fastened. Once part of a Roman house, it was unearthed after World War II bombing. **■TIP→ The mosaic can be viewed for free by looking down through a grate beside an uninspiring apartment building a stone's throw from the Crkva Sv. Marije od Trstika (Chapel of St. Mary of Formosa).** ✉ *Between Sergijevaca ulica and Flaciusova ulica, left off Sergijevaca ulica, two blocks before the Forum.*

Katedrala uznesenja Blazene Djevice Marije (*Cathedral of the Assumption of the Blessed Virgin Mary*). Built originally in the 4th century by the town's defense walls and facing the sea, Pula's star ecclesiastical attraction—more often called simply St. Mary's Cathedral—was transformed in the second half of the 5th century into a three-nave basilica. Extensive reconstruction began in the 16th century, with the adjacent campanile constructed in the late 17th century from stones taken from the Arena. Note that the Roman-era mosaic on the floor of the central nave bears a 5th-century donor's inscription. ✉ *Kandlerova ulica 27* ⏲ *Closed Oct.–Apr. (open by appointment only).*

Roman Theater. If you make your way down from the Fortress along the eastern slope of the hill, toward the Archaeological Museum (closed for renovation as of this writing) and the Twin Gates, you will pass right through the ruins of the 1st-century Roman Theater, a quiet, sublime spot to rest and reflect. ✉ *Malo rimsko kazalište, Kastel, Fortress Hill.*

Sveta Srca Gallery (*Sacred Hearts Gallery*). This small gallery, located in a deconsecrated church built in 1908, is the off-site exhibition space of Pula's Archaeological Museum. One of the most renowned of Pula's artistic venues, the Sveta Srca Gallery has had exhibitions of abstract landscapes, modern art, light installations, and the Istrian diet through time. ✉ *De Villeov uspon 8* ☎ *052/353–185* 🌐 *www.ami-pula.hr* 🎟 *20 Kn.*

NEED A BREAK

Narodni trg. For a lively and aromatic atmosphere in which to have a shot of espresso, buy a banana, or just wander about gazing at food stands, check out Pula's market square, Narodni trg. On one side of its stately, two-story market building—whose iron-and-glass construction was state-of-the-art when it opened to great fanfare in 1903—you'll find fruit and vegetable stands and, on the other side, cafés; inside are a fish market (downstairs) and fast-food eateries (second floor). ✉ ***Narodni trg 9.***

WHERE TO EAT

$$$$ EUROPEAN

Alla Becaccia. Located in the village of Valbandon, close to Fažana, Alla Becaccia offers hearty meat dishes with an emphasis on game—the owner is a hunter. A huge fireplace dominates the dining room in the simple but tasteful interior, and the kitchen door is always open. **Known for:** meat and fish grilled on wood; game and steaks; quiet setting. $ *Average main: 150 Kn* ✉ *Pineta 25, Fažana* ☎ *052/520–753* 🌐 *www.beccaccia.hr* ⏲ *Closed Nov. Closed Tues.*

$$$$ SEAFOOD Fodor's Choice ★

Batelina. This quirky, innovative restaurant is considered by many locals—and foodies around the world—to be the best seafood restaurant in Croatia. Run by a family of fishermen, Batelina is popular for its delicious appetizers, often created from what Anthony Bourdain, on his visit here, described as "trash fish." Specialties include fish tripe stew, shark-liver pâté, bonito tartare, cuttlefish stew, and fish carpaccio. **Known for:** owner David Skoko, one of the best chefs in Croatia; accepting cash only; being booked days in advance. $ *Average main: 100 Kn* ✉ *Čimulje 25* ☎ *052/573–767* 💳 *No credit cards* ⏲ *Closed Aug. and Dec.–mid-Jan., and Sun. No lunch.*

$$$$ MEDITERRANEAN

Farabuto. In residential Pula, far from tourist attractions, Farabuto has a short menu of fresh and tasty seafood and just few meat dishes, all based on what's available from Pula's green and fish market. The modern and innovative cuisine is well presented in Farabuto's small, cozy interior. **Known for:** local crowd; casual neighborhood vibe; fresh seafood. $ *Average main: 130 Kn* ✉ *Sisplac ulica 15* ☎ *052/386–074* ⏲ *Closed Sun. Oct.–May. No lunch Sun. June–Sept.*

$$ PIZZA **Jupiter.** In a quiet street a couple of blocks' walk above the Forum, this is Pula's premier place for budget, Italian-style fare. Try any of its more than 20 types of pizza, grilled meat, or a plate of pasta as you sip a glass of house red wine at one of the rustic wooden tables on the rear terrace. **Known for:** pizzas from a wood-burning oven; good value for money; summer crowds. *Average main: 60 Kn* *Castropola 42* *052/214–333* *www.pizzeriajupiter.com.*

$$ VENETIAN **Vodnjanka Pula.** One of the few restaurants in downtown Pula offering honest and authentic Croatian dishes, no-frills Vodnjanka is a short walk from the farmers' market. Lunch is the best time to enjoy its flavorful, unpretentious home-cooked dishes—a truly local experience that brings back the forgotten flavors of old times. **Known for:** a reasonably priced home-cooked meal; cash only; small and cozy. *Average main: 60 Kn* *D. Vitezića 4* *098/175–7343* *No credit cards* *Closed Sun.*

WHERE TO STAY

$ RENTAL FAMILY **D&A Center Apartments.** In the heart of the old town, just a couple of blocks from the Forum and the "golden gate" (Slavoluk Sergijevaca), these seven bright, modern, and clean apartments and studios were completely refurbished in 2015. **Pros:** centrally located; modern and well maintained. **Cons:** no parking; no views; no common areas. *Rooms from: €110* *Giardini 3* *098/976–9586* *dacenterapartments.com* *7 apartments* *No meals.*

$ HOTEL **Hotel Amfiteatar.** This hotel in a converted three-story town house close to the Arena and just one block from the seafront has 18 rooms with smart minimalist furniture, free Wi–Fi, and spacious bathrooms. **Pros:** central location; good restaurant with open-air terrace. **Cons:** "sea views" are disappointing; only one room has a balcony; top-floor rooms have only skylights (no windows). *Rooms from: €115* *Amfiteatarska 6* *052/375–600* *www.hotelamfiteatar.com* *18 rooms* *Breakfast.*

$$$$ HOTEL **Hotel Park Plaza Histria.** With its superb location at the tip of the Verudela peninsula overlooking both the marina and the sea, this large hotel has stylish, modern rooms that are comfortable and well appointed with comfy beds, flat-screen TVs, Wi-Fi, and balconies. **Pros:** quiet seaside location; balconies in all rooms and suites; panoramic views from some rooms; good in-room and on-site facilities. **Cons:** can feel overcrowded and impersonal; a bit of a hike from town; disappointing sea views from some rooms. *Rooms from: €250* *Verudela 17* *052/590–000* *www.arenaturist.com* *Closed Jan.–Mar.* *368 rooms* *Breakfast; Some meals.*

NIGHTLIFE AND PERFORMING ARTS

NIGHTLIFE

Club life in Pula tends to begin in early April and continue through late October or early November. Pubs are open year-round.

Club Uljanik. Conveniently located in the city center, with posters announcing its various musical events ubiquitous about town, Club Uljanik is an exceedingly popular counterculture haven with DJ nights all year and live music on its spacious terrace. ✉ *Jurja Dobrile 2* ☎ *092/236–8289* 🌐 *www.clubuljanik.hr.*

E&D Lounge Bar. Set in a landscaped garden with a small swimming pool surrounded by lounge chairs, E&D Lounge Bar is the perfect place to laze during the day with a coffee or a beer and views over the sea or dance at night with DJ parties. During the summer the bar also serves light Mediterranean dishes. ✉ *Verudela 22* ☎ *052/213–404.*

Pietas Julia. This large, seafront dance club also features a coffee bar and pizzeria. This is the place to dance a night away in Pula, with DJs playing electronic, house, techno, and R&B music. A great selection of cocktails makes this popular among Pula's hip crowd. ✉ *Riva 20* ☎ *091/181–1811, 052/881–881* 🌐 *www.pietasjulia.com.*

PERFORMING ARTS

Being the most prominent place in town, the Arena hosts a fair share of the city's core art events.

Outlook Festival. Celebrating sound-system culture with the latest dance music from house to dubstep, the Outlook Festival takes place in the first week of September at the 19th-century Punta Christo Fort and the surrounding area. Four days of music and parties—including infamous boat and beach parties—make Outlook one of the most popular summer festivals in Istria. Previous lineups have included Busta Rhymes, Lauryn Hill, Barrington Levy, DJ Premier, DJ EZ, and many others. ✉ *Fort Punta Christo, Štinjan* 🌐 *www.outlookfestival.com.*

Pula Film Festival. The decades-old annual festival occurs around mid-July, before the Motovun Film Festival. It features both Croatian and, in recent years, an increasing number of international works. ✉ *Pula* 🌐 *www.pulafilmfestival.hr.*

SPORTS AND THE OUTDOORS

Unlike some smaller towns farther up the coast, such as Rovinj, downtown Pula is a bit too much of a port and industrial center to allow for a dip in the sea in between visits to cultural attractions. Now for the good news: the **beaches** aren't far away. A short drive or bus ride to the Verudela or Stoja resort areas, each around 4 km (2½ miles) south of downtown, will provide the clear water (and rocky shores) Croatia has in no short supply. You might also try the long stretch of relatively isolated beach between the two, on the Lungomare. If you have a car or a bicycle, this lovely little stretch of undeveloped coast is close to town and popular with locals as well as tourists. Head south about 2 km (1½ miles) along the main road out of Pula and follow the signs to the right toward Stoja, a resort-cum-camping area. Once there, proceed left and then back north along the pine-fringed coastal road Lungomare as it makes its way to the Verudela resort area.

If you have a car at your disposal, drive 10 km (6¼ miles) southwest of central Pula to the Premantura peninsula. The relatively remote shoreline there, at the very southern tip of Istria, is even more scenic, punctuated by cliffs and caves, and the crowds are mercifully thinner.

SHOPPING

Pula is no shopping mecca, but it does have a handful of stores with quality goods from Istria, as well as Croatian delicacies, wines, crafts, and more. On Monday and Tuesday evenings in July and August (from 8 to 11) the Forum hosts an open-air fair of Istrian handicrafts. A walk through the Triumphal Arch of the Sergians onto bustling Sergijevaca ulica will show you much of what the city has available, shopping-wise; the stores listed here are on the fringe of this central business zone.

Pula Green Market. Join locals stocking up on fresh and seasonal products early in the morning. The **Jelenic charcuterie** offers homemade, traditional Istrian cured meat like cooked ham, prosciutto, and homemade sausages. **Kumparicka Dairy** produces unpasteurized, fresh, and aged (up to 30 months) goat cheeses. ✉ *Narodni trg 9* ☎.

Trapan Wine Station. Don't miss a trip to Trapan Wine Station, in Šišan, less than 10 km (6 miles) from Pula. A visit to the trendy winery includes wine tasting and a tour. Popular labels include Uroboros and Ponente, both white wines made of 100% Istrian Malvasia, and Che, a sparkling wine made of 100% Terrano. ✉ *Giordano Dobran 63, Šišan* ☎ *052/574–770* 🌐 *www.trapan.hr* 🕓 *Closed Sun., and Nov.–Apr.*

VODNJAN

12 km (7½ miles) north of Pula.

Vodnjan may look a bit run-down at first glance, but there are three good reasons to come here: its saintly mummies; its quiet, narrow, centuries-old streets populated by a higher percentage of Italian speakers than you'll find almost anywhere else in Istria; and the Vodnjanka restaurant's scrumptious fare.

GETTING HERE AND AROUND

There are 10 buses daily between Pula and Vodnjan, at 15 Kn each way, payable directly to the driver.

EXPLORING

Chiavalon Olive Oil Tasting Room. Sandi Chiavalon was barely 13 years old when he planted his first olive trees and decided to become an olive-oil producer. Less than two decades later, Chiavalon's extra virgin olive oil was chosen among the 15 best olive oils in the world by the prestigious Flos Olei. A visit to the Chiavalon tasting room is well worth a detour; just call in advance to arrange the tasting, some of which are accompanied by delicious Istrian fare like cheese, prosciutto, and sausages. ✉ *Vladimira Nazora 16* ☎ *098/860–566, 052/511–906* 🌐 *www.chiavalon.hr* 🕓 *Closed Sun.* *Reservations essential.*

FAMILY **Crkva svetog Blaža** (*St. Blaise's Church*). From the tourist office on the main square, stroll down ulica Castello to Crkva svetog Blaža, an 18th-century structure built in the style of architect Palladio that not only has the highest campanile in all of Istria but is also the unlikely home of the mummies or mummified body parts of six saints impressively preserved without embalming. Among the best preserved are St. Nicolosa Bursa and Leon Bembo the Blessed. Nicolosa, whose relatively elastic skin and overall postmortem presentability make her one of the best-preserved human bodies in Europe, was born in Koper (Istria) in the 15th century and was a nun in Venice and elsewhere; she's the one with the garland of flowers still on her head. Leon Bembo the Blessed was a 12th-century Venetian priest who was tortured in religious riots while ambassador to Syria. And then there is St. Sebastian, a Roman-officer-turned-Christian who was whipped and strangled around AD 288 in Rome after initially surviving torture by arrows. The head, spinal column, neck muscles, and related parts of this very famous saint are on display here. As for St. Barbara, from 3rd-century Nicomeda (in present-day Turkey), only her leg remains; she so disagreed with her father's pagan, slave-keeping lifestyle that he personally killed her with a sword. Admittance to the mummy room, behind the main altar, includes an English-language recording that sums up the saints' lives and roads to mummihood. ✉ *Župni ured Sv. Blaža, Sv. Roka 4* ☎ *052/511–420* 🌐 *www.zupavodnjan.com* 🎫 *50 Kn* 🕒 *Closed Oct.–June (open by appointment).*

WHERE TO EAT AND STAY

$$$$ VENETIAN Fodor's Choice ★ ✕ **Vodnjanka.** This restaurant is the place to go for the most mouthwatering homemade pasta dishes you can imagine, not least *fuži* with wild asparagus and prosciutto, which is simply unforgettable. The inner of two small rooms, with its six tables and framed family-style photographs, is positively homey, while the outer room features bizarre but fantastic wall art by sculptor/painter Lilia Batel. **Known for:** Istrian cuisine; quirky decorations; roof terrace. $ *Average main: 140 Kn* ✉ *Istarska 22* ☎ *052/511–435* 🕒 *Closed Jan., and Sun.*

$ B&B/INN 🏨 **La Casa di Matiki.** Located in the countryside near the village of Žminj, La Casa di Matiki may not be a fully working farm, but you'll find donkeys, chickens, and three dogs here, and you can even opt to sleep on hay in the converted barn. **Pros:** peaceful location far from the crowds; excellent breakfast with homemade and homegrown products; swimming pool. **Cons:** remote location means a car is essential. $ *Rooms from: €85* ✉ *Matiki 14, Žminj* ☎ *098/299–040* 🌐 *www.matiki.com* 💳 *No credit cards* 🛏 *8 rooms* 🍽 *No meals*; *Breakfast.*

NACIONALNI PARK BRIJUNI

Ferry from Fažana, which is 15 km (9 miles) northwest of Pula.

When Austrian industrialist Paul Kupelwieser set off for Brijuni by boat from Fažana in 1885, the archipelago had long been a haven for the Austro-Hungarian military and for malaria. Kupelwieser was to change all that. In 1893 he bought the 14 islands and islets, eradicated the disease with the help of doctors, and fashioned parks from Mediterranean scrub. Thus arose a vacation retreat par excellence—not for rich Romans, as had been the case here 17 centuries earlier, but for fin-de-siècle Viennese and other European high-society sorts. Archduke Franz Ferdinand summered here, as did such literary lights as Thomas

Mann and Arthur Schnitzler; James Joyce came here to celebrate his 23rd birthday. Two world wars ensued, however, and the islands' fate grew cloudy as they changed hands—coming under Italian rule and, later, Yugoslavian. From 1949 to 1979 the largest island, Veli Brijun, was the official summer residence of Marshal Josip Broz Tito, Yugoslavia's "president for life." Here he retreated to work, rest, and pursue his hobbies. World leaders, film and opera stars, artists, and writers were his frequent guests; and it was here that, together with Nasser of Egypt and Nehru of India, Tito forged the Brioni Declaration, uniting the so-called nonaligned nations (countries adhering to neither NATO nor the Warsaw Pact). The archipelago was designated a national park in 1983 and opened to the public.

4

Fodor's Choice ★ **Nacionalni Park Brijuni.** The Brijuni islands are a group of 14 small islands that were developed in the late 19th century. You'll need to pass through Fažana to get here, and though the town seems to offer little more than the usual collection of touristy restaurants along its small harbor, it is at least refreshingly quiet compared with some other tourist-traveled spots along Istria's west coast. Fažana's main cultural attractions—all just a short walk from the harbor—are the 16th-century **Church of Saints Kosmas and Damian** and the smaller 14th-century **Church of Our Lady of Mount Carmel,** which you enter through an atmospheric loggia and whose ceiling features several layers of fascinating 15th-century Renaissance frescoes. But you are presumably here to visit the archipelago. Call or email the Brijuni National Park office in Fažana at least one day in advance to make a reservation; you can also do so in person, but especially in midsummer there is a substantial risk that there won't be space. (Though various private tourist agencies in Fažana and Pula offer excursions, they do not generally measure up, in cost or quality, to making your arrangements directly with the national park. Some of the tourist agencies simply reserve you a spot on the "official" tour, adding their own commission when doing so.) Take the 15-minute National Park ferry from Fažana; the entire tour of the park takes about four hours. Your first view is of a low-lying island with a dense canopy of evergreens over blue waters. Ashore on Veli Brijun, the largest island, a **tourist train** takes you past villas in the seaside forest and relics from the Roman and Byzantine eras. The network of roads on this 6½-km-long (4-mile-long) island was laid down by the Romans, and stretches of original Roman stonework remain. Rows of cypresses shade herds of deer, and peacocks strut along pathways. The train stops at the **Safari Park,** a piece of Africa transplanted to the Adriatic, its zebras, Indian holly cattle, llamas, and elephants all gifts from visitors from faraway lands. In the **museum,** an archaeological exhibition traces life on Brijuni through the centuries, and a photography exhibition, "Tito on Brijuni," focuses on Tito and his guests. ✉ *Brionska 10, Fažana* ☎ *052/525–883, 052/525–882* 🌐 *www.np-brijuni.hr* 🎫 *July and Aug., 210 Kn; June and Sept., 200 Kn; March–May and Oct., 170 Kn; Nov.–Feb., 125 Kn* ⏲ *Closed Nov.–Apr.*

WHERE TO STAY

You can save money by booking a room in Fažana and taking a day trip to the islands.

$$ HOTEL **Heritage Hotel Chersin.** Set in a beautifully restored old house in the center of Fažana, Heritage Hotel Chersin is a small and cozy family-run hotel perfect for couples. **Pros:** wonderful location; lovely design and ambience; on-site restaurant. **Cons:** wooden floors and beds a bit squeaky. *Rooms from: €150 ✉ Piazza Grande 8, Fažana ☎ 095/398–5350 🌐 www.hotel-chersin.com ⏲ Closed mid-Oct.–mid-Apr. 8 rooms 🍽 Breakfast.*

ROVINJ

35 km (22 miles) northwest of Pula.

Fodor's Choice ★ It is hard to imagine how Rovinj could be more beautiful than it is. In a fantastic setting, with centuries-old red-roofed houses clustered around the hill of a former island, Istria's cultural mecca is crowned by the monumental Baroque Crkva Sv. Eufemije (Church of St. Euphemia), which has a typical Venetian bell tower topped by a gleaming bronze figure of St. Euphemia. Far below, a wide harbor crowded with pleasure boats is rimmed with bright awnings and colorful café umbrellas. Artists, writers, musicians, and actors have long gravitated to this ravishing place to carve out apartments in historic houses. Throughout the summer, the winding cobbled streets are crowded with vacationers from all reaches of Europe, who are more often than not staying in nearby resort developments. South of the harbor lies the beautiful nature park of Zlatni Rt, planted with avenues of cedars, oaks, and cypresses and offering numerous secluded coves for bathing.

GETTING HERE AND AROUND

A shuttle bus runs from Pula airport to Rovinj. Buses travel daily between Pula central bus station and Rovinj and between Zagreb and Rovinj. The town is easily reachable by car, but the best way to get around Rovinj is on foot or bicycle, but due to stairs along almost all the steep streets, you cannot really cycle within the Old Town.

EXPLORING

Practically all of Rovinj's key cultural and commercial attractions are packed into the compact one-time island and present-day peninsula that juts like the tip of a hitchhiker's thumb westward into the sea. The main square, Trg M. Tita, is at the southern juncture of this little peninsula with the mainland; from there you can either cut straight up the center of the peninsula (i.e., west) along Grisia toward the cathedral or walk around the outer edge of the peninsula, or you can go south along the harbor to some fine restaurants and the beaches of Zlatni Rt beyond.

Exploring

Crkva Sv Eufemije 1
Dvigrad 5
Galerija Sv. Toma 2
Kuća o Batani ... 3
San Tommaso Winery 6
Trg M. Tita 4

Restaurants

Barba Danilo 7
Giannino 4
Maestral 8
Monte 1
Orca 6
Pizzeria Da Sergio 2

Hotels

Hotel Adriatic ... 3
Hotel Lone 11
Hotel Monte Mulini . 10
Island Hotel Katarina 9
Stancija 1904 ... 5

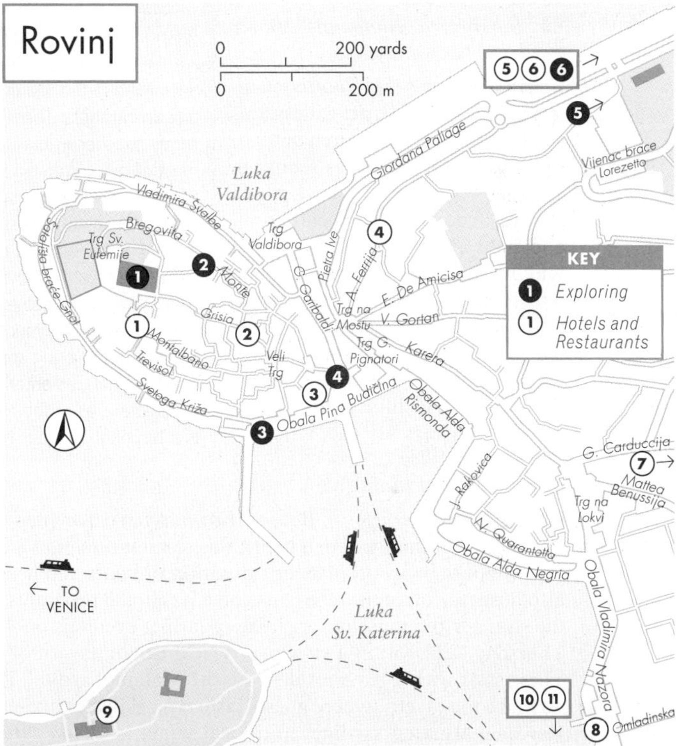

4

NEED A BREAK

Havana Club. The Adriatic may not be quite as warm as the Caribbean, but at the Havana Club—a spacious, tropical-themed cocktail-bar-cum-café right on the harbor—you can sip a piña colada or a canchánchara (rum, lime, and honey). There's a great selection of rums and premium gins plus nonalcoholic cocktails, as well as iced tea and coffee. Kick back and relax in a wicker chair under a bamboo umbrella while listening to reggae. That's not to mention the Cuban cigars you can puff for anywhere between 60 Kn and 140 Kn. Ah, the life! ✉ ***Obala Alda Negria*** ☎ ***091/588–3470*** ⏲ ***Closed Oct.–Apr.***

Fodor's Choice ★ **Crkva Sv. Eufemije** (*Church of St. Euphemia*). Inside this 18th-century Baroque church, the remains of Rovinj's patron saint are said to lie within a 6th-century sarcophagus. Born near Constantinople, Euphemia was martyred in her youth, on September 16 in AD 304, under the reign of Emperor Diocletian. The marble sarcophagus containing her remains mysteriously vanished in AD 800 when it was at risk of destruction by iconoclasts—and, legend has it, it somehow floated out to sea and washed up in faraway Rovinj. (Note the wall engraving just to the right of the entrance of St. Euphemia holding Rovinj in her arms.) On September 16 of each year many people gather to pray by her tomb. In the church a large mural in the sarcophagus room portrays Euphemia being picked at by two lions who, legend has it, didn't eat her after all. ✉ *Trg Sv. Eufemije* ☎ *052/815–615*

Church free, campanile 20 Kn Closed Nov.–May.

Galerija Sv. Toma (*St. Thomas Gallery*). Today a public art gallery, this small, bright yellow church dates to the Middle Ages but was rebuilt in 1722. It's on your way back down the hill from the main cathedral, and right after you pass by it, you will pass under a lovely, arched hall some 50 feet long and with a wooden-beamed ceiling. On your left, you'll notice a small courtyard, encircled by pastel painted houses with green and blue shutters and colorful flowers in the window. *Bregovita ulica Free Closed Oct.–June, and Mon.*

SWIMMING IN ROVINJ

Swimming in the sea in Rovinj is a rocky business. There are no sandy beaches in the town itself; most of the swimming is done off the rocks or cement slabs (with ladders in some places) that jut into the sea. Head out to Crveni Otok (Red Island) or Uvala Lone (Lone Bay) for a pebble beach and a place to lay your towel, but don't forget to bring some rubber water sandals, as entering the water there, as in the rest of Istria, is a bit rough on your feet.

Kuća o Batani (*House of Batana Ecomuseum*). Devoted to Rovinj's *batana* (traditional wooden boat), this small museum in a typical multistory house has a permanent exhibition of boats and fishing tools. It also hosts various cultural events and educational programs, and during the summer the museum organizes gourmet evenings on Tuesday and Thursday (220 Kn) in a *spacio,* a typical Rovinj tavern or wine cellar. These start with a batana ride from the Mali mol around Rovinj's Old Town to the tavern, where guests taste typical dishes like salted anchovies or marinated sardines and local wine. *Obala Pinia Budicina 2 052/812–593 www.batana.org 10 Kn Closed Dec.–Mar.*

OFF THE BEATEN PATH

San Tommaso Winery. This small family-run winery in Golaš, a small village 17 km (10½ miles) south of Rovinj, is housed in a beautifully restored farmhouse with exposed stones and large wooden beams. It features a wine cellar, tasting room with a big open fireplace, and a small ethnographic museum displaying old family photos and equipment that once was used in the wine-making process in Istria. Don't let their Malvazija Istarska fool you! Although the wine is fresh, easy to drink, and sweet, it is still 14% alcohol. They also produce a few reds, a rosé, and the sweet dessert wine Muscat Žuti. If the owner, Janja, happens to be there, ask her to let you taste her raisin wine, which isn't for sale. *Golaš 13, Bale 098/309–594 www.santommaso-debeljuh.hr Closed Mon., and Nov.–Apr.*

Trg M. Tita. Standing on the Old Town's main square, you can't help but notice the **Balbi Arch,** which at one time was the gate to Rovinj's fish market. Notice the Venetian lion with an open book (a symbol of acceptance of Venetian rule without a fight) and a Venetian head on one side, and a Turkish head on the other, the symbolism of which hasn't yet been explained. At the top, between the two Balbi coats of arms, is a Latin epigraph. Also quite prominent on the square is the city's pinkish-orange **watchtower,** whose base houses the tourist agency. Although it looks Venetian, the tower was erected in 1907. That said, the winged-lion relief on one side is indeed from the 16th century. *Trg Maršala Tita.*

OFF THE BEATEN PATH

Dvigrad. When its residents abandoned Dvigrad suddenly in the mid-17th century—fleeing the combined misfortune of plague and attacks by Uskok raiders—and established nearby Kanfanar, surely they didn't foresee that more than three centuries later tourists would delight in what they left behind. In any case, if exploring ruins is your (or your child's) thing, this is the place for you. Along an isolated road 23 km (14 miles) east of Rovinj, outside the sleepy town of Kanfanar (a short detour if you're headed north toward Poreč, Motovun, or Grožnjan), this huge maze of dirt paths surrounded by high stone walls makes for an adventuresome, imagination-stirring walk. Indeed, just enough restoration has been done to let your imagination "reconstruct" the rest: some of the walls are vine-covered, and much of the place is overgrown with vegetation. Nor is there a single explanatory sign, in any language. All this combines to give you the sense that you are discovering this eerie ghost town of a fortress city, even if a few other tourists are also wandering about. The battlements are impressively intact, and toward the center of the fortress you will find the remains of St. Sophia's Church, replete with depressions in the ground that contained the crypts of very important persons. To get here, take the main road east out of Rovinj toward Kanfanar. Just before you cross the railroad tracks and enter Kanfanar, you'll see a sign pointing to Dvigrad, which is to your left; from the sign the ruins are about 4 km (2½ miles) down an isolated, scrub-lined road. ✉ *Kanfanar*.

4

WHERE TO EAT

$$$$ MEDITERRANEAN Fodor's Choice ★

✕ **Barba Danilo.** Don't let this restaurant's location—in a campsite outside of town—fool you: this fine-dining seafood restaurant is by far the best restaurant in Rovinj, and possibly in all Istria. Forget the standard starter-main-dessert kind of meal and instead indulge in a variety of innovative cold and warm appetizers made with the freshest local ingredients. **Known for:** upscale dining experience; imaginative dishes; a variety of cold and warm seafood starters. Ⓢ *Average main: 150 Kn* ✉ *Polari 5* ☎ *052/830–002* 🌐 *barbadanilo.com* ⏲ *Closed Dec.–Mar., and Sun. Apr.–mid-June, Oct., and Nov.*

$$$$ MEDITERRANEAN

✕ **Giannino.** Tucked away on a small square in a residential area of the Old Town, Gannino is equally popular among locals and tourists for its fresh and delicious Mediterranean fare such as Adriatic shrimp in vinegar and pasta with lobster. White tablecloths make the place look classy, but the atmosphere is convivial and relaxed and the staff very friendly. **Known for:** fresh fish and seafood; run by the same family since 1982; elegant plating. Ⓢ *Average main: 150 Kn* ✉ *Agusta Ferrija 38* ☎ *052/813–402* 🌐 *restoran-giannino.com/en/* ⏲ *Closed Nov.–Mar., and Tues.*

$$$$ MEDITERRANEAN

✕ **Maestral.** You won't find a bad seat at this outdoor seafront restaurant with fantastic views of the Old Town. An extensive menu, the friendly staff, a laid-back vibe, and affordable prices draw crowds here all day. **Known for:** great views; outdoor dining; fisherman's pie and squid stew. Ⓢ *Average main: 100 Kn* ✉ *Obala V. Nazora 3* ☎ *052/830–565* ⏲ *Closed Oct.–Apr.*

$$$$ MEDITERRANEAN ✕ **Monte.** A Michelin star, the very first one in Croatia, promises upscale, out-of-this-world Italian-Istrian dishes served in a special setting just below famous St. Euphemia's Church. Crisp white tablecloths on wrought-iron patio tables dot the shady terrace. **Known for:** one Michelin star; multicourse tasting menus; exceptional wine pairing. *Average main: 300 Kn ✉ Montalbano 75 ☎ 052/830–203 www.monte.hr ⏲ Closed mid-Oct.–Easter. No lunch.*

$$$$ MEDITERRANEAN ✕ **Orca.** Local, fresh, traditional food makes this restaurant on the outskirts of town a favorite among locals. Its location on the main road may not draw visitors in, but the food is excellent and a great value. **Known for:** friendly staff; traditional restaurant with old-fashioned interior; big portions. *Average main: 150 Kn ✉ Gripole 70 ☎ 052/816–851 www.orca-rovinj.com ⏲ Closed Nov., and Tues. Oct.–May.*

$$ PIZZA ✕ **Pizzeria Da Sergio.** With 50-plus varieties of delicious thin-crust pizzas, there's plenty to choose from at this conveniently located venue along the narrow road leading up to the main cathedral. Pizzas are delicious, and all baked in a wood-burning oven. *Average main: 60 Kn ✉ Grisia 11 ☎ 052/816–949 No credit cards ⏲ Closed Mon. Nov.–Easter. No lunch Nov.–Easter.*

WHERE TO STAY

$$$$ HOTEL **Hotel Adriatic.** Founded in 1912, this harborside boutique hotel is the oldest (still functioning) one in town, and after an extensive 2015 renovation, is modern, artsy, and as cosmopolitan as anything in New York or London. **Pros:** first-class view of Old Town square and harbor; breakfast served on the terrace; superb design. **Cons:** no spa facilities; off-site parking; neither direct beach nor swimming pool. *Rooms from: €400 ✉ P. Budicin 16 ☎ 052/803510, 052/800–250 reservation center www.maistra.com 18 rooms Breakfast.*

$$$$ HOTEL **Hotel Lone.** Superbly designed by an all-star Croatian team, the large Hotel Lone blends perfectly with its lush surroundings; rooms are modern, spacious, and comfortable, with sleek bathrooms and huge balconies. **Pros:** contemporary design; cool ambience and airy interior; easy access to the beach; located within a wonderful forest park. **Cons:** pool is shared with nearby Eden Hotel; service a bit lax; large hotel also caters to business travelers. *Rooms from: €330 ✉ L. Adamovića 31 ☎ 052/800–250 reservation center, 052/632–000 www.maistra.com 248 rooms Breakfast.*

$$$$ HOTEL **Hotel Monte Mulini.** Considered one of the top luxury hotels in Croatia, the Hotel Monte Mulini has a stunning location just a 20-minute walk from Rovinj's Old Town, in a landscaped park next to the nature park Zlatni Rt and 164 feet from the sea. **Pros:** great location by the sea; within walking distance of town; first-class facilities; spacious rooms. **Cons:** pricey; heated outdoor swimming pool sometimes too cold. *Rooms from: €560 ✉ A. Smareglia 3 ☎ 052/636000, 052/800–250 reservation center www.maistra.com ⏲ Closed Nov.–Easter 113 rooms Breakfast.*

$$ HOTEL **Island Hotel Katarina.** Located on Santa Katarina Island, just a 15-minute boat ride from the Old Town, Island Hotel Katarina is partly housed in an old family castle from the early 20th century with basic and outdated but spacious rooms, some with breathtaking views over the Old Town. **Pros:** wonderful island location; surrounded

by beautiful parks; nice views. **Cons:** dependent on a boat schedule; outdated decor in the rooms. *Rooms from: €165 Otok Katarina 1 052/800–250 www.maistra.com Closed Oct.–May 120 rooms Breakfast; Some meals.*

$$ RENTAL **Stancija 1904.** This lovingly restored turn-of-the-century villa 30 minutes east of Rovinj is an excellent place to stay—and a good example of what you're likely to find if you venture into the agritourism section of the Istria brochure. **Pros:** secluded property but still convenient to major tourist sites; friendly owners; great homemade meals offered on-site for guests only. **Cons:** no swimming pool or spa facilities; car is essential. *Rooms from: €165 Smoljanci 2–3, Svetvincenat 052/560–022, 098/738–974 www.stancija.com Closed Oct.–Easter 3 rooms Breakfast.*

4

NIGHTLIFE AND PERFORMING ARTS

Croatian Summer Salsa Festival. The last week of June, the Croatian Summer Salsa Festival offers eight days of dance, fun, beach/pool parties, workshops, and DJs to over 2,000 attendees. *www.crosalsafestival.com.*

Mediterraneo Bar. With a lovely terrace at the sea's edge friendly staff, a great selection of drinks, a relaxed atmosphere, and more affordable prices than similar bars in the vicinity, Mediterraneo is popular among locals and visitors alike. Pass through the low archway and head down a staircase to the fun terrace with colorful tables, stone benches, and cushions for those willing to have a drink sitting on the rocks. Even dolphins occasionally visit. The bar is closed November to April. *Santa Croce 24 091/532–8357.*

Piassa Granda Wine Bar. Rovinj's must-visit bar for wine aficionados, Piassa Granda features over 70 white, red, rosé, dessert, and sparkling wines by the glass. Istrian wines dominate the wine list. Run by two sisters, both passionate about wine, this is a perfect place to taste, enjoy, and learn about Istrian wines and wine makers. Located at the small square right in the Old Town, Piassa Granda also serves simple food like bruschetta, salad, local cheeses, and cold cuts. It's closed November to April. *Veli trg 1 099/407–9427.*

Puntulina Wine & Cocktail Bar. Take the steps down to Puntulina's terrace, where you can enjoy a glass of Istrian or other Croatian wine in a pleasant atmosphere yards from the sea, with light pop music setting the tone, plus amazing sunsets. And, yes, you can take a few more steps down if you wish, to the rocks, and take a dip before or after being served—this is where Rovinj's free, public swimming area begins. It's not especially a "night" spot, so you may want to confine your wine-sipping to daylight hours. There's also an excellent restaurant on the upper level. *Sv. Križ 38 052/813–186 www.puntulina.eu Closed Nov.–Mar.*

Wine Bar San Tommaso. This wine bar at Rovinj's seafront promenade is small, with only four interior tables, but the outdoor terrace—right at the seafront—is a great place to enjoy your glass of wine and nibble a variety of cheeses and cold cuts. Wines offered here include San Tommaso's own wines and others from Rovinj and its surroundings. *Obala A. Rismonda BB 052/815–915 Closed Nov.–Mar.*

SPORTS AND THE OUTDOORS

DIVING

As elsewhere along the coast, the Rovinj area has its share of places to dive, and several diving centers to go along with them—most of which will take you by boat for supervised dives to shipwrecks and other fascinating spots, not least the famous wreck of the *Baron Gautsch*, an Austrian passenger ferry that sank in 1914 just 13 km (8 miles) from Rovinj.

Puffer. This diving center offers shore dives, off-site island and wreck dives, and night diving (€15–€60). The *Baron Gautsch* shipwreck dive is the most popular around Rovinj, but at €60 it's also the most expensive. Puffer also offers diving courses, a two-hour discovery dive, and specialized courses for advanced divers. ✉ *Hotel Istra, Otok Sveti Andrija* ☎ *095/902–5543* 🌐 *www.rovinj-diving.hr*.

SHOPPING

Rovinj is worth visiting for its beauty, not its boutiques. The souvenir market is nothing to write home about, but there are at least a couple of shops with fine Istrian and/or Croatian products worth checking out.

House of Batana. Original souvenirs based on Rovinj's fishing heritage—including key-chains; T-shirts; and replicas of its traditional vessel, the batana—can be bought at the House of Batana museum. Besides batana-inspired souvenirs, you can pick up a small recipe book with old, almost-forgotten recipes from Rovinj fishermen, also available in English. ✉ *Obala Pina Budicina 2* ☎ *052/812–593* 🌐 *www.batana.org*.

Profumo di Rovigno. The Salvi family offers an array of unique perfumes, toiletries, and home fragrances under their Profumo di Rovigno brand. Needless to say, all products at their tiny store on the main shopping street are inspired by Rovinj. ✉ *Carera 45-47* ☎ *052/813–419* 🌐 *www.profumodirovigno.com*.

EN ROUTE

Wine Cellar Krunčići. A first-class spot to get a tour of Istrian vineyards and taste the local wine, Wine Cellar Krunčići has tastings on a stone patio attached to a farmhouse. Owner Ivica Matošević is usually on hand to tell you about his vintages, including the Alba wine, an Istrian Malvasia considered one of the region's best. Call ahead to arrange tastings. ✉ *Krunčići 2, Kruncici* ☎ *052/448–558, 098/367–339* 🌐 *www.matosevic.com* ⏲ *Closed Oct.–May*.

POREČ

55 km (34 miles) northwest of Pula.

A chic, bustling little city founded as a Roman *castrum* (fort) in the 2nd century BC and swarming with tourists more than 2,000 years later, Poreč may not be quite as lovely as Rovinj—nor does it enjoy the benefits of a hilltop panorama—but it is nonetheless a pretty sea of red-tile roofs on a peninsula jutting out to sea. Within the historic center, the network of streets still follows the original urban layout. Dekumanova, the Roman *decumanus* (the main traverse street), has maintained its character as the principal thoroughfare. Today it is a worn flagstone passage lined with Romanesque and Gothic mansions and patrician palaces, some of which now house cafés and restaurants. Close by lies the magnificent UNESCO-listed Eufrazijeva Basilica (St. Euphrasius Basilica), Istria's prime ecclesiastical attraction and one of the coast's major artistic showpieces. Although the town itself is small, Poreč has ample capacity for overnight stays, thanks to the vast hotel complexes of Plava and Zelena Laguna, situated along the pine-rimmed shoreline a short distance from the center. Although you can cover the main sights in two or three hours, Poreč surely merits a one-night stay, or more if you figure in a day trip to a nearby attraction such as the Baredine Cave or the Limski kanal.

GETTING HERE AND AROUND

Getting to Poreč is easier straight from Pula than from Rovinj, as you simply take the main inland highway north for 42 km (26 miles) and then follow the signs before turning west onto the secondary road that leads you another 13 km (8 miles) to Poreč—a 45- to 60-minute drive in all, depending on the traffic and how much pressure you apply to that pedal.

Contacts Tourist Information Center Poreč. ✉ *Zagrebačka 9, Poreč* ☎ *052/451–293* 🌐 *www.myporec.com.*

EXPLORING

FAMILY **Aquacolors Poreč.** Whether you're looking for an adrenaline-filled day or just a relaxing day by the pool, Aquacolors water park has you covered. With 12 slides and more than a full acre of pools, it's the largest water park in all Croatia. A looping, 61-meter-long (200-foot-long) slide rockets you down at high speed, while a 204-meter-long (1/3-mile-long) lazy river eases you along on an inflatable tube. ✉ *Molindrio 18, Poreč* ☎ *052/219–671* 🌐 *www.aquacolors.eu* 🎟 *135 Kn–210 Kn* ⏲ *Closed Oct.–June.*

Fodor's Choice ★ **Eufrazijeva Basilica** (*St. Euphrasius Basilica*). The magnificent Eufrazijeva Basilica is among the most perfectly preserved early Christian churches in Europe, and one of the most important monuments of Byzantine art on the Adriatic. It was built by Bishop Euphrasius in the middle of the 6th century and consists of a delightful atrium, a church decorated with stunning mosaics, and an octagonal baptistery. Added in the 17th-century were a bell tower you can climb (for a modest fee) and a 17th-century Bishop's Palace, whose foundations date to the 6th century; the basement contains an exhibit of stone monuments and mosaics previously on the basilica floor. The church interior is dominated by biblical mosaics above, behind, and around the main apse. In the apsidal semidome, the Virgin holding the Christ child is seated in a celestial sphere on a golden throne, flanked by angels in flowing white robes. On the right side there are three martyrs, the patrons of Poreč; the mosaic on the left shows Bishop Euphrasius holding a model of the church, slightly askew. High above the main apse, just below the beamed ceiling, Christ holds an open book in his hands while apostles approach on both sides. Other luminous, shimmeringly intense mosaics portray further ecclesiastical themes. ✉ *Eufrazijeva 22, Poreč* ☎ *No phone* 🎟 *40 kn* ⏲ *Closed Sun.*

Trg Marafor. This square toward the tip of the peninsula was the site of Poreč's Roman forum, whose original stonework is visible in spots amid the present-day pavement. Beside it is a park containing the ruins of Roman temples dedicated to the gods Mars and Neptune. ✉ *Poreč.*

NEED A BREAK

Torre Rotonda Cocktail & Coffee Bar. Do not be deterred by the cannon facing you as you enter the 15th-century tower that now houses the Torre Rotonda café and bar. Climb up a spiral staircase to a second floor with several intimate nooks, or go one more flight to the roof for an unbeatable view of Poreč and its harbor. ✉ *Narodni trg 3a, Poreč* ☎ *098/255–731* 🌐 *www.torrerotonda.com* ⏲ *Closed Oct.–Apr.*

OUTSIDE OF TOWN

FAMILY **Jama Baredine** (*Baredine Cave*). Far from sun and sea though it may be, the Baredine Cave has long been one of the Poreč area's top natural attractions. About 8 km (5 miles) northeast of town, near Nova Vas, this wonderful world of five limestone halls includes not only the miniature olm (known as the cave salamander) and insects but, of course, stalactites, stalagmites, and dripstone formations—from "curtains" 30 feet long to "statues" resembling the Virgin Mary, the Leaning Tower of Pisa, and the body of the 13th-century shepherdess Milka, who supposedly lost her way down here while looking for her lover Gabriel (who met the same fate). One of the halls includes a hatch some 70 yards deep that leads to underground lakes. Groups leave every half hour on a 40-minute guided tour. Those without car transport may wish to join an excursion to the cave from Poreč or another nearby town. ✉ *Nova Vas* ☎ *052/421–333, 098/224350* 🌐 *www.baredine.com* 🎫 *70 Kn* ⏲ *Closed Nov.–Mar.*

Limski kanal. There's even a bit of Norwegian-style fjord in Croatia. The Limski kanal is a 13-km-long (8-mile-long) karst canyon, whose emerald-green waters are flanked by forested valley walls that rise gradually to heights of more than 300 feet inland. The canyon was formed in the last Ice Age, and it is Istria's most fertile breeding area for mussels and oysters—hence, you'll find the excellent Viking seafood restaurant on-site. Tours are available from both Poreč and Rovinj with various agencies and independent operators, whose stands and boats are impossible to miss. A reservation a day or two in advance can't hurt, though, particularly in midsummer. Expect to pay approximately 150 Kn for the four-hour tour or 250 Kn for a daylong tour that includes a "fish picnic." You can also visit the Limski kanal on your own by car. And hiking enthusiasts can take a trail to the Romualdova Cave, open daily from June to September. ✉ *D21, halfway between Rovinj and Poreč, Kruncici.*

Vrsar. This pretty, medieval hilltop town just 10 km (6 miles) south of Poreč is situated near the fjord's northern juncture with the sea (and yet another place you can catch a tour of the fjord). Famous since Roman times for its high-quality stone, which helped build Venice, Vrsar is home to the 12th-century Romanesque church Sv. Marija Od Mora (St. Mary of the Sea), which has three naves. In his memoirs, the Venetian adventurer Casanova fondly recalled the local red wine, Teran. Just a couple of miles south, by the way, is Croatia's oldest and largest naturist resort, FKK Park Koversada. 🌐 *infovrsar.com.*

WHERE TO EAT

$$$$ EUROPEAN ✕ **Konoba Daniela.** In the village of Veleniki just a few miles from Poreč, this rustic, family-run tavern has exposed stone walls, wooden beams, and an outdoor terrace in an enclosed courtyard. With its simple and honest food, friendly staff, and huge portions, Tavern Daniela offers excellent value for money. **Known for:** excellent steak tartare; many seafood options; friendly service. *Average main: 100 Kn ✉ Veleniki 15a, Veleniki ☎ 052/460–519 ⊕ www.konobadaniela.com ⊗ Closed mid-Feb.–mid-Mar.*

$$ PIZZA ✕ **Pizzeria Nono.** Right across the street from the main tourist office, the Nono is teeming with folks saying "yes, yes!" to scrumptious budget fare from pizzas and salads to such seafood standards as grilled squid. **Known for:** affordable prices; streetside terrace; summer crowds. *Average main: 60 Kn ✉ Zagrebačka 4, Poreč ☎ 052/453–088 ⊗ Closed Feb., Mon. Oct.–Apr., and 2 wks in Nov.*

$$$$ CONTEMPORARY ✕ **Restaurant Divino.** For upscale dining in Poreč, the lovely seafront terrace at Restaurant Divino is hard to beat. Its sophisticated but not stuffy atmosphere, contemporary dishes, wine pairing, and friendly service make this one of the best places in town. **Known for:** fine dining; elegant seafront terrace; lunch specials. *Average main: 150 Kn ✉ Obala Maršala Tita 20, Poreč ☎ 052/453–030 ⊕ www.divino.hr ⊗ Closed mid-Jan.–mid-Feb.*

$$$$ CONTEMPORARY ✕ **Sv. Nikola Restaurant.** Those with a discriminating palate and a not-so-discriminating pocketbook should try this sparkling, air-conditioned restaurant right across from the harbor. The menu offers such delicacies as fish fillet in scampi and scallops sauce, cream soup with truffles and mushrooms, and beefsteak, but it's the elegant seafront terrace that makes this the top dining spot in Poreč. **Known for:** special-occasion dining; harbor-facing terrace; exquisite food. *Average main: 150 Kn ✉ Obala maršala Tita 23, Poreč ☎ 052/423–018 ⊕ www.svnikola.com.*

WHERE TO STAY

$$$$ HOTEL **Grand Hotel Palazzo.** Its outstanding location on the head of a small peninsula in Poreč's Old Town sets this hotel apart; built in 1910, it housed the very first hotel in town. **Pros:** excellent location; surrounded by the sea on three sides; historical building with character; outdoor pool and spa. **Cons:** smallish rooms; lacks its own beach; can be noisy at night. *Rooms from: €230 ✉ Obala Maršala Tita 24, Poreč ☎ 052/858–800 ⊕ www.hotel-palazzo.hr 74 rooms Breakfast.*

$ B&B/INN **Korta Gira.** Only 5 km (3 miles) from downtown Poreč, this small B&B on a family farm feels like a world apart. **Pros:** quiet and relaxing yet not far from Poreč; warm, friendly hosts; homemade products at breakfast. **Cons:** car is essential; outside town. *Rooms from: €120 ✉ Buići 8, Poreč ☎ 091/427–0521 ⊕ www.bbkortagira.com 3 rooms Breakfast.*

$$$$ HOTEL **Valamar Riviera Hotel.** On the seafront promenade, where Poreč's oldest hotels are found, the Valamar Riviera is an adults-only hotel with a chic restaurant and smallish but comfortable rooms, most of which have sea views. **Pros:** easy access to the Old Town; private beach served

by taxi-boat; popular restaurant with outdoor dining. **Cons:** noise from the promenade reaches the rooms; limited parking in front of hotel. *$ Rooms from: €220 ✉ Obala M. Tita 15, Poreč ☎ 052/465–000 reservation center, 052/400–800 🌐 www.valamar.com ⏱ Closed Oct.–Apr. 105 rooms 🍽 Breakfast; Some meals.*

NIGHTLIFE AND PERFORMING ARTS

Jazz in Lap Festival. Live jazz performances can be heard once a week through July and August, usually on Wednesday evening, behind the 18th-century Baroque palace housing the Zavičajni muzej (Regional Museum). ✉ *Decumanus 9, Poreč.*

Fodor's Choice ★ **Poreč Open Air Festival of Life.** Poreč celebrates life with a variety of shows, concerts, street performances, and special events daily from mid-June to mid-September. Town squares, streets, and the island Sveti Nikola become open-air stages during the festival. Many activities are free. MTV Summerblast, a two-day festival event full of concerts and partying under the stars, happens at the end of August. ✉ *Poreč* 🌐 *www.porecopenair.com.*

Street Art Festival. In the third week of August, Poreč's annual Street Art Festival enlivens the Old Town's streets and squares with musical, theatrical, art, multimedia, and acrobatic events. ✉ *Poreč.*

Tequila Beach Bar. An open-air beach bar in the shadow of pines at Pical Beach, just half a mile north of the Old Town, this is a favorite among locals for a nightcap with live rock performed by bands from all over Croatia. Resident DJs play mostly rock, funk, and pop. ✉ *Pical Beach, below Valamar Hotel Zagreb, Poreč.*

Villa Club. Located near the marina, right by the beach, the Villa Club is a popular hangout with lounge chairs, wicker canopy beds, and lounge music during the day. Night brings DJs, thematic parties, live bands playing dance music, and go-go dancers until dawn. ✉ *By the beach south of the marina, Poreč* 🌐 *www.villa-club.net.*

SPORTS AND THE OUTDOORS

BEACHES

Walk 10 minutes south of Poreč along the shore, past the marina, and you'll meet with the thoroughly swimmable, if typically rocky, pine-fringed beaches of the Brulo and Plava Laguna resort area. Keep walking until you're about 5 km (3 miles) south, and you'll be right in the center of the Zelena Laguna, which, though more concrete than rock, is one of the best-equipped tourist resorts on the Adriatic coast. Every day from May through September, two charming "tourist trains," tiny open-walled buses, run hourly from 9 am to 11 pm between the town center and the resort, as well as the Hotel Luna to the north—costing you 20 Kn but saving you the walk. Another option is the boat that runs between Zelena Laguna and the center May through September daily from 10 am to 11 pm, with stops at other resort areas in between. Tickets can be purchased on board.

DIVING

Starfish Diving Center. This outfitter offers aspiring or advanced divers daily diving tours to local shipwrecks, reefs, and caves. A four-day certification course is also available. ✉ *Autocamp Porto Sole, 10 km (6 miles) south of Poreč, Vrsar* ☎ *098/335–506, 098/334–816* 🌐 *www.starfish.hr.*

NOVIGRAD

15 km (9½ miles) northwest of Poreč.

Imagine a mini Rovinj of sorts, not quite so well preserved, it's true, and without the hill. This is Novigrad—a pretty little peninsula town that was the seat of a bishopric for more than 1,300 years, from 520 to 1831, and, like Rovinj, was at one time an island (before being connected with the mainland in the 18th century). With its medieval structure still impressively intact, along with its Old Town wall, it merits a substantial visit and perhaps a one-night stay as you make your way up and down the coast or before heading inland toward the hill towns of Grožnjan and Motovun. At first glance, as you enter town on an uninspiring main road bordered by communist-era, concrete-box apartment buildings, you might wonder if it was worth coming this far. Continue on and you'll arrive at a little gem: to your right is a pint-size, protected harbor, the Old Town is in front of you, and to your left is a peaceful park. The bustling harborside square has a few bars and restaurants. A nearby ice-cream stand is manned by enterprising, acrobatic young men who wow the crowds by hurling scoops 50 or more feet into the air to open-mouthed colleagues who then discreetly spit them into napkins, garnering much applause (and generating long lines). If you continue walking past the harbor on the left, you'll arrive at Vitriol, one of the most popular sunset bars in all of Istria.

GETTING HERE AND AROUND

There are daily buses from Pula to Novigrad. The town is also connected by bus with Zagreb, Rijeka, and Trieste. Novigrad is easily reachable by car, but the best way to get around town is on foot or by bicycle. The electric tourist train connects the resort complex to the south with Novigrad harbor from June to September.

EXPLORING

The 13th-century **Crkva svetog Pelagija** (Church of St. Pelagius), built on a 6th-century foundation and containing some elaborate Baroque artwork, stands near the tip of the peninsula with its towering late-19th-century campanile topped by a statue of St. Pelagius. As in Rovinj, the main church faces the sea.

On nearby Veliki trg is Novigrad's pale-red **city hall,** topped by a watchtower and contrasting sharply with the yellow building beside it. Here and there, Gothic elements are in evidence on the medieval architecture about town (e.g., two windows on a 15th-century building at Velika ulica 33).

4

NEED A BREAK

Istralandia. The first water park in Istria opened in 2014, featuring 20 waterslides, including an almost 90-foot-high free-fall waterslide; family rafting in inflatable rafts; three pools, including a children's pool with water castle, pirate ship, and several smaller slides; sand volleyball; and a badminton court—a great place to spend a day! Direct buses from Poreč, Novigrad, and resort towns in between run throughout the day in July and August. ✉ ***Nova Vas*** ☎ ***052/866-900*** 🌐 ***www.istralandia.hr*** 🎫 ***130 Kn–180 Kn*** ⏲ ***Closed Oct.–June.***

WHERE TO EAT

$$$$ SEAFOOD Fodor's Choice ★ ✕**Damir e Ornella.** Tucked away on a quiet side street, this superb (and pricey) little family-run establishment is a secret wonder you may want to share only with your fellow gourmands who appreciate raw-fish specialties. You can also enjoy grilled seafood and gnocchi, although you don't go here for a simple plate of pasta, but instead to indulge in a four-course meal. **Known for:** Mediterranean-style sashimi; intimate atmosphere; booking days in advance. $ *Average main: 500 Kn* ✉ *Ul. Zidine 5* ☎ *052/758–134* 🌐 *www.damir-ornella.com* ⏲ *Closed Nov. and Feb. No lunch Sept.–May.*

$$$$ CONTEMPORARY ✕**Restaurant Marina.** Set on the first floor of what looks like a typical family house, this seafood restaurant has a surprisingly elegant and stylish interior. Husband-and-wife duo Marina and Davor don't have a fixed menu; offerings are recited by the young owner. **Known for:** innovative seafood dishes; tasting menus; food and wine pairing. $ *Average main: 340 Kn* ✉ *Sv. Antona 38* ☎ *099/812–1267, 052/726–691* ⏲ *Closed Jan. and Feb., and Tues.*

$$$$ SEAFOOD ✕**Tavern Čok.** Just steps from the Old Town, this family-run restaurant offers fresh and tasty seafood dishes and a great selection of homemade pasta. Choose a seat in the rustic and cozy interior, as the covered outdoor terrace overlooks the main road. **Known for:** fresh seafood; rustic interior. $ *Average main: 150 Kn* ✉ *Sv. Antona 2* ☎ *052/757–643, 098/255–894* ⏲ *Closed Jan., and Wed.*

WHERE TO STAY

$$ HOTEL **Hotel Cittar.** The facade of this hotel is part of the medieval Old Town wall; inside, a glass-covered vestibule imaginatively separates the wall from the hotel lobby. **Pros:** central location; pleasant patio and breakfast room; friendly staff. **Cons:** somewhat sterile modern interior; limited parking near hotel. $ *Rooms from: €140* ✉ *Prolaz Venecija 1* ☎ *052/758–780* 🌐 *www.cittar.hr* ⏲ *Closed Dec.* *12 rooms* 🍽 *Breakfast.*

$$$ HOTEL **Hotel San Rocco.** Nine km (6 miles) up the road from Novigrad (on the road to Buje), the Hotel San Rocco is a real change of pace from the coast: among rolling hills surrounded by olive trees and vineyards, this upscale boutique hotel makes an impressive entrée to the Istrian interior. **Pros:** good (though pricey) restaurant on-site; magnificent views; elegant rural relaxation close to town. **Cons:** not regularly accessible by public

transportation; terrace is within earshot of busy road. $ *Rooms from: €190* ✉ *Srednja ulica 2, Brtonigla–Verteneglio* ☎ *052/725–000* 🌐 *www.san-rocco.hr* *14 rooms* *Breakfast.*

$$$ HOTEL **Nautica Hotel.** Sparkling bathrooms and plasma-screen TVs in every room promise comfort of the highest order in this modern hotel a few steps from the marina in Novigrad. **Pros:** great location with lovely views over marina; hearty breakfast. **Cons:** nautical theme a bit over-the-top. $ *Rooms from: €175* ✉ *Sv. Anton 15* ☎ *052/600–400* 🌐 *www.nauticahotels.com* *42 rooms* *Breakfast.*

$$$$ HOTEL **Rivalmare.** With just 13 spacious contemporary rooms—some with lovely sea views and balcony—this boutique hotel is popular for its chic minimalist look, elegance, design furniture, and superb location right at the seafront. **Pros:** small and intimate; top location; on-site parking. **Cons:** no free parking; no swimming pool; extra charge for sun loungers at the beach. $ *Rooms from: €250* ✉ *Rivarella 19* ☎ *052/555–600* 🌐 *www.rivalmare.hr* *Closed Dec.–Mar.* *13 rooms* *Breakfast.*

EN ROUTE

As you head north to Umag or northeast toward the interior hill towns, remember that you're driving through some of Istria's most fertile olive-oil territory. The tourist offices in Novigrad and Umag can give you a map outlining an olive oil (and wine) route with directions to several production facilities that offer tastings.

UMAG

15 km (9 miles) northwest of Novigrad.

Yet another onetime island, the peninsula town of Umag draws the fewest tourists of any of the major towns along Istria's western coast, even if it has more than its share of the usual beach resorts nearby. Perhaps it's the frustration with waiters who, while twiddling their thumbs in front of their restaurants, call out to every passing tourist, "Italiano? Deutsch? English?" and, less often, "Français?"

And yet Umag is a nice enough place to stroll for a couple of hours if you are passing this way, even if you might not be moved to stay for the night. Although the town grew up under the rule of Rome, practically none of its ancient roots are apparent in what remains of the historic core, which dates to the Middle Ages.

GETTING HERE AND AROUND

The best way to get to Umag is by car. This quaint historic town is best explored on foot.

EXPLORING

Cuj Winery. The Cuj olive oils (and wines) are a true labor of love and passion. Owner Danijel Kraljevic—Cuj—will infuse you with both when you visit his wine and olive oil estate in the village of Farnažine near Umag. A beautifully restored, old stone building houses an olive mill, wine cellar, and tasting room with an open fireplace. He produces three single-sort extra virgin olive oils—Buža, Črna, and Bjelica—and one multisort extra virgin olive oil—Selekcija. Call in advance to arrange a visit. ✉ *Farnažine BB* ☎ *098/219–277* 🌐 *www.cuj.hr.*

Kabola Winery. Near the small medieval hill town of Momjan, the Kabola Winery is a must-visit for wine and olive-oil aficionados. A wine cellar, small wine museum, and tasting room are set in a traditional Istrian farmhouse; views over the surrounding landscapes are breathtaking. Kabola produces only one extra virgin olive oil, a blend of three kinds of olives: indigenous Istarska Bjelica mixed with Leccino and Pendolino. Fresh, well rounded, and balanced, it marries perfectly with seafood, cheese, and salads. Call in advance to arrange a visit. ✉ *Kanedolo 90, Momjan* ☎ *099/720–7106, 052/779–208* 🌐 *www.kabola.hr* ⏲ *Closed Sun.*

Fodor's Choice ★ **Kozlović Winery.** At the Kozlović family's stylish, modern winery, which blends perfectly with the scenic countryside, you can taste their single extra virgin olive oil along with their wines. Next door is the Stari Podrum, one of the best taverns in Istria. ✉ *Vale 78, Momjan* ☎ *052/779–177* 🌐 *www.kozlovic.hr* ⏲ *Closed Sun.*

WHERE TO EAT

$$$$ MEDITERRANEAN ✕ **Restaurant Sole.** Its large parking area and bland exterior don't do justice to this family-run restaurant with excellent food and a friendly atmosphere. Based more on seafood than meat, everything on the menu is prepared using fresh, locally sourced, and homegrown produce. **Known for:** fresh seafood; family-run establishment where father is the chef and mother and son are servers; homegrown veggies and salads. [$] *Average main: 150 Kn* ✉ *Juricani, Sošići 58* ☎ *052/730–123* 🌐 *www.konoba-sole.hr* ⏲ *Closed Tues. Closed mid-Sept.–mid-Oct.*

$$$$ VENETIAN FAMILY ✕ **Tavern Nono.** Extremely popular and always busy, Tavern Nono is located in Petrovija, just a mile east of Umag. This family-run tavern offers hearty Istrian seafood, meat, and pasta dishes in a cozy and friendly atmosphere. **Known for:** traditional Istrian food; kid-friendly dining with a playground and a small farm behind the restaurant; popularity among locals and tourists. [$] *Average main: 120 Kn* ✉ *Umaška 35, Petrovija* ☎ *052/740–160* 🌐 *www.konoba-nono.com* ⏲ *Closed Mon. Oct.–May.*

EN ROUTE

Istria's interior hilltop villages have been much celebrated in recent years, both for their beauty and their gastronomical traditions. We recommend renting a car, even for one day, for a drive into the interior in the late afternoon, when fewer tour buses are likely to be on the road. Aside from Motovun and Grožnjan, you'll find Oprtalj, Roč, Hum, and Gračišće are all picturesque villages with their own medieval churches, old clock towers, and small-town restaurants.

MOTOVUN

38 km (24 miles) southeast of Umag, 30 km (19 miles) northeast of Poreč.

Fodor's Choice ★ It is an understatement to say that a day exploring the undulating green countryside and medieval hill towns of inland Istria makes a pleasant contrast to life on the coast. Motovun, for one, is a ravishing place. The king of Istria's medieval hill towns, with a double ring of defensive walls as well as towers and gates, may even evoke a scene straight from *Lord of the Rings*. If you opt to travel inland for only a day or two, Motovun is *the* place to visit. Be warned, though: the town sees lots of tour buses. That said, a walk around the ramparts offers views across the oak forests and vineyards of the Mirna Valley. On the town's main square stands a church built according to plans by Palladio. In late July the famed **Motovun Film Festival** transforms the town into one of Croatia's liveliest (and most crowded) destinations for about five days.

GETTING HERE AND AROUND

The best way to get to Motovun is by car, and travelling here by bus isn't a viable option. This small hilltop town is best explored on foot.

4

WHERE TO EAT AND STAY

$$$$ VENETIAN **Mondo.** On a narrow cobblestone street just a few yards from the town's gate, this tavern is perhaps the best place to eat in town, with a truffle-centric menu and a breezy terrace perfect for alfresco dining. The pleasant rustic interior has roughly plastered stone walls. **Known for:** truffle-stuffed menu; being featured on Anthony Bourdain's No Reservations and in the New York Times. *Average main: 140 Kn* ✉ *Barbacan 1* ☎ *052/681–791* *Closed Jan.–Mar. Closed Tues.*

$$$$ VENETIAN **Pod Voltom.** Centrally located, Pod Voltom offers authentic local dishes, many flavored with either black or white truffles, plus open-air dining on a romantic terrace by the town walls with terrific sunset views. Look out for excellent homemade *fuži* (Istrian pasta), succulent steaks, and a delicious panna cotta. **Known for:** truffle-inspired dishes; rustic interior with beautiful brick walls; lovely outdoor terrace with outstanding views. *Average main: 140 Kn* ✉ *Trg Josefa Ressela 6* ☎ *052/681–923* *Closed Jan., Feb., and Wed. Oct.–Dec. and Mar.–May.*

$$$$ VENETIAN Fodor's Choice ★ **Tavern Tončić.** This rustic tavern with exposed stone walls, wooden beams, and large open fireplace offers traditional hearty Istrian meat dishes. Located off the beaten path well past Oprtalj, the outdoor terrace has scenic views over the rolling hills, valley, and mountain in the background. **Known for:** delicious traditional Istrian food; remote location; essential reservations. *Average main: 100 Kn* ✉ *Čabarnica 42, Zrenj* ☎ *052/644–146* *www.agroturizam-toncic.com* *No credit cards* *Closed weekdays. Closed July.*

CLOSE UP

Truffles in Istria

November 2, 1999, in the village of Livade near Motovun, Giancarlo Zigante and his sharp-nosed dog unearthed a record-breaking, 1.31-kilogram (2.89-pound) white truffle. What he foraged—as attested to by the 100 guests he served in an effort to promote the cause of the Istrian truffle—was the most delicious fungus you are likely to find.

Truffles grow underground, in a symbiotic relationship with the roots of oaks and certain other trees. As such, they cannot readily be seen. It is their scent that gives them away—a swoon-inducing scent. Sows were once the truffle hunter's favored companion, as truffles smell a lot like male hogs. (To be fair, the earthy aroma and pungent taste of truffles, which has also been likened to garlic, is prized by gourmands the world over.) These days, dogs are the truffle hunter's best friend.

Truffles are extremely rare. Most efforts to cultivate them domestically have failed, not least because you first need to grow a forest full of trees whose roots are just right for truffles. Prices fluctuate, but the white truffle, prized for its superior scent—the "white diamond," it's often called—sells for up to $10,000 a pound. In addition to the white truffle, Istria is also home to three sorts of black truffle, which sell for a mere $1,500 a pound.

In Istria truffles have been extracted since ancient times. Even Roman emperors and Austro-Hungarian aristocrats had a taste for truffles, not least because of the aphrodisiac qualities attributed to them. Truffles were once consumed and gathered like potatoes—that's how plentiful they were. That was in the 1800s. No longer, of course. Still, their fine shavings impart an unforgettable, earthy aroma and an irresistibly pungent, vaguely garlicky taste to pastas, salads, omelets, beef specialties, sauces, and more.

Economics and truffle scarcity being what they are, the Istrian truffle has become a hot commodity indeed. These days, for example, much of what is sold by Italy as Italian white truffles actually comes from Croatia—not least from the moist woods around Motovun, near the river Mirna.

Karlić Tartufi. The Karlic family has been truffle hunting for over half a century, and a visit to their estate in Paladini near Buzet is a must for aficionados of this rare fungus. The family offers truffle-hunting tours followed by truffle-inspired meals, and their shop sells a variety of truffle products, such as fresh and frozen black and white truffles and truffle-infused olive oil, honey, and various tapenades. ✉ *Paladini 14, Village Paladini, Buzet* ☎ *052/667–304* 🌐 *www.karlictartufi.hr* 🎫 *From €65.*

Istriana Travel. If you'd like to join a truffle hunt, reserve a spot on a truffle-hunting excursion that departs from the village of Vrh from April to December. Accompanied by an English-speaking guide, you'll meet a truffle hunter and his trained truffle-sniffing dogs at the hunter's house, spend 45 minutes hunting in the woods, and enjoy a light lunch or dinner. ✉ *Vrh 46/3, Buzet* ☎ *052/667–022, 091/541–2099* 🌐 *www.trufflehuntingcroatia.com* 🎫 *From €55.*

$ HOTEL **Hotel Kaštel.** Just outside the Motovun town walls—but nonetheless nestled in a cloistered niche atop the hill—this peaceful, old-fashioned hotel makes an ideal retreat if you prefer green hills to sea and islands. **Pros:** quiet location; indoor pool and spa facilities; nice views over the valley from some rooms. **Cons:** uphill walk to the hotel; no car access. *Rooms from: €115* *Trg Andrea Antico 7* *052/681–607, 052/681–735* *www.hotel-kastel-motovun.hr* *Closed Jan.–Apr.* *33 rooms* *Breakfast.*

EN ROUTE As you near Grožnjan, you can take a small detour for a stop in the hilltop villages of Oprtalj and Završje. Drive up the hill and take a stroll around Oprtalj's hushed little streets and square where the 15th-century church of Sveti Juraj and 16th-century bell tower still stand. Just a bit farther, halfway between Oprtalj and Grožnjan, mystical Završje is today almost deserted. Large houses now covered in creeping ivy, as well as the town gate, a leaning tower, a church, and the remains of defensive walls witness Završje's past glory.

4

GROŽNJAN

18 km (11 miles) northeast of Motovun.

Close to Motovun and a reasonable drive from Poreč, Novigrad, or Umag, Grožnjan is also among Istria's preeminent and most beautiful hill towns, with a Renaissance loggia adjoining the town gate. Much visited by busloads of summer tourists, it is quite empty the rest of the year. In 1358, after at least 250 years in existence as a walled city, Grožnjan came under Venetian rule and remained so for more than 400 years. Though most of its population left after World War II, when decades of Italian rule came to an end and it officially became part of Yugoslavia, from the mid-1960s the government encouraged artists and musicians to settle here. This explains the number of painting and sculpture galleries you will encounter in this otherwise unassuming village. During the summer, an international federation of young musicians meets for training and workshops, presenting concerts beneath the stars throughout July and August.

GETTING HERE AND AROUND

The best way to get to Grožnjan is by car, as no buses connect it to Pula or other coastal towns. This small hilltop town is best explored on foot.

EXPLORING

Crkva svetog Vida i Modesta (*Church of St. Vitus and St. Modestus*). Walk straight ahead from the small parking area just outside Grožnjan and you will come to the Crkva svetog Vida i Modesta. Reconstructed in Baroque style from an earlier, 14th-century church, it stands on a relatively unassuming, parklike space a bit removed from the gallery scene, with panoramic views of the surrounding countryside and plateaus of Istria all the way to the sea. *Obzidna 2, at the main entrance to Grožnjan on the left.*

NEED A BREAK

Kaya Energy Bar and Design. Bar-cum-furniture-and-jewelry-store Kaya is a great place for a rendezvous in Grožnjan. On a breezy day, sit on the terrace under the trees and enjoy beautiful vistas. Look for local craft beer San Servolo, refreshing natural juices, and homemade cakes. The interior is worth a peek as well, with unique furniture, lights, and decorations. ✉ *Vincenta iz Kastva 2* ☎ *052/776–051.*

Zigante Tartufi. Grožnjan may be small and out of the way, but enough tourists visit to merit yet another outlet in the Zigante family's Zigante Tartufi chain. The shop sells truffles and everything truffle-related you can imagine, as well as local products from aromatic herb brandies to honey to dried porcini. It's attached to the town's loggia. ✉ *Ul Gorjan 5* ☎ *052/776–099 store* 🌐 *www.zigantetartufi.hr* ⏲ *Closed Nov.–Mar.*

WHERE TO EAT

$$$$ STEAKHOUSE

✕ **Beer and Steakhouse San Servolo.** It's always time for a cold one at the Beer and Steakhouse San Servolo, attached to the brewery of the same name, where you get a tasty selection of six unfiltered and unpasteurized Istrian craft beers together with an expansive menu of hearty dishes. Located on a lonely country road about a 15-minute drive from Grožnjan, this beer lover's hot spot has breathtaking views of the countryside and the hill town of Buje. **Known for:** craft beer; grilled meat; lively atmosphere. [$] *Average main: 120 Kn* ✉ *Momjanska ulica 7, just outside Buje, 9 km (6 miles) northwest of Grožnjan, Momjan* ☎ *052/894–6065* 🌐 *www.bujska-pivovara.com* ⏲ *Closed Tues.*

EASTERN ISTRIA: LABIN AND RABAC

Labin is 44 km (28 miles) northeast of Pula.

Few travelers take time to explore Istria's often-overlooked eastern coast. Although the region's mostly mountainous terrain offers a relative dearth of large towns abounding in historical sights and easy-to-access, swimmable stretches of sea, the region does contain one notable exception: Labin.

GETTING HERE AND AROUND

There are nine buses daily from Pula to Labin, from which you can easily reach Rabac by bus. The best way to get around Rabac and Labin is on foot. An electric tourist train in Rabac runs between the resorts Maslenica and Girandella from mid-June to mid-September.

EXPLORING

Labin. Perched in all its compact medieval redolence atop a hill a short drive or walk from the sea, Labin is Croatia's former coal-mining capital and the birthplace of Matthias Flacius Illyricus, a Reformation-era collaborator of Martin Luther. Its narrow, historic streets are well deserving of a good walk—followed, if time allows, by a dip in the sea at Rabac, the relatively crowded and less inspiring complex of hotels and beaches 3 km (2 miles) away. From Labin's endearing little main square, **Titov trg,** with its 16th-century loggia and bastion, it's an easy stroll to Šetalište San Marco, a semicircular promenade with a spectacular view of the sea. Walk to the end and take a sharp left up the cobblestone road. Once you reach the top of the hill, you can climb another 98½ feet up for an even better view from the town's onetime fortress, the **Fortica.** From here Labin's relatively bustling commercial center, which seemed nonexistent a few minutes ago, comes fully into view below, as do the dry, craggy hills of inland Istria. Making your way down the other side of the hill back toward the main square, you will pass the **Crkva Rođenja Blažene Djevice Marije** (Church of the Birth of the Virgin Mary). With a facade featuring a 14th-century rose window and a 17th-century Venetian lion of the sort you will encounter elsewhere in Istria, the church is a mix of architectural styles dating back to a late-16th-century renovation, though its foundations may date to the 11th century. ✉ *Labin* 🌐 *www.rabac-labin.com.*

4

Rabac. Your first thought on arriving (buses run hourly from Labin for 12 Kn) at Rabac may be: why come all the way to Europe for a place that looks much like a generic beach resort anywhere? Its series of huge, honeycomb-shape, Italian-owned hotel monstrosities with names like Narcis, Hedera, and Mimosa are truly the last place the writer of these lines, for one, would want to stay. But wait. Make a *right* on entering town rather than a left, then walk down the hill by the road or the steps to the harbor. Once you reach the harbor, go *left* and then along the harborside promenade, rather than right. Doing so will reveal a side of Rabac that, although still somewhat touristy, retains something of the idyllic—with its quiet harbor replete with small yachts, motorboats, and other pleasure craft, not to mention dozens of tiny, harborside coves you can walk down into for a quick dip via short flights of concrete steps. ✉ *Rabac* 🌐 *www.rabac-labin.com.*

WHERE TO EAT AND STAY

$$$$
MEDITERRANEAN

✕ **Due Fratelli.** When the family is not catching fish, they are preparing it at their well-regarded, folksy restaurant with a cool, grapevine-shaded terrace. The menu offers fresh, delicious seafood specialties and a good selection of meat and poultry dishes. **Known for:** fresh fish; traditional Istrian dishes; relaxed atmosphere. [$] *Average main: 110 Kn* ✉ *Montozi 6, Labin* ☎ *052/853577* 🌐 *www.due-fratelli.com* ⏲ *Closed Jan. Closed Mon. Oct.–May.*

$$$$
INTERNATIONAL
Fodor's Choice ★

✕ **Velo Kafe.** Whether it be a coffee, homemade cake, and an ice cream on the shaded ground-floor terrace, a full dinner on the first-floor terrace, or hearty Istrian fare in the basement dining room, it's all to be found at this popular restaurant conveniently located at Titov Trg, Labin's main square. The menu is extensive, and it includes specialties like nettle gnocchi with salmon, steak in black-pepper sauce, and lobster pasta. **Known for:** three floors, three experiences (café, restaurant, and tavern); great location; homemade cakes and sweets. [$] *Average main: 100 Kn* ✉ *Titov Trg 12, Labin* ☎ *052/852–745* 🌐 *www.velokafe.com.*

$$$ HOTEL **Hotel Adoral.** This family-run hotel has an excellent location right across the seafront promenade just a few yards from the water, and its spacious, modern, and well-equipped rooms have balconies overlooking the sea. **Pros:** location right at the seafront; modern and spacious rooms; attentive staff. **Cons:** checkout time could be a bit later. *Rooms from: €200* *Obala M. Tita 2a, Rabac* *052/535–840* *www.adoral-hotel.com* *15 rooms* *Breakfast.*

$$ HOTEL **Hotel Peteani.** On the main road leading up to Labin's Old Town, this boutique hotel offers a fresh and playful designer interior, facilities such as saunas, and one of the best restaurants in town. **Pros:** small and friendly hotel; superb design; excellent on-site restaurant. **Cons:** some traffic noise in street-facing rooms. *Rooms from: €150* *Aldo Negri 9, Labin* *052/863–404* *www.hotel-peteani.hr* *14 rooms* *Breakfast.*

5

KVARNER

Updated by Vera Brljevic and Frank Galparsoro

Majestic scenery and natural diversity characterize the Kvarner region: the mainland is dominated by a tiny stretch of coast backed by high-rising mountains, while some of the largest Croatian islands fill the heart of Kvarner Bay. Hike the wild Gorski Kotar Mountains, explore Krk Island on two wheels, beach-hop on the island of Cres, enjoy the mild climate and abundant vegetation of Lošinj, and experience the best of Croatian cuisine along the Opatija Riviera.

The Kvarner Gulf is a large, deep bay with the Istrian peninsula to the north and Dalmatia to the south. Four major islands, Cres, Krk, Lošinj, and Rab, along with numerous smaller specks of land, fill the heart of the bay and can be viewed from the gentle resort towns strung around the coastal arc. The lush, rolling hills of this coastal strip wind their way around the gulf from Opatija. East of Rijeka, the scenic Magistrala costal highway cuts into the solid rock of the foothills on its way to the southern tip of Croatia.

The wild Gorski Kotar mountain district is on the mainland northeast of Rijeka. Across the narrow range sits the inland part of Primorsko-goranska županija (Primorje–Gorski Kotar county), a region of small towns and thick forests that you pass through if you're traveling overland to Zagreb. Although the entire northern stretch of the Croatian coast exhibits a strong Italian influence, thanks to centuries of control from across the Adriatic, most of the mainland resorts developed during Habsburg rule. Robust and sophisticated Austro-Hungarian architecture and infrastructure predominate in these towns.

In contrast, the islands tend toward the cozier, less aspirational features of Italy. Dwellings are simpler, often of stone, and set in less geometric layouts.

Krk, entered via a short bridge from the eastern shore of the gulf region, reflects the mainland's arid nature more than its brethren. On Cres, the northern stretches are a twisted knot of forest peaks and rocky crags, while gentler, cultivated slopes appear toward the center. Pine forests marching down to the shores provide welcome shade in the middle of the day. On the island's central part, hollows have filled up to make freshwater lakes that provide the island's drinking water, counterbalancing the salty sea that licks at the land just a hill crest away. At the foot of Cres, a hop across a narrow stretch of the Adriatic brings you to Lošinj. This lush oasis owes much of its charm to the gardens and villas that were built here during the seafaring heydays of the 19th century. As you approach from the north, the silhouette of Rab resembles the humped back of a diving sea monster. The high north of the island is dry and barren, almost a desert of rock and scrub, whereas the lower southern hemisphere is lush and fertile.

GREAT ITINERARIES

IF YOU HAVE 3 DAYS

With only three days, start off on **Krk** to enjoy a little island life, heading straight to the action on Baška beach. From here, either choose another town like Malinska or Krk Town, or make your way to **Rijeka,** visiting the fruit and vegetable market and possibly taking in a cultural exhibit or two. On the final day, scoot farther west for some classic seaside resorting in **Opatija,** and don't miss an afternoon stroll along the Lungomare.

IF YOU HAVE 5 DAYS

Begin your trip either in Opatija or Krk, reversing the three-day itinerary to suit your fancy, and add a visit to the relatively wild island of **Cres.** Ferries connect northern Cres (Porozina) to Brestova west of Opatija and central Cres (Merag) with Krk at Valbiska. A day divided between swimming at the beaches and relaxing in a café or ice-cream parlor in Cres Town can be enhanced by a second day exploring the more remote areas of the island, taking in some of the smaller villages or the rugged north.

IF YOU HAVE 7 DAYS

With a full week, explore the marina at **Mali Lošinj** for one day (reachable by bus from Cres Town). You'll have to work your way back to Rijeka or Krk at this point to get to Rab, as ferries don't connect Cres and Lošinj to Rab. On your way, spend an extra day on the Opatija Riviera, taking in the pretty towns of **Lovran** and **Volosko.** From Rijeka jump on a bus or a catamaran and head south to sample some of the region's only sandy beaches on the beautifully lush island of **Rab.** Spend at least a day admiring the medieval churches and campaniles of **Rab Town.**

5

ORIENTATION AND PLANNING

GETTING ORIENTED

The Kvarner region is a stretch of Adriatic coast dotted with some of the largest Croatian islands. Rijeka, the region's administrative center and largest town, is within a five-hour drive of European hubs like Munich, Milan, Vienna, Budapest, Zagreb, and Ljubljana. The Kvarner's principal city, Rijeka, is a somewhat dilapidated port (although the 21st century has seen it making a reasonably committed effort at a comeback), with good road and rail connections to Zagreb. Genteel Opatija was founded by the Habsburgs in the mid-19th century as Croatia's first seaside resort. The regional airport is found on the island of Krk.

PLANNING

WHEN TO GO

The Kvarner region gets very busy in high summer, so don't even dream of heading, for instance, to Opatija or Krk in August without accommodations lined up. Late May through early June and September are ideal times to visit, since you can expect good weather, warm seas, and open facilities. Early May and October are good if you're looking for

TOP REASONS TO GO TO KVARNER

The ultimate waterfront path: Opatija's Lungomare—more than 11 km (7 miles) long—is ideal for a leisurely stroll anywhere between Lovran and Volosko.

Fun in the sun: For a day of seaside family fun—windsurfing, swimming, and ice-cream stands galore—visit Krk's Baška beach, on the southern end of the island.

Beautiful remote beaches: Take a taxi boat or join one of the many daily excursions to the remote beaches below the hilltop village of Lubenice on Cres Island. The famed Sv. Ivan beach is one of the prettiest in Croatia. Not far from it, at the beach Žanja, you can visit a sea cave.

Towering views: The view from the top of the Great Bell Tower, Rab Town's tallest and most beautiful (there are four), is of a perfectly preserved medieval square.

Yacht gazing: Watch yachts come in to the picturesque harbor of Lošinj and dock in front of stately 19th-century villas on both sides of the marina.

peace and quiet, but remember that few tourist-related activities are on offer and you still need to book accommodations in advance.

GETTING HERE AND AROUND

AIR TRAVEL

Rijeka's airport is on Omišalj on Krk Island, with regular bus service provided by Autotrans to downtown Rijeka and the beach towns on Krk island as well as to Mali Lošinj and Cres (though not to Rab). The airport is served by Ryanair from London, Stockholm, and Brussels; Norwegian Air Shuttle from Oslo; Croatia Airlines from Munich; and Eurowings from Cologne, Berlin, and from several other cities in Germany. ■ **TIP→ The list of new destinations and airlines changes every year, so always do your research.**

Airport Contacts **Rijeka Airport.** ✉ *Hamec 1, Omišalj* ☎ *051/842–040* 🌐 *www.rijeka-airport.hr.*

BOAT AND FERRY TRAVEL

The Jadrolinija ferries no longer travel between Dubrovnik and Rijeka, however ferries do run between Brestova and Porozina on the island of Cres, connecting the mainland to the islands. From June to September, as many as 13 ferries depart daily. Prices vary according to season, but expect to pay €2.40 a person (€15.50 if you have a car) during the summer; rates fall as much as 20% in the low season. Ferries also run between Valbiska on the island of Krk and Merag on the island of Cres.

Every day in high season, U.T.O Kapetan Luka ferries leave Rijeka at 5 pm to call at Ilovik, Sušak, Unije, Cres, and Mali Lošinj; the entire trip from Rijeka to Mali Lošinj takes around four hours. Meanwhile, a catamaran service heads out to Rab at 5 pm and drops into the northern Dalmatian island of Pag about 2½ hours later. Tourist boats and water taxis offering transport on shorter stretches are also abundant at many resorts.

Contacts **Jadrolinija.** ☎ *051/211–444* 🌐 *www.jadrolinija.hr.* **U.T.O. Kapetan Luka.** ☎ *051/618–176* 🌐 *www.krilo.hr.*

BUS TRAVEL

There's daily international bus service to Rijeka from Italy (Trieste), Slovenia (Ljubljana), Austria (Vienna), and Germany (Frankfurt, Munich, and Stuttgart). You can also reach destinations all over mainland Croatia from Rijeka. Timetable information is available at the Rijeka Bus Terminal. GetByBus, a Croatia-based company, offers instant online booking for many bus operators and lines in Croatia.

Buses travel from Rijeka to all the major towns on the mainland and the islands at least once a day. If you're traveling independently, you'll find that buses to the various islands are roughly scheduled to tie in with ferry services.

Contacts **Autotrans.** ✉ *Rijeka Bus Terminal, Žabica 1, Rijeka* ☎ *051/660–660* 🌐 *www.autotrans.hr.* **GetByBus.** 🌐 *www.getbybus.com.* **Rijeka Bus Terminal.** ✉ *Žabica 1, Rijeka.*

CAR TRAVEL

Although local buses and ferries are an excellent, stress-free method of touring the region, touring the Kvarner by car does offer the opportunity to nose your way around some of the smaller and more remote villages on the islands and up in the mountains. In addition, despite a poor safety record and heavy traffic in high season, there are few roads more scenic than the Magistrala. A car is also useful if you plan to leave Kvarner and head for Istria (passing through the Učka Tunnel). However, good train and bus services to Zagreb, as well as bus service to Dalmatia, mean that a vehicle is not really essential for moving on to other areas.

TRAIN TRAVEL

There are three trains daily from Rijeka to Zagreb (journey time is approximately 4 hours) and two trains daily to Ljubljana (2½ hours).

Contacts **Hrvatske Željeznice (Croatian Railways).** ☎ *060/333–444* ✉ *informacije@hzpp.hr* 🌐 *www.hzpp.hr.* **Rijeka Train Station.** ✉ *Trg kralja Tomislava 1, Rijeka* ☎ *051/211–304.*

ABOUT THE RESTAURANTS

Without wanting to force square pegs into round holes, there are essentially four types of restaurants in Kvarner, if not the whole of the country. Unsurprisingly, many of them fall heavily under the influence of the Italian *tricolore*. In place of faith, hope, and charity, expect white pasta, green salads, and red pizza. The many pizza and pasta spots tend to be the cheaper and more casual alternatives.

Possibly the most delightful Croatian establishment is the *konoba*. Originally, the konoba was a humble cottage or shed, where fishermen would gather after returning to shore and toast to surviving another day's trip out to sea by raising a few glasses, followed by a sample of their catch cooked to soak up the booze. These rustically styled fish restaurants have cropped up everywhere in the last few years.

In Rijeka try *jota,* a thick soup with sauerkraut or pickled beets with cured meat, or famed Kvarner scampi. *Palenta kompirica* is a cornmeal with potatoes, a specialty of Gorski Kotar, the hilly area between Rijeka and Karlovac. The Gorski kotar region also serves hearty game stews, cured meat, and baked potatoes with bacon and cheese. On Krk try *Krk–Šurlice,* the local version of pasta; handmade on a spindle, it's often served with wild-game goulash. Cres has a fierce rivalry with the northern Dalmatian island of Pag regarding who serves the best lamb in Croatia. Calamari cooked in herbs and wine is a good bet on Lošinj. In Kvarner, *mrkač* is the local word for octopus; it's *hobotnica* in the rest of the country. If you order white fish, either grilled (*na žaru*) or baked in salt (*u soli*), you'll be charged by the kilogram, whereas squid (either grilled or fried) and shrimp (often cooked in white wine, *na buzaru*) come in regular portions. The classic accompaniment to fish is chard (*blitva*) and potatoes (*krumpir*). Many choices will come smothered in olive oil and garlic. Krk is home to the most highly regarded wines from the region, with the dry white *Vrbnićka žlahtina* a strong candidate for "best." *Rakija* (fruit and herb brandies) are, of course, the common end to a meal and the start of a long night.

ABOUT THE HOTELS

Opatija, Krk, and Lošinj have a healthy selection of quality hotels, but outside these (relatively) major resorts, hotels become a rarer commodity. Much more common is renting a house or apartment. There are multitudes of these holiday homes available across the region. Expect anything from a room in a block that shares a common kitchen, to a full-blown private house. Terraces are a standard and range from a simple tiled slab with metal rails to prevent you toppling off to a beautifully appointed perch shaded by a vine-smothered trellis and with an open grill for alfresco cooking. If you want to save money, consider renting a room in a private home. This arrangement rarely involves food, so you'll have to get up and out in the morning for your breakfast. Croats are a house-proud people, so in general rented rooms are likely to be very clean and comfortable, with private bathrooms. Your welcome will probably be very warm, with drinks—especially strong coffee—thrust under your nose the moment you step across the threshold. There's no better way to get a real feel for how Croats live. *Hotel reviews have been shortened. For full information, visit Fodors.com.*

WHAT IT COSTS IN EUROS (€) AND CROATIAN KUNA (KN)

	$	$$	$$$	$$$$
Restaurants	under 35 Kn	35 Kn–60 Kn	61 Kn–80 Kn	over 80 Kn
	under €5	€5–€8	€9–€10	over €10
Hotels	under 925 Kn	925 Kn–1,300 Kn	1,301 Kn–1,650 Kn	over 1,650 Kn
	under €121	€121–€170	€171–€216	over €216

Restaurant prices are the average cost of a main course at dinner or, if dinner is not served, at lunch. Hotel prices are the lowest cost of a standard double room in high season.

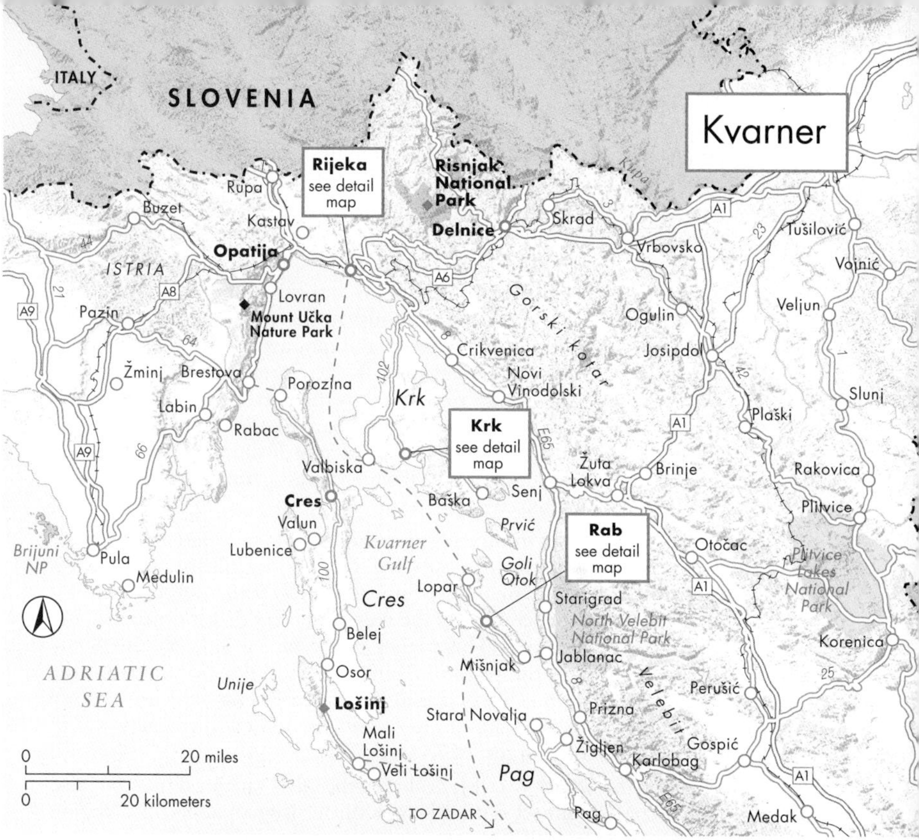

VISITOR INFORMATION

Tourist information offices can help you with information about accommodations and activities and excursions like diving, windsurfing, and sightseeing. Most offices give out maps and ferry schedules for free.

Contacts Cres Tourist Information. ✉ *Cons 10, Cres Town* ☎ *051/571–535* 🌐 *www.tzg-cres.hr.* **Krk Tourist Information.** ✉ *Vela placa 1/1, Krk Town* ☎ *051/221–414* 🌐 *www.tz-krk.hr.* **Lošinj Tourist Information.** ✉ *Priko 42, Mali Lošinj* ☎ *051/231–884* 🌐 *www.visitlosinj.hr.* **Opatija Tourist Information.** ✉ *Maršala Tita 128, Opatija* ☎ *051/271–310* 🌐 *www.visitopatija.com.* **Rab Tourist Information.** ✉ *Trg Municipum Arba 8, Rab* ☎ *051/724–064* 🌐 *www.rab-visit.com.* **Rijeka Tourist Information.** ✉ *Korzo 14, Rijeka* ☎ *051/335–882* 🌐 *www.visitrijeka.eu.*

RIJEKA

165 km (103 miles) southwest of Zagreb.

Water is the essence of Kvarner, and the region's largest city expresses this simply. Whether in Croatian or Italian (Fiume) the translation of the name to English is the same: *river.* Although the history of Croatia's third city goes back to the days of Imperial Rome, modern Rijeka evolved under the rule of Austria-Hungary. The historic core retains vestiges of the old Habsburg monarchy from the time when Rijeka served as the empire's outlet to the Adriatic. During the 1960s, under Yugoslavia, the suburbs expanded rapidly. Rijeka is the country's largest port, with a huge shipyard, massive dry-dock facilities, refineries, and other heavy industries offering large-scale employment. Since the breakup of Yugoslavia, however, Rijeka's role as a shipping town has declined significantly.

At the city's core sits Korzo, a pedestrian street of shops and cafés running parallel with the harbor and just to the south of where the land begins to rise toward the peaks of the mountains that back the bay. The high ground ensures that the suburbs stretch out to the east and the west, with little space to expand to the north. The general rule is that Rijeka is more of a transit town than a holiday destination, and it's not known for its points of interest, apart from the hilltop fortress of Trsat. However, the city is well worth investigating more thoroughly than most would have you believe.

Many visitors stay in the nearby seaside resort of Opatija, and locals will often head that way in their free time as well. That said, Rijeka is a perfectly pleasant small city (approximately 130,000 people call it home); if it did not command the wonderful bay that it does, it would also be unremarkable. This makes it one of the more authentically Croatian spots in the region in summer. Those looking to avoid the hordes could do much worse than to stay in Rijeka—albeit with very few options for accommodation—and use the excellent network of ferries to explore the rest of Kvarner.

Rijeka is the home port of Jadrolinija, the coast's major ferry company. Local ferries connect with all the Kvarner islands and will take you farther afield as well.

GETTING HERE AND AROUND

Rijeka is linked with Zagreb by the new A6 motorway, which is clean and fast, though tolls add up on the journey. To reach the Dalmatian coast from Rijeka, you'll have to backtrack 75 km (47 miles) away from the coast and get on the motorway heading south toward Split and Dubrovnik. Rijeka is also the start of the Jadranska Magistrala (the coastal highway), which follows the coast south, all the way to the Montenegro border.

EXPLORING

TOP ATTRACTIONS

City Market. A set of three turn-of-the-20th-century halls hosts the city's main market, one of the liveliest spots in Rijeka on a weekday or Saturday morning. Get here before midday to enjoy the trading in full cry. The original constructions from the 1880s have suffered a little from later additions, but the fish market, the last to be built, is a wonderful example of art nouveau design. The castings by well-known Venetian artist Urbano Bottasso ape the fish and crustaceans being sold below. The streets surrounding the market are filled with no-frills eateries that are good for a quick lunch, and it's a good bet that their offerings will

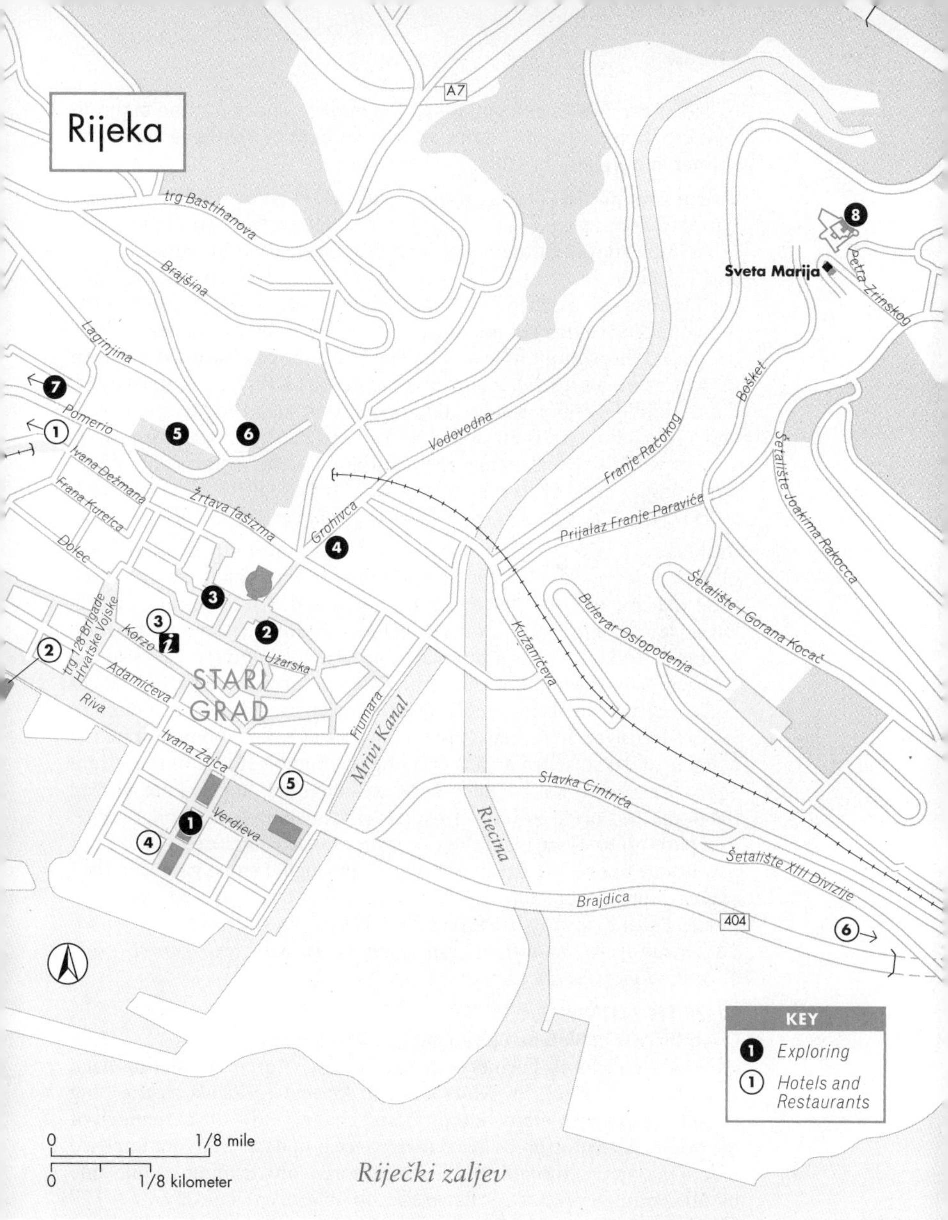

Exploring

City Market 1
Crkva Uznesenja Blažene Djevice Marije i Kosi toranj 2
Guvernerova palača 5
Kastav 7
Peek + Poke Musej Djetinjstva 4
Prirodoslovni muzej 6
Stara Vrata 3
Trsat 8

Restaurants

Bistro Mala Riba 1
Konoba Feral 5
Konoba Fiume 4

Hotels

Botel Marina 2
Grand Hotel Bonavia 3
Hotel Jadran 6

be fresh. ■ **TIP→ Before you leave the market, check out the magnificent Croatian National Theatre, which was built by Viennese architects Fellner and Helmer in 1885.** ✉ *Demetrova 3.*

Guvernerova palača (*The Governor's Palace*). High on a hill, the palace affords a grand view over the harbor from all the front windows. Built in 1893 by Alajos Hauszmann, who also worked on Budapest's castle and Palace of Justice for the then-governor of Hungary, the building itself is no eyesore either. The large columned facade communicates the self-confidence of the robust Habsburg empire, as do the numerous statues placed throughout its grounds. The **Maritime & Historical Museum of the Croatian Littoral,** which investigates the Kvarner's seafaring traditions and the region's cultural heritage from both the Mediterranean and Central Europe, is housed here. You can also admire the rest of the interior while viewing a temporary exhibition in the atrium or attending a meeting or concert in the impressive Marble Hall. ✉ *Muzejski trg 1* ☎ *051/213–578, 051/553–666* 🌐 *www.ppmhp.hr* 🎫 *15 Kn.*

Fodor's Choice ★ **Trsat** (*Trsat Castle*). The medieval castle was built on the foundations of a prehistoric fort. In the early 1800s, it was bought by an Austrian general of Irish descent, who converted it into a kind of pre-Disneyland confection that even includes a Greek temple with Doric columns. Today it hosts a popular café, offering stunning views of the Kvarner Bay; throughout the summer, open-air theater performances and concerts take place here. Across the street, the pilgrimage church of **Sveta Marija** (St. Mary) was constructed in 1453 to commemorate the Miracle of Trsat, when angels carrying the humble house of the Virgin Mary are said to have landed here. Although the angels later moved the house to Loreto in Italy, Trsat has remained a place of pilgrimage. The path up to Trsat from the city center takes you close to Titov trg, at a bridge across the Rječina. It passes through a stone gateway, then makes a long, steep climb up 538 steps. Local Bus 2 will get you here, too. ✉ *Petra Zrinskog BB* ☎ *051/217–714 castle, 051/452–900 church* 🎫 *Church free; castle free; castle exhibits 10 Kn* ⏲ *No church visits during religious services.*

WORTH NOTING

Crkva Uznesenja Blažene Djevice Marije i Kosi toranj (*Church of St. Mary of the Assumption*). Formerly the city's main church and dating back to the Middle Ages, St. Mary's is still known to locals as the "big church." However, many additions and changes now obscure much of the original architecture. The relatively recent updates have not imposed severe geometry, though: the bell tower remains leaning to one side by 40 centimeters or so. ✉ *Pavla Rittera Vitezovica 3* ☎ *051/214–177* ⏲ *Closed daily after 12:30 pm.*

Peek + Poke Muzej Djetinjstva (*Peek + Poke Museum of Childhood*). Return to your childhood through the museum's exhibit of toys and games. Among the 600 items on display, mostly donated by people from Croatia and around the world, the oldest is a doll dating to 1894. The collections are displayed thematically: construction games, a "fossil" zone displaying the oldest items, board games, literature, a school corner, a doll collection, outdoor games and toys, and vintage computer and game consoles. Among the most interesting items are Richter's Stone Building Set from 1902 and a large replica of the Croatian National Theater made of Lego blocks. ✉ *Ivana Grohovca 2* ☎ *091/780–5709* 🌐 *www.peekpoke.hr* 🎫 *30 Kn* 🕒 *Closed Sun. May–Nov.; Sun.–Fri. Nov.–May.*

Prirodoslovni muzej (*Natural History Museum*). Exploring the geology and biology of the region invariably involves holding a sizable chunk of marine life up to the eyes. The shark and ray display here is predictably popular, starring a brigade of stuffed sharks swimming in strict formation while suspended from the ceiling. A multimedia center based on an aquarium adds to the extensive collection of nonmammalian species, which boasts 90,000 specimens in total, but includes rocks, plants, and other less animated elements of the locality. The botanical garden contributes more exotic plants to the array from the museum's grounds. Considering the fearsome appearance of some of the more fascinating inhabitants of the museum, it may be worth considering putting off a visit here until the end of your stay on the coast, lest your imagination get the better of you while bathing off the beaches. ✉ *Lorenzov prolaz 1* ☎ *051/553–669* 🌐 *www.prirodoslovni.com* 🎫 *10 Kn* 🕒 *Closed on public holidays.*

5

Stara Vrata (*The Roman Gate*). This enormous stone arch—the oldest structure in the city—is an ancient town gate. Today it's partly engulfed by additions from more recent times, but it was from this site many centuries ago that the chain of mountain fortresses in the region was commanded by the Romans. These days, the Roman elite's enthusiasm for comfort is catered to with a handful of park benches amid what is left of the ancient walls and columns. ✉ *Ulica Stara Vrata.*

OFF THE BEATEN PATH

Kastav. One of the finest spots from which to admire the splendors of the Kvarner bay is Kastav, 11 km (7 miles) northwest of Rijeka. Originally a medieval fortress comprising nine defensive towers, the old hilltop village sits at 1,200 feet in elevation and is home to 900-some people. Without the crowds of Rijeka, you, along with city residents that spend their leisure time here, can concentrate more properly on the quality of your relaxation. The local vintage, Kastavska Belica, is a decent white wine that is gulped merrily at Kastav Cultural Summer and on the feast day of patron St. Helena (as featured on the coat of arms), May 22. Having been home to wealthy and powerful clans in times past, the tiny town has many splendid—if not officially noted—buildings from throughout the ages. ✉ *Kastav* 🌐 *www.kastav-touristinfo.hr.*

WHERE TO EAT

$$$$ SEAFOOD

✕ **Bistro Mala Riba.** Located on the main road Matulji–Kastav, this cozy tavern sports a delicious line-up of Kvarner-style tapas best enjoyed on the pleasant outdoor terrace overshadowed by pine trees. Seafood lovers will have a hard time choosing between menu items—fish marinated in lemon juice, sea-snail salad, fried olives, barley and squid stew—and may find themselves coming back for more. **Known for:** seafood Kvarner-style tapas; cozy atmosphere; friendly service. [$] *Average main: 90 Kn* ✉ *Tometići 33a, Tometići, Kastav* ☎ *051/277–945* 🌐 *www.mala-riba.com.*

$$$ SEAFOOD ✕ **Konoba Feral.** Frequented by locals, this excellent informal seafood restaurant lies on a side road conveniently close to the City Market. House specialties are *crni rižot* (cuttlefish-ink risotto), seafood tagliatelle, and shellfish. Fish is charged by weight. **Known for:** affordable traditional dishes; popular with locals; cozy atmosphere. *Average main: 80 Kn* ✉ *Matije Gupca 5B* ☎ *051/212–274* 🌐 *www.konoba-feral.com* ⏲ *No dinner Sun.; no dinner mid-Sept.–June.*

$$$$ MEDITERRANEAN ✕ **Konoba Fiume.** Tucked away in an alley right next to Rijeka's fish market, quaint Fiume fills with locals at lunchtime. Unpretentious and friendly with a small streetside terrace, the tavern serves mostly seafood but also meat and pasta dishes. **Known for:** friendly atmosphere; fresh seafood; affordable prices. *Average main: 90 Kn* ✉ *Vatroslava Lisinskog 12* ☎ *051/312–108* ⏲ *Closed Sun. No dinner.*

WHERE TO STAY

The selection of hotels in Rijeka reflects the city's status as a simple transit town.

$ HOTEL **Botel Marina.** Docked at the pier in Rijeka, the first Croatian boat hotel features 35 modern rooms, from doubles to dorms, furnished with comfy beds and en suite bathrooms—a cool place to stay. **Pros:** centrally located; nice ambience; friendly staff. **Cons:** no elevators, so carrying luggage to the rooms on lower decks can be inconvenient; smallish rooms. *Rooms from: €82* ✉ *Adamićev gat* ☎ *051/410–162* 🌐 *www.botel-marina.com* *35 rooms* *Breakfast.*

$$ HOTEL **Grand Hotel Bonavia.** In the city center, one block back from the Korzo, this modern high-rise has comfortable rooms with specially designed furnishings and original oil paintings. **Pros:** spacious rooms; good service; excellent location. **Cons:** getting a bit outdated; also caters to business guests. *Rooms from: €125* ✉ *Dolac 4* ☎ *051/357–100* 🌐 *www.bonavia.hr* *121 rooms* *Breakfast.*

$ HOTEL **Hotel Jadran.** It's a good 20-minute walk (or 10-minute bus ride) from central Rijeka to this pleasant hotel right on the water, but views of the Gulf of Kvarner don't come much better than this. **Pros:** substantial breakfast; unfettered sea views. **Cons:** a bit out of town to take in any nightlife; walk into town is along a busy street. *Rooms from: €115* ✉ *Šetalište XIII divizije 46* ☎ *051/216–600* 🌐 *www.jadran-hoteli.hr* *69 rooms* *Breakfast.*

NIGHTLIFE AND PERFORMING ARTS

NIGHTLIFE

BARS

Celtic Cafe Bard. A hangout spot for beer lovers, this bar on a small town square next to St. Vitus Cathedral is decorated with wood and brass. This cozy spot offers an excellent choice of Croatian and international beer in a friendly atmosphere to the rhythm of Celtic music and some jazz. Closed Sunday. ✉ *Trg Grivica 6b* ☎ *051/215–235.*

Cukarikafe. Perhaps the most popular daytime café-bar in Rijeka, this shabby chic spot is packed with unique decor, much of it culled from the dump and flea market. People from all walks of life come here for the excellent selection of wine by glass, beer, local spirits, teas, and freshly squeezed juices. ✉ *Trg Jurja Klovića 4* ☎ *099/583–8276.*

Karolina. In an upmarket pavilion right on the quayside, Karolina serves cocktails and wine to the smart set as they watch the tide flow in and out of the bay. ✉ *Gat Karoline Riječke* ☎ *091/490–4042.*

Phanas Pub. The best party place in town, this nautically themed pub is like an old sailboat with its dark wood, long bar, and maritime decorations. Music ranges from acoustic and R&B to dance, and you can enjoy it until 6 am from Thursday through Sunday. ✉ *Ivana Zajca 9.*

River Pub. For those who might remember summer nights sitting on a terrace, drinking, dancing, chatting, and actually being able to hear what others are saying, the River Pub is the place to make it all come back. ✉ *Frana Supila 12* ☎ *051/324–673* ⏲ *Closed Sun.*

Tunel. In a real tunnel under the railway in the Skoljić area of town, one of Rijeka's favorite bars has a great atmosphere, friendly staff, and cool crowd. Some nights jazz, rock, and funk bands take the small stage; other nights DJs play electronic music. They have a good choice of local brandies, Croatian wines, and international beers. ✉ *Školjić 12* ⏲ *Closed Sun.*

5

PERFORMING ARTS

FESTIVALS

Rijeka Carnival. From the end of January until mid-February the streets of the city are taken over by crazy antics and costumes during the Rijeka Carnival. The carnival kicks off with the Carnival Queen Pageant, continues with weeks of fun activities and masked parties all over town, and ends with the Children's Carnival Parade and the International Carnival Parade. ✉ *Rijeka* 🌐 *www.rijecki-karneval.hr.*

Summer on Gradina. From mid-July to the beginning of September, this cultural festival brings theater plays, live concerts, and conceptual and themed events to Trsat Fortress. ✉ *Trsat Fortress, Petar Zrinskog BB* 🌐 *www.trsatskagradina.com.*

SHOPPING

Appearance is of great importance to Croatians, and the local ladies will invariably be exhibiting style and glamour even as they sip coffee or shop for vegetables on any given weekday morning. To serve this fashion-conscious crowd, many hip little boutiques offer the latest styles in imported clothing and shoes (mostly from Italy). Prices are generally higher than what you'd pay in Italy, so unless you're caught short needing some posh clothes, it's better for your wallet to do your high-fashion shopping elsewhere. The Korzo, a pedestrian strip that strides through the center of Rijeka, is the best place to go, should you be unable to contain your shopping urges.

Fresh local produce, fish, cheeses, olive oils, wines, and rakijas are the items that should be on your Kvarner shopping list. The best place to buy these is the City Market on Verdijeva. Although there are "professional" traders present, many of the stallholders are still locals who bring their home-produced wares to sell. Noisy and colorful, Rijeka's central market is the place to haggle over fresh produce, swap gossip, and, of course, drink coffee. Pick up a picnic lunch of cheeses, salads, fruit, and nuts here, then pop into one of the multitude of bakeries for freshly baked *burek* (cheese and meat pies) to complete the feast. Although a little tricky to transport, homemade olive oil, apple-cider vinegar, and rakija—usually sold in recycled bottles—are good buys as well. Smaller containers of dried herbal tea leaves and seasonings like rosemary and oregano are a good alternative if your luggage is already tightly packed.

Mala galerija. All things that glitter or smash easily are available at the Mala galerija. Although not entirely exclusive to Rijeka (you'll find similar, if more ostentatious, artifacts in Venice), the Morčić is the figure of a Moor wearing a white turban and is associated with the luck that all seafarers rely on. This small shop has many items bearing the "little Moor." ✉ *Užarska 25* ☎ *051/335–403* 🌐 *www.mala-galerija.hr* ⏲ *Closed Sun.*

ZTC. This mall right at the seafront is the favorite shopping destination of Rijeka residents. Shops include fashion brands like Benetton, H&M, and S'Oliver; Lush and L'Occitane cosmetics; and sport store Hervis. ✉ *Zvonimirova 3* ☎ *051/561–014* 🌐 *www.ztc-shopping.hr.*

SPORTS AND THE OUTDOORS

BEACHES

Since it serves as the country's largest port, there aren't too many beautiful beaches in the middle of Rijeka. However, you don't imagine locals stay here the whole summer without having a few spots they try to keep secret from the tourists, do you? Favorite beaches easily accessible from the city include the **Bivio Cove,** near Kantrida to the west. In the opposite direction around the coast, **Uvala Žurkovo,** at Kostrena, is wonderful. Within the city itself, the popular place is **Pecine** to the east, where you can swim off rocky beaches and admire the local villas.

FISHING

The Croatian coast is well known for its population of bluefin tuna.

Ministry of Agriculture, Forestry & Water Management. You need a fishing license to hunt for any marine life using a line or gun. Prices start from 60 Kn per day. In Rijeka licenses are available from the local office of the Ministry of Agriculture, Forestry & Water Management, or online through the ministry's website. ✉ *Demetrova 3* ☎ *051/213–626* 🌐 *www.mps.hr.*

RISNJAK NATIONAL PARK

40 km (25 miles) northeast of Rijeka.

The northern outpost of the forested and karst-peaked Gorski kotar region, Veliki Risnjak is the major peak in this national park, peering over Rijeka from 5,013 feet. The thick pine-forest meadows are stuffed with wildflowers in the spring, and limestone peaks, crevices, and caves cover around 60 square km (25 square miles).

EXPLORING

Risnjak National Park. Risnjak is a popular destination year-round. In winter you'll find a healthy contingent of snow aficionados desperately trying to avoid a trip up to Austria to sample the real thing. In summer, however, as the sun and the tourists beat down upon the coast, this is perhaps the best place to be. The cooling mountain air—the average temperature in the region in July is around 16°C (60°F)—is a bonus to Risnjak's virtually deserted landscape.

You'll be free to commune with the locals, which include deer, bear, wildcat, and lynx (*ris*), from which the park takes its name. Geologic and botanical features are occasionally explained by English-language information points over which you may stumble on one of the more popular walking routes. Marked trails can occupy you for an hour's evening stroll to a full seven-day trek on the monstrous Rijeka Mountain Transversal from one side of Gorski kotar to the other. Hiking huts are strung across the peaks to accommodate such ambitious expeditions. More information regarding these multiday hiking trips is available from the Croatian Mountaineering Association.

The park information office is in the village of Crni lug, at the eastern entrance to the park. You can easily explore the gentler trails on day trips from either Rijeka or Delnice. Paths from the villages of Razloge and Kupari lead up to the source of the wild Kupa River, which can then be followed down the slopes through the "Valley of the Butterflies." ✉ *Bijela vodica 48, Crni Lug* ☎ *051/836–133* 🌐 *www.np-risnjak.hr/en/* 🎟 *45 Kn* ⏲ *Information office closed Oct.–Apr.*

OPATIJA

15 km (9 miles) southwest of Rijeka.

In the late 19th century, Opatija (Abbazia in Italian) was among the most elegant and fashionable resorts in Europe. Its history as a resort town dates from the 1840s, when villas were built for members of minor royalty. In 1873 the start of rail service from Vienna and Budapest, along with an aggressive publicity campaign, put Abbazia on the tourist map as a spa of the first magnitude. With the high mineral content of the sea water, iodine in the air, and an annual average of 2,230 hours of sunshine, it qualified as a top-rated climatic health resort, and emerged as a favorite wintering spot for Central European nobility and high society.

A hint of the formality that shrouded Opatija in its heyday still survives; the narrow pines and grand buildings remind one of the Italian lakes. This means that many visitors from all over Europe continue to head to the Opatija Riviera in the summer. At the same time, this stretch of coast has not gone unnoticed by the locals. Until recent years the town was a weekend haunt for some younger, motorized Rijeka citizens. Thanks to these driving forces, the upmarket hotel guests still share the resort with some of the region's more upwardly mobile restaurants. However, their number is dwindling, while the town's once admirable nightlife has packed up and headed back to the cooler parts of Rijeka, leaving Opatija to wealthy and more elderly visitors from the surrounding countries. These guests seem more eager to sip the waters than wine and spirits.

The main street, ulica Maršala Tita, runs parallel to the coast for the length of town, and you can go from one end of town to the other on foot in about half an hour, passing numerous terrace cafés along the way. The best seafood restaurants are in the neighboring fishing village of Volosko, a 15-minute walk along the seafront. The mild climate year-round and resulting subtropical vegetation, frequently sunny skies, and shelter from cold north winds provided by Mt. Učka give Opatija pleasant weather for much of the year. In summer, fresh sea breezes tend to dispel any oppressive heat, making the city an ideal seaside resort.

EXPLORING

TOP ATTRACTIONS

Lungomare. If you enjoy walking by the sea, set off along the magnificent paved, waterfront Lungomare. Built in 1889, this 12-km (7½-mile) path leads from the fishing village of Volosko through Opatija—passing in front of old hotels, parks, and gardens and around yacht basins—and all the way past the villages of Ičići and Ika to Lovran. In the middle you'll find the popular town beach that fronts the center of Opatija. Close to many cafés, ice-cream shops, and other essentials, the beach also has a couple of protected sections of water for safe swimming. ✉ *Obalno Šetalište Franza Josefa.*

Mount Učka Nature Park. From gentle hiking to mountain biking, climbing and paragliding, all are available in the 160 square km (62 square miles) of Mount Učka Nature Park, a series of peaks that help shelter the Liburnia Riviera (which is actually the official name for the stretch of coast centered on Opatija) and the islands from weather systems to the north. Paths toward the summit of the range start from all the resorts along the coast. A climb up to the highest peak, Vojak (4,596 feet), with a fine stone lookout tower at its summit, can be well worth it, particularly on a clear day. The view offers a cheap (but somewhat distant) tour of the islands of Kvarner Bay, the Italian Alps, and perhaps even an indistinct version of Venice. Most routes up to the heights lead through forest, so you can make the trek in summer without overheating. Along the way you'll find natural springs from which to quench your thirst, along with ponds, tumbling waterfalls (in the wetter months), impressive natural stone columns and several hundred caves. The local inhabitants include deer, wild boar, and, in the northernmost sections of the park, bears. Humans have been living in these hills for centuries also, rearing cattle, farming, and working the forest; you'll come across numerous tiny villages and historic sites if you roam far enough. If you're running short of time, there are many mountain-biking tracks throughout the park offering the chance to expand your lungs on the way up and test your nerve rattling back down to the coast. ✉ *Liganj 42, Lovran* ☎ *051/293–753* 🌐 *www.pp-ucka.hr* 🎫 *Free.*

WORTH NOTING

Park Angiolina. The grounds of Park Angiolina are a wonderful spread of palm-punctuated lawns with a botanical garden. The vegetation is strikingly lush, including cacti, bamboo, and magnolias, plus neatly kept beds of colorful flowers and sweet-scented shrubs. Indeed, Opatija as a whole is a town saturated with botanical splendor. Iginio Scarpa, an aristocrat from Rijeka and the first settler in Opatija, began importing exotic plants, and the tradition has survived into the present. The camellia is the symbol of the city. ✉ *Between Maršala Tita and the seafront* 🌐 *www.visitopatija.com* 🎫 *Free.*

OFF THE BEATEN PATH

Lovran. Just 5 km (3 miles) southwest of Opatija, the lovely town of Lovran is home to good swimming coves, Habsburg villas, and paths up to Mount Učka Nature Park. Massive chestnut trees dot the medieval town, giving shady relief from the sun on long summer days. If the crowds of Opatija leave you no place for peace and quiet, walk along the Lungomare through Ičići and Ika (or take Bus No. 32) to Lovran, where you can take in the sea air that lured Austrian royalty to winter here. If you find yourself on the Opatija Riviera in October, don't miss Lovran's **Marunada,** or chestnut festival. Contact the Lovran Tourist Office (Trg Slobode 1, Opatija ☎ *051/291–740* 🌐 *www.tz-lovran.hr*) for information. ✉ *Lovran.*

5

WHERE TO EAT

$$$$ VENETIAN

✕ **Istranka.** With a delightful covered terrace flanked by a twisting tree, this small restaurant is Opatija's best option for those who are not the greatest fans of seafood (although if that's you, what you're doing in Kvarner is a mystery). Taking its influence from the neighboring region of Istria, the menu concentrates more on landlubber food: hams, cheeses, and of course, the famous Istrian truffle! **Known for:** traditional Istrian cuisine; affordable prices; friendly service. $ *Average main: 90 Kn* ✉ *Bože Milanoviča 2* ☎ *051/271–835* ⏲ *Closed Jan.*

$$$$ SEAFOOD

✕ **Plavi Podrum3.** Although this is one of the more traditional fish restaurants in Volosko, don't be fooled into thinking it's not classy. The owner has been "Sommelier of the Year" a few years in a row in this young century. **Known for:** tasting menus; excellent wine list; special occasion. $ *Average main: 180 Kn* ✉ *Obala Frana Supila 12, Volosko* ☎ *051/701–223* 🌐 *www.plavipodrum.com* ⏲ *Closed Jan.*

$$$$ SEAFOOD Fodor's Choice ★

✕ **Tramerka.** Located in Volosko, just above more famed Plavi Podrum, this small seafood tavern offers fresh, creative seafood dishes in a cozy interior with exposed stone walls; a tiny streetside terrace has only a few tables. Locals rave about their bonito tartare, monkfish stew, and dirty calamari (baby calamari too small to be thoroughly cleaned before cooking, thus "dirty"). **Known for:** fish tapas; creative food; friendly atmosphere. $ *Average main: 100 Kn* ✉ *Dr. Andrije Mohorovicica 15, Volosko* ☎ *051/701–707* ⏲ *Closed Mon. and Jan.*

WHERE TO STAY

$$ HOTEL **Hotel Astoria by OHM Group.** Sleek flat-screen TVs and Wi-Fi in every room aren't what you'd expect in a hotel in this price category in a city popular with Austrian pensioners. **Pros:** boutique touches like flat-screen TVs and deluxe toiletries; big breakfasts. **Cons:** superior rooms are on the small side; not directly on the seafront. *Rooms from: €150 ✉ Maršala Tita 174 ☎ 051/706–350 ⊕ www.hotel-astoria.hr 50 rooms Breakfast.*

$$$$ HOTEL **Milenij Hotel Opatija.** On the coastal promenade, this bright pink villa is part old and part new; rooms are furnished accordingly, with either Louis XV–style antiques heavily striped in silk or modern designer pieces. **Pros:** centrally located and at seafront; homemade pralines and a good choice of other cakes and pastries in hotel's café. **Cons:** small pool with few lounge chairs; lack of parking spaces. *Rooms from: €299 ✉ Maršala Tita 109 ☎ 051/202–000 ⊕ www.milenijhoteli.hr 99 rooms Breakfast.*

$$$ HOTEL **Remisens Premium Hotel Ambasador.** This 10-floor skyscraper may not look appealing from the outside, but this five-star hotel is surprisingly elegant on the inside, with an airy lobby area and floor-to-ceiling windows overlooking the sea. **Pros:** view from sea-facing rooms is gorgeous; nice pool area; friendly staff. **Cons:** parking fees; hotel also caters to business travelers. *Rooms from: €210 ✉ Feliksa Peršića 5 ☎ 051/710–444 reservation center, 051/743–333 ⊕ www.remisens.com 200 rooms Breakfast.*

$$$ HOTEL Fodor's Choice ★ **Remisens Premium Hotel Kvarner.** The former summer residence of European royalty, Kvarner's oldest hotel first opened its doors to guests in 1884. **Pros:** Habsburg-era grandeur; spacious patio overlooking the sea. **Cons:** noise from wedding parties sometimes hosted in the Crystal Ballroom. *Rooms from: €200 ✉ Pava Tomašica 2 ☎ 051/271–233, 051/710–444 reservation center ⊕ www.remisens.com ⊗ Closed Nov.–Mar. 58 rooms Breakfast.*

NIGHTLIFE AND PERFORMING ARTS

There was a time when folk from Rijeka used Opatija as their playground; then, the town offered superb nightlife options. These days, however, the big city along the coast is reclaiming its post as the cultural hot spot of the region, and Opatija has been busy transforming itself back into Central and Eastern Europe's health resort. The wealthy, older Italians and Austrians who dominate here have done little to inspire energetic evenings.

Monokini. Right on the main road that winds through town along the seafront, Monokini has a shaded, streetside terrace with plenty of comfortable seating, whereas inside all is funky and modern. You'll find good music, a friendly staff, good drinks, cocktails and a selection of teas, and an atmosphere that invites locals to meet up here for a chat. *✉ Maršala Tita 96 ☎.*

SPORTS AND THE OUTDOORS

Mount Učka Nature Park, accessible from virtually any point along the coast, offers the easiest opportunity for active exploring, including mountain-bike and hiking trails up through the forested slopes.

OUTFITTERS

Raspadalica. This outfitter can help out if you want to do some exploring on two wheels, on foot, underground, or in the air: paragliding and free flying above the clouds in Mount Učka Nature Park. They also offer Robinson Crusoe–style camping (no hot water, electricity, or other amenities). ✉ *Ćićarija, Buzet* ☎ *098/924–7300* 🌐 *www.raspadalica.com.*

CRES

Brestova is 30 km (18 miles) southwest of Opatija, then a 20-minute ferry ride.

Twisting down the entire length of the Kvarner Bay on its western side is Cres, whose latest claim to fame is that it is the largest of all Croatian islands. For many years, squat neighbor Krk was awarded this distinction, but recent recalculations have rectified a long-standing error. Cres has been known as one of the most unspoiled islands in the Adriatic for a long time. More difficult to get to than Krk, and with a wilder and more rugged topography, Cres is quite frankly a delight. Its natural stretches are punctuated with olive groves and tiny towns and villages that remain authentic for the most part.

GETTING HERE AND AROUND

Ferries to Cres take about 20 minutes, embarking from Brestova, which is on the mainland southwest of Opatija, to Porozina; another ferry goes from Valbiska on Krk to Merag, on the east side of Cres.

EXPLORING

Cres Town. Tucked into a well-protected bay, midway down the island, Cres Town is set around a lovely little fishing harbor, small but perfectly formed, with numerous Gothic and Renaissance churches, monasteries, and palaces. For the most part these are in the Old Town, which sits protected by winged Venetian lions atop three 16th-century gates, the only remains of a defensive wall. A small harbor (*Mandrać*), as well as a municipal loggia built in the 15th-century, remain the soul of the town.

The **town beach,** at Kovačine campsite, holds a Blue Flag award for cleanliness. To get there, follow the path around the harbor from the main road and keep going for at least 15 minutes along the promenade, where you'll find spots to jump into the water and the odd café or restaurant to keep you fueled. Although the seaside here is man-made, it somehow doesn't detract too much from the experience. ✉ *Cres Town* 🌐 *www.tzg-cres.hr.*

Fodor's Choice ★ **Lubenice.** One of the most tempting beaches on the island is on the western coast of Cres at the foot of a steep cliff, at the top of which is the tiny village of Lubenice, which offers great views out to sea and up the western coast. This picturesque collection of houses that surround the 15th-century Church of St. Anthony the Hermit has been clinging to its outcrop for around 4,000 years. The hamlet is popular among arty types and hosts exhibitions and music performances in the summer. From the beach below, a short walk through vineyards will bring you to Žanja Cove, which has a blue grotto, a cave at water level that enjoys brilliant blue light as strong sunlight filters through the azure water. ✉ *Lubenice* 🌐 *www.tzg-cres.hr.*

Osor. At the southwestern tip of Cres is the town of Osor, whose strategic position on the channel between the island Cres and Lošinj ensured that wealth flowed into the town from trade ships. A tour of the town makes for a pleasant afternoon. Reflecting its former status, there's even a cathedral, and many important archaeological sites have been discovered in the vicinity. ✉ *Osor* 🌐 *www.visitlosinj.hr.*

Osor Archaeological Collection. Housed at city hall, this collection contains booty from throughout the ages, including artifacts from across the Roman empire. ✉ *Gradska vijecnica, Osor* ☎ *051/233–892* 🌐 *www.muzej.losinj.hr* 🎟 *35 Kn* ⏲ *Closed Mon. mid-June–mid-Sept.; Sun. and Mon. mid-Sept.–mid-June.*

Valun. Across the bay from Cres, the village of Valun has a nice beach. The town's claim to fame is the "Valun Tablet," a gravestone that is one of the oldest known examples of Glagolitic script. The tablet is now kept in the parish church, right on the waterfront. Get to Valun by car or by taking the wooden boat that sits just outside the Cres Harbor wall; it's easily spotted from the main square. ✉ *Valun.*

WHERE TO EAT

$$$ MEDITERRANEAN

✕ **Hibernicia.** A nice little terrace right by the bell tower in the heart of the stone hilltop village of Lubenice is the perfect location for a light lunch of *pršut* (prosciutto), cheese, olives, and a glass of local wine. For a more hearty meal, order lamb-stew gnocchi or lamb liver with polenta, since lamb is a specialty on Cres. **Known for:** relaxed atmosphere; simple traditional food; friendly staff. $ *Average main: 80 Kn* ✉ *Lubenice 17, Lubenice* ☎ *051/525–040* ▬ *No credit cards* ⏲ *Closed Oct.–Apr.*

$$$$ MEDITERRANEAN

✕ **Konoba Bonifačić.** The subtitle on the road signs reads *nonina kuhinja* (granny's cooking), and you were a spoiled child indeed if your grandma turned out dishes of this standard for you. The shady garden in the heart of ancient Osor is a perfect setting in which to enjoy the typical plates of the konoba: meat, seafood, pasta, and salads. **Known for:** lovely garden terrace; traditional cuisine; relaxed atmosphere. $ *Average main: 90 Kn* ✉ *Osor 64, Osor* ☎ *051/237–413* 🌐 *www.jazon.hr* ⏲ *Closed Oct.–Easter. No lunch.*

$$$$ MEDITERRANEAN Fodor's Choice ★

✕ **Konoba Bukaleta.** Cres is famous for its lamb, and although the majority of restaurants have it on the menu, Bukaleta is *the* place for the best on the island. Located in the small village of Loznati, just 10 km (6 miles) south of Cres Town, Bukaleta has been run by the same family for over 30 years. **Known for:** the place for lamb; friendly service; casual ambience. $ *Average main: 100 Kn* ✉ *Loznati 9a, Loznati* ☎ *051/571–606* ⏲ *Closed Oct.–Apr.*

$$$$ SEAFOOD ✕ **Riva.** The colorful square on the edge of Cres Town harbor is lined with many restaurants serving seafood, pasta, and risotto, and Riva is an excellent choice. Tables edge out onto the flagstones of the square, meaning the steady stream of strollers through the town will eye your plate with appreciative glances. **Known for:** fresh seafood; harbor view terrace. $ *Average main: 130 Kn* ✉ *Riva creskih kapetana 13, Cres Town* ☎ *051/571–107* ⏲ *Closed Nov.–Easter.*

WHERE TO STAY

Reflecting its splendid, undeveloped nature, Cres offers very few hotels, though there are plenty of apartments and guest rooms available for rent on the island.

$$ HOTEL **Hotel Kimen.** Tucked away in a shady pine forest just a stone's throw from the town beach and a 10-minute walk from the center, Kimen's four stories provide the only hotel accommodation in Cres Town. **Pros:** enviable position on an attractive cove; close to town center. **Cons:** smallish rooms; a bit outdated. $ *Rooms from: €130* ✉ *Melin I 16, Cres Town* ☎ *051/573–305* 🌐 *www.hotel-kimen.com* ⏲ *Closed mid-Oct.–Apr.* *128 rooms* *Breakfast.*

$ HOTEL **Zlatni lav.** A delightful 20-minute drive south from Cres Town, in the small, west coast resort of Martinšćica, Zlatni lav is a large, new building looking across 300 feet of land to the Adriatic. **Pros:** spectacular views; friendly staff. **Cons:** far from any nightlife; breakfast can be improved upon. $ *Rooms from: €120* ✉ *Martinšćica 18d, Martinšcica* ☎ *051/574–020* 🌐 *www.hotel-zlatni-lav.com* ⏲ *Closed mid-Oct.–Apr.* *29 rooms* *Breakfast.*

NIGHTLIFE AND PERFORMING ARTS

The half-dozen or so bars around the main harbor are great for casual drinking and chatting while you sit outside on balmy evenings listening to the clinking chains of boats. Head inside for quicker quaffing and shouting above Croatian high-energy pop music, where you'll share the space with German yachtsmen. If you're looking for livelier options, unfortunately you're on entirely the wrong piece of land for that sort of nonsense.

SPORTS AND THE OUTDOORS

BOATING

Alan Excursion Boat. This wooden sailing ship offers differing routes around the island's coast. A full-day trip to Blue Cave including a lunch and selected drinks costs 270 Kn. The ship offers regularly scheduled sailings. ✉ *Cres Harbor* ☎ *091/257–1070.*

CYCLING

Camp Kovačine. The staff at Camp Kovačine, which is nicely set under shady pines and right on the main town beach, can rent you bikes and boats, organize diving trips, beach volleyball, and even paragliding.

✉ *Melin I/20, Cres Town* ☎ *051/573–150 sales office, 051/571–423 front desk* 🌐 *www.camp-kovacine.com* ⊗ *Closed mid-Oct.–Mar.*

DIVING

Diving Cres. If you prefer to explore beneath the waves, Diving Cres can be found in the Camp Kovačine, about a 10-minute walk from the harbor. A single-orientation dive can be tried for €60. ✉ *Campsite Kovačine, Melin I/20, Cres Town* ☎ *051/571–706* 🌐 *www.diving.de.*

LOŠINJ

Mali Lošinj is 55 km (35 miles) from Cres Town.

As you approach the southern tip of Cres, you'll see the steep slopes of Osorčica Mountain on nearby Lošinj. Sheltered from poor weather by the Alps and closer ranges such as the Velebit, the excellent climate prompted the creation of a health resort here in 1892.

Blink and you might miss the bridge that connects Cres to Lošinj, unless you happen to arrive when the span is raised to allow a ship through the narrow channel that splits the two islands. In fact, until Roman times the two islands were one, connected near Osor. Mother Nature's inconsiderate arrangement did much to frustrate trade ships; entire vessels would be hauled across the few feet of land that blocked the route here rather than sail around the southern tip of the archipelago. Eventually, some bright spark decided to cut the present-day channel, opening the shipping lanes. Lošinj is an elongated, low-lying island covered with a pine forest. Viewed from the hills of Cres, the slim green outline of the main island and its surrounding islets, with a backbone of hills in the middle, resembles a long frog splayed out in the water, basking in the sun and contrasting beautifully with the water. Lošinj's past and present are very much connected to the shipping industry. The sea captains who populated the towns of Veli and Mali Lošinj when the island reached its golden age in the 19th century are very much responsible for bringing exotic plant life here from around the world and for building the fine villas that have made this a colorful destination for vacationers, who contribute much more to the island's economy today. The smaller islands that make up the archipelago include Unije, Susak, and Ilovik—all of which are large enough to provide some type of accommodation—and even smaller islands such as Vele and Male Srakane, Orjule, and Sveti Petar, which can be reached by tourist boats from the resorts on Lošinj.

EXPLORING

Čikat Bay. The road that runs along the Mali Lošinj harbor leads to Čikat Bay, a pine-covered area dotted with impressive Habsburg-era villas and pebbled beach coves. Nearby hotels and campsites, plus good parking, lots of cafés, and ice-cream stands make these beaches popular. There's a gracious promenade along the bay that's perfect for strolling, a windsurfing school for the adventurous, and paddleboat rentals. ✉ *Mali Lošinj.*

Kula (*The Tower*). Opposite the harbor, but now hidden by a row of houses, are the battlements of a defensive tower that dates from the 15th century. The squat construction, known as the Tower, now houses a museum and an art gallery staging temporary exhibitions by notable Croatian artists. The permanent exhibition tracing the town's history includes a copy of a Greek statue of Apoksiomen, which was discovered on the seabed in 1999. ✉ *Kaštel bb, Veli Lošinj* ☎ *051/236–594* 🌐 *www.muzej.losinj.hr* 🎫 *35 Kn* ⏲ *Closed Mon. mid-June–mid-Sept.; Sun. and Mon. mid-Sept.–mid-Oct. and Easter–mid-June.*

FAMILY Fodor's Choice ★ **Lošinj Marine Education Centre.** A community of around 180 bottlenose dolphins makes its home just off the coast of Lošinj, and the nonprofit Lošinj Marine Education Centre will tell you all about them. Excellent displays and videos take you right into their underwater world, fascinating stuff for kids and adults alike. You may even end up adopting your own dolphin, although you can't take it home with you. For a mere €30 you'll receive an adoption certificate, a photo of your adopted dolphin, membership for a year, and, of course, that warm fuzzy feeling of doing something good for the world. ✉ *Kaštel 24, Veli Lošinj* ☎ *051/604–666* 🌐 *www.blue-world.org* 🎫 *20 Kn* ⏲ *Closed Sun. in May, June, and Sept.; weekends Oct.–Apr.*

5

Mali Lošinj. With 8,000 inhabitants sheltered around an inlet, Mali Lošinj is the largest island settlement in the Adriatic. In the 19th century, Mali and Veli Lošinj experienced a golden age, when many wealthy sea captains lived on the island. Brightening the waterfront, the mansions and villas they constructed contribute greatly to the towns' appeal. A number of attractive churches will catch your gaze as you wander around town. Somewhat scruffy and announcing its presence with a tall square tower that tapers to a spike at the summit, the 15th-century **St. Martin's Church** was the original centerpiece around which the town was built. The cemetery it lords over amalgamates much of the history of the town. If you wish to dig a bit deeper, **The Church of Our Little Lady** (aka Church of the Nativity of Our Lord) houses many fine examples of religious art. ✉ *Mali Lošinj, Mali Lošinj* 🌐 *www.visitlosinj.hr.*

Miomirisni otočki vrt (*Garden of Fine Scents*). After a few days of dipping your toes in the water and basking in the sun, you might be itching for a diversionary outing. The Miomirisni otočki vrt is a pleasant place to spend the afternoon—rain or shine—sitting on the terrace admiring the sea of lavender on the hilltop. A donkey, a rabbit, and a small sheep delight visitors, especially children. A small shop in a wooden building sells organic products like soaps, marmalades, and of course, lavender oil. ✉ *Bukovica 6, Mali Lošinj* ☎ *098/326–519* 🌐 *www.miomirisni-vrt.hr* 🎫 *Free* ⏲ *Closed Jan. and Feb.*

Veli Lošinj. The sea captains of Veli Lošinj evidently preferred to escape their working environment during their time off, and thus built their villas away from the waterfront, surrounding themselves with exotic plants brought back from their travels. Archduke Karl Stephen built a winter residence in Veli Lošinj; it's now a sanatorium surrounded by wonderful gardens, again with a range of exotic plants and an arboretum. It's possible to stay in the sanatorium, even for the healthy. A

CLOSE UP

Slow Down: Islands of Lošinj

If the pace of life on the major islands is too hectic, knock your engine down to quarter-speed and head out to one of the tiny islands that pepper the seas around the coast of Lošinj. The island of **Unije** is by far the largest, managing to fit in a population of 90, although many of them are summer-only residents. The tiny town of the same name has a few restaurants settled around a large pebble bay, although exploring the northern coasts, by foot or by boat, should reveal many private swimming spots. **Ilovik** is the southernmost island of the group. Its nickname, "Island of Flowers," is accurate; oleanders and roses surround almost every home. Watch yachts at close quarters cutting through the channel between Ilovik and the islet of Sveti Petar, on which there was once a convent. The graveyard remains, and burial processions by fishing boat still take place. Paržine, on the southeastern coast, has a large sandy beach.

If you're from New Jersey, you may have a good chance of being related to one of the 188 people living on **Sušak** since many folk from here have settled in the Garden State. Sušak, flung farther out into the sea than any of the other islands, is a very different beast. First, while the rest of the Kvarner is composed of limestone karst, Sušak consists entirely of sand, so its coast is far gentler both in elevation and indentation. Not wanting to be outdone, the population retains a distinctive character and culture. The only wheeled transport on the island are wheelbarrows.

short walk beyond the main harbor is the little fishing cove of Rovenska. Beyond, there's a pebble beach and some nice restaurants. The breakwater was established by Habsburg archduke Maximilian. ✉ *Veli Lošinj, Veli Lošinj.*

Church of St. Anthony the Hermit. The intimate harbor is the centerpiece of Veli Lošinj, at the entrance to which is the delightful Church of St. Anthony the Hermit, with a separate bell tower in pink and cream stone. Built on the site of a former church in 1774, the church has always had a congregation of seafarers, who have filled it with religious art and altars from spots such as Venice. ✉ *On the Veli Lošinj waterfront* ⏲ *Closed Sun. and Sept.–July.*

WHERE TO EAT

$$$$ MEDITERRANEAN

✕ **Artatore.** Ten km (6 miles) north of Mali Lošinj, in the small village of Artatore, you'll find the restaurant of the same name. Locals claim the restaurant, which they call *Kod Janje* (Chez Janje), is the best on the entire island. **Known for:** a seafood lover's paradise; longevity: the place has been open for 45 years. $ *Average main: 200 Kn* ✉ *Artatore 132, Mali Lošinj* ☎ *051/232–932* ⏲ *Closed Nov.–Easter.*

$$$$ SEAFOOD Fodor's Choice ★

✕ **Baracuda.** Many of the yachts that line the harbor unload their human cargo at this small restaurant, which enjoys a big reputation for fresh fish dinners. Tuna carpaccio, shark on the grill, and lobster *na buzaru* (cooked with wine) are all great. **Known for:** fresh fish and seafood;

great location on the marina; friendly staff. *Average main: 130 Kn* ✉ *Priko 31, Mali Lošinj* ☎ *051/233–309* ⏲ *Closed mid-Oct.–Apr.*

$$$$ MEDITERRANEAN **Bora Bar.** Creative Italian dishes like tuna carpaccio with celery root and truffles are what you'll find at this friendly restaurant in the Rovenska bay. The place bills itself as a "tartuferia," which is a cozy café that serves snacks, sandwiches, and dishes that feature truffles. **Known for:** homemade pasta; truffle-infused dishes; seafront terrace. *Average main: 130 Kn* ✉ *Rovenska 3, Veli Lošinj* ☎ *051/867–544* 🌐 *www.borabar.net* ⏲ *Closed Oct.–Easter.*

WHERE TO STAY

$$$ HOTEL **Hotel Apoksiomen.** Named after a Greek statue that was recovered from the seabed near Mali Lošinj in 1999, this renovated villa imposes itself on the seafront close to the main square and offers a good example of how to run a small establishment. **Pros:** seafront location in the heart of town; delicious pastries at the café. **Cons:** rooms don't match the gorgeous hotel exterior; parking is off-site and costs 90 Kn. *Rooms from: €180* ✉ *Riva Lošinjskih kapetana 1, Mali Lošinj* ☎ *051/520–820* 🌐 *www.apoksiomen.com* ⏲ *Closed Nov.–Apr.* *25 rooms* *Breakfast.*

$$$ HOTEL **Vitality Hotel Punta.** The attractive colored blocks of this newly renovated four-star property in Veli Lošinj line the seashore in a style that complements the island's traditional architecture surprisingly well. **Pros:** good on-site facilities; near both the sea and the town of Veli Lošinj. **Cons:** small pool complex; large hotel complex can feel a bit impersonal. *Rooms from: €200* ✉ *Šestavine 17, Veli Lošinj* ☎ *051/662–000* 🌐 *www.losinj-hotels.com* ⏲ *Closed Nov.–Mar.* *289 rooms* *Breakfast.*

NIGHTLIFE AND PERFORMING ARTS

Both Mali and Vela Lošinj offer a healthy selection of bars, where you can sit outside on warm evenings, sip drinks, and chat. Those looking for brighter lights had better move on to Krk or the mainland.

SPORTS AND THE OUTDOORS

BIKING

Rent-A-Bike Junior (*Rent-A-Bike Best Price*). You can rent bikes for 15 Kn per hour or 65 Kn per day. ✉ *Velopin 15, Mali Lošinj* ☎ *099/409–9943.*

DIVING AND SAILING

Diver Sport Center. The center offers a full-day guided diving boat cruise with lunch and drinks for about 660 Kn per person. ✉ *Uvala Čikat 13, Mali Lošinj* ☎ *051/233–900* 🌐 *www.diver.hr.*

FLIGHTSEEING

Airport Lošinj. To put it all in perspective, from Airport Lošinj you can take a panoramic 15-minute flight over the archipelago for about 500 Kn. The airport is open year-round. ✉ *Privlaka 19, Mali Lošinj* ☎ *051/231–666* 🌐 *www.airportmalilosinj.hr.*

KRK

Krk Town is 50 km (31 miles) southeast of Rijeka.

It's no surprise—since Krk is one of the largest Croatian islands, hosts the regional airport, and is connected to the mainland by a bridge—that the robust island is one of the most developed in the country. The dusty edges and agricultural interior get very busy during the high season, and if you visit then you will likely find yourself in traffic jams along the snaking routes between the resort towns. Add the sight of the oil refinery on the mainland near the bridge and the terminal for tankers near Omišalj on the northern coast of the island, and you may think twice about heading here. The sights aren't exactly what you'd call picturesque, but don't be put off so easily. Krk still offers many of the same delights found in the rest of the region: great beaches, interesting history, and pretty old towns. Although other islands may offer a slower pace, Krk compensates by offering more facilities and convenience. With numerous accommodation options and more entertainments, it may very well be the best choice for families with easily bored children in tow.

EXPLORING

Baška. On the southern end of the island, this town has a great beach as well as the conveniences of civilization. However, this means that you must sometimes fight to find a spot in season. The 2-km (1-mile) beach is fronted by houses (and hotels at the southern end), which are often painted in bright colors and adorned with interesting nooks and stairways, all lending a fun and slightly eccentric air to the town. Cute backstreets behind the houses offer a selection of nice cafés and ice-cream shops. ✉ *Baška* 🌐 *www.tz-baska.hr.*

Crkva Sv. Lucije (*Church of St. Lucy*). Driving into Baška, you'll pass through Bašcanska draga, and then find yourself in Jurandvor. While on this road, take the chance to visit the Church of St. Lucy, which has achieved cultlike status since the discovery of the glagolithic Baška Tablet on its grounds in 1851. ✉ *Jurandvor* ☎ *051/860–184* 🌐 *www.azjurandvor.com* 🎫 *25 Kn* ⏲ *Closed Nov.–Apr.*

Krk Town. In terms of its importance and the pride of the 4,000 locals, the island's capital could perhaps even be called a city. It's not completely clear when the old city walls were first built, but the oldest mention of the walls dates back to the 1st century BC. The present-day walls, however, date mainly to the Middle Ages. The city walls have four gates.

The seafront has a pleasant green area that takes you past cafés and a fish market. The main square, **Vela Placa,** is just behind the first row of houses. There's a beach underneath the town walls with a lovely view of the town.

The **old town hall** on Vela Placa was built in the 15th century. Its clock shows all 24 hours: daytime on the upper part, nighttime on the lower.

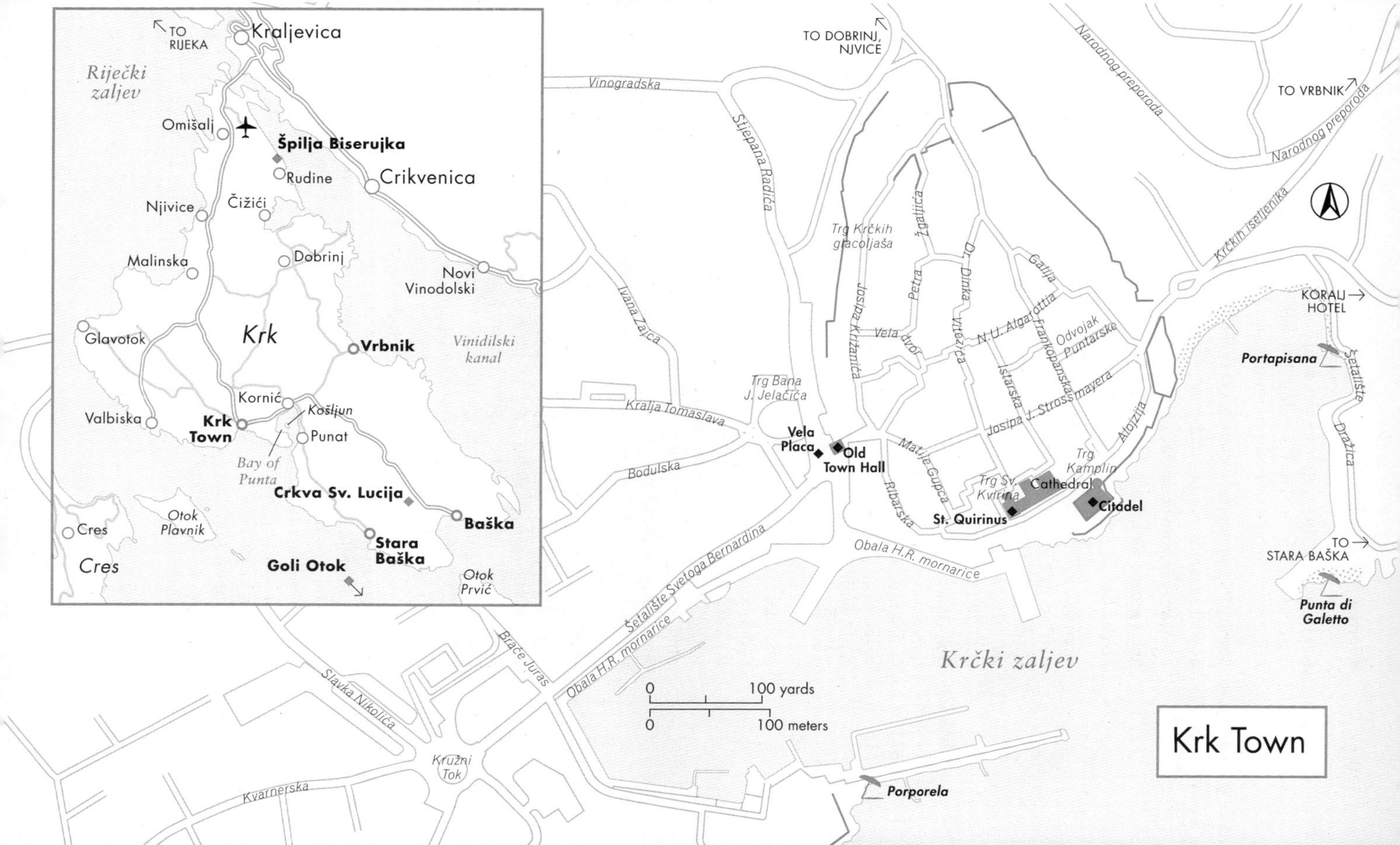
Krk Town
Kraljevica
TO RIJEKA
Riječki zaljev
Omišalj
Špilja Biserujka
Rudine
Crikvenica
Njivice
Čižići
Malinska
Dobrinj
Novi Vinodolski
Glavotok
Krk
Vrbnik
Vinidilski kanal
Kornić
Košljun
Valbiska
Krk Town
Punat
Bay of Punta
Crkva Sv. Lucija
Baška
Cres
Otok Plavnik
Stara Baška
Cres
Goli Otok
Otok Prvić
TO DOBRINJ, NJIVICE
Vinogradska
Narodnog preporoda
TO VRBNIK
Stjepana Radića
Trg Krčkih glacoljaša
Žgaljića
Dr. Dinka Vitezića
Petra
Josipa Križanića
Galija
Krčkih iseljenika
KORALJ HOTEL
Ivana Zajca
Vela dvor
N.U. Algarottia
Frankopanska
Odvojak Puntarske
Portapisana
Šetalište
Trg Bana J. Jelačića
Kralja Tomaslava
Istarska
Josipa J. Strossmayera
Atojzija
Dražica
Vela Placa
Old Town Hall
Matije Gupca
Trg Kamplin
Bodulska
Ribarska
Trg Sv. Kvirina
Cathedral
Citadel
St. Quirinus
TO STARA BAŠKA
Obala H.R. mornarice
Šetalište Svetoga Bernardina
Punta di Galetto
Brače Juras
Obala H.R. mornarice
Krčki zaljev
Slavka Nikolića
0
100 yards
0
100 meters
Kružni Tok
Kvarnerska
Porporela

Krk Town has two well-known visual anchors. The first is the imposing **citadel** that sits on Trg Kamplin. The bell tower of **St. Quirinus** is the other, with its angular onion dome typical of Krk. ✉ *Krk Town*.

NEED A BREAK

Stanic. This wonderful gallery is chockablock with works by local artists, as well as lamps, mirrors, and souvenirs. If you're not into shopping, you can simply remain downstairs at the café-bar, or the many other watering holes around Vela Placa. ✉ *Vela Placa 8, Krk Town* ☎ *051/220–052* 🌐 *www.helena.hr.*

Stara Baška. If you're looking for a more secluded spot, head to this town that sits just above the beaches that trim a wide cove and peninsula. The road here is a single track through the tiny village, so you may find yourself performing intricate maneuvers in your car should you be unlucky enough to meet the local water truck that keeps the houses supplied.

OFF THE BEATEN PATH

Goli Otok. Like Communist history? Consider a day trip to this uninhabited former Yugoslavian prison island just off the coast of Rab. Goli Otok means "naked island" and was so named for the lack of vegetation and habitable conditions on the island. After Tito broke ranks with Stalin in 1948, the island became infamous as a place where Yugoslav political prisoners were confined. Men were incarcerated here while women were taken to nearby Grgur island. The treatment of these prisoners is wholly unknown, as very few prisoners lived to tell of their experiences, but a stone quarry indicates that prisoners were forced to do hard labor quarrying stone. Conditions on Goli Otok were harsh, with blistering temperatures in the summer, and brutal *Bura* winds ripping across the barren island in the winter. Any mention of Goli Otok was strictly forbidden in Yugoslavia until after Tito's death. The prison was completely abandoned in 1989, but prison barracks remain there. You can make a short trip to this legendary gulag by taxi boat with one of the many charter companies in Baška or Punat on Krk island.

Špilja Biserujka (*Biserujka Cave*). North of Vrbnik, near Rudine, this cave is only one of many caverns on Krk; however, it's the only one open to the public. The stalactites, stalagmites, and calcine pillars inside are lighted for your pleasure. ✉ *½ km (1/3 mile) from Rudine* ☎ *098/211–630, 051/852–203* 🌐 *www.spilja-biserujka.com.hr* 🎫 *30 Kn* ⏲ *Closed Nov.–Apr.*

Vrbnik. Lovers of majestic views or high-diving should head to this clifftop town on the northeast coast. Clustered on a hilltop 157 feet above a small harbor, it's a mass of confusing, winding streets. The bumpy terrain means that staircases crop up around most corners. One of the oldest settlements on Krk, Vrbnik may be a little ramshackle, but it's utterly charming. That's certainly what the busloads of tourists seem to think anyway. Vrbnik's fragrance is of the vine; you'll see old barrels lying around everywhere. These might once have been filled with Žlahtina, a great white wine that some claim is the best to come from the Kvarner region. The vineyards are but a short hop from town.

WHERE TO EAT

In the summer you'll be sharing tables with busloads of tourists at many of Krk's best restaurants, all of which tend to be outside the capital. However, Krk Town has many restaurants that will serve you perfectly reasonable renditions of less ambitious fare, such as fish, pasta, and pizza.

$$$$ MEDITERRANEAN **Nada.** Considered top-notch by many islanders and Croatians who know their stuff, this tiny downstairs konoba provides an authentic Croatian atmosphere. The terrace is a great place to try Kvarner specialties and sample some of the island's best charcuterie and cheeses; a more elaborate meal can be had at the large restaurant upstairs. **Known for:** popular island restaurant; family-run; lovely terrace to chill with a glass of local wine. *Average main: 150 Kn* *Glavača 22, Vrbnik* *051/857–065* *www.nada-vrbnik.hr* *Closed Nov.–Easter.*

$$$$ MEDITERRANEAN **Pod Prevolt.** This small, family-run tavern, located in the village of Milohnići, is a bit off the beaten path, but it's well worth a detour. Its name, which means "under the vaulted porch," is inspired by the entrance to the traditional house. **Known for:** excellent homemade food; small, cozy, and family-run; off the beaten path. *Average main: 90 Kn* *Milohnići 21B, Malinska* *051/862–149* *Closed Oct.–Apr.*

$$$$ SEAFOOD Fodor's Choice ★ **Rivica.** One of the best-known restaurants in the region, Rivica has a long tradition but lacks any pretense. Try a poached fish fillet with fennel and olives while you sit on the terrace shaded from the sun. **Known for:** top-notch food; great location by the sea; friendly staff. *Average main: 130 Kn* *Ribarska obala 13, Njivice* *051/846–101* *www.rivica.hr* *Closed Dec.–Mar.*

WHERE TO STAY

$$$ HOTEL **Atrium Residence Baska.** Located just a few steps away from the famed Baška beach, Atrium Residence has spacious, well-appointed rooms and apartments. **Pros:** seafront location; great beach views; spacious rooms. **Cons:** standard rooms have French balconies; parking located at the sister hotel Corinthia; lack of in-hotel facilities (guests can use facilities of the nearby hotels). *Rooms from: €200* *Emila Geistlicha 39, Baška* *051/656–890 reception, 052/465–000 reservations* *www.valamar.com* *Closed Oct.–Apr.* *64 rooms* *Breakfast.*

$$ HOTEL **Hotel Kanajt.** Set in a 16th-century building that served as a bishop's residence and surrounded by palms, pine, and olive trees, this hotel in Punat has rooms that are modern, clean, and comfortable. **Pros:** comfortable rooms, some with really large terrace; relaxing garden; historic building; easy parking. **Cons:** good beaches are a bit away from the hotel; not all rooms have balcony. *Rooms from: €165* *Kanajt 5, Punat* *051/654–340* *www.kanajt.hr* *22 rooms* *Breakfast.*

$$$ HOTEL **Hotel Pinia Malinska.** Located in the small seaside village of Porat, just next to Malinska, this hotel has a wonderful setting by the sea, surrounded by greenery; the hotel's beach—a nice pebbly beach, though a bit on a small side—is just a few meters down. **Pros:** great location by the sea; good on-site restaurant; spacious rooms. **Cons:** hotel beach can get very busy in July and August; a bit far from the center of Malinska.

$ Rooms from: €200 ✉ Porat BB, Malinska ☎ 051/866–333 ⊕ www.hotel-pinia.hr ⊙ Closed Nov.–Apr. 45 rooms Some meals.

$$$ HOTEL FAMILY **Valamar Koralj Hotel.** For long days on the beach and all conveniences on tap, this hotel on the edge of Krk Town is a decent choice, though those who plan busy evenings may want to find somewhere closer to the center. **Pros:** great for families with kids in summer; good for couples off-season; peaceful location amid pine trees. **Cons:** small rooms; some rooms without balcony; better rooms quite pricey for the quality. *$ Rooms from: €175 ✉ Ul. Vlade Tomašiča, Krk Town ☎ 051/655–400 hotel, 052/465–000 reservations ⊕ www.valamar.com ⊙ Closed Oct.–Apr. 194 rooms Some meals.*

NIGHTLIFE

Krk Town and Baška are the places to head for relatively low-key drinks in the evening. The center of the capital and the stretch of town above the beach at Baška offer numerous bars with music and tables out under the stars. A firm family favorite, Krk is definitely not the place for cutting-edge nightlife. However, if you really can't live without getting your club fix, there are a couple of large venues offering house DJs. Note that clubs are open only in the summer months.

Cocktail Bar Volsonis. One of the livelier nightspots in Krk Town, this bar has the appropriate, though somewhat mysterious, ruins of a wonderful sacrificial altar to love goddess Venus down in the basement. In fact, all of Volsonis is incorporated into a 2,000-year-old archaeological site that the owners, Maria Elena and Goran, found under the house. Electronic music plays on weekends in the underground Catacombs, or you can chill out with a glass of wine, beer, or coffee in their secret garden. *✉ Vela Placa 8, Krk Town ☎ 051/880–249 ⊕ www.volsonis.hr.*

SPORTS AND THE OUTDOORS

BICYCLING

You can bike around the island for transportation or exercise.

Cycling Union Krk. The best place to rent a bicycle is at the Cycling Union, either in Krk, or at the Marina in Punat. *✉ Omišaljska 14, Krk Town ☎ 099/672–0424 ⊕ www.cyclingunionkrk.info.*

DIVING

Dive Center Krk. The most interesting sights in Kvarner Bay are wrecks. At Divesport on the Bay of Punta, a full-day diving trip (two dives) sets you back about 400 Kn, plus 185 Kn for equipment rental, if you need it. *✉ Dunat 50, Kornic ☎ 051/867–303 ⊕ www.dive-center-krk.com.*

HIKING

There are many marked paths in the area around Baška. For a longer hike, consider visiting the splendid remote villages at Vela and Mala Luka; take this path as part of a group, and be aware that the section of the trail through the canyon may flood if there's rain. For some nice hikes around Baška, consider the path from Baška to Mjesec Hill (5½ km [3 miles], 2 hours). Offering spectacular views over the bay, this easy route passes by St. John's Church, where you can take a breather while you contemplate higher things. The route from Baška to Jurandvor (5 km [3 miles], 2 hours) takes you through the Baška Valley and leaves you with a visit to the Church of St. Lucy, home of the Baška Tablet. The short hike between Baška and Stara Baška will give you a little exercise; a delightful stretch of small, quiet beaches is the reward for a short hike.

Krk Tourist Office. For more hiking information, contact the Krk Tourist Office. ✉ *Trg Sv. Kvirina 1, Krk Town* ☎ *051/221–359* 🌐 *www.krk.hr.*

WATERSKIING

Cable Krk. Always fancied spraying majestic jets of water across the aquamarine seas, but sorting out a boat and someone to drive just seems too much trouble? Well, the answer lies with Cable Krk, on a calm bay just outside the resort of Punat, toward Krk Town. A large wooden pier with a bar and restaurant to entertain your companions is the gateway to a cableway, which is not much different than a drag-lift at a ski resort. The cable pulls you around a short course, with instruction on hand to help you get your sea legs. One hour costs about 100 Kn. ✉ *Dunat, Kornic* ☎ *091/262–7303* 🌐 *www.wakeboarder.hr.*

5

DELNICE

50 km (31 miles) east of Rijeka.

Delnice, which sits on the road between Rijeka and Zagreb, is itself not much to write home about. However, it makes a good base for exploring the mountains of the Gorski kotar region that sits above Kvarner Bay. This is the place to head for hiking trails that swing away from civilization. It's also a convenient stopover if you're taking the slow route back to Zagreb and your transport home. Take a day or two to swap the brilliant blue domination and ramshackle culture of the coast for the bright green mountains and hearty way of life in Gorski kotar.

WHERE TO EAT

$$$$ EASTERN EUROPEAN

✕ **Volta.** The small town of Fužine is very close to Delnice and is well known for its pine-bordered lake. *Volta,* which means vaults, tells you exactly what to expect from this vaulted, cellar-style dining room, fronted by a conservatory. The simple, publike interior is a cut above most of the restaurants in the Gorski kotar, which tend to be a little old-fashioned. **Known for:** horse and game meat; local crowd; hearty meals. Ⓢ *Average main: 100 Kn* ✉ *Franja Račkog 8, Fužine* ☎ *051/830–030* ⊙ *Closed Feb.*

WHERE TO STAY

$ B&B/INN

Mountain Center Petehovac. There is no better place to stay in Gorski kotar than up in the hills, surrounded by thick pine forest, and that's exactly where you'll find Mountain Center Petehovac. **Pros:** location in nature; good and very affordable food; views over the surrounding area. **Cons:** basic facilities; basic rooms. Ⓢ *Rooms from: €60* ✉ *Polane 1a* ☎ *051/814–901* 🌐 *www.petehovac.com.hr* *18 rooms* *Breakfast.*

SPORTS AND THE OUTDOORS

HIKING

Delnice is a good base for hiking around Risnjak and the Gorski kotar range, which have many marked walking and hiking paths.

RAFTING AND CANOEING

Gorski Tok. The Kupa River either meanders or rushes down through the mountains toward the coast. You can join expeditions organized by Gorski Tok, which start at 10 am and 2:30 pm from a point near Delnice and tackle the rough or the smooth sections of the river. The company also runs canoe safari trips, in case the water level is low. ✉ *Kralja Tomislava 11, Brod na Kupi* ☎ *098/177–2585* 🌐 *www.gorski-tok.hr.*

RAB

120 km (75 miles) southeast of Rijeka.

Fodor's Choice ★ Rab presents an utterly fascinating landscape. When you drive southward, down the Magistrala, you see that the island resembles the humped back of a diving sea monster. Once you've mounted this beast, via a short ferry ride from Stinica to Mišnjak, you travel along the center of its back, which is almost entirely bald to the north, letting all its hair hang out to the south. The high northern coast, which bears the brunt of the northern Bora winds, is dry, rocky, and barren. Crouching below this crusty ledge, the southern half of the island could hardly differ more, and has possibly the lushest terrain found on any Croatian island. Low, green hills dip into the seas, while the ancient Dundo forest grows so voraciously that it's almost impossible to walk in.

EXPLORING

Sitting on a narrow peninsula halfway up the island's southern coast, the compact, well-preserved medieval village is best known for its distinctive skyline of four elegant bell towers, and its many churches. Author Rebecca West, who traveled through Yugoslavia in the 1930s, called Rab Town "one of the most beautiful cities of the world" in her masterpiece, *Black Lamb and Grey Falcon.* Closed to traffic, the narrow cobbled streets of the Old Town, which are lined with Romanesque churches and patrician palaces, can be explored in an hour's leisurely stroll. The urban layout is simple: three longitudinal streets run parallel to the waterfront promenade and are linked together by steep passages traversing the hillside. The lower street is Donja ulica, the middle street Srednja ulica, and the upper street Gornja ulica.

The oldest part of Rab Town is **Kaldanac,** the very tip of the narrow peninsula that juts into the sea. From here the ancient city grew in the 15th century to include Varoš, farther north, and later was widened and fortified by walls during a brief Venetian rule.

Komrčar Park. On the edge of town, the green expanse of Komrčar Park, laid out in the 19th century, offers avenues lined with pine trees for gentle strolling and access down to the sea. Although the Old Town and its immediate surroundings are Rab's chief treasures, the city is

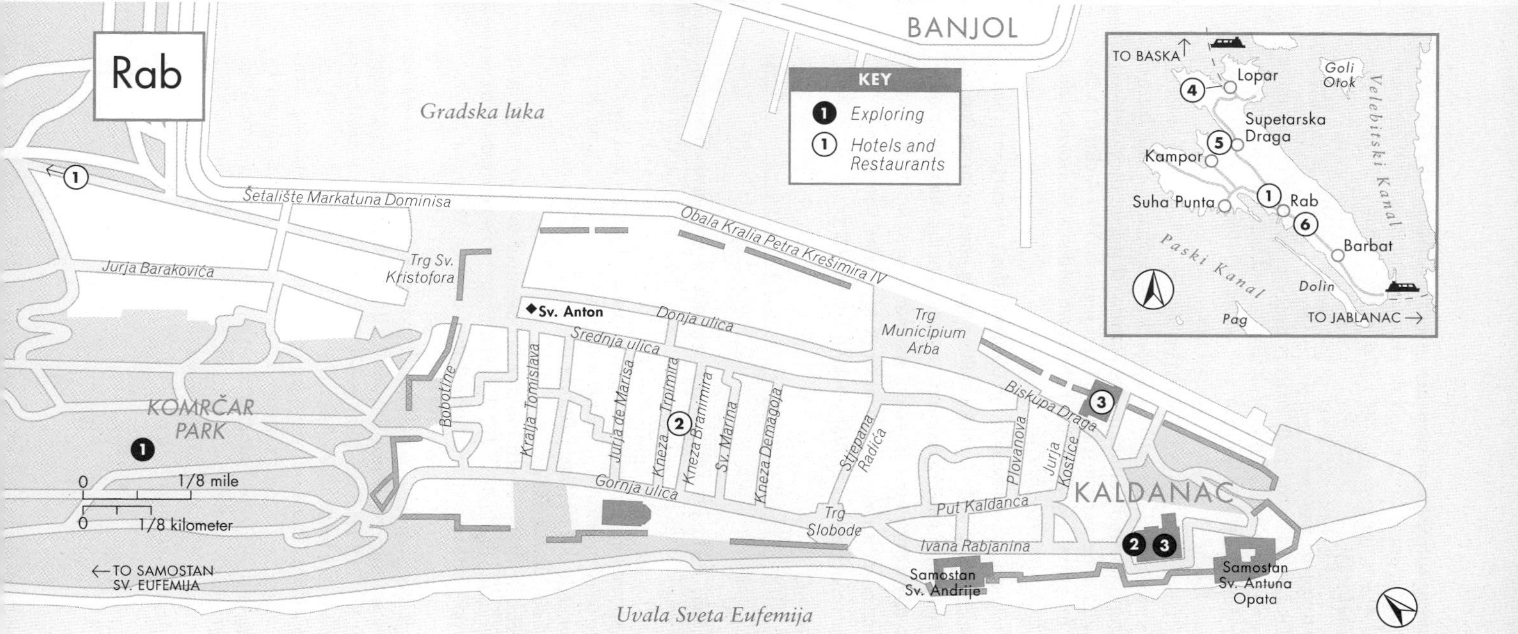

Exploring	▼
Komrčar Park	1
Sveta Marija Velika	3
Veli Zvonik	2

Restaurants	▼
Konoba Rab	2
Marco Polo	6
Restaurant More	5

Hotels	▼
Arbiana Hotel	3
Hotel Imperial	1
Tourist Resort San Marino	4

also a gateway to the great stretches of beach that rim the towns of Kampor, Suha Punta, Lopar, and neighboring islands. ✉ *Northwest of the Old Town, just behind the seafront promenade, Obala Kralja Petra Krešimira IV.*

Sveta Marija Velika (*Cathedral of St. Mary*). The Romanesque Sveta Marija Velika, built in the 12th century and consecrated by the pope in 1177, is the biggest church in Rab Town, and was built on the site of Roman ruins. ✉ *Ivana Rabljanina* 🌐 *www.rab-visit.com* ⏲ *Closed Oct.–May and June–Sept. from 1–7:30 pm.*

Veli Zvonik (*Great Bell Tower*). The tallest and most beautiful of Rab's campaniles, the freestanding Veli Zvonik forms part of the former cathedral complex and dominates the southwest side of the peninsula. Built in the 12th century, it stands 85 feet high. **■ TIP→ A climb to the top offers breathtaking views over the town and sea.** ✉ *Gornja ulica* 🎫 *15 kn* ⏲ *Closed Oct.–May.*

NEED A BREAK

Kuća rapske torte. Tucked away in the Old Town, this café-cum-shop has a wonderful courtyard that's ideal for chilling out in after exploring Rab Town. Don't miss the famed *rapska torta*, a traditional Croatian cake made of almonds, maraschino liqueur, lemon, and orange peel. Inside you can see first hand how the cake is made, or stock up on wine, homemade cookies, and other pastries. ✉ ***Dinka Dokule 2*** ☎ ***051/771–122*** ⏲ ***Closed Nov.–Apr.***

WHERE TO EAT

$$$$ MEDITERRANEAN

✕ **Konoba Rab.** Tucked away in a narrow side street between Srednja ulica and Gornja ulica in Rab Town, this konoba is warm and inviting, with exposed-stone walls and rustic furniture. Grilled fish and meat are the house specialties, along with a good choice of pastas and risottos. **Known for:** cozy interior; traditional food; hard-to-find location. [$] *Average main: 130 Kn* ✉ *Kneza Branimira 3* ☎ *051/725–666* ⏲ *Closed Nov. and Feb. No lunch Sun.*

$$$$ MEDITERRANEAN

✕ **Marco Polo.** With its superb food and convenient location right next to the large campsite Padova III, this restaurant draws crowds in to its large outdoor terrace and small but elegant interior. Veggies are homegrown, seafood is local and always fresh, and meat dishes like Viennese schnitzel or beef tenderloin never disappoint. **Known for:** extensive menu; nice setting; good portions and affordable prices. [$] *Average main: 100 Kn* ✉ *Banjol 468, Banjol* ☎ *051/725–846* 🌐 *www.marco-polo-rab.com* ⏲ *Closed Oct.–Apr.*

$$$$ MEDITERRANEAN

✕ **Restaurant More.** This family-owned restaurant has an amazing location with seating right on the quay. The fish served here is caught by the owner, so the phrase "catch of the day" really means something. **Known for:** lovely waterfront location; fresh fish and other seafood. [$] *Average main: 100 Kn* ✉ *Supetarska Draga 321, Supetarska Draga* ☎ *051/776–202* 🌐 *www.more-rab.com* ⏲ *Closed Oct.–Apr.*

WHERE TO STAY

You'll see plenty of private rooms advertised on the Internet, as well as signs on the side of the road. If you want to seek out private accommodations, perhaps the best place to start is the website of the tourist office in the closest main town. Costs vary wildly, but private rooms are almost always a cheaper alternative to hotels.

$$$ HOTEL **Arbiana Hotel.** It's hard to imagine a more romantic setting than this harborside inn in a perfectly restored medieval villa with balconies overlooking Rab marina and the hills of Barbat in the distance. **Pros:** boutique-hotel feel; personal service. **Cons:** no pool or beach access; not all rooms have balconies. *Rooms from: €200 Obala Kralja Petra Kresimira IV br.12 051/725–563 www.arbianahotel.com Closed mid-Oct.–mid-Apr. 28 rooms Breakfast.*

$$$ HOTEL **Hotel Imperial.** Amid the greenery of Komrčar Park, this peaceful 1930s-era resort hotel is just a stone's throw from the center of Rab Town. **Pros:** good location in a wooded park near Rab Town; good facilities; lovely historical building. **Cons:** old-fashioned design; limited parking spaces in high season; double rooms a bit smallish. *Rooms from: €180 Palit 051/724–522 www.imperialrab.com 136 rooms Breakfast.*

$$$ HOTEL FAMILY **Tourist Resort San Marino.** A complex of five hotels stretches across the peninsula at this family-friendly resort wrapping around the gentle Paradise Beach. **Pros:** access to Paradise Beach couldn't be better; good choice of on-site activities. **Cons:** sprawling complex lacks personality; rooms are on the small side and lack luxuries. *Rooms from: €180 Lopar 408, Lopar 051/775–144 www.imperialrab.com Closed Oct.–May 495 rooms Breakfast.*

NIGHTLIFE

For such a small town, Rab has a surprisingly active nightlife, although it's certainly not extreme by any stretch of the imagination. Trg Municipium Arbe on the waterfront is lined with bars and can get noisy as the night progresses. All-night house parties are found at Santos Beach Club on Puderica Beach, 2 km (1 mile) from Barbat toward the ferry terminal.

Forum. A favorite among locals, Forum is short on luxury, but not on entertainment, beers, and great cocktails. *Donja 9a.*

San Antonio. Those after a little glitz to show off their suntan can head to the center of Rab Town nightlife at San Antonio. *Trg Municipium Arba 4 051/724–145 www.sanantonio-club.com.*

SPORTS AND THE OUTDOORS

BOATING

Sahara Tours. Whether you want to explore the Croatian coast or dive into the clear blue waters of the Adriatic Sea, Sahara Tours can help with motorboat rentals. Prices start at about 600 Kn per day, depending on the power. *Lopar BB, Lopar 051/775–633 www.sahara-lopar.com.*

DIVING

Aqua Sport. A single dive costs about 350 Kn including equipment; a full diving course costs 2,440 Kn. In addition, you can dive at various sites from their boat, and your nondiving companions are welcome to go along for the ride. ✉ *Supetarska Draga 331, Supetarska Draga* ☎ *051/776–145* 🌐 *www.aquasport.hr*.

ZADAR AND NORTHERN DALMATIA

Updated by Sierra Christianson and Ivan Verunica

Safely protected from the northern Adriatic shore and continental Croatia by the imposing Velebit Mountain, northern Dalmatia offers a whole new set of aesthetic and cultural values. The islands get smaller and more abundant and the architecture, which varies between Roman, Venetian, socialist and modern influences, still carries the elegance of locally quarried limestone. Make Zadar, a fast-growing historical city, the focal point of your sojourn, but do not overlook Nin and the islands, especially Kornati and Telašćica. Admirers of intact, rough nature will revel in the Paklenica National Park.

Where exactly does Northern Dalmatia begin? Zadar may be the region's cultural and urban capital—it is, after all, the first sizable city you encounter in Dalmatia on your way south from Zagreb or Rijeka—but it is not where the region begins, either culturally or geographically. Look instead to the southern reaches of Velebit Mountain, where that coastal range gives way to the flat, sandy coastline of Nin and environs. Practically speaking, though, you enter Dalmatia proper when you cross the long, bright-red span of the Maslenica Bridge going south on the route from Zagreb to Zadar.

Though it's easy enough to drive on straight to Zadar, you won't regret stopping for a visit in Nin. While today it's an unassuming little town with well-preserved 17th-century architecture, more than 1,000 years ago—and for centuries afterward—it was one of the most important Croatian towns of all.

Much of the region is not on the mainland at all but rather comprises the Zadar archipelago, including Pag Island, and, farther south, the Adriatic's largest archipelago, Kornati National Park. Farther inland, only miles from the coast, is a sweeping expanse of countryside still visibly recovering from the Yugoslav war of the 1990s, where tourists rarely tread. Benkovac, the region's center, is home to an imposing 16th-century fort; nearby are the massive ruins of the ancient city of Asseria. Zadar itself, with its mix of Roman, Venetian, communist-era, and modern architecture, has a bustling and beautiful historic center and is also the main point of access by ferry to the islands, which include the beautiful Telašćica Nature Park.

GREAT ITINERARIES

Unless you stop at Paklenica National Park, head straight for Zadar and work outward from there, depending on how much time you have. It's easier to take day trips to visit the closer parts of the Zadar archipelago, as well as Nin. To see the further reaches of the archipelago, stay over in Sali or plan on doing a full nine-hour boat tour out of Zadar. Keep Benkovac and environs in mind if you have some time to spare and might appreciate a look at the relatively tourist-free interior, including the ruins of the ancient city of Asseria.

IF YOU HAVE 3 DAYS

Plan on two nights in **Zadar** with excursions to the island of Dugo Otok or Ugljan Island, which are in the **Zadar archipelago.** For your final day and night, go either to **Sali** to see **Telašćica Nature Park** or, if you're hankering for mountains, spend one night in Starigrad and see **Paklenica National Park** (unless you've already stopped there on the way south or might do so on your return north).

IF YOU HAVE 5 DAYS

Spend your first three days as outlined in the three-day itinerary, but spend the third night in Zadar. Then spend one night in **Starigrad** or environs to devote some quality time to Paklenica National Park, and do a loop that includes a night on **Pag Island,** too.

IF YOU HAVE 7 DAYS

Follow the itinerary above, adding a trip to the island of **Molat** for a few active days of paddling, biking, and exploring the island's maritime history.

6

ORIENTATION AND PLANNING

GETTING ORIENTED

Getting to Zadar is easiest by car. Be it on the A1 highway from Zagreb, down a winding coastal road from Rijeka or from nearby Split, the roads are good and there are signs aplenty. If you are skipping the Kvarner region, Croatian Airlines operates flights from Pula as well as from Zagreb, and the Zadar intl is also served from England and Germany during the summer months.

WHEN TO GO

If you don't mind crowds, midsummer is a good time to visit Northern Dalmatia—when the Adriatic is at its optimal temperature for beach-going, and when you can also delight in the varied music, dance, and drama of the Zadar Summer Theatre (late June to early August), the Full Moon Festival (late July) in and around Zadar, the Pag Carnival (late July or early August), and Sali's annual Saljske užance, which features raucous, horn-blown "donkey music" and donkey races (early August). However, if you don't mind missing out on midsummer culture and crowds, late spring to early autumn is preferable—when you can relax on relatively quiet beaches and enjoy discounts of up to 20% on accommodations relative to high season prices.

PLANNING

GETTING HERE AND AROUND

If you're driving or bussing it from the north, you can stop for an excursion to Pag Island and at Paklenica National Park before arriving in Zadar. The pretty little town of Nin, meanwhile, is just a half-hour north of Zadar and most easily done as a day trip (or even a half-day trip). Though many daily ferries can take you to the Zadar archipelago, Sali (two hours from Zadar by ferry) is a good place to base yourself for a night or two if you want to explore the outer reaches and have the best access to Telašćica Nature Park. A drive or bus trip to Murter will get you within a short boat ride of the spectacular Kornati National Park.

AIR TRAVEL

Zadar's airport is in Zemunik Donji, 9 km (5½ miles) southeast of the city. Croatia Airlines, which offers service between Zadar and Zagreb as well as Paris and other European cities, runs buses (20 Kn one-way) between the airport, the city bus station, and the harborside near the ferry port on the Old Town's peninsula.

Fodor's Choice ★ **Zadar Archipelago.** This Zadar-based company runs day trips by boat from Zadar to the islands of Kornati National Park. All tours have a maximum of 12 travelers, allowing for a more individual approach rather than the general tourist offering of uncomfortably packed boats. ✉ *Obala kneza Trpimira 2, Zadar* ☎ *99/627–3333* 🌐 *www.zadar-archipelago.com.*

BOAT AND FERRY TRAVEL

Jadrolinija's local ferries (*trajektne linije*) and passenger boats (*brodske linije*) run daily routes that connect Zadar not only with the surrounding islands but also with Southern Dalmatia and Italy. The offices are by the Harbor Gate in the city walls, across from the ferry port.

Jadrolinija runs ferry routes from the port of Zadar, just outside the city walls on the western side of the Old Town, to Sali. The trip, which takes about two hours and costs 40 Kn, takes you initially south in the Zadarski kanal, then through a narrow strait between Ugljan and Pašman islands before proceeding to the island of Dugi Otok, where you stop briefly in Zaglav before heading on to Sali. If you don't want to base yourself in Murter, you can take a cruise straight from the Borik marina just outside Zadar all the way to Kornati National Park, that almost mythical archipelago even farther south. The *Zadar Archipelago,* which holds 12 passengers, will take you on a full-day journey (9 am to 7 pm) to the national park, including stops at Telašćica Nature Reserve, Vrulje bay, Sali and the islands of Mana and Levrnaka.

Contacts Jadrolinija. ✉ *Liburnska obala 7, Zadar* ☎ *023/254–800* 🌐 *www.jadrolinija.hr.*

BUS TRAVEL

Though sometimes crowded in midsummer, Zadar's bus station will almost certainly figure prominently in your travel plans unless you're driving or flying directly here. The trip to or from Zagreb takes around 4½ hours, for around 105 Kn. Timetables are available at the station. The luggage room (*garderobe*) is open from 6 am to 10 pm, and costs 1.50 Kn per hour.

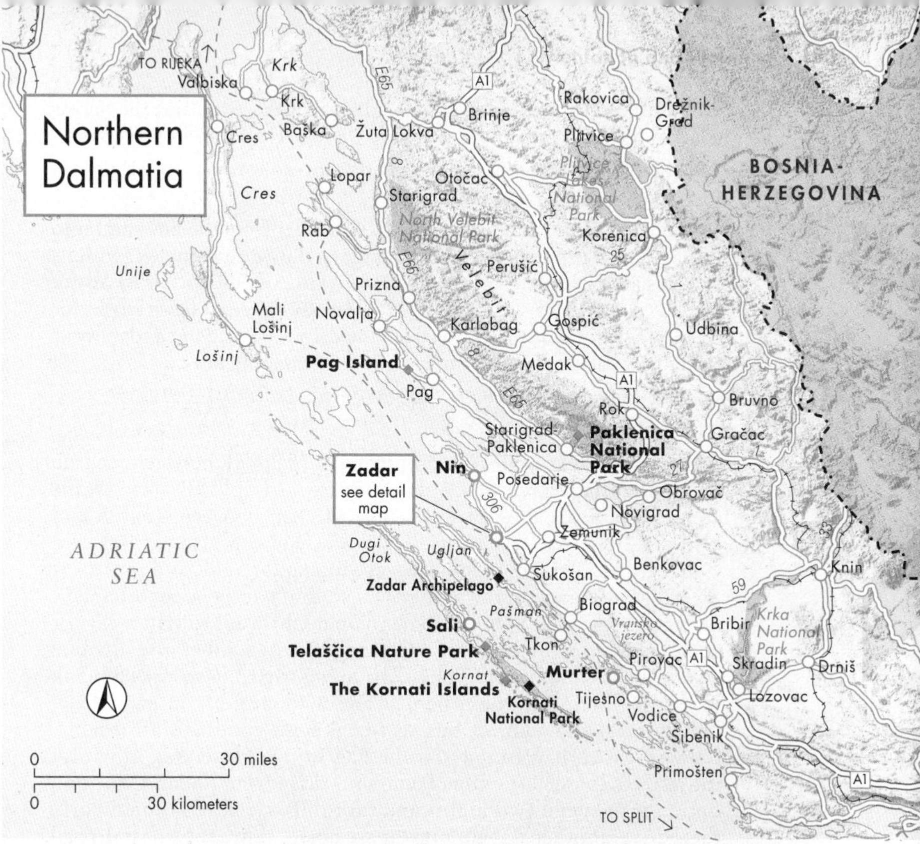

Getting to Nin from Zadar is easy by bus. The half-hour trip follows the coastal road north; the fare is 11 Kn one-way, with buses running daily out of Zadar's station every 45 minutes or so.

Getting to Murter—to its tiny main square, Trg Rudina, which is where you're dropped off and picked up—from Zadar is certainly doable, if a bit complicated. You can transfer either at Šibenik or at Vodice. Although the former option looks longer on the map, given the crowded confusion at Vodice's small station, Šibenik—around 12 buses daily from Zadar—may be a less trying experience (and a surer way of getting a seat) even if it might take a bit longer; about nine buses go on from Šibenik to Murter (via Vodice). Travel time via Šibenik is 2½ hours or more (i.e., 90 minutes from Zadar to Šibenik, up to an hour of waiting time, then another 45 minutes to Murter via Vodice). The total cost is around 70 Kn via Šibenik and around 50 Kn if you go straight to Vodice (travel time is less than two hours, plus an even harder-to-predict wait time, because the bus from Šibenik might be contending with heavy traffic).

Numerous buses ply the one-hour route daily between Zadar and Starigrad for access to Paklenica National Park. The one-way cost to or from Starigrad—via the Zadar–Rijeka bus—is between 20 Kn and 38 Kn, depending on the company. There are two stops in Starigrad; the national park information office is between the two, and the access road to the park is near the first stop (if you're coming from Zadar).

Around half a dozen buses daily ply the one-hour route from Zadar to Pag Town, on Pag Island (55 Kn).

Last but not least, the easiest way to get either from the bus station to Zadar's town center, or from the center to the Borik complex (with its beaches, hotels, and restaurants) on the northern outskirts, is by any of several, user-friendly local buses. You can buy tickets at news kiosks for 8 Kn (single ride) or for 10 Kn from the driver; be sure to validate your ticket on boarding by inserting it into the stamping device.

Contact Zadar Bus Station. ✉ *Ante Starčevića 1, Zadar* ☎ *023/319–057.*

CAR TRAVEL

Zadar is the first major stop on the A1 highway between Zagreb and Dalmatia, which proceeds south toward Split. Barring traffic congestion, especially on weekends, the trip between Zagreb and Zadar is doable in 2½ hours. That said, you can also easily get to Zadar by bus, whether from Zagreb, Rijeka, or Split, and rent a car there if necessary. As the Zadar bus station can be a chaotic place at times, especially in midsummer, you might want to rent a car for some excursions—to Murter, for example, which otherwise involves a somewhat complicated, time-consuming trip to or toward Šibenik with a transfer. But you'll be just fine without a car in and immediately around Zadar, as bus service is both good and affordable. How to get to Pag Island? By the Pag Bridge route, Pag Town (at the island's center) is within a one-hour drive from Zadar. One good option is to spend two nights and take in Paklenica National Park, then drive another 25 minutes or so north along the coastal road toward Rab Island and Rijeka, and take the ferry from the village of Prizna—roughly midway between Rijeka and Zadar, just south of Rab Island—to Žigljen, in the north of the island (14 Kn per person, 89 Kn for a car); or do the same in reverse.

TRAIN TRAVEL

It's possible to travel between Zadar and Zagreb by train. Five trains run daily from Zadar to Knin (in just over two hours with almost 20 stops in between), and from Knin you can transfer within an hour to a train that gets you to Zagreb in roughly four hours—that's around seven hours in all from Zadar to Zagreb, for about 130 Kn one-way. Unless you want to see some relatively war-wearied parts of the interior, though, you'll do well to simply hop aboard one of the many daily Zagreb-bound buses at Zadar's bus station, which get you to the capital in less time and for less money (around 100 Kn). Trains also run between Knin and Split, and service and travel times are improving yearly on all these routes.

ABOUT THE RESTAURANTS

Fresh seafood is the cuisine of choice in Northern Dalmatia, as it is elsewhere on Croatia's coast. Beyond standard coastal fare, look for Dalmatian specialties including Pag Island lamb and *Paški sir* (Pag cheese); *pršut* (prosciutto), and *šokol* (smoked pork neck) from Posedarje; and sheep's cheese and peppery meat dishes from inner Dalmatia. And of course, there's Zadar's famous maraschino liqueur—compliments of the area's uniquely zesty cherry and the Maraška company—whose facility is just across the town's pedestrian bridge and whose brand name graces the bottles of the best maraschino.

ABOUT THE HOTELS

As elsewhere along practically every populated area of the Croatian coast, package-hotel resorts are easy to find, in particular in the Borik complex on the northern outskirts of Zadar. Top-notch pensions and intimate, elegant small hotels are in somewhat short supply, though a whole host of private rooms and apartments can be found, often for half the price of larger, more established accommodations, either through the local tourist-information office or through private travel agencies. And, as is the practice in other parts of Croatia, short stays (i.e., fewer than three days) often mean a surcharge of around 20%. *Hotel reviews have been shortened. For full information, visit Fodors.com.*

WHAT IT COSTS IN EUROS (€) AND CROATIAN KUNA (KN)

	$	$$	$$$	$$$$
Restaurants	under 50 Kn	50 Kn–120 Kn	121 Kn–250 Kn	over 250 Kn
	under €8	€8–€20	€21–€40	over €40
Hotels	under 450 Kn	450 Kn–900 Kn	901 Kn–1,500 Kn	over 1,500 Kn
	under €60	€60–€120	€121–€200	over €200

Restaurant prices are the average cost of a main course at dinner or, if dinner is not served, at lunch. Hotel prices are the lowest cost of a standard double room in high season.

VISITOR INFORMATION

If there's no English speaker at the office you happen to contact, try the Zadar County Tourist Information office or the city of Zadar's corresponding office.

Contacts Zadar Tourist Information. ✉ *Mihe Klaića, Zadar* ☎ *023/316–166* 🌐 *www.visitzadar.net.*

ZADAR

347 km (217 miles) southwest of Zagreb.

Dalmatia's capital for more than 1,000 years, Zadar is all too often passed over by travelers on their way to Split or Dubrovnik. What they miss out on is a city of more than 73,000 that is remarkably lovely and lively despite—and, in some measure, because of—its tumultuous history. The Old Town, separated from the rest of the city on a peninsula some 4 km (2½ miles) long and just 1,640 feet wide, is bustling and beautiful: the marble pedestrian streets are replete with Roman ruins, medieval churches, palaces, museums, archives, and libraries. Parts of the new town are comparatively dreary, a testament to what a world war followed by decades of communism, not to mention a civil war, can do to the architecture of a city that is 3,000 years old.

A settlement had already existed on the site of the present-day city for some 2,000 years when Rome finally conquered Zadar in the 1st century BC; the foundations of the Forum can be seen today. Before the Romans came, the Liburnians had made it a key center for trade with the Greeks and Romans for 800 years. In the 3rd century BC the Romans began to seriously pester the Liburnians, but required two centuries to bring the area under their control. During the Byzantine era, Zadar became the capital of Dalmatia, and this period saw the construction of its most famous church, the 9th-century St. Donat's Basilica. It remained the region's foremost city through the ensuing centuries. The city then experienced successive onslaughts and occupations—both long and short—by the Ostrogoths, the Croatian-Hungarian kings, the Venetians, the Turks, the Habsburgs, the French, the Habsburgs again, and finally the Italians before becoming part of Yugoslavia and, in 1991, the independent republic of Croatia.

Zadar was for centuries an Italian-speaking city, and Italian is still spoken widely, especially by older people. Indeed, it was ceded to Italy in 1921 under the Treaty of Rapallo (and reverted to its Italian name of Zara). However, its occupation by the Germans in 1943 led to intense bombing by the Allies during World War II, which left most of the city in ruins. Zadar became part of Tito's Yugoslavia in 1947, prompting many Italian residents to leave. Zadar's most recent ravages occurred during a three-month siege by Serb forces and months more of bombardment during the Croatian-Serbian war between 1991 and 1995. But you'd be hard-pressed to find outward signs of this today in what is a city to behold.

GETTING HERE AND AROUND

Zadar is the only sizable city in Northern Dalmatia and quite likely your first destination in the area. It has an international airport that connects it to Europe during the summer season (mostly via budget airlines) and Zagreb and Pula year-round. You can also drive in via the A1 highway or the Adriatic "magistrala" road, but a car will be of little use in the city itself, where narrow alleys are best explored on foot. There are ample regular bus lines from Zagreb, Rijeka, and Split, but be advised that the bus station is not in walking distance from the old city. Zadar's port is very busy with lines serving local islands and a daily international line to Ancona, Italy.

TOURS

FAMILY **Malik Adventures.** Discover remote islands, sheltered coves, and steep cliffs only a short catamaran sail from Zadar with the energetic crew of Malik Adventures. The juxtaposition of intense adventure activities during the day with a night of slowly paced, exquisite local cuisine and island life may be the defining point of your vacation. This serene island is a rejuvenating break between touring cities. ✉ *Molat 40* ☎ *091/784–7547* 🌐 *www.malikadventures.com.*

Secret Dalmatia. Not the biggest, but certainly one of the best organized companies, Secret Dalmatia specializes in showing you parts of

Zadar

Exploring

Archaeological Museum 8
Crkva Sv. Donata 6
Crkva Sv. Marije 7
Crkva Sv. Šimuna 10
Forum 5
Franjevački samostan i Crkva sv. Franje Asiškog 3
Greeting to the Sun 2
Katedrala Sv. Stošije 4
Kopnena Vrata 12
Museum of Ancient Glass .. 13
Narodni trg 9
Sea Organ 1
Square of Five Wells 11

Restaurants

Bistro Gourmet Kalelarga 5
Bruschetta 4
Foša 9
Mama Mia 12
Niko 10
Pasta & Svasta 7
Pet Bunara 8
Restoran Kornat 1

Hotels

Almayer Art and Heritage Hotel ...3
Art Hotel Kalelarga 6
Falkensteuner Hotel Adriana .. 11
Hotel Bastion 2

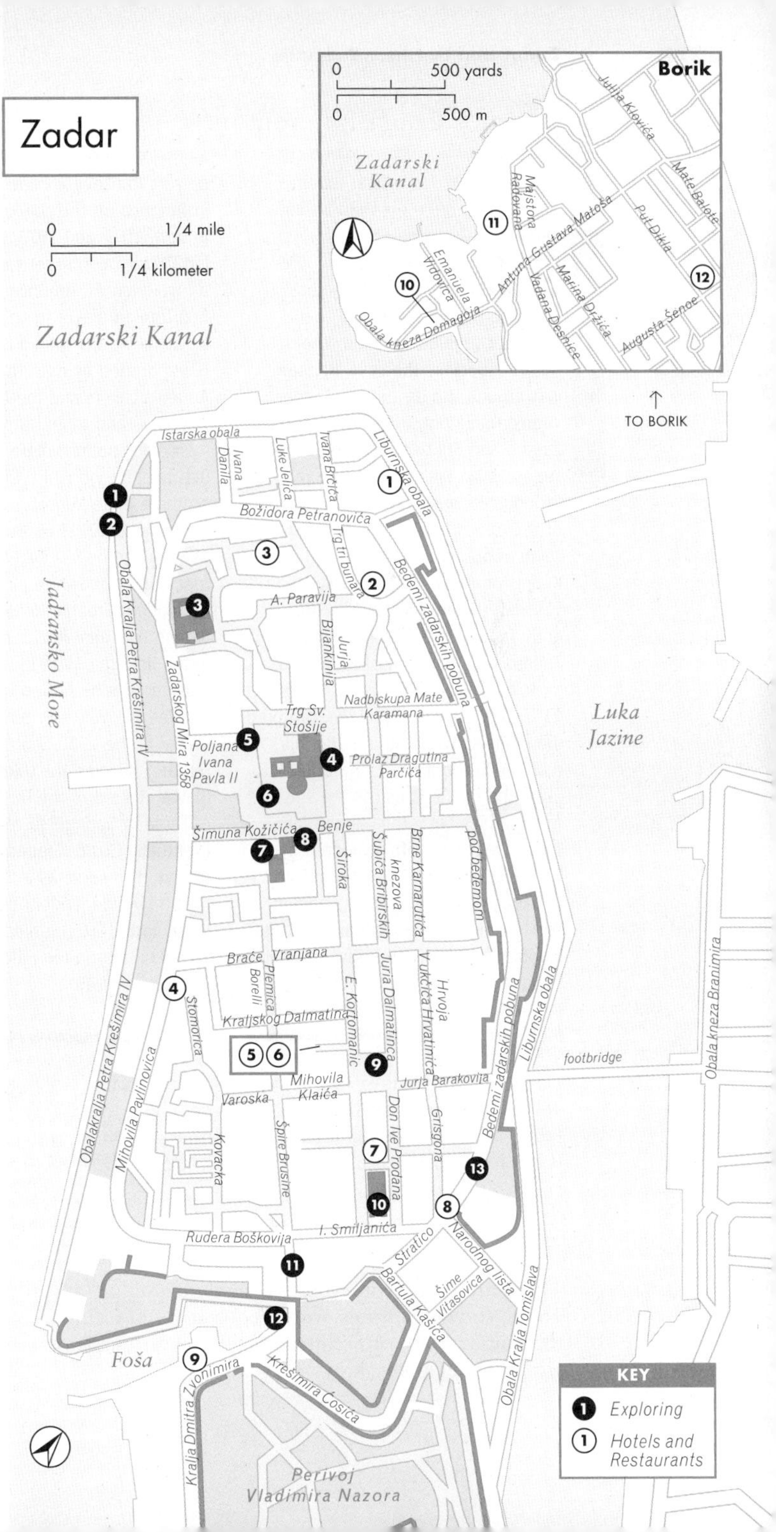

CLOSE UP

Zadar's Court Phenomenon

In 2005, team Zadar beat Cibona Zagreb to win the Croatian basketball league's championship for the first time in 19 years. The city was delirious with joy. Basketball has long rivaled soccer in Croatia for sheer popularity, and in Zadar this is especially the case. Its team was among the best in the former Yugoslavia, alongside Cibona Zagreb and Split's team, then called Jugoplastika Split. To see one reason for yourself, walk south from the foot of the pedestrian bridge in the Old Town about 10 minutes along Obala Kralja Tomislava to the grassy area on your left (where the bay reaches an end) and consider the huge statue of Zadar's preeminent basketball hero as he towers even higher than the 6 feet 11 inches he was in real life, captured meditatively with ball in hand. His name is Krešimir Ćosić. (Appropriately, the statue is across the street from Zadar's basketball auditorium Jazine, replaced with a modern gym in 2010.) Born in Zagreb but raised in Zadar, Ćosić enrolled at Brigham Young University in Utah in 1970 after leading Yugoslavia to a silver medal in basketball in 1968. His decision opened the way for other foreign players to likewise hone their skills in America on the collegiate level. In both 1972 and 1973, Ćosić—who led BYU in scoring for two years in a row—won All-America honors, the first foreign player to do so. In 1973 he achieved the added distinction of being drafted by both the NBA's Los Angeles Lakers and the ABA's Carolina Cougars—and saying "no thanks." He went back home, where he continued to shine on court. Ćosić played on three more Yugoslav Olympic teams, in 1972, 1976, and finally, 1980, when he led his team to a gold medal in Moscow. He played not only for leading Croatian teams but also for the two-time Italian champions, Virtus Bologna. With the close of his playing days he turned to coaching and led the Yugoslav team to a silver medal in the 1988 Seoul Olympics. He later became the third foreign player elected to the Basketball Hall of Fame in Springfield, Massachusetts. Eventually Ćosić stepped away from the court to serve as a diplomat for his newly independent country in Washington, D.C. He died on May 25, 1995, after a long illness, at the young age of 46.

Dalmatia that might not be on the tourist map. The owner, Alan, is very outgoing and reliable, and his team have Dalmatia well covered, from hidden little wineries to sailboats. Young and professional, their English is excellent. ✉ *Turanj 426* ☎ *091/567–1604* 🌐 *www.secretdalmatia.com.*

EXPLORING

There are helpful interpretive signs in English all around the Old Town, so you certainly won't feel lost when trying to make sense of the wide variety of architectural sites you might otherwise pass by with only a cursory look.

TOP ATTRACTIONS

Fodor's Choice ★ **Crkva Sv. Donata** (*St. Donatus Church*). Zadar's star attraction, this huge cylindrical structure is the most monumental early Byzantine church in Croatia. Originally called Church of the Holy Trinity, it was probably inspired by plans set forth in a book by the Byzantine emperor Constantine Porphyrogenet, *On Ruling the Empire*. Centuries later it was rededicated to St. Donatus, the bishop here from 801 to 814. Legend has it that Donatus, an Irishman, was the one who had it built, using stone from the adjacent Forum. The stark, round interior features a circular center surrounded by an annular passageway; a sanctuary consisting of three apses attached to the lofty mantle of the church walls, set off from the center by two columns; and a gallery reached by a circular stairway. Although the church no longer holds services, its fine acoustics make it a regular concert venue. During the off-season (November to March), when the church is closed, someone at the Archaeological Museum next door may have a key to let you in. ✉ *Šimuna Kožičića Benje* ☎ *023/316–166* 🌐 *www.amzd.hr* 🎫 *20 Kn* ⏲ *Closed Nov.–Mar.; by appointment only.*

Franjevački samostan i Crkva sv. Franje Asiškog (*St. Francis Church & Franciscan Monastery*). Dalmatia's oldest Gothic church, consecrated in 1280, is a stellar example of a so-called Gothic monastic church, characterized by a single nave with a raised shrine. Although the church underwent extensive reconstruction in the 18th century, behind the main altar is a shrine dating to 1672; inside the shrine you can see choir stalls in the floral Gothic style that date to 1394. In 1358 a peace treaty was signed in this very sacristy under which the Venetian Republic ended centuries of attack and handed Zadar over to the protection of the Croat-Hungarian kingdom. ■ **TIP→ You can walk around the atmospheric inner courtyard for free, but you pay a fee to enter the church itself.** From mid-October through March or April, the church may keep irregular hours. ✉ *Samostan Sv. Franje, Trg Sv. Frane 1* ☎ *023/250–468* 🌐 *www.svetifrane.org* 🎫 *15 Kn.*

Katedrala Sv. Stošije (*St. Anastasia's Cathedral*). Dalmatia's largest basilica was shaped into its magnificent Romanesque form in the 12th and 13th centuries from an earlier church; though it was damaged severely during World War II, it was later reconstructed. The front portal is adorned with striking Gothic reliefs and a dedication to the archbishop Ivan from the year 1324. The interior includes not only a high, spacious nave but also a Gothic stone ciborium from 1332 covering the 9th-century altar; intricately carved 15th-century choir stalls by the Venetian artist Matej Morozon; and, in the sacristy, an early Christian mosaic. St. Anastasia is buried in the altar's left apse; according to legend, she was the wife of a patrician in Rome but was eventually burned at the stake. Bishop Donatus of Zadar obtained the remains in 804 from Byzantine Emperor Niceforos. ■ **TIP→ The late-19th-century belfry, which is separate from the main church building, offers a sweeping view to those who climb to the top for a fee, but even the 20 steps up to the ticket desk rewards you with a decent view of the square below.** ✉ *Trg Sv. Stošije 2* ☎ *023/251–708* 🎫 *Church free, belfry 10 Kn* ⏲ *Closed Sun.*

FAMILY Fodor's Choice ★ **Sea Organ.** Comprising 35 pipes under the quay stretching along a 230-foot stretch of Zadar's atmospheric Riva promenade, the Sea Organ yields a never-ending (and ever free) concert that delights one and all. Designed by architect Nikola Bašić with the help of other experts, the organ's sound resembles a whale song, but it is in fact the sea itself. It's hard not to be in awe as the sound of the sea undulates in rhythm and volume with the waves. ✉ *Obala kralja Petra Krešimira IV, toward the end of the western tip of the peninsula.*

WORTH NOTING

Archaeological Museum. Founded in 1832, Zadar's archaeological museum is one of the oldest museums in this part of Europe. It occupies a plain but pleasant modern building beside the convent complex of Crkva Sv. Marije (St. Mary's Church). It is home to numerous artifacts from Zadar's past, from prehistoric times to the first Croatian settlements. Head upstairs to move back in time. The third floor focuses on ceramics, weaponry, and other items the seafaring Liburnians brought home from Greece and Italy, whereas the second floor covers the classical period, including a model of the Forum square as it would have looked back then; a smaller exhibit addresses the development of Christianity in Northern Dalmatia and contains rare artifacts from the invasion of the Goths. On the first floor you'll find an exhibit from the early Middle Ages, taking you to the 12th century. ✉ *Trg Opatice Čike 1* ☎ *023/250–613* 🌐 *www.amzd.hr* 💳 *15 Kn* ⏲ *Closed Sun. Oct.–May.*

Crkva Sv. Marije (*St. Mary's Church*). Legend has it that a local noblewoman founded a Benedictine convent on this site in 1066, and the adjoining St. Mary's Church in 1091. Rebuilt in the 16th century, the church was supposed to incorporate a new Renaissance look into the remnants of its earlier style: its rounded gables remained, continuing to express a certain Dalmatian touch; early Romanesque frescoes are still evident amid the largely Baroque interior; and your eyes will discover 18th-century rococo above the original columns without being any worse for the effect. Most noteworthy for modern-day visitors, however, is the adjoining convent complex, two wings of which house one of Zadar's most treasured museums. The **Permanent Exhibition of Religious Art,** whose highlight is commonly called "The Gold and Silver of Zadar," is a remarkable collection of work from centuries past by local gold- and silversmiths (including Italians and Venetians who lived here), from reliquaries for saints and crucifixes to vestments interwoven with gold and silver thread. ✉ *Poljana Opatice Čike* ☎ *023/254–820* 💳 *Museum 30 Kn.*

Crkva Sv. Šimuna (*St. Simeon's Church*). Built in the 5th century as a three-nave basilica, it was later reconstructed in Gothic style, and again in Baroque style, though the terra-cotta and white exterior pales in comparison to some of the city's other churches. St. Simeon's Church is best known for housing the gilded silver sarcophagus of Zadar's most popular patron saint. The chest, which depicts intricately detailed scenes from St. Simeon's life and the city's history, was commissioned in 1381 by Elizabeth, wife of Croat-Hungarian King Ludwig I of Anjou, and made by Francesco De Sesto of Milan, one of Zadar's best silversmiths. As for St. Simeon, legend has it that his body wound up here while being transported from the Holy Land to Venice by a merchant who got caught in a storm, took refuge here, fell ill, and died—but not before drawing attention to the saintliness of the body he'd brought with him. Palm trees outside the church lend the site a pleasant, Mediterranean touch. ✉ *Crkva Sv. Šime, Trg Petra Zoranića 7* ☎ *023/211–705* 💵 *Free.*

Forum. Established in the 1st century BC by the first emperor Augustus, the Roman Forum is, more than 2,000 years later, pretty much a wide empty space with some scattered ruins. However, since it was rediscovered in the 1930s and restored to its present condition in the 1960s, the Forum has been one of Zadar's most important public spaces. A raised area on the western flank indicates the site of a onetime temple dedicated to Jupiter, Juno, and Minerva, and if you look closely you will notice what remains of its altars that served as venues for blood sacrifices. The only surviving column was used in the Middle Ages as a "Pillar of Shame," to which wayward individuals were chained. Fragments of a second column were removed from the Forum in 1729 and put back together again near the Square of Five Wells, where the column still stands today. ✉ *Zeleni trg.*

Greeting to the Sun (*Pozdrav Suncu*). Close to the Sea Organ, the Greeting to the Sun is a 22-meter circle of multilayered glass plates set into the stone-paved waterfront. Under the glass, light-sensitive solar modules soak up the sun's energy during daylight hours, turning it into electrical energy. Just after sunset, it puts on an impressive light show, illuminating the waterfront in shades of blue, green, red, and yellow. It was installed in 2008 and was created by local architect Nikola Bašić, who also made the Sea Organ. ✉ *Obala Kralja Petra Krešimira IV, toward the western tip of the peninsula.*

6

Kopnena Vrata (*The Land Gate*). A walk around the walls of Zadar's Old Town is a walk around what was, once, the largest city-fortress in the Venetian Republic. One of the finest Venetian-era monuments in Dalmatia, the Land Gate was built in 1543 by the small Foša harbor as the main entrance to the city. It takes the form of a triumphal arch, with a large, central passage for vehicles and two side entrances for pedestrians, and is decorated with reliefs of St. Chrysogonus (Zadar's main patron saint) on his horse, and the shield of St. Mark (the coat of arms of the Venetian Republic). ✉ *Ulica Ante Kumanića.*

Museum of Ancient Glass. Occupying the 19th-century Cosmacendi Palace, on the edge of the Old Town, this museum opened in 2011. It displays one of the world's finest collections of Roman glassware outside Italy, with a vast array of ancient pieces unearthed from archaeological sites across Dalmatia. Highlights include the delicate vessels used by Roman ladies to keep their perfumes, skin creams, and essential oils, as well as sacred goblets used to celebrate Mass. ■ **TIP→ The museum shop offers a fine choice of replicas of Roman glassware, which make great gifts to bring home.** ✉ *Poljana Zemaljskog odbora 1* ☎ *023/363–831* 🌐 *www.mas-zadar.hr* 💵 *30 kn* ⏲ *Closed Sun. Oct.–mid-June.*

Narodni trg (*People's Square*). One of the Old Town's two main public spaces, the ever bustling Narodni trg is home of the Gradska Straža (City Sentinel), which was designed by a Venetian architect in late-Renaissance style with a large central clock tower. The sentinel's stone barrier and railing, complete with holes for cannons, were added later. This impressive tower once housed the ethnographic section of the National Museum and is today a venue for various regular cultural exhibits. ✉ *Narodni trg.*

HOW SWEET—AND DRY—IT IS

Zadar's famous maraschino cherry liqueur, one of the world's few liqueurs produced by distillation, manages to be subtly sweet and robustly dry at the same time. Look for bottles labeled Maraška, the Zadar company that produces this transparent spirit from the area's zesty sour cherries. It is typically enjoyed as either an aperitif or digestif.

Square of Five Wells. The square is the site of a large cistern built by the Venetians in the 1570s to help Zadar endure sieges by the Turks. The cistern itself has five wells that still look quite serviceable, even though they have long been sealed shut. Much later, in 1829, Baron Franz Ludwig von Welden, a passionate botanist, established a park above an adjacent pentagonal bastion that was also built to keep the Turks at bay. ✉ *Pet Bunara.*

WHERE TO EAT

$$ MEDITERRANEAN

Bistro Gourmet Kalelarga. Located within the Art Hotel Kalelarga just off the square, sleek Bistro Gourmet Kalelarga serves up authentic local specialties complemented by a carefully arranged wine list and best enjoyed on the charming outdoor terrace. Be sure to ask your server to help you take advantage of seasonal dishes, especially if you find yourself here during asparagus season in early spring. **Known for:** Zadar orange and Maraška–sour cherry cakes; chic design; creative tasting plates. $ *Average main: 70 Kn* ✉ *Art Hotel Kalelarga, Ul. Majke Margarite 3, 23000, Zadar* ☎ *023/233–000* 🌐 *www.arthotel-kalelarga.com/en/gourmet* 🌐 *www.arthotel-kalelarga.com/en/gourmet.*

$$ MEDITERRANEAN

Bruschetta. With outdoor tables on a lovely terrace, overlooking the sea in the Old Town, Bruschetta serves reasonably priced and well-presented Mediterranean cuisine. Popular with locals and visitors alike, it's especially known for its pizzas and pasta dishes, but it also does excellent steaks and fresh fish, as well as an irresistible tiramisu. **Known for:** local seafood; view of the water; late night eats. $ *Average main: 100 Kn* ✉ *Mihovila Pavlinovica 12* ☎ *023/312–915* 🌐 *www.bruschetta.hr.*

$$$$ SEAFOOD Fodor's Choice ★

Foša. Boasting an appealing outdoor terrace overlooking a quiet little harbor, Foša is a combination of age-old Dalmatian style and modern trends, in architecture, design, and gastronomy. It's old-world tastes give foundation to creative modern dishes, such as the tuna carpaccio beautifully complemented by a dab of wasabi cream or the sea bass marinated in a potent emulsion of local fennel root, citrus, and honey. **Known for:** terrace views of the town walls; tasting menus; local tuna. $ *Average main: 500 Kn* ✉ *Kralja Dimitra Zvonimira 2* ☎ *023/314–421* 🌐 *www.fosa.hr.*

$$ PIZZA ✕ **Mama Mia.** Mama Mia is a popular place for locals and tourists, and with good reason: delicious, generous portions at fair prices and pizzas big enough to share (not that you'll want to). Pizza is definitely the star here, with an impressive spread of toppings to choose from, but if you're not a pizza fan the cuttlefish risotto and daily specials never disappoint. **Known for:** oversize dishes; wood-fired pizza; good value. $ *Average main: 80 Kn* ✉ *Put Dikla 54* ☎ *023/337–713.*

$$ MEDITERRANEAN Fodor's Choice ★ ✕ **Niko.** Just across from a public beach and near the Borik resort complex, this distinguished restaurant has been serving up a delicious array of seafood, beef, veal, pork, and pasta dishes since 1963. You can choose between such lower-end fare as spaghetti with scampi or more expensive delights like scampi on the skewer. **Known for:** beachside; historical; something for everyone. $ *Average main: 120 Kn* ✉ *Obala Kneza Domagoja 9* ☎ *023/337–880* 🌐 *www.hotel-niko.hr.*

$$ ITALIAN ✕ **Pasta & Svasta.** Charming and cozy (with limited but coveted seating) this tucked-away spot offers a consistently pleasant experience, especially on a clear night when you can sit in the courtyard, enjoying a tasty house wine that complements both the lighter fare and pasta plates. Knowledgeable waiters will help you pair the fresh pastas and sauces; don't overlook the pillowy gnocchi. **Known for:** local aperitifs; lovely courtyard; secluded location. $ *Average main: 80 Kn* ✉ *Poljana Šime Budinića 1* ☎ *099/731–0232.*

6

$$$ MEDITERRANEAN Fodor's Choice ★ ✕ **Pet Bunara.** For a break from the tourist bustle, head for the Pet Bunara, a slow food restaurant situated in a quiet little nook just off the Pet Bunara square. The fare is creative and changes weekly, if not daily, according to local produce available. **Known for:** secluded; homemade fig jam; all local food. $ *Average main: €25* ✉ *Stratico Street, near Trg pet Bunara* ☎ *023/224–010* 🌐 *www.petbunara.hr.*

$$$ SEAFOOD ✕ **Restoran Kornat.** Just outside the city walls on the tip of the peninsula and on the ground floor of a four-story concrete-box building, the Kornat serves original, first-rate cuisine, with an emphasis on seafood—try the monkfish fillet with truffle sauce—plus a limited choice of hearty meat dishes, including leg of lamb with roasted potatoes. Desserts include melon with champagne. **Known for:** excellent seafood; wide-ranging wine list; interesting desserts. $ *Average main: 120 Kn* ✉ *Liburnska obala 6* ☎ *023/254–501* 🌐 *www.restaurant-kornat.com.*

WHERE TO STAY

There are very few hotels in or near Zadar's Old Town—the pension-style Venera used to be the only option until the opening of the Bastion Hotel in 2008. As you leave the center, you'll find either fairly expensive, top-end hotels or relatively simple, budget places, but not much in the middle price ranges. In midsummer, you can step off the ferry from Pula at midnight and be reasonably assured that some relatively trustworthy person—more likely than not a pensioner who speaks more Italian than English—will offer you a room in a centrally located apartment for around 300 Kn for two people. But your best bet is to book a room—for a slightly higher cost—through a travel agency, which also offers excursions to nearby islands and national parks.

$$$$ HOTEL **Almayer Art and Heritage Hotel.** Nestled into the historic Old Town, this family-owned boutique hotel in a 19th-century building was renovated in 2017 to both preserve its historical character and give the space a modern, open, and artistic feel. **Pros:** beautiful interior and courtyard; green space; close to attractions and the beach. **Cons:** limited rooms so often fully booked in high season; parking can be problematic. *Rooms from: €239 Braće Bersa 2 023/335–357 www.almayer.hr 9 rooms No meals.*

$$$$ HOTEL Fodor's Choice ★ **Art Hotel Kalelarga.** Carefully curated modern furnishings create a cool relief after a day of hustling through Zadar's narrow streets. **Pros:** excellent restaurant; one of the few hotels in the Old Town; good off-season packages. **Cons:** atmosphere can be stuffy; pricey. *Rooms from: €260 Majke Margarite 3 023/233–000 www.arthotel-kalelarga.com 10 rooms Breakfast.*

$$$$ RESORT **Falkensteiner Hotel Adriana.** Flanked beachside by a grove of tall pines and encircled by a security fence (more to keep nonguests from enjoying the hotel's outdoor pool than for the sake of safety), this is an appealing place to stay even if the long, narrow lobby does resemble an airport terminal. **Pros:** bright, spacious rooms; lovely private beach; substantial discounts for stays of three nights or more. **Cons:** pricey; in a huge, somewhat characterless complex; far from the town center. *Rooms from: €282 Majstora Radovana 7, Borik 023/206–300 www.falkensteiner.com 48 rooms Some meals.*

$$$$ HOTEL Fodor's Choice ★ **Hotel Bastion.** Elegant, with artistic decoration and a refined ambience, Hotel Bastion offers a chic respite for travelers with a taste for sophistication. **Pros:** perhaps the best slow-food restaurant in the country; location in the Old Town; stylish interior. **Cons:** small, so often fully booked in high season; Old Town is pedestrian only and parking nearby can be problematic; guests pay to use the spa. *Rooms from: €219 Bedem zadarskih pobuna 13 023/494–950 www.hotel-bastion.hr 23 rooms, 5 suites Breakfast.*

NIGHTLIFE AND PERFORMING ARTS

NIGHTLIFE

BARS AND CLUBS

Bamboo Caffe & Lounge Bar. The big wooden deck clad with wooden benches, deck chairs, and grass umbrellas right on the beach certainly has its appeal. Bamboo Caffe & Lounge Bar overlooks the old city and outward to the islands. They know how to keep it simple, and their version of simple is pretty good. *Obala Kneza Domagoja BB 098/756–998 www.restorani-zadar.hr/beach-bar-bamboo.*

The Garden Lounge. Cloistered in a walled garden right atop the city walls, the Garden Lounge is a minimalist and exceedingly popular place to drink, soak in the sun and the views, play a game of chess, and even dance to the jazz, Latin, and downtempo electronica. It's open daily from 10 am to 1:30 am. *Bedemi Zadarskih Pobuna 023/364–320 www.watchthegardengrow.eu/the-garden-zadar/.*

PERFORMING ARTS

SUMMER FESTIVALS

Musical Evenings in Saint Donat. Despite its name, performances of this month-long series of classical music concerts and recitals, staged between early-July and early-August, are held in the Roman Forum, Saint Anastasia Cathedral, Saint Donat Church, and Marina Dalmacija, down the road in Bibinje. ✉ *Trg Petra Zoranića 1* 🌐 *www.donat-festival.com.*

Zadar Snova (*Zadar of Dreams*). The eclectic Zadar Snova festival, held the first two weeks of August, welcomes everything from contemporary dance and films to comic-strip exhibits and workshops to theatrical events to a rich array of music, and more. ✉ *I. Meštrovića 9* 🌐 *www.facebook.com/zadarsnova/info.*

Zadar Summer Theatre. From late June to early August the annual Zadar Summer Theatre festival sees a whole range of music, dance, and drama performed in various squares, churches, and other buildings about town. ✉ *Zadar.*

SPORTS AND THE OUTDOORS

BEACHES

Feel free to take a short dip off the quay in the Old Town—the most atmospheric place to do so being the **Riva** promenade and especially the tip of the peninsula directly over the Sea Organ, as nature's music accompanies your strokes. But for a more tranquil swim, head to the **Kolovare** district, just southeast of the Old Town, with its long stretch of park-flanked beach punctuated here and there by restaurants and cafés. There's also the resort complex in **Borik,** where relatively shallow waters and a sandy bottom may be more amenable to kids. Last but not least, by driving or bussing it 30 minutes north along the coast you can reach the famously sandy beaches of **Zaton** and **Nin.** For true peace and quiet, though, your best bet is an excursion by ferry and then on foot, by bicycle, or in a rental car out to some more isolated stretch of beach on an island of the Zadar archipelago.

BICYCLING

Zadar Archipelago. ✉ *Obala kneza Trpimira 2* ☎ *099/627–3333* 🌐 *www.zadar-archipelago.com.*

SHOPPING

As hip as it otherwise is, Zadar is low on high fashion and has few outlets for quality souvenirs (as opposed to the usual kitsch, which there is plenty of). That said, those interested will be happy to know that jewelry stores are in no short supply. Also, one of the first shopping opportunities you will pass if you enter the Old Town via the main pedestrian bridge is a large enclosed hall with an antiques market inside; look for the open doorway to your right on Jurja Barakovića, just before you reach H. Vukšića Hrvatinića (9–2 and 5–10 daily).

Fodor's Choice ★ **Arsenal.** Where the Venetians repaired their galleys in the 18th-century is today a multipurpose cultural space that hosts art exhibitions and concerts, as well as a lounge bar, a restaurant, and a wine shop. ✉ *Trg Tri Bunara 1* ☎ *023/253–821* 🌐 *www.arsenalzadar.com.*

Fodor's Choice ★ **Boutique MAR&VAL.** This boutique is a multibrand store full of unique pieces from prominent Croatian fashion designers. ✉ *Don Ivo Prodan 3* ☎ *023/213–239.*

Croatian Design Superstore. If you find yourself in Zadar over the summer months, make sure to check out the Croatian Design Superstore, an unusual gifts and souvenirs shop open only in July, August, and September. It hosts everything from high fashion and furniture to design crafts and gastro treats, and rest assured that everything is locally made. ✉ *Rector's Palace, Poljana Šime Budinića* 🌐 *www.croatiandesignsuperstore.com.*

Galerija Morsky. Galerija Morsky sells fine paintings by local artists. ✉ *Ulica Borelli 3* ☎ *091/780–6101.*

NIN

14 km (9 miles) northeast of Zadar.

On a tiny, 1,640-foot-wide island in a shallow, sandy lagoon that affords a spectacular view of the Velebit range to the northeast, Nin is connected to the mainland by two small bridges. The peaceful town of 1,700, a compact gem whose present-day size and unassuming attitude belie a stormy history, is well worth a visit, whether on the way to Zadar or as a day trip from there, assuming that the beautiful sand beaches stretching for miles around Nin don't inspire you to stay a bit longer.

Nin was a major settlement of the Liburnians, an Illyrian people who also settled Zadar, hundreds of years before the Romans came, conquered, and named it Aenona. A vital harbor for centuries, it was the first seat of Croatia's royalty, and was long the region's episcopal see, whose bishop was responsible for the conversion to Christianity of all Croatian territory. In 1382 the Venetians seized it and prospered from the trade in salt, livestock, and agriculture. However, the Venetian-Turkish wars eventually brought devastating onslaughts, including Nin's destruction in 1571; later, the Candian Wars of 1645–69 led to the decimation of Nin and the surrounding area yet again.

Aside from its historic buildings and monuments that testify to a rich past, Nin's draw also includes the only sandy beaches on this stretch of the Adriatic, not to mention the area's medicinal seaside mud. Since the sea here is shallow, water temperatures are warmer than in the rest of the Adriatic; moreover, the water is more saline, accounting for Nin's major export product—salt. But what would a Croatian coastal town be without the usual resort complex on its fringes? Holiday Village Zaton is a 15-minute walk from the Old Town.

If you're coming from Zadar, soon before you reach Nin proper, look to your left (your right if headed back toward Zadar) to see the squat, stony, 12th-century form of **St. Nicholas's Church** on a hillock out in the middle of a field, looking rather like a cake ornament, with a lone Scotch pine at the foot of the little hill keeping it company, as it were. You can enter Nin via one of two small bridges—the most likely of the two being the charming, pedestrian **Donja most** (Lower Bridge), only yards from the tourist-information office, which provides a helpful map that folds small enough to fit in your palm. If you're coming by car, you can park in a lot on the right just beyond the office and then cross the bridge, or else find a semi-legal spot along the road roughly opposite the lot, which plenty of enterprising visitors prefer.

GETTING HERE AND AROUND

The best way to Nin is a 15-km (9-mile) drive from Zadar, be it by car or one of the hourly regular buses. Once there, you can only get around on foot.

EXPLORING

Arheološki muzej (*Archaeological Museum*). Nin's shallow coast and centuries of sand deposits preserved numerous remains from prehistory to the Middle Ages under the sea. The Arheološki muzej has a rich collection for a town of this size, including replicas of two small, late-11th-century fishing boats discovered only in 1966 and carefully removed from the sea in 1974. One of these boats has been completely reconstructed, the other only to the extent to which it had been preserved underwater. The main themes in each room are elucidated in clear English translations. ✉ *Trg Kraljevac 8, 23232, Nin* ☎ *023/264–160* 🌐 *www.nin.hr/en/cultural-heritage/museum-nin-antiquities* 🎟 *20 Kn.*

Crkva Sv. Anselma (*St. Anselmo's Church*). The 18th-century Crkva Sv. Anselma, dedicated to a 1st-century martyr believed to have been Nin's first bishop, was built on the site of Nin's former, 9th-century cathedral, the first cathedral of the medieval Croatian principality. To the right of the altar is a 15th-century statue of the Madonna of Zečevo, inspired by the appearance of the Virgin Mary to a woman on a nearby island. Though the church is plain—the ceiling is adorned with only a nice chandelier and a smoke detector—the foundations of the onetime cathedral are still much in evidence. Beside the church is the belfry, and next door is the treasury, which houses a stunning little collection of reliquaries containing various body parts of St. Anselmo. ✉ *Branimirova, near Višeslavov trg* ☎ *098/509–307* 🌐 *www.nin.hr/en/cultural-heritage/sv-anselmo* 🎟 *Free.*

Crkva Sv. Križa (*Church of the Holy Cross*). Croatia's oldest church, the 8th-century Crkva Sv. Križa is also known locally as the "world's smallest cathedral." Indeed, the unadorned, three-naved whitewashed structure—which has a solid, cylindrical top and a few tall, Romanesque windows (too high to peek inside)—has an unmistakable monumental quality to it even though it's no larger than a small house. There's little to see inside, though it is sometimes open, erratically, in summer; check with the tourist office or the Archaeological Museum. ✉ *Petra Zoranića* ☎ *098/509–307* 🌐 *www.nin.hr/en/cultural-heritage/sv-kriz* 🎟 *Free.*

Nin Saltworks. Historically, Nin's riches came from an unlikely source: salt. Making the best of a rare geographical location with lots of sun, lots of wind, and shallow sea basins, Nin Saltworks produces salt in a traditional, ecological way to this date. To commemorate salt's vast influence on the development of the city, Nin opened up a small but charming salt museum that opens our eyes to how this common table adornment was produced back in the day. While there, make sure to pick up a bag of *fleur du sel*, or "flower of salt," ultrarich in minerals. For a fee, you can take a tour led by a professional guide (offered on the hour). ✉ *Ilirska cesta 7* ☎ *023/264–764* 🌐 *www.solananin.hr* 🎫 *Free; standard tour 45 Kn (inquire for additional tours)* 🕒 *Closed Sun. and public holidays.*

Temple of Diana. Around the corner from the Archaeological Museum are the ruins of the large Temple of Diana, one of the few remaining testaments in Nin to the Roman era. ✉ *Sv. Mihovila.*

WHERE TO EAT

$$ MEDITERRANEAN FAMILY ✕ **Bepo.** Even if you are not staying at Holiday Village Zaton, you might find yourself at Zaton's Konoba Bepo in search of a good meal because Nin does not have many worthy alternatives. Bepo's charming atmosphere is lively, and their menu is a good representation of local Mediterranean fare. **Known for:** regional olive oil; local favorite; traditional desserts. 💲 *Average main: €15* ✉ *Zaton Holiday Resort, Dražnikova 76t* ☎ *023/280–336* 🌐 *www.konoba-bepo.hr.*

$$ EASTERN EUROPEAN ✕ **Konoba Branimir.** Located yards away from the Church of the Holy Cross—indeed you might enter the restaurant by mistake, thinking you are proceeding to the churchyard from a back entrance—this pleasant spot's well-prepared fare ranges from fresh seafood to meats, and desserts such as pancakes with fig marmalade. Note that the spaghetti, though listed as a children's meal, makes for a hearty "light" (and budget) meal even for an adult. **Known for:** pancakes with local fig marmalade; hearty fare. 💲 *Average main: €15* ✉ *Višeslavov trg 2* ☎ *023/264–866.*

$$ PIZZA ✕ **Pizzeria Peperoni.** Baked in a beautiful wood-fired stone oven, and with 24 delicious and distinct varieties, pizza is the unsurprising specialty in this lively restaurant in the Old Town. Excellent salads featuring fresh vegetables and seafood as well other Dalmatian specialties are also offered. **Known for:** wood-fired pizza; affordable; friendly environment. 💲 *Average main: 55 Kn* ✉ *Trg Kraljevac 3* ☎ *098/875–693* 🌐 *www.restaurant-nin.taxipizzapeperoni.hr.*

SPORTS AND THE OUTDOORS

With its long sandy **beaches,** the coastline in and around Nin, and Pag Island just to the north, is widely regarded as the most beautiful—and most swimmable—in Dalmatia.

DIVING

Scuba Adriatic. The Holiday Village Zaton resort complex, a 15-minute walk from Nin, is home to Scuba Adriatic, which offers diving excursions for advanced and beginning divers, formal diving instruction, as well as a two-hour "Discovery Diving" course. ✉ *Holiday Village Zaton* ☎ *098/686–999* 🌐 *www.scubaadriatic.com.*

SALI AND TELAŠĆICA NATURE PARK

Sali is approximately 30 km (19 miles) southwest of Zadar; Telašćica Nature Park is 10 km (6 miles) southeast of Sali.

Situated toward the southeastern tip of the 52-km-long (32-mile-long) island, which is no more than 4 km (2½ miles) wide, Sali is Dugi Otok's largest settlement—with around half of the island's 1,800 inhabitants, the rest of whom reside mostly in its 10 other villages—but it's an awfully peaceful little place you arrive in after the two-hour ferry ride from Zadar.

GETTING HERE AND AROUND

Sali is on Dugi Otok Island and functions as a gateway to Telašćica Nature Park. You can get to Sali via the regular ferry line from Zadar to Dugi Otok or hop on one of many organized tours leaving from the area. Telašćica is a special treat, of course, for those chartering their own boat.

EXPLORING

The largest and most westerly island of the Zadar archipelago, facing the open sea, Dugi Otok culminates at its southern end with a spectacular nature preserve in and around Telašćica Bay, the town of Sali being the ideal access point.

Sali. Once an out-of-the-way fishing village, Sali draws tourists these days due to its location in and near such natural splendors. It is home to several old churches, including the 12th-century **St. Mary's Church,** whose Baroque altar was carved in Venice. Adding to the village's appeal is its annual **Saljske užance** (Donkey Festival) during the first full weekend in August, which includes an evening ritual during which lantern-lit boats enter Sali harbor and there are donkey races and *tovareća muzika* (donkey music) produced by locals blowing or braying raucously into horns. Spending at least a night or two here can provide a relatively peaceful, nature-filled respite from the rigors of tourism on the mainland or, for that matter, on more tourist-trodden reaches of the Zadar archipelago. ✉ *Sali.*

Telašćica Nature Park. Telašćica Nature Park encompasses Telašćica Bay, which cuts 7 km (4½ miles) into the southern tip of Dugi Otok with an inner coastline so indented that it is really a series of smaller bays and a handful of islands. Flanked by high vertical cliffs facing the open sea to the west, with low, peaceful bays on the other side, it has a variety of vegetation. Relatively lush alpine forests and flower-filled fields as well as vineyards, olive groves, and onetime cultivated fields give way, as you move south, to bare rocky ground of the sort that predominates on the Kornati Islands, whose northern boundary begins where

Telaščica Nature Park ends. Aside from Telaščica's other attractions, most of which are accessible only by boat, one of the park's key highlights—accessible by land on a 20-minute drive from Sali—is the salt lake **Jezero mir,** which was formed when a karst depression was filled by the sea. Small boats (generally with 8–12 passengers) bound for both Telaščica Nature Park and the northern fringes of Kornati National Park leave the east side of Sali's harbor (i.e., where the Zadar ferry arrives) at approximately 11:15 each morning and return by 6 or 6:30 in the evening. Verify ferry times at 🌐 *www.croatiaferries.com.* Expect to pay 200 Kn per person, sometimes less. The best way to arrange ferry passage is in person—by going to the harborside square near the post office around 8 pm on the day before you wish to leave (which means at least a one-night stay in Sali), when boat captains gather there looking for passengers for the next day's excursion. However, the tourist-information office in Sali can put you in touch with operators by phone as well. ✉ *Put Danijela Grbina, Sali* ☎ *023/377–096* 🌐 *www.telascica.hr.*

Zadar archipelago. The Zadar archipelago is so close and yet so far away. Ugljan and Pašman are just two of the myriad islands comprising the lacelike islands, and yet they are among the largest and the easiest to reach from Zadar. More than 15 ferries a day run the 5-km (3-mile) distance between Zadar and Ugljan, a 19-km-long (12-mile-long) island whose narrow width of just a couple of kilometers runs parallel to the mainland, with its midway point across from Zadar. From the ferry landing on Ugljan, your best bet may be to head north along the seafront 10 minutes on foot to the heart of **Preko,** a fine access point to several worthwhile destinations (very) near and (not too) far. Going south will get you in roughly the same time to the unassuming fishing village of Kali. From Preko's harbor you can walk about 1 km (½ mile) farther north to a shallow bay locals like to swim in; or better yet, take a taxi-boat to **Galevac,** a charming wooded islet less than 100 yards from Preko that not only has splendid swimming but also a 15th-century Franciscan monastery set in a lush green park. And then there's the **Tvrđava Sv. Mihovila** (Fortress of St. Michael), a 13th-century landmark atop a hill roughly an hour's walk west of town. Though largely in ruins, the fortress offers spectacular views not only of nearby Zadar, to the west, but on a cloudless day the Italian coast as well. Meanwhile, 10 km (6 miles) farther north is the quiet village of **Ugljan,** accessible from the ferry port by a handful of buses daily. For a somewhat sleepier island experience, hop aboard one of eight buses daily from Preko to the village of **Pašman.** Continuing on, you can eventually get to Tkon, Pašman island's largest village, from which some 10 ferries daily can get you back to the mainland south of Zadar. ✉ *Zadar.*

WHERE TO EAT

$$ EASTERN EUROPEAN

✕ **Konoba Kod Sipe.** If you want to have a hearty meal well above the tourist fray in Sali, you'll have to do some climbing (over 100 steps!) to reach this rustic restaurant with tables on barrels, fishnets hanging from the ceiling's wooden beams, an enticing open hearth, and an outdoor terrace shaded by grapevines. Set in a villagelike atmosphere that feels very off the beaten path, Konoba Kod Sipe serves everything from grilled calamari and pork chops to cuttlefish spaghetti and "octopus under a baking lid." To find Konoba Kod Sipe, start at the steps between the Suvenirica Porat store and the Gelateri Contes café, near the tip of the harbor, and walk up more than 100 steps, passing two pretty little churches on your left along the way. **Known for:** octopus under a baking lid; rustic barrel-theme decor; local favorite. $ *Average main: €15* ✉ *Ulica Sv. Marije, Sali* ☎ *023/377–137* ▭ *No credit cards.*

$ MEDITERRANEAN ✕ **Konoba Trapula.** Located in the cool shade of a stone alleyway behind Sali's harbor, Konoba Trapula has the charm of a place you can find only by word of mouth, as well as delicious, fresh seafood, such as *brudet* (seafood stew) and perfectly prepared tuna steak. The polished, dark wood tables and the nautical decor remind you of the restaurant's proximity to the sea. **Known for:** perfectly cooked seafood; nautical atmosphere; secluded location. $ *Average main: 35 Kn* ✉ *Sali ll 74, Dugi otok, Sali* ☎ *091/234–3274.*

WHERE TO STAY

The tourist information office can put you in touch with locals who rent private rooms, at around 220 Kn per night in high season. Large hotels will generally accept payment in either euros or kunas.

$$ HOTEL **Hotel Sali.** A 10-minute walk from the harbor on the quiet waters of Saśćica, the next bay north, this low-key hotel occupies a pair of two-story, concrete-boxish buildings perched on a lovely, pine-covered hill leading down to a beach on a pristine bay. **Pros:** lovely setting on private beach; diving center yards away. **Cons:** rooms have smoky smell; hotel bland and boxlike on the outside; few frills. $ *Rooms from: €85* ✉ *Adresa, Sali* ☎ *023/377–049, 023/377–078* 🌐 *www.hotel-sali.hr* *52 rooms* *Breakfast.*

MURTER AND THE KORNATI ISLANDS

70 km (44 miles) southeast of Zadar.

Built near the ruins of the 1st-century Roman settlement of Colentum, Murter has that unmistakable tourism-driven hustle and bustle in midsummer that Sali doesn't—both because it is the key gateway to one of Croatia's chief offshore natural splendors, Kornati National Park, and because it is easily accessible by road from Zadar.

GETTING HERE AND AROUND

Murter Island is serviced by a regular ferry line from the town of Tisno, halfway between Zadar and Šibenik. If you're visiting Kornati National Park only for a day, there are many daily boats leaving from Zadar (north of the park) and Vodice (south of the park).

EXPLORING

Fodor's Choice ★ **Kornati National Park.** The largest archipelago in the Adriatic, Kornati National Park comprises more than 100 islands that are privately owned, mostly by residents of Murter, who purchased them more than a century ago from Zadar aristocrats. The new owners burned the forests to make room for sheep, which in turn ate much of the remaining vegetation. Although anything but lush today, the islands' almost mythical beauty is ironically synonymous with their barrenness: their bone-white-to-ochre colors represent a striking contrast to the azure sea. However, owners tend vineyards and orchards on some, and there are quite a few small buildings scattered about, mostly stone cottages—many of them on **Kornat,** which is by far the largest island, at 35 km long (22 miles long) and less than a tenth as wide. Indeed, some of these cottages are available for so-called *Robinson turizm* (ask at the Murter tourist office, or inquire around town). In 1980 the archipelago became a national park. It was reportedly during a visit to Kornati in 1936 that King Edward of England decided between love for his throne and love for Wallis Simpson, the married woman who was to become his wife a year later. ■ **TIP→ The entrance ticket is included in the price of the excursion, departing from Zadar.** ✉ *An archipelago lying off the coast of North Dalmatia, between the mainland coastal cities of Zadar and Šibenik, Zadar* ☎ *098/875–746* 🌐 *www.kornat-excursions.hr.*

Murter. However you go to Murter, you'll pass through Biograd-Na-Moru, a relatively big, bustling—but thoroughly tourist-trampled—town, where the resorts have long come to predominate in what was once a charming place; Biograd-Na-Moru also serves as another access point for ferries to the Kornati Islands.

Murter, a town of 2,000 on the island of the same name that lies just off the mainland, is accessible by road from the main coastal route that runs south from Zadar toward Split. As important as tourism is to its present-day economy, boatbuilding has, not surprisingly, long been vital to Murter as well. This is not to mention its olive oil, which was once so famous that it made its way to the imperial table in Vienna. ✉ *Murter.*

WHERE TO EAT

$$ MEDITERRANEAN FAMILY

✕ **Konoba Boba.** Beyond its outstanding selection of seafood, Boba offers a variety of regional delicacies sure to please even finicky diners. The outdoor terrace and shaded gardens provide a quiet respite, and while the restaurant is very popular it doesn't feel crowded. **Known for:** popular among locals; diverse regional dishes; garden terrace. 💲 *Average main: €15* ✉ *Butina 22, Murter* ☎ *098/948–5272.*

$$$ SEAFOOD

✕ **Tic-Tac.** In this elegant little restaurant near the main square, with tables lining the length of the narrow, historic alleyway, you can begin with an appetizer such as mussels in wine sauce and move on to monkfish tail or grilled scampi—both in wine sauce. The chef likes putting seafood in wine sauce here, to gratifyingly delicious effect. **Known for:** historic location; seafood in wine sauce. 💲 *Average main: €40* ✉ *Hrokešina 5, Murter* ☎ *022/435–230* 🌐 *www.tictac-murter.com.*

WHERE TO STAY

Check with local agencies, which can find you a private room for around €30 for two.

$$ HOTEL **Hotel Tisno.** A waterfront mansion located close to the National Park Kornati and Krka, Hotel Tisno—like many regional lodging options—marries historical elegance with modern amenities. **Pros:** beautiful surrounding scenery; complimentary bikes; friendly staff. **Cons:** limited number of rooms, so book in advance; decor is pleasant but lacks personality. *Rooms from: €110* ✉ *Zapadna Gomilica 8, Tisno* ☎ *022/438–182* 🌐 *www.hoteltisno.hr* *9 rooms* *Breakfast.*

PERFORMING ARTS

FESTIVALS

Tisno Music Festivals. An array of hip music festivals come to the strait of Tisno every summer, including Garden Festival, Electric Elephant, Soundwave Croatia, SuncéBeat, and Stop Making Sense. Dates can vary, so check festival specific websites for up-to-date information. ✉ *Tisno* 🌐 *www.tz-tisno.hr/en.*

6

SPORTS AND THE OUTDOORS

DIVING

With its shipwrecks, reefs, and underwater cliffs, Kornati National Park is among Croatia's most popular diving destinations. You cannot dive alone here, so you must book your dive through a qualified center. The permit for diving in the park is 150 Kn, which includes the park entrance fee.

Aquanaut Diving Center. Aquanaut Diving Center offers a small menu of choice courses and excursions (to more than 100 sites), including a daylong boat trip that includes two dives and a stopover in the Kornati Islands. Nondiving companions are also welcome to join at a reduced fee. ✉ *Luke, near intersection of Kornatski, across from supermarket, J. Dalmatinca 1, Murter* ☎ *098/202–249* 🌐 *www.divingmurter.com.*

Najada Diving. Najada Diving offers supervised shore dives as well as half-day group excursions that include two dives. Among the highlights on its menu of excursions to more than 30 sites is a visit to the wreck of the World War II cargo ship *Francesca.* ✉ *Luke 57, on the jetty behind the supermarket, Murter* ☎ *022/436–020* 🌐 *www.najada.com.*

PAKLENICA NATIONAL PARK

50 km (31 miles) northeast of Zadar.

For mountain scenery at its most spectacular and mountain tourism at its most advanced, you need go no further from Zadar than Paklenica National Park.

EXPLORING

Paklenica National Park. The Velebit mountain range stretches along the Croatian coast for more than 100 km (62 miles), but nowhere does it pack in as much to see and do as in this relatively small, 96-square-km (37-square-mile) park at the southern terminus of the range. Here, less than an hour from Zadar, is a wealth of extraordinary karst features—from fissures, crooks, and cliffs to pits and caves. The park comprises two limestone gorges, Velika Paklenica (which ends, near the sea, at the park entrance in Starigrad) and Mala Paklenica, a few kilometers to the south; trails through the former gorge are better marked (and more tourist-trodden).

All that dry rockiness visible from the seaward side of the range turns resplendently green as you cross over the mountains to the landward side. Named after the sap of the black pine, *paklina,* which was used long ago to prime boats, the park is in fact two-thirds forest, with beech and the indigenous black pine a key part of this picture; the remaining vegetation includes cliff-bound habitats featuring several types of bluebells, and rocky areas abounding in sage and heather. The park is also home to 4,000 different species of fauna, including butterflies that have long vanished elsewhere in Europe. It is also the only mainland nesting ground in Croatia for the stately griffin vulture.

The park has more than 150 km (94 miles) of trails, from relatively easy ones leading from the Velika **Paklenica Canyon** (from the entrance in Starigrad) to the 1,640-foot-long complex of caverns called Manita Peć, to mountain huts situated strategically along the way to the Velebit's highest peaks, Vaganski Vrh (5,768 feet) and Sveto brdo (5,751 feet). The most prominent of the park's large and spectacular caves, **Manita Peć** is accessible on foot from the park entrance in Starigrad; you can enter for a modest additional fee, but buy your ticket at the park entrance. Rock climbing is also a popular activity in the park. Meanwhile, mills and mountain villages scattered throughout Paklenica evoke the life of mountain folk from the not-too-distant past.

About a half-mile down the park access road in Starigrad, you pass through the mostly abandoned hamlet of **Marasovići,** from which it's a few hundreds yards more downhill to the small building where you buy your tickets and enter the park (from this point on, only on foot). From here it's 45 minutes uphill to a side path to Anića kuk, a craggy peak, and from there it's not far to Manita Peć. However, if you don't have time or inclination for a substantial hike into the mountains, you will be happy to know that even the 45-minute walk to the entrance gate and back from the main road affords spectacular, close-up views of the Velebit range's craggy ridgeline and the gorge entrance. Also, be forewarned that if you are looking to escape the crowds, you will be hard-pressed to do so here in midsummer unless you head well into the mountains or, perhaps, opt for the park's less frequented entrance at Mala Paklenica; more likely than not, you will be sharing the sublimities of nature with thousands of other seaside revelers taking a brief respite from the coast.

A further point of interest at the park are the Bunkers, an intricate system of underground shelters built by Marshall Tito in the early 1950s. With relations between Yugoslavia and the USSR then at their worst, Tito used the geographical benefits of the gorges to build an A-bomb shelter. All the work was done in complete secrecy and very few people knew of the Bunkers. After Stalin's death, they were closed down and only reopened in 1991.

Although the park headquarters is on the main coastal road in the middle of Starigrad, fees are payable where you actually enter the park on the access road. Beyond the basic park admission and the supplemental fee to enter Manita Peć cave, the park offers every imaginable service and presentation that might encourage you to part with your kunas, from half-day group tours (400 Kn) to presentations every half hour from 11 to noon and 4 to 7 on the park's birds of prey and on falconry. ✉ *Dr. Franje Tuđmana 14a, Starigrad* ☎ *023/369–202* 🌐 *www.paklenica.hr* 🎫 *50 Kn, guided tour 400kn.*

6

WHERE TO EAT

$ MEDITERRANEAN

✕ **Restaurant Dinko.** With generous portions and a location just a short way down the road from Paklenica National Park, Restaurant Dinko is perfect for feeding hungry climbers, hikers, and park visitors. Dinko's sticks to the basics, serving fresh seafood and traditional Croatian dishes in a rustic outdoor setting. **Known for:** neighboring national park; outdoor rustic atmosphere; knowledgeable staff. $ *Average main: 35 Kn* ✉ *Paklenicka 1, Starigrad-Paklenica, Zadar* ☎ *091/512–9455* 🌐 *www.dinko-paklenica.com.*

$$ EASTERN EUROPEAN

✕ **Taverna-Konoba Marasović.** An excellent choice for travelers looking to experience traditional Croatian-style architecture, this konoba is a transformed village house replete with period furniture and a customary front terrace. The kitchen prepares local, seasonal ingredients with care, producing meals that will satisfy the desire for an authentic Dalmatian experience. **Known for:** regional dishes; rustic atmosphere; traditional architecture. $ *Average main: €13* ✉ *Trg Marasovica, Starigrad* ☎ *023/359–339* ✉ *np-paklenica@paklenica.hr.*

WHERE TO STAY

$$$ HOTEL

Hotel Alan. Once inside this high-rise hotel, you might easily forget that you are, in fact, in a concrete box that still looks rather like a college dormitory. **Pros:** great views; beach and pool; bright and modern interiors. **Cons:** bland high-rise look on the outside; pricey; smallish rooms. $ *Rooms from: €150* ✉ *Dr. Franje Tuđmana 14, Starigrad* ☎ *023/209–050, 023/369–203* 🌐 *www.hotel-alan.hr* *138 rooms* 🍽 *Breakfast.*

$$ HOTEL **Hotel Rajna.** On an isolated stretch of the main road just before you enter Starigrad from the south—and close to the national park access road—this friendly little hotel is a bit concrete-boxish in appearance. **Pros:** pleasantly isolated spot near park-access road; fine mountain views; good on-site dining; friendly service. **Cons:** 15-minute walk from the village center; bland on the outside; rooms a tad worn. *Rooms from: €60 ✉ Dr. Franje Tuđmana, Starigrad ☎ 023/359–121, 023/369–888 🌐 www.hotel-rajna.com 10 rooms Breakfast.*

SPORTS AND THE OUTDOORS

TOURS

Koma-Maras. Koma-Maras rents bicycles and sells tickets for various excursions in the national park as well as tickets for daylong boat trips up the lovely Zrmanja River gorge and its waterfalls, which are near Obrovac, toward the southern end of the Velebit range; the boat tours cost about 300 Kn per person. There's an ATM by the agency entrance. *✉ Dr. Franje Tuđmana 14, Starigrad ☎ 023/359–206, 023/359–207 🌐 www.koma-maras.hr.*

PAG ISLAND

48 km (30 miles) northeast of Zadar.

Telling an urbane resident of architecturally well-endowed Zadar that you are headed to Pag Island for a night or two will make them think you want to wallow on a sandy beach all day and party all night. Indeed, Pag Island has developed a reputation in recent years as a place to sunbathe and live it up rather than visit historic sites. The town of Novalja, in the north, has quite a summertime population of easy-livin' revelers. But to be fair, this narrow island, one of Croatia's longest, stretching 63 km (40 miles) north to south, has long been famous for other reasons, among them its cheese, salt, and, not least, its lace. Moreover, Pag Town in particular has an attractive historic center, a surprising contrast to the modern, resortish feel of its outskirts, and a contrast to the breathtaking natural barrenness of so much of the island.

Inaccessible for centuries except by sea, Pag Island saw a dramatic boost in tourism starting in 1968 with the completion of the Paškog mosta (Pag Bridge), which linked it with the mainland and the Zagreb–Split motorway. The first thing you notice on crossing over the bridge onto the island is that practically all vegetation disappears. You are on a moonlike landscape of whitewashed rocks scattered with clumps of green hanging on for dear life. But, sure enough, soon you also notice the sheep so instrumental in producing both Pag cheese—that strong, hard, Parmesan-like product that results from the sheep munching all day long on the island's salty herbs—and, yes, Pag lamb. Then, five minutes or so apart, you pass through a couple of small villages and, finally, the huge salt flats stretching out along the road right before you pull into Pag Town.

GETTING HERE AND AROUND

Pag is easiest to reach by car or bus from Zadar via the toll-free Pag Bridge. There are 10 to 15 inexpensive bus connections a day. If driving along the magistrala from Rijeka, you will do well to take the ferry from Prizna, while nondrivers have the option of a daily fast boat connection from Rijeka to Novalja at the southern tip of the island.

EXPLORING

> **PAG CHEESE**
>
> Thanks to its many sheep, Pag Island is known as the home of one of Croatia's most esteemed cheeses: *Paški sir* (Pag cheese). You can buy some for 150 Kn per kilogram, or 15 Kn for a decagram, which is a small piece indeed. If that sounds expensive, just try ordering a bit as an appetizer in a restaurant, where it's more than twice as much. You can easily find it on sale in private homes on some of the narrow streets off the main square. Celebrated local complements to the cheese include the lamb, an herb brandy called *travarica,* and Pag prosciutto.

Lest you think the modern vacation homes lining the bay are all there is to Pag Town, park your car (or get off the bus) for a walk into the historic center, the narrow streets of which provide not only a rich sense of centuries past but also a refuge of shade on a hot summer day. Pag Town was founded in 1443, when Juraj Dalmatinac of Šibenik, best known for designing Šibenik's magnificent cathedral, was commissioned by the Venetians to build a fortified island capital to replace its predecessor, which was ravaged by invaders in 1395. Today a few odd stretches remain of the 23-foot-high wall Dalmatinac built around the town, and a walk around the center reveals several Renaissance buildings and palaces from his era, as well as Baroque balconies and stone coats of arms from the 15th to 18th centuries. Pag Town's compact main square, **Trg Kralja Petra Krešimira IV,** is home to three of the town's key landmarks, two of them original buildings designed in the mid-14th century by Juraj Dalmatinac. The bay stretches far, with sandy, shallow beaches aplenty—making Pag Island a great place to sunbathe and swim for a day or two, especially with children. The best and biggest beaches, amid pretty groves of pine and Dalmatian oak, are in Novalja.

Crkva Sveta Marija (*St. Mary's Church*). This three-nave basilica's simple front is decorated with a Gothic portal, an appropriately lacelike Renaissance rosette, and unfinished figures of saints. A relief over the entrance depicts the Virgin Mary protecting the townsfolk of Pag. Begun in 1466 under Dalmatinac's direction, it was completed only decades later, after his death. Inside, note the elaborate, 18th-century Baroque altars, and the wood beams visible on the original stone walls. The church is open daily 9–noon and 5–7. ✉ *Glavni Trg, 6 Ulica Jurja Dalmatinca, Pag* 🌐 *www.tzgpag.hr/en/grad-i-otok-pag-en/2013-01-08-15-53-2/marijina-uznesenja-en.*

Knežev dvor (*Duke's Palace*). Across the square is the imposing Knežev dvor with its magnificent, richly detailed portal, a sumptuous

CLOSE UP

White Gold

There was a time when *paške čipke* was passed off abroad as Greek, Austrian, or Italian. Those days are long over. Today an officially recognized "authentic Croatian product" that is sometimes called "white gold," Pag lace is the iconic souvenir to take home with you from a visit to Pag Island—unless you are confident that a hulking block of Pag cheese won't spoil. An integral component of the colorful folk costumes locals wear during festivals, this celebrated white lace is featured most saliently as the huge peaked head ornament ladies don on such occasions, which resembles a fastidiously folded, ultra-starched white cloth napkin.

Originating in the ancient Greek city of Mycenae, the Pag lace-making tradition endured for centuries before being popularized far and wide as a Pag product beginning in the late 19th century. A lace-making school was founded in Pag Town in 1906, drawing orders from royalty from distant lands. In 1938, Pag lace makers participated in the world exhibition in New York.

Pag lace differs from other types of lace in two key respects: a thin thread and exceptional durability. Using an ordinary mending needle against a solid background, and usually proceeding without a plan, the maker begins by creating a circle within which she (or he) makes tiny holes close together; the thread is then pulled through them. The completed lace has a starched quality and can even be washed without losing its firmness. It is best presented on a dark background and framed.

The process is painstaking, so Pag lace is not cheap: a typical small piece of around 20 centimeters in diameter costs at least 200 Kn from a maker or perhaps double that from a shop.

15th-century edifice built to house the duke. Until the early 1990s, it housed a grocery store and a café; now it is a cultural and exhibition venue, hosting concerts, plays, and manifestations during the summer months. The upper floors have been converted into the City Hall. ✉ *Glavni Trg, Pag.*

Stari grad. A mere 20-minute walk south of the present town center lie the ruins of the previous, 9th-century town. You can wander around for free, taking in the Romanesque-style Crkva Sveta Marija (St. Mary's Church), first mentioned in historical records in 1192; the ruins of a Franciscan monastery; and a legendary, centuries-old well whose filling up with water after a drought was credited to the intervention of the Holy Virgin. On August 15, one of only two days St. Mary's Church is open to the public (the other is September 8), a procession of locals carries a statue of the Virgin Mary from here to the church of the same name on present-day Pag's main square. On September 8 they return. To get to Stari grad, walk across the bridge and keep left on Put Starog Grada, the road that runs south along the bay. ✉ *Pag.*

WHERE TO EAT

$$ EASTERN EUROPEAN **Bistro Na Tale.** An easy choice if you're looking to sample Pag's signature local lamb or specialty *Paški sir* (cheese produced by sheep consuming grass laced with salty sea water). While more unique eateries are to be had, Bistro Na Tale is nevertheless a popular spot that serves quality dishes in a pleasant atmosphere. **Known for:** signature regional dishes; popular among locals; terrace overlooking the salt flats. *Average main: €18 Radiceva 2, Pag 023/611–194 Closed Dec. 23–Feb. 1.*

$ EASTERN EUROPEAN **Konoba Bodulo.** The menu may be small at this family-owned spot, but it manages to squeeze in everything from staple pastas and risottos to grilled meats and steak—and the service is friendly. You can enjoy this combination under the courtyard's grapevine or next to the interior's stone walls, with Croatian pop for background music. **Known for:** versatile menu; traditional rustic atmosphere. *Average main: 42 Kn Vangrada 19, Pag 023/611–989.*

$$ EASTERN EUROPEAN **Konoba Giardin.** The Konoba Giardin has mastered the art of cooking with flame, producing delectably grilled entrées from a real wood fire nestled within a brick oven. Select a whole fish from the day's fresh catch, sold by the kilogram, or share a grill platter of mixed cuts of beef piled high atop potatoes and salads. **Known for:** flambé technique; live guitar music; local wine. *Average main: €18 Vanđelje 1, Kolan 023/698–007 www.konoba-giardin.com.*

WHERE TO STAY

$$$ B&B/INN Fodor's Choice ★ **Boškinac.** Nestled amid vineyards and olive groves, refined serenity awaits guests to Boškinac. **Pros:** phenomenal restaurant; great vineyard tour; luxurious everything. **Cons:** remote; vehicle needed. *Rooms from: €170 Novaljsko Polje BB, Novalja 053/663–500 www.boskinac.com 11 rooms Breakfast.*

$$$ RESORT **Luna Island Hotel.** If you're looking for a place to relax and have your meals, spa treatments, and lounge chair easily available within just a few steps, at Luna Island Hotel you have arrived. **Pros:** air-conditioning; beachside location; far from the party beach of Zrće (the Ibiza of Croatia). **Cons:** vehicle is helpful; pleasant yet bland furnishings; pricey. *Rooms from: €200 Jakisnica BB, Pag 05/365–4700 lunaislandhotel.com 96 rooms Breakfast.*

PERFORMING ARTS

FESTIVALS

Pag Carnival. Pag Carnival, featuring a range of music on and around the main square, dance and folk-song performances—and, not least, the annual reenactment of a 16th-century folk drama, *Paška robinja* (Slave Girl of Pag), which tells the story of buying back an enslaved girl, the granddaughter of the ruler Ban Derenčin, who was defeated by the Turks. The Pag Carnival takes place immediately before Lent, which is usually in February, but varies from year to year. There is also a shorter carnival held in the last weekend of July. See the tourist office website for specific dates. *Pag.*

Pag Music Festivals. An array of hip music festivals come to the island of Pag every summer. Some island festivals include Hideout Festival, Sonus Festival, and Fresh Island Festival. ✉ *Pag.*

SHOPPING

Galerija Paške Čipke (*Pag Lace Gallery*). You needn't venture farther than the main square and surrounding narrow streets of Pag Town to find a white gold jewelry seller—whether an old lady or an equally enthusiastic child. Of course, you can also try Pag Town's very own Galerija Paške Čipke (mid-June through mid-September, daily 9–1) or any of several local shops that you are certain to encounter near the main square in Pag Town. ✉ *Trg Krajla Petra Krešimira IV, Pag* 🌐 *www.tzgpag.hr/en/grad-i-otok-pag-en/kulturna-bastina/paska-cipka-en.*

SPORTS AND THE OUTDOORS

BEACHES

Deciding where to swim once you reach Pag Town is a no-brainer; you can pick practically anywhere in the huge, sheltered bay that stretches out from the short bridge in the town center. If you have kids, all that sand and shallow water is a real plus compared to Zadar and so many other stretches of Croatia's often deep, rocky coast. Most of the 27 km (17 miles) of public beaches in the bay are accessible by car. For even better swimming, if that is possible, try heading north to Novalja and environs. The tourist-information office has a free map showing the locations of the best beaches.

SPLIT AND CENTRAL DALMATIA

Updated by Elizabeth Hughes and Robert Komljen

Central Dalmatia's wild beauty is often characterized as harsh, hot, and edgy because of its scorching summers, rocky coastal beaches, steep mountains, and rugged inland. It is precisely that combination of wild raw beauty that makes central Dalmatia stand out from its northern and inland neighbors and what attracts outsiders. The capital city of Dalmatia, Split, is an historic city that was once an industrial and trade center that has transformed dramatically since the war for independence.

Split has blossomed in the past 10 years into a bustling coastal destination. The layers of history contained within the walls of the Diocletian palace beg to be uncovered with more than just a few snapshots and a stroll through the labyrinth-like side streets. The modern life of the citizens that currently live in and around the old walls contrast sharply with its ancient history, and make Split the most eclectic of all Croatian cities.

From Split you can take an overnight ferry to Ancona, Italy, or hop on one of the regular ferries or catamarans to one of the outlying islands. Split is also Central Dalmatia's main base for yacht-charter companies. A 90-minute drive up the coast, northwest of Split, lies Šibenik, home to a Gothic-Renaissance cathedral. Once an important industrial center, Šibenik has fallen into economic decline, but it still makes a good base for visiting the cascading waterfalls of Krka National Park, and the peaceful riverside town of Skradin. Moving back from Šibenik toward Split is Trogir. The historic city of Trogir is a remarkable conglomeration of Roman, Greek, and Venetian ancient stone architecture contained on a tiny island that residents call their living museum. A 30-minute drive down the coast from Split brings one to Omiš and the mouth of the River Cetina. This river forms a steep-sided valley renowned for adventure sports like rafting and rock climbing (called free climbing in Croatia). However, for many people, what makes Central Dalmatia so special are the islands. The nearest, Brač, most often recognized for its famous Zlatni Rat (Golden Cape) beach is an island of exceptional beauty that will leave you with a lasting impression because of the traditions, culture, and history that remain undiscovered yet pervade every aspect of the food, work, and life on this island. West of Brač lies the island of Šolta. Although there is little of cultural interest here, those lucky enough to be sailing along the south side of the island will find several idyllic bays that are accessible only by sea. South of Brač rises the island of Hvar, home to Central Dalmatia's most exclusive party destination, Hvar Town. Sixteenth-century Venetian buildings ring three sides of the Hvar Town harbor with its magnificent main square that is overlooked by a Baroque cathedral and a proud hilltop castle that beckons visitors to take in the view from higher ground. Farther out to sea still lies wild, windswept Vis, Croatia's most distant inhabited island. There are

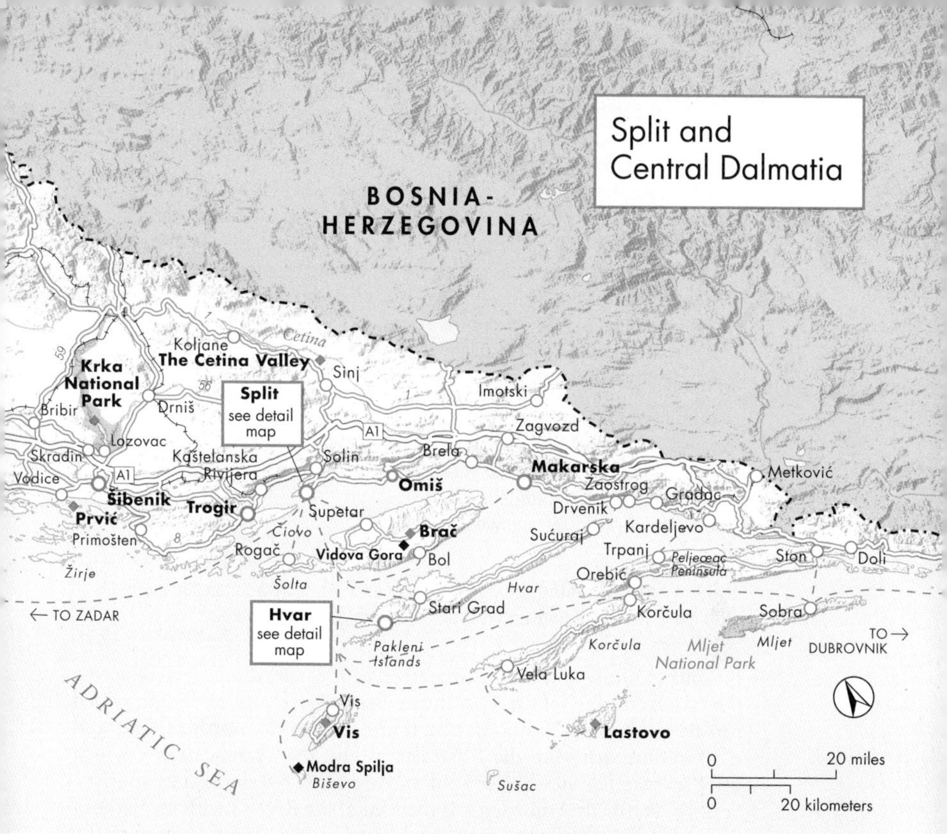

only two real settlements here: Vis Town and Komiža, the latter making the best starting point for a day trip to Modra Spilja (Blue Cave) on the island of Biševo. Back on the mainland, a two-hour drive down the coast south of Split brings you to Makarska, a popular seaside area built around a bay filled with fishing boats and backed by the rugged silhouette of the Biokovo Mountains. Biokovo's peak, Sveti Jure (5,780 feet) is the third highest of Croatia's mountains and offers stunning views over the entire region.

Lastovo, Croatia's second–most distant inhabited island (after Vis), remains firmly off the beaten track. Although it is part of Southern Dalmatia, it is only connected to Split via ferry and catamaran services.

ORIENTATION AND PLANNING

GETTING ORIENTED

Split is the main jumping-off point for exploring all of Dalmatia, not just Central Dalmatia. From there it is easy to catch a bus, boat, train, or rental car in any direction to see everything Dalmatia offers, on and off the beaten path. In each direction of Split, there are many nearby places worth exploring. Directly south of Split are the islands of Brač and Šolta, both easily accessed by ferry in less than one hour. Northeast

TOP REASONS TO GO

Roman splendor: Explore Diocletian's Palace, a massive 3rd-century Roman edifice that contains Croatia's most defiant and alternative population within its walls. Arrange to take a tour in the early morning hours before the buzz of daily life drowns out the voices of the past in this amazing historical location.

Island hopping: Come to Hvar and hire a taxi boat or a one-day sailing charter to bring you to your own private island and experience the purity of island life and what it inspires.

Hiking and swimming: Plunge into the clear waters of Sutivan on Brač after climbing to Vidova Gora, the highest point on all the Croatian islands, or walking the Dolce Vita trail through the island's olive groves where the country's premier olive oil is produced.

Sailing adventures: Sail into Komiža harbor on Vis island aboard a yacht after a long day on the water, perhaps having visited Modra Spilja (the Blue Cave) on the nearby island of Biševo.

Natural beauty: Climb Biokovo Mountain at sunrise, take a moonlight swim in Tucepi, and be awed by the Makarska Riviera's majestic mountain from above and below.

of Split is Omiš and the Cetina river valley, and directly west across the bay from the Split port is the ancient walled city of Trogir, which can be reached in 20 minutes by taxi boat. To the north of Split and a 30-minute drive are the Klis fortress and the Vranjaca cave, which offer spectacular views over Split and are often overlooked by tourists. Southwest toward Dubrovnik is the Makarska Riviera with its plethora of hidden coved beaches that can be reached in about 45 minutes by car from Split. In the opposite direction of Makarska, along the main coastal highway, there is Krka National Park, about a two-hour drive from Split but also accessible by boat via Skradin Bay. Međugorje, which is across the border in Bosnia and Herzegovina, is less than a two-hour drive from Split and is also a short distance from Mostar.

WHEN TO GO

High season runs from July through August, when the region is inundated with foreign tourists. The Split airport is connected to over 100 locations during this time, and up to 58 different air companies have scheduled flights into Split, making it the most accessible of all Croatian destinations. Prices at this time rise significantly, restaurant staff are overworked, beaches are crowded, and it can be difficult to find a place to sleep if you haven't reserved in advance. On top of everything, it can be very hot. On the upside, museums and churches have extended hours, open-air bars and clubs bring nightlife to the fore, and there are numerous cultural festivals with performances starring international musicians, dancers, and actors assuring you that this is the most happening place to be in summer.

Low season runs from November through April, when many hotels and restaurants close completely. The exception being over Christmas and New Year, when some more sophisticated establishments (for example,

GREAT ITINERARIES

Central Dalmatia warrants weeks of discovery; even many locals admit that they haven't even seen it all. However, if your time is limited, the itineraries listed below aim to give you a taste of the major attractions.

IF YOU HAVE 3 DAYS

Devote Day 1 to **Split,** exploring the historic monuments within the walls of Diocletian's Palace and attending an open-air opera performance if the Split Summer Festival is in progress. On the next day, take an early-morning ferry to Supetar on the island of Brač, then a local bus to **Bol,** for an afternoon bathing on Croatia's finest beach, Zlatni Rat. Catch the late-afternoon catamaran to Jelsa on the island of Hvar, then a local bus to **Hvar Town,** the region's hippest island resort, where you should sleep. Next morning, either check out Hvar's Venetian-style architecture or take a taxi boat to Pakleni Otoci for a swim. Catch the late-afternoon ferry back to Split for your final night.

IF YOU HAVE 5 DAYS

Spend your first day in Split. On the next morning, drive or take a local bus to **Trogir,** a compact settlement of stone houses built on an island linked to the mainland by a bridge, then proceed up the coast for an afternoon in **Šibenik,** where the most visited monument is the Gothic–Renaissance cathedral. Spend the night in either Šibenik or **Skradin.** Give Day 3 to the waterfalls and dense woodland of **Krka National Park,** returning to Split for the night. Days 4 and 5 should be dedicated to the islands of **Brač** and **Hvar** *(see above)*, returning to Split for the final night.

IF YOU HAVE 7 DAYS

Spend your first day in Split, the second and third days in Trogir, Šibenik, Skradin, and Krka National Park, as outlined above, returning to Split on the third night. Days 4 and 5 can then be given over to the islands of Brač and Hvar (*as described above*), returning to Split for the fifth night. On the next morning, either drive or take a local bus down the coast to **Omiš,** from which you can set off up the **Cetina Valley** and participate in adventure sports (by prior arrangement). In the evening, continue down the coast to **Makarska,** where you should sleep. On the final day you can explore Makarska and its beaches, or venture up Biokovo Mountain for spectacular views over the entire region. Return to Split for your last night.

in Hvar Town) open their doors for the holidays. The weather can be unreliable during this time, but if you're lucky you could find yourself drinking morning coffee in the sunshine below a deep blue sky, against a backdrop of snowcapped mountains and quite possibly leave you feeling like you have discovered your own private paradise.

However, for most people the best time to visit is midseason, May through June and September through October. During these periods you'll miss the crowds, the weather should be sunny and dry, and the sea will still be warm for swimming; the region's hotels and restaurants will be open, but their pace slow enough to lend an air of true relaxation.

PLANNING

GETTING HERE AND AROUND

AIR TRAVEL

Split is served by Split Airport (SPU) at Kaštela, 25 km (16 miles) northwest of the city center. The island of Brač is served by Brač Airport at Veško Polje, 14 km (9 miles) northeast of Bol.

The national carrier, Croatia Airlines, operates domestic flights from Split to Zagreb, Dubrovnik, Pula, and Osijek. During the summer high season you can fly directly to Split from Amsterdam, Bari, Brussels, Catania, Copenhagen, Frankfurt, Gothenburg, Hamburg, Helsinki, Istanbul, Lisbon, London, Lyon, Manchester, Milan, Munich, Oslo, Palermo, Paris, Prague, Rome, Sarajevo, Skopje, Stockholm, Tel Aviv, Turin, Vienna, Warsaw, and Zurich. Also through summer, Croatia Airlines flies nonstop from the island of Brač to Zagreb, Munich, and Frankfurt. Adria and British Airways also fly to Split. In addition, through the summer the low-cost airlines EasyJet and Wizzair operate between London and Split.

Airline Contacts Adria Airways. ✉ *Praška 9, Zagreb* ☎ *021/203–331* 🌐 *www.adria.si.* **Air Mediterranee.** ☎ *1/312–999* 🌐 *www.air-mediterranee.fr.* **Austria Airlines.** ✉ *Maksimirska 112a, Zagreb* ☎ *1/626–5900* 🌐 *www.austrian.com.* **British Airways.** ✉ *Split Airport, Kaštel Štafilic* ☎ *021/797–303.* **Croatia Airlines.** ☎ *021/303–305* 🌐 *www.croatiaairlines.com.* **EasyJet.** 🌐 *www.easyjet.com.* **Jet2.com.** 🌐 *www.jet2.com.* **Lufthansa.** ☎ *1/390–7284* 🌐 *www.lufthansa.com.* **Wizzair.** 🌐 *www.wizzair.com.*

Airport Contacts Split Airport. ☎ *021/203–555 general info, 021/203–218 lost and found* 🌐 *www.split-airport.hr.* **Brač Airport.** ✉ *Veško field, Supetar* ☎ *021/559–711 general info* 🌐 *www.airport-brac.hr.*

Airport Transfer Contacts Pleso prijevoz. ☎ *021/203–119* 🌐 *www.plesoprijevoz.hr.*

BOAT AND FERRY TRAVEL

From June through September, Jadrolinija and Blue Line both run regular services to Ancona (Italy), departing at 9 pm from Split and arriving in Ancona at 7 am the following day. The same vessels depart at 9 pm from Ancona to arrive in Split at 7 am. Journey time is approximately 10 hours in either direction. In peak season only, Blue Line also runs day crossings departing from Ancona at 11 am on Saturday, Sunday, and Monday. Through winter these services are reduced slightly.

From June to September the Italian company SNAV runs Croazia Jet, a daily catamaran service between Ancona (Italy) and Split, departing at 5 pm from Split and arriving in Ancona at 9:30 pm. The same vessel departs at 11 am from Ancona to arrive in Split at 3:30 pm. The journey time is 4½ hours in either direction. The same company runs Pescara Jet, a daily catamaran service between Pescara (Italy) and Split, stopping at Stari Grad (island of Hvar) en route. The vessel departs at 5 pm from Split and arrives in Pescara at 11 pm, then leaves Pescara the following morning at 10:30, arriving in Split at 4:15 pm. On Saturday only, a corresponding catamaran connects from Stari Grad (Hvar) to

Bol (Brač). Jadrolinija operates coastal ferries that run from Rijeka to Dubrovnik. Ferries depart from Rijeka twice a week in the evening, and arrive in Split in the early morning on the following day (journey time is approximately 10 hours) and then continue down the coast to Dubrovnik (journey time is approximately 9 hours), stopping at Stari Grad (island of Hvar) and Korčula en route. From Dubrovnik, they then cover an overnight stretch to Bari in Italy. Jadrolinija runs daily ferries to Supetar (island of Brač), Stari Grad (island of Hvar), and Vis from Split. Jadrolinija runs a daily catamaran from Split to Hvar Town (island of Hvar), which then continues to Vela Luka (island of Korčula) and Ubli (island of Lastovo). A separate service runs to Bol (island of Brač) and then continues to Jelsa (island of Hvar). It is now possible to book most boat and ferry travel online, sometimes at a reduced price. It is highly recommended to purchase online in advance whenever possible, especially during high season when waiting until the last minute could often mean waiting an extra day.

Contacts Blue Line. ☎ *021/352–533* 🌐 *www.blueline-ferries.com.* **Jadrolinija.** ✉ *Split ferry port, Gat Sv. Duje BB, Split* ☎ *021/338–333* 🌐 *www.jadrolinija.hr.* **Krilo.** ✉ *Poljička cesta, Jesenice* ☎ *021/645–476* 🌐 *krilo.hr.* **SNAV.** ☎ *021/322–252* 🌐 *www.snav.it.*

BUS TRAVEL

International buses arrive daily from Trieste, Ljubljana, Belgrade, Sarajevo, Munich, and Stuttgart. There are buses once a week from Vienna, and London via Paris.

There are good bus connections to destinations all over Croatia. There are approximately 30 buses per day to Zagreb, 12 to Dubrovnik (in Southern Dalmatia), 14 to Zadar (in Northern Dalmatia), and 12 to Rijeka (in Kvarner). Buses traveling south to Dubrovnik stop at Makarska en route, while those going north to Zadar stop at Šibenik. In addition, regular local buses run every 30 minutes up the coast to Trogir and down the coast to Omiš. Timetable information is available from the Split bus station, or from their website *(see below)*.

Contacts Split Bus Station. ✉ *Obala Kneza Domogoja 12, Split* ☎ *060/327–777* 🌐 *www.ak-split.hr.*

CAR TRAVEL

While visiting Split and the nearby islands of Brač, Hvar, and Vis, you are certainly better off without a car. However, you may wish to rent a vehicle to drive up the coast to Šibenik and Krka National Park, or down the coast to Omiš and Makarska, although these destinations are also well served by buses. Renting a car once you arrive on the islands is also an affordable option to be able to see the entire island at your own pace.

Contacts Dollar Thrifty. ✉ *Trumbićeva Obala 17, Split* ☎ *021/895–320* 🌐 *www.subrosa.hr* ✉ *Split Airport, Kaštel Štafilic* ☎ *021/399–000* 🌐 *www.subrosa.hr.* **Hertz.** ✉ *Trubićeva Obala 2, Split* ☎ *021/360–455* 🌐 *www.hertz.hr* ✉ *Split Airport, Kaštel Štafilic* ☎ *021/203–292* 🌐 *www.hertz.hr.* **Rapidus rent-a-car.** 🌐 *www.rapidus.hr/en-hvar.php.*

TAXI TRAVEL

In Split the main taxi ranks lie at each end of the Riva (Obala Hrvatskog Preporoda), in front of the *pazar* (open-air market), and in front of Hotel Bellevue. You will also find taxis waiting outside the train station (Obala Kneza Domagoja). Or you can call for a taxi in Split.

TRAIN TRAVEL

There are three day trains and two night trains (with sleeper cars) daily between Split and Zagreb (journey time 5½ hours daytime; 8½ hours nighttime). In addition, there are three day trains daily between Split and Šibenik (journey time approximately 3½ hours, with a change at Perković).

Contact Split Train Station. ✉ *Obala Kneza Domogoja 9, Split* ☎ *060/333–444* 🌐 *www.hzpp.hr.*

RESTAURANTS

Eateries fall into two main categories: you can eat in a *restoran* (restaurant) or *konoba* (tavern). Restaurants are more formal affairs, catering mainly to tourists and offering Croatian cuisine plus a choice of popular international dishes. In contrast, a konoba serves typical regional dishes; many offer a *marenda* (cut-price lunch), and at those you are likely to see locals as well as tourists. Central Dalmatian specialties are mainly seafood-based. *Rižot* (risotto) reflects the region's historic ties with Venice, as does *brodet* (fish stewed in a rich tomato, onion, and wine sauce). Fish are divided into two categories: "white" fish, including *brancin* (branzino, or sea bass) and *san pjero* (John Dory), are more expensive, while "blue" fish, including *srdele* (sardines) and *skuša* (mackerel), are cheaper but less frequently on offer. In restaurants, be aware that fresh fish is priced by the kilogram, so prices vary dramatically depending on how big your fish is. A popular new trend in dining are the wine bars that have popped up all over Dalmatia featuring the region's best local wines, cheeses, and prosciutto. Some offer a wide selection of original tapas, and almost all are eager to educate their clientele about local wines and provide suggestions.

HOTELS

Central Dalmatia's best and most expensive hotels are in Hvar Town on the island of Hvar. The region's socialist-era resort hotels are gradually being privatized and refurbished, and a number of small family-run and boutique luxury hotels have opened as well. However, many visitors still prefer to rent a private room or apartment, a solution that offers value for money, direct contact with the locals, and (if you are lucky) an authentic stone cottage opening onto a terrace lined with potted geraniums and a blissful sea view. The season runs from Easter to late October, and peaks during July and August, when prices rise significantly and when it may be difficult to find a place to sleep if you have not booked in advance. *Hotel reviews have been shortened. For full information, visit Fodors.com.*

	WHAT IT COSTS IN EUROS (€) AND CROATIAN KUNA (KN)			
	$	$$	$$$	$$$$
Restaurants	under 35 Kn	35 Kn–60 Kn	61 Kn–80 Kn	over 80 Kn
	under €5	€5–€8	€9–€10	over €10
Hotels	under 925 Kn	925 Kn–1,300 Kn	1,301 Kn–1,650 Kn	over 1,650 Kn
	under €121	€121–€170	€171–€216	over €216

Restaurant prices are the average cost of a main course at dinner or, if dinner is not served, at lunch. Hotel prices are the lowest cost of a standard double room in high season.

TOURS

There are many tour options to choose from in Split. New agencies pop up every year offering different options of the same basic tours. There are some agencies more committed to preserving the natural beauty, culture, and traditions of Dalmatia. These agencies are very proud of Croatia and seek to provide tourists with authentic and individual experiences that are not focused on mass tourism.

Opcija Tours. Opcija Tours is well known not only for their walking tours of Diocletian's Palace but also for their private one-day charters to nearby islands and restaurants. ✉ *Papalićeva ulica 2, Split* ☎ *021/345–244* 🌐 *www.opcijatours.hr.*

FAMILY Fodor's Choice ★ **Secret Dalmatia.** Custom-designed tours are the best choice for adventurous foodies who want to experience Dalmatia's culinary heritage in a deeper, authentic way. The company started with wine and food tours and has grown to include sailing and biking trips that showcase not only great food, wine, and chefs, but also Croatia's blue seas and rolling hills and forests in the hinterlands. Splurge on a cooking class with Tatijana on Trogir. Tatijana is a creative culinary diva who brings the roots of Mediterranean life through her cooking and kitchen conversation. ✉ *Ulica Marina Držića 15, Split* ☎ *091/567–1604* 🌐 *www.secretdalmatia.com.*

Split Excursions. Split Excursions offers tours both of the city and the surrounding area, including Plitvice National Park. ✉ *Trg Republike 1, Split* ☎ *021/360–061* 🌐 *www.split-excursions.com.*

VISITOR INFORMATION

Contacts Bol Tourist Information Center. ✉ *Porat Bolskih Pomoraca BB, Bol* ☎ *021/635–638* 🌐 *www.bol.hr.* **Hvar Town Tourist Information Center.** ✉ *Trg Sv. Stjepana 42, Hvar* ☎ *021/741–059* 🌐 *www.tzhvar.hr.* **Lastovo Tourist Office.** ✉ *Pjevor BB, Lastovo* ☎ *020/801–018* 🌐 *www.lastovo-tz.net.* **Makarska Tourist Information Centre.** ✉ *Obala Kralja Tomislava 2, Makarska* ☎ *021/611–688* 🌐 *www.turistbiro-makarska.com.* **Šibenik Tourist Information Center.** ✉ *Obala palih omladinaca 3, Šibenik* ☎ *022/214–411* 🌐 *www.sibenik-tourism.hr.* **Split & Dalmatia County Tourist Board.** ✉ *Prilaz brace Kaliterna 10/I, Split* ☎ *021/490–032* 🌐 *www.dalmatia.hr.* **Split Tourist Information Center.** ✉ *Hrvatskog narodnog preporoda 9, Split* ☎ *021/348–600* 🌐 *www.visitsplit.com.* **Trogir Tourist Information Center.** ✉ *Trg Ivana Pavla II 1, Trogir* ☎ *021/885–628* 🌐 *www.tztrogir.hr.* **Vis Tourist Information Center.** ✉ *Šetalište Stare Isse 5, Vis Town* ☎ *021/717–017* 🌐 *www.tz-vis.hr.*

7

SPLIT

Split is 365 km (228 miles) south of Zagreb.

Split's ancient core is so spectacular and unusual that a visit is more than worth your time. The heart of the city lies within the walls of Roman emperor Diocletian's retirement palace, which was built in the 3rd century AD. Diocletian, born in the nearby Roman settlement of Salona in AD 245, achieved a brilliant career as a soldier and became emperor at the age of 40. In 295 he ordered this vast palace to be built in his native Dalmatia, and when it was completed he stepped down from the throne and retired to his beloved homeland. Upon his death, he was laid to rest in an octagonal mausoleum, around which Split's magnificent cathedral was built.

In 615, when Salona was sacked by barbarian tribes, those fortunate enough to escape found refuge within the stout palace walls and divided up the vast imperial apartments into more modest living quarters. Thus, the palace developed into an urban center, and by the 11th century the settlement had expanded beyond the ancient walls.

Under the rule of Venice (1420–1797), Split—as a gateway to the Balkan interior—became one of the Adriatic's main trading ports, and the city's splendid Renaissance palaces bear witness to the affluence of those times. When the Habsburgs took control during the 19th century, an overland connection to Central Europe was established by the construction of the Split–Zagreb–Vienna railway line.

After World War II, the Tito years saw a period of rapid urban expansion: industrialization accelerated, and the suburbs extended to accommodate high-rise apartment blocks. Today the historic center of Split is included on UNESCO's list of World Heritage Sites.

GETTING HERE AND AROUND

Central Dalmatia's capital, this coastal city is easy to get around and offers ferries to popular tourist spots like the islands of Brač and Hvar. There are also local buses available to visit surrounding towns like Bol and Trogir.

EXPLORING

The Old Town (often referred to as the Grad), where most of the architectural monuments are found, lies within the walls of Diocletian's Palace, which fronts on the seafront promenade, known to locals as the Riva. West of the center, Varoš is a conglomeration of stone fishermen's cottages built into a hillside, behind which rises Marjan, a 3½-km-long (2-mile-long) peninsula covered with pinewoods. Southeast of the center, the ferry port, bus station, and train station are grouped close together on Obala Kneza Domagoja. The newly constructed waterfront area, known as Westcoast to locals, is a three-minute walk from the Riva and is modernly designed and offers a fresh new spacious view of Split.

TOP ATTRACTIONS

Fodor's Choice ★ **Dioklecijanova Palača** (*Diocletian's Palace*). The original palace, which took about 10 years to complete, was built in AD 298. The palace was both a luxurious villa and a Roman garrison. Its rectangular shape has two main streets that divide the palace into four quarters: Dioklecijanova Ul, which runs north to south, and Poljana Krajlice Jelene, which runs east to west. Each of the four walls have a main gate, the largest and most important being the northern Zlatna Vrata (Golden Gate), which once opened onto the road to the Roman settlement of Salona. The entrance from the western wall was the Željezna Vrata (Iron Gate), and the entrance through the east wall was the Srebrena Vrata (Silver Gate). The Mjedna Vrata (Bronze Gate) on the south wall faces directly onto the sea, and during Roman times boats would have docked here. The city celebrated the palace's 1,700th birthday in 2005 and continues to share the heritage of its Roman emperor by annually marking the last Friday in July as Diocletian's Night. ■ **TIP→ Hire an experienced private guide that can give you a walking tour in the early morning hours in order to experience the true history of the palace walls.** There are more than 1,000 people living within the walls of what was once a Roman emperor's palace; this and the summer crowds can make it difficult to uncover this treasure as it once was and a compelling reason for visiting in the early hours or off-season. ✉ *Obala Hrvatskog Narodnog Preporoda, Grad.*

Fodor's Choice ★ **Galerija Meštrović** (*Meštrović Gallery*). A short walk from the Riva, this must-see gallery is in a tranquil location overlooking the sea and is surrounded by extensive gardens. Ivan Mestrovic, considered to be the Rodin of Croatia, designed this building as his summer residence during the 1920s and '30s. Some 200 of his sculptural works in wood, marble, stone, and bronze are on display, both indoors and out. The gallery is a green oasis in the center of the city with an open-air café that is frequented by children and families during the day and young locals in the evening. It's a great place to escape the crowded city streets and relax while enjoying a refreshing drink surrounded by a stunning collection of a master's work. ✉ *Šetalište Ivana Meštrovicá 46, Meje* ☎ *021/340–800* 🌐 *www.mdc.hr* 🎫 *40 Kn* ⏲ *Closed Mon.*

Kaštelet-Crikvine. Entrance to the Galerija Meštrović is also valid for nearby Kaštelet, which is down the road from the Meštrović Gallery. The Holy Cross chapel contains a magnificent collection of Ivan Meštrović's work that was produced over a period of 40 years and depicts the life of Christ in a series of bas-relief wood carvings that many consider Meštrović's finest work. Viewing the entire work should not be rushed and is worth visiting in conjunction with his other works in the gallery. ✉ *Šetalište Ivana Meštrovicá 39, Meje* 🌐 *mdc.hr/mestrovic/kastelet* 🎫 *30 Kn (includes Galerija Meštrović)* ⏲ *Closed Mon.*

Vestibul. The cupola of this domed space would once have been decorated with marble and mosaics. Today there's only a round hole in the top of the dome, but it produces a stunning effect: the dark interior, the blue sky above, and the tip of the cathedral's bell tower framed in the opening. ✉ *Peristil, Grad.*

Zlatna Vrata (*Golden Gate*). Formerly the main entrance into the palace, Zlatna Vrata, on the north side of the palace, is the most monumental of the four gates—two guards in Roman costume stand here through summer. Just outside the Zlatna Vrata stands Meštrović's gigantic bronze

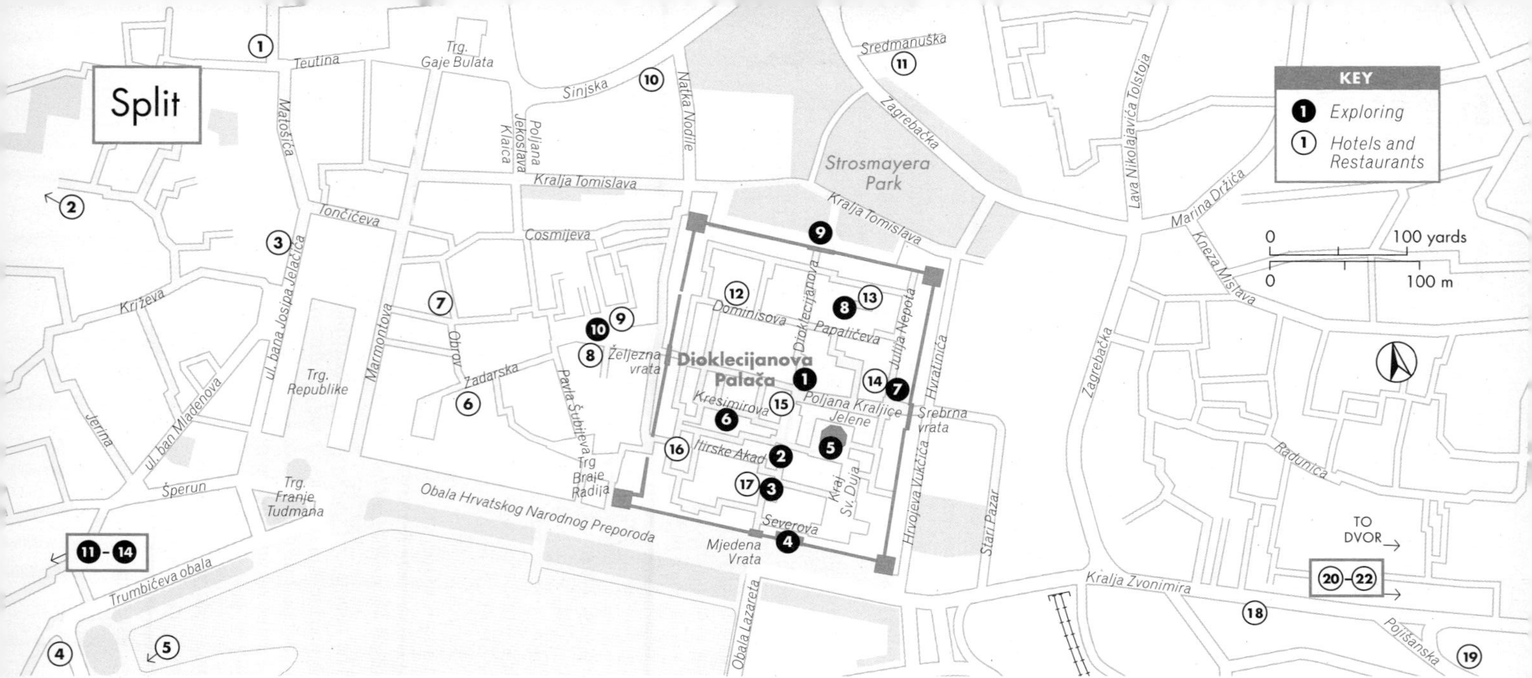

Exploring

Dioklecijanova Palača 1
Etnografski Muzej 4
Galerija Meštrović 12
Galerija Vidović 7
Gradski Muzej 8
Jupiterov Hram/ Temple of Jupiter 6
Kaštelet-Crikvine 14
Katedrala Sveti Dujam 5
Marjan 13
Muzej Hrvatskih Arheološki Spomenika .. 11
Narodni trg 10
Peristil 2
Vestibul 3
Zlatna Vrata 9

Restaurants

Adriatic Grašo 5
Adriatic Oyster and Sushi Bar 13
Articok 3
Caffe-restoran Dvor 20
Corto Maltese
Freestyle Food 7
Fife 4
Kod Joze 11
No Stress 9
Paradox 1
To Je Tako 15
Uje/Oil Bar 12

Hotels

Divota Apartment Hotel ... 2
Hotel Cornaro 10
Hotel Luxe 18
Hotel Marmont 6
Hotel Peristil 14
Hotel Slavija 16
Hotel Split 22
Hotel Vestibul Palace ... 17
Le Meridien Lav 21
Palace Judita Heritage Hotel 8
Villa Diana 19

statue of Grgur Ninski (Bishop Gregory of Nin). During the 9th century, the bishop campaigned for the use of the Slav language in the Croatian Church, as opposed to Latin, thus infuriating Rome. This statue was created in 1929 and placed on Peristil to mark the 1,000th anniversary of the Split Synod, then moved here in 1957. Note the big toe on the left foot, which is considered by locals to be a good luck charm and has been worn gold through constant touching. ✉ *Dioklecijanova, Grad.*

WORTH NOTING

Etnografski Muzej (*Ethnographic Museum*). Occupying a splendid location within the walls of Diocletian's Palace, the museum displays traditional Dalmatian folk costumes and local antique furniture. ■ **TIP→ If you are staying in Split for more than three days, be sure to pick up your free Split Card, which gives you free entry to certain museums and galleries and reduced rates at others, including some restaurants and cafés. Just ask the staff at your hotel or go to the nearest Tourist Information Bureau to pick one up.** ✉ *Iza Vestibula 4, Grad* ☎ *021/344–161* 🌐 *www.etnografski-muzej-split.hr* 🎟 *15 Kn, free if you have the SplitCard* ⏲ *Closed Sun.*

Galerija Vidović (*Vidović Gallery*). Emanuel Vidović (1870–1953) is acknowledged as Split's greatest painter. Here you can see 74 of his works, donated to the city by his family. Large, bold canvases depict local landmarks cast in hazy light, while the sketches done outdoors before returning to his studio to paint are more playful and colorful. ✉ *Poljana Kraljice Jelene BB, Grad* ☎ *021/360–155* 🌐 *www.galerija-vidovic.com* 🎟 *10 Kn; guided tours in English 100 Kn* ⏲ *Closed Mon.*

Gradski Muzej (*City Museum*). Split's city museum is worth a quick look both to marvel at the collection of medieval weaponry and to see the interior of this splendid 15th-century town house. The dining room, on the first floor, is furnished just as it would have been when the Papalić family owned the house, giving some idea of how the aristocracy of that time lived. ✉ *Papalićeva 1, Grad* ☎ *021/360–171* 🌐 *www.mgst.net* 🎟 *20 Kn* ⏲ *Closed Mon. Nov.–Apr.*

Jupiterov Hram/ Temple of Jupiter (*Jupiter's Temple*). Roman Emperor Diocletian constructed this temple to worship the god Jupiter. It was converted during the Middle Ages into a baptistery by Christians, who were greatly persecuted during the emperor's reign. The entrance is guarded by a black-granite sphinx that stands in front of the cathedral. The sphinx, brought to the palace from ancient Egypt by Diocletian, was partially destroyed by Christians as revenge for the persecution they suffered during his rule. Inside, beneath the coffered barrel vault and ornamented cornice, the 11th-century baptismal font is adorned with a stone relief showing a medieval Croatian king on his throne. Directly behind it, the bronze statue of St. John the Baptist is the work of Meštrović. ✉ *Kraj Sv. Ivana, Grad* 🎟 *15 Kn.*

Katedrala Sveti Dujam (*Cathedral of St. Dominius*). The main body of the cathedral is the 3rd-century octagonal mausoleum designed as a shrine to Emperor Diocletian. During the 7th century, refugees from Salona converted it into an early Christian church, ironically dedicating it to Sv. Duje (St. Domnius), after Bishop Domnius of Salona, one of the many Christians martyred during the late emperor's persecution campaign. The cathedral's monumental main door is ornamented with magnificent carved wooden reliefs, the work of Andrija Buvina of Split, portraying 28 scenes from the life of Christ and dated 1214. The interior contains a hexagonal Romanesque stone pulpit from the 13th century that is richly carved. The high altar, surmounted by a late-Gothic canopy, was executed by Bonino of Milan in 1427. Nearby is the 15th-century canopied Gothic altar of Anastasius by Juraj Dalmatinac. The elegant 200-foot Romanesque-Gothic bell tower was constructed in stages between the 12th and 16th centuries; the tower is sometimes closed in winter during bad weather. Climb to the top of the bell tower for a spectacular view of the entire palace and of Split. ✉ *3 Ul. Kraj Sv. Duje, Grad* 🎫 *Cathedral 25 Kn (including crypt); bell tower 15 Kn.*

Marjan (*Marjan Hill*). Situated on a hilly 3½-km-long (2-mile-long) peninsula that is covered with pine trees and Mediterranean shrubs, Marjan Hill has been a protected nature reserve since 1964. It is known to locals as the "lungs of the city" because of its vast green area and is frequented by locals on weekends as a nearby recreational area. There are stunning views from the top, and rocky beach areas circling the peninsula. A network of paths crisscross the grounds that are suitable for biking and jogging. There are seven small churches throughout the park; one in particular is St. Jerome (Sv. Jere), built in 1500 into a rock face and which includes Renaissance-style stone reliefs on the walls. The beaches on this side are more relaxed and offer shade but there is limited access for cars, which helps to preserve the green of the park. There are bikes to rent and water sports available. ✉ *Cattanijin put 2, Marjan* 🌐 *www.marjan-parksuma.hr.*

NEED A BREAK

Vidilica. A lounge-style café terrace with breathtaking views, this is a good spot for lunch or a sunset dinner. They're even open for breakfast for those who want to come and enjoy the sunrise. ✉ ***Prilaz Vladimira Nazora 1, Marjan*** 🌐 ***95/871–8792.***

Muzej Hrvatskih Arheološki Spomenika (*Museum of Croatian Archaeological Monuments*). One of the oldest Croatian museums, it houses more than 20,000 Croatian archaeological artifacts, only a quarter of which are on display. The most interesting exhibits are fine stone carvings decorated with plaitwork designs, surprisingly similar to the geometric patterns typical of Celtic art. In the garden are several *stećci*, monolithic stone tombs dating back to the Bogomils. The museum also conducts archaeological excavations in the southern Croatian regions between the Cetina and Zrmanja rivers and has a large collection of cultural/historical guidebooks on early medieval monuments in Croatia. ✉ *Stjepana Gunjace BB, Meje* ☎ *021/323–901* 🌐 *www.mhas-split.hr* 🎫 *20 Kn.*

Narodni trg (*People's Square*). This is the main city square (*pjaca*) and can be accessed from Diocletian's Palace through the western or Iron Gate. This was, and still is, the primary gathering place for Splicani (people from Split). In the 15th century the Venetians constructed several important public buildings here: the Town Hall (that today houses a contemporary art gallery, with erratic opening hours), plus the

CLOSE UP

Emperor Diocletian

Many powerful state leaders tend toward eccentricity, and Roman emperor Diocletian was no exception. Born to a humble family in Dalmatia, he went on to govern the empire for 20 years, proving to be an astute and innovative leader. However, he was also something of a megalomaniac. Believing himself to be Jupiter's representative on Earth, he set about persecuting Christians, ordering religious scriptures to be burnt, churches destroyed, and thousands of believers executed. He dressed in robes of satin and gold, along with a crown embedded with pearls and shoes studded with precious stones. His imperial apartments were guarded by eunuchs, and anyone who came into his presence was obliged to fall prostrate on the ground out of respect. The best known of his many massive building schemes is the Baths of Diocletian in Rome, a vast complex of marble and mosaics, constructed by 10,000 Christian prisoners for the pleasure of some 3,000 bathers.

Rector's Palace and a theater; the latter two were sadly demolished by the Habsburgs in the 19th century. The Austrians, for their part, added a Secessionist building at the west end of the square. Once the heart of the city for civic life, it is now a prime location for people-watching from one of the many restaurants or cafés that line the white marble square. ✉ *Narodni trg, Grad.*

Peristil (*Peristyle*). From Roman times to the present day, this has been the main public meeting place within the palace walls. The spacious central courtyard is flanked by marble columns topped with Corinthian capitals and richly ornamented cornices linked by arches. There are six columns on both the east and west sides, and four more at the south end, which mark the monumental entrance to the Vestibul. During summer, occasional live concerts are held here. ✉ *Grad.*

NEED A BREAK

Luxor Café. This is a perfect place to sit over coffee or a glass of local wine and absorb the 2,000 years of magnificent architecture that surround you. There are no longer outdoor tables, but there are cushions on the stone steps outside where you can have your drink and watch life inside the palace walls pass by. There are also English-language newspapers and magazines available for browsing. Luxor stages occasional live music and open-air dancing in summer. ✉ ***Kraj Sv. Ivana 11, Grad*** ☎ ***021/341–082.***

WHERE TO EAT

In the past two years the gastro scene in Split has exploded. There are a great number of new and exciting places to eat that showcase the region's growing culinary sophistication. This comes as a great relief for foreign travelers looking for more than a good pizza and fresh grilled fish, the only options once found in most restaurants. A new generation of young well-traveled entrepreneurs have come back to Croatia and are giving the food scene a much needed face-lift. The fact that in Split there are three sushi bars, an authentic Turkish mezza, a specialty olive oil and farm food restaurant, numerous healthy lunch options, several fine-dining options, and, of course, the original wine and cheese bar that spurred a Croatian trend speaks volumes about the dining changes that have hit Split in recent years.

$$$$ SEAFOOD **Adriatic Grašo.** Above the ACI Marina, at the foot of Marjan Hill and close to the gardens of Sveti Stipan, this seafood restaurant has a light and airy minimalist interior and a summer terrace where you can watch the yachts sail in and out of port. In the vein of "slow food," the kitchen gives great care to seasonal ingredients and presentation. **Known for:** famous basketball player owner; the views; classic Croatian fine dining. *Average main: 120 Kn ✉ Uvala Baluni BB, Zvoncac ☎ 021/398–560 🌐 www.adriaticgraso.com.*

$$$$ SUSHISEAFOOD **Adriatic Oyster and Sushi Bar.** Croatians are not known for being big sushi lovers, but this sushi bar, with its fresh seafood and simple dishes, is winning people over. Eighty percent of the menu comes directly from the Adriatic ocean and as much as possible of everything else is sourced within a 50-km (30-mile) radius of the premises, from the yellowfin tuna to the award-winning *Paški sir* (sheep's cheese) and Dalmatian prosciutto. **Known for:** locally sourced ingredients; superfresh seafood; good wine list. *Average main: €20 ✉ Carrarina Poljana, 4, Grad ☎ 021/610–644 🌐 www.adriaticsushioyster.hr.*

$$$$ MEDITERRANEAN **Apetit.** A small, low-key restaurant, tucked away on the second floor of a 15th-century palazzo just off the main square, Apetit serves traditional dishes that are made with fresh, locally sourced, high-quality ingredients. Some favorites to look out for are *tuna ala pašticada* (fresh tuna cooked in wine and served with gnocchi) or the house specialty, *rezanci Apetit* (homemade tagliatelle with shrimp, salmon, and zucchini). **Known for:** delicous tuna; Istrian heritage beef; homemade tagliatelle. *Average main: 90 Kn ✉ Šubićeva 5, Grad ☎ 021/332–549 for reservations 098/173–0736 🌐 www.apetit-split.hr.*

$$$ FUSION **Articok.** Articok is a cool new hipster location that serves exciting food with well-selected ingredients. The owner is a designer and has taken great care to ensure that an enjoyable dining experience is accompanied by an equally satisfying visual experience. **Known for:** fish tacos; superfresh ingredients; friendly staff. *Average main: €10 ✉ Bana Josipa Jelačića 19 ☎ 095/670–0004 🌐 www.instagram.com/articoksplit.*

$$$$ MEDITERRANEAN **Caffe-restoran Dvor.** Located in a quiet area a few miles out of town, Dvor offers up a superior rendition of Croatian seafood, professional service, and a broad selection of local and international wines, all with garden seating and outstanding views over the sea. There's an outdoor grill as well as parking, which is a luxury in Split. **Known for:** stunning outdoor location; superb tasting menu; nice selection of wine. *Average main: 120 Kn ✉ Put Firula 14 ☎ 021/571–513.*

$$$ MEDITERRANEAN FAMILY **Corto Maltese Freestyle Food.** Decorated with a bit of the wit and themes from the beloved Italian comic strip of Corto Maltese, Freestyle Food offers traditional Croatian ingredients prepared in a healthy way and explained on a funny, irreverent menu. With lots of seafood and salad options, the presentation of food is eclipsed only by the flavor. **Known for:** quirky menu descriptions; healthy cooking techniques; attentive

staff. [$] *Average main: 70 Kn* ✉ *Obrov 7, near fish market* ☎ *021/587–201* 🌐 *www.cortomaltese.rocks.*

$$$ MEDITERRANEAN
✕ **Fife.** This casual local hangout offers traditional dishes commonly found on Dalmatian dinner tables. Fife is a popular local eatery where the seating both inside and out is often crowded, especially in summer. **Known for:** lots of affordable fish dishes; tasty chicken tomato stew; local favorite. [$] *Average main: 65 Kn* ✉ *Trubičeva Obala 11, Matejuška* ☎ *021/345–223* ▬ *No credit cards.*

$$$$ MEDITERRANEAN
✕ **Kod Joze.** This typical Dalmatian konoba is relaxed and romantic, with exposed stone walls and heavy wooden furniture that are set off by candlelight. The waiters are wonderfully discreet, and the *rižot frutta di mare* (seafood risotto) delicious. **Known for:** discreet service; excellent seafood risotto; al fresco dining. [$] *Average main: 120 Kn* ✉ *Sredmanuška 4, Manuš* ☎ *021/347–397.*

$$$$ EASTERN EUROPEAN
✕ **Konoba Varoš.** The dining-room walls are hung with seascapes and fishing nets, and the waiters wear traditional Dalmatian waistcoats. The place can seem a little dour at lunchtime, but mellows when the candles are lighted during the evening. [$] *Average main: 120 Kn* ✉ *Ban Mladenova 7, Varoš* ☎ *021/396–138.*

$$$$ CONTEMPORARY
✕ **No Stress.** Situated on the *pjaca,* smack-dab in the middle of everything, this bistro does not define itself by its great location but by its premium ingredients, eclectic menu, and trendy drinks. They bake their own whole-wheat bread and have branded some traditional Hvar wines, Bogdanusa and Pharos, with their own label. **Known for:** good people-watching; excellent breakfasts; eclectic menu. [$] *Average main: 150 Kn* ✉ *Iza Loza 1, Grad* ☎ *099/498–1888* 🌐 *www.bistro-nostress.com.*

$$$$ WINE BAR
Fodor's Choice ★
✕ **Paradox.** Split's top tapas and wine bar has moved to a new rooftop location and expanded its menu. The superb waitstaff are well versed in their craft and eager to share their knowledge of more than 100 different wine labels and the foods with which to pair them. **Known for:** happening place; snazzy new rooftop location; well-trained staff. [$] *Average main: 150 Kn* ✉ *Poljane Tina Ujevica 2, Grad* ☎ *021/395–854* ⏲ *Closed Mon.*

$$$ SEAFOOD
✕ **Šperun.** This cozy restaurant has become popular because of its reasonably priced menu and quaint atmosphere. The Italo-Dalmatian menu features pasta dishes, seafood risottos, and old-fashioned local fish specialties such as *bakalar* (salt cod cooked in a rich tomato and onion sauce) and *brudet* (fish stew). **Known for:** classic Croatian fare; hearty fish stew for lunch; small dining room. [$] *Average main: 80 Kn* ✉ *Šperun 3, Varoš* ☎ *021/346–999.*

$$ MEXICAN
✕ **To Je Tako.** This cozy little place offers a local version of Latin American street food—very unusual dishes for Croatia—and it's much more interesting than typical Croatian fast food. To Je Tako offers breakfast, lunch, and dinner, as well as a good craft beer selection and gluten-free options, at great prices. **Known for:** good food at great prices; unusual cuisine for Croatia; tacos and empanadas. [$] *Average main: 35 Kn* ✉ *Ulica Kraj Svetog Ivana 5* ☎ *021/553–021* ▬ *No credit cards.*

$ MEDITERRANEAN
✕ **Uje/Oil Bar.** Stop in at Uje and sample some of the region's best olive oil, as well as a choice selection of Croatia's best cheese, prosciutto,

7

and wine. This quaint back-alley tapas bar or *pikulece,* a term the owner cleverly coined to mean tapas in Dalmatian dialect, showcases popular local chefs during the off-season, changes the menu regularly, and sources many ingredients from a local organic family farm. **Known for:** good selection of oil oils for sale; showcases local chefs in the off season; delicious tapas. *Average main: 20 Kn* ✉ *Dominisova 3, Grad* ☎ *095/200–8008* 🌐 *www.uje.hr.*

WHERE TO STAY

Split is no longer just a transit destination, and travelers today have excellent options for making it their primary vacation spot. The demand for more upscale and affordable sleeping options has been met with a solid selection from which travelers can choose. From luxury boutique hotels and apartments to clean and modern hostels to green hotels and spa and wellness centers, there are new places popping up constantly around the city. Even the most affordable places will feel overpriced in high season, so do your research to find the best deals.

$$ B&B/INN FAMILY Fodor's Choice ★ **Divota Apartment Hotel.** Set in row of ancient stone houses in the charming neighborhood of Veli Varoš, these 24 beautifully renovated apartments and rooms have been lovingly re-imagined to create a clean, bright, modern accommodation that preserves historic elements, like the steep tiled roofs and tiny shuttered windows. **Pros:** spa and concierge services available; unique hotel experience; great location. **Cons:** apartments are close together; reception is located in a separate nearby office; kitchenettes in some apartments are basic. *Rooms from: €158* ✉ *Plinarska 75, Varoš* ☎ *021/782–700* 🌐 *divota.hr* *24 rooms* *Breakfast.*

$$$$ HOTEL **Hotel Cornaro.** This sleek four-star hotel is a short walk from the city's car-free city center and close to all the main attractions. **Pros:** hearty breakfasts; a spa and rooftop bar; al fresco dining. **Cons:** parking is €15 per day. *Rooms from: €229* ✉ *Sinjska 6* ☎ *021/644–200* 🌐 *www.cornarohotel.com* *34 rooms, plus 2 luxury suites* *Breakfast.*

$$$ HOTEL **Hotel Luxe.** Located just outside the palace walls and close to the port, this contemporary hotel makes a great base for exploring the city. **Pros:** nearby free parking; a well organized and functional fitness and wellness area; children under 16 are free. **Cons:** additional meals must be catered by a nearby restaurant; some rooms on first floor have no sea view. *Rooms from: €200* ✉ *K. Zvonimira 6, Grad* ☎ *021/314–444* 🌐 *www.hotelluxesplit.com* 🌐 *www.hotelluxesplit.com* *27 rooms, 3 suites* *Breakfast.*

$$$$ HOTEL **Hotel Marmont.** This beautifully refurbished, 15th-century stone building is in the heart of the city and offers guests a quiet retreat from the hustle and bustle of Split's Old Town. **Pros:** 10% discount for hotel guests in restaurant; smart and pleasant staff. **Cons:** no parking nearby; some rooms have unattractive views of adjacent walls or windows. *Rooms from: €350* ✉ *Zadarska 1, Grad* ☎ *021/308–060* 🌐 *www.marmonthotel.com* *21 rooms, 1 suite* *Breakfast.*

$$ HOTEL **Hotel Peristil.** One of only a handful of hotels within the palace walls, Hotel Peristil lies behind the cathedral, just inside Srebrena

Vrata, the city gate leading to the open-air market. **Pros:** good value for money based on location; small (so guests receive individual attention); lovely open-air restaurant terrace. **Cons:** often fully booked; nearby parking difficult; limited facilities. *Rooms from: €162 Poljana Kraljice Jelena 5, Grad 021/329–070 www.hotelperistil.com 12 rooms Breakfast.*

$$$ HOTEL **Hotel Slavija.** Split's first hotel when it opened in 1900, Slavija occupies an 18th-century building within the palace walls. **Pros:** elevator; nightlife nearby; several four-bed family rooms. **Cons:** no restaurant; parking is not convenient; can get loud during high season. *Rooms from: €208 Buvinina 2, Grad 021/323–840 www.hotelslavija.com 25 rooms Breakfast.*

$$$$ HOTEL **Hotel Split.** Located on the outskirts of the city, Hotel Split offers every guest an comfortable, eco-friendly room with sea-views and quality furnishings. **Pros:** spa and fitness facilities; panoramic elevator; easy access into city. **Cons:** on-site parking €8 per day; crowded breakfast area during peak season. *Rooms from: €290 Strožanačka 20, Podstrana 021/420–420 www.hotel-split.hr 40 rooms All-inclusive.*

$$$$ B&B/INN Fodor's Choice ★ **Hotel Vestibul Palace.** Three palaces from different eras have been combined to form this intimate Old Town standout with interiors that have been carefully renovated to expose Roman stone- and brick-work, along with more modern, minimalist designer details. **Pros:** history and standout architecture; superb concierge service; breakfast buffet; private boat available for excursions. **Cons:** expensive for most of the season; often fully booked; not great if you have trouble with stairs. *Rooms from: €400 Iza Vestibula 4, Grad 021/329–329 www.vestibulpalace.com 7 rooms, 4 suites Breakfast.*

$$$$ RESORT FAMILY **Le Meridien Lav.** A world unto its own, this vast, self-contained complex lies 8 km (5 miles) south of Split. **Pros:** beautifully designed modern interior; excellent sports facilities; luxurious spa. **Cons:** far from the center of Split (8 km [5 miles]); expensive; large (so the hotel can seem somewhat impersonal). *Rooms from: €240 Grljevačka 2A, Podstrana 021/500–500 www.lemeridienlavsplit.com 364 rooms, 17 suites Breakfast.*

$$$$ B&B/INN **Palace Judita Heritage Hotel.** Only a couple of steps away the Diocletian Palace, the Palace Judita is quite possibly the best lodging in the city. **Pros:** beyond comfortable; perfect location; you'll still be talking about it when you get home. **Cons:** the hotel is small, so it's always full; you'll need to book a couple of months in advance; in the pedestrian-only area of Split. *Rooms from: €300 Narodni trg 4, Grad 021/420–220 www.juditapalace.com 11 rooms Breakfast.*

$$ B&B/INN FAMILY **Villa Diana.** On a peaceful side street just a five-minute walk east of the Old Town, Villa Diana is a traditional Dalmatian stone building with green wooden shutters. **Pros:** close to Old Town; more affordable alternative to nearby larger, more expensive hotels; intimate setting that provides individual attention. **Cons:** often fully booked; located on a busy road leading into Split. *Rooms from: €149 Kuzmanića 3, Radunica 021/482–460 www.villadiana.hr 5 rooms, 1 suite Breakfast.*

NIGHTLIFE AND PERFORMING ARTS

Split is much livelier at night during the summer season, when bars stay open late, discos hold open-air parties by the sea, and the Split Summer Festival offers a respectable program of opera and classical-music concerts.

NIGHTLIFE

Through summer, many bars have extended licenses and stay open until 2 am. The clubbing scene is rather tame, but the local twentysomethings frequent the discos. In August, rock musicians from Croatia and the other countries of the former Yugoslavia perform open-air concerts. There's no particular source of information about what's on, but you'll see posters around town if anything special is planned.

BARS

Academia Ghetto Klub. With a colorful, bohemian interior and a courtyard garden lit with flaming torches, Ghetto Klub pulls in the cool, young, artsy crowd and hosts occasional exhibitions and concerts. ✉ *Dosud 10, Grad* ☎ *021/346–879.*

Teak. Close to Zlatna Vrata, Teak is a small café with an exposed-stonework-and-wood interior plus tables outside throughout summer. It's popular with highbrow locals, who come here to leaf through the piles of international newspapers and magazines. ✉ *Majstora Jurja 11, Grad.*

To Je To. This happening café-bar showcases a careful selection of Croatian craft beers and locally roasted organic coffee beans. The owners are passionate about their coffee and beer and keep things fun with karaoke, live music, quiz nights, and other specialty events. The bar's name translates as "That's It," and that is exactly how you feel once you get here, "That's It"—let's stay! The fun vibe of To Je To is sure to leave you with a smile. ■ TIP→ **Check out the Wake the Dead specialty coffee after a late night out or a hard-to-find-in-Croatia red ale by Red Baron.** ✉ *Nigerova ulica 2, Grad* 🌐 *www.tojetosplit.com* 🌐 *www.tojetosplit.com.*

Tropic Club Equador. One of several amusing but vaguely pretentious bars overlooking Bačvice Bay, Tropic Club Equador serves pricey cocktails to a background of live DJ music (with a Caribbean vibe) and fake palms. ✉ *Kupalište Bačvice, Bacvica* ☎ *021/323–574.*

CLUBS AND DISCOS

Club Bačvice. After hanging out on a local *zidic* (wall for hanging out), and "preparing" (i.e., drinking) for the nightclub scene, most young people then make their way to the Bačvice beach complex. Club Bačvice is at the center of this, but there is a whole slew of venues along the way with pulsating music 'til the wee hours. ✉ *Preradovićevo šetalište 2, Bacvica.*

Gaga. Just behind the main pjaca, Gaga is the primary evening hangout within the palace walls. The cocktails are less expensive and the music is good. In summer it is frequented mostly by young tourists sharing their Croatian experiences. ✉ *Iza Lože 5, Grad* ☎ *021/348–257.*

Kocka. Run by a coalition of local youth organizations, Kocka is the primary underground alternative club. Over the past 20 years they have hosted thousands of bands and artists from the region and from around the world with shows, exhibits, and other events. Located in the basement of the *Dom omladina,* the stage area can hold up to 700, listening to everything from dub and trip-hop to ska and metal. Irregular hours during summer. ✉ *Ulica Slobode 28* ☎ *021/540–537* 🌐 *www.kum-split.hr.*

Vanilla. In summer Vanilla hosts pool parties for "Yacht Week" party-goers and foreign DJs every Friday night. Located about a 20-minute walk from the center of town near the public pools, they have a great terrace and a rotating bar. During the year, it is a trendy place for fans of Croatian pop and folk music. ✉ *Poljudsko šetalište BB* ☎ *098/292–522* 🌐 *www.vanilla.hr.*

PERFORMING ARTS

FESTIVALS

Split Summer Festival. Running from mid-July to mid-August, the Split Summer Festival includes a variety of open-air opera, classical-music concerts, dance, and theatrical performances, the highlight being opera on Prokurative (Republic Square) and other venues. **■ TIP→ Tickets can be purchased online or from the theater box office. Book your accommodation in advance, as hotel rates and occupancies go up during the festival.** ✉ *Croatian National Theater, Trg Gaje Bulata 1, Grad* ☎ *021/347–377* 🌐 *www.splitsko-ljeto.hr* 🎫 *€10–€40.*

FILM

Kino Bačvice. Kino Bačvice is an open-air summer cinema in the pine woods above Bačvice Bay. The Bačvice location is one of three movie locations that operates as one complex. Predominantly English-language, top Hollywood films are shown in original version with subtitles. Special movie event nights that feature different foreign and local films are mostly shown at the Bačvice location. Discount seats on Monday. ✉ *Trg Republike 1, Bacvica* 🌐 *www.ekran.hr* 🎫 *25 Kn.*

SPORTS AND THE OUTDOORS

BEACHES

FAMILY **Uvala Bačvica.** The largest beach area in Split is a 10-minute walk east of the Old Town. If you don't mind the crowds, you can rent beach chairs and umbrellas, and there's a string of cafés and bars along this stretch of coast. It's one of the few sandy beaches on the Dalmatian coast, with a shallow swimming area. **Amenities:** food and drink; parking (fee); showers. **Best for:** partiers; *picigin,* a local water volleyball–type game; swimming. ✉ *Šetalište Petra Preradovića, Bacvica.*

SAILING

Well connected to the rest of Europe by plane and ferry—and within just a few hours' sailing of several of the Adriatic's most beautiful islands—Split is the center of the yacht-charter business in Dalmatia.

ACI Marina. The 355-berth ACI Marina is southwest of the city center. It stays open all year and is a base for dozens of charter companies organizing sailing on the Adriatic. Prices for berth rental and amenities can be found on their website. ✉ *Uvala Baluni 8, Zvoncac* ☎ *021/398–599* 🌐 *www.aci-club.hr.*

SHOPPING

Dalmatian women—and those from Split in particular—are renowned for their sense of style. Despite a poor local economy, you'll find a good number of exclusive boutiques selling original women's clothes, jewelry, and housewares, not to mention numerous shoe and dress shops with goods imported from Italy. Art galleries throughout the region will often feature some unique handmade products that are not able to be found elsewhere because of the difficulty local artists and crafters have in distributing their work. The city's most memorable shopping venue remains the *pijaca,* the colorful open-air market held each morning just outside the palace walls, where you can find everything from lavender and Brač stone souvenirs to purses and dresses, fresh vegetables and Dalmatian delicacies. Dalmatia is known for producing some of the country's best wine, olive oil, and *pršut* (prosciutto), all of which can be found in the market in Split.

Vinoteka Terra. Vinoteka Terra is a stone cellar close to Bačvice Bay, where you can taste Croatian regional wines, accompanied by savory appetizers, before purchasing bottles. They also offer truffle products and olive oils and a range of artistically designed wooden boxes for packing. ✉ *Prilaz Braće Kaliterna 6, Bacvica* ☎ *021/314–800* 🌐 *vinoteka.hr.*

ŠIBENIK

75 km (47 miles) northwest of Split.

Šibenik's main monument, its Gothic-Renaissance cathedral, built of pale-gray Dalmatian stone and designated a UNESCO World Heritage Site, stands on a raised piazza close to the seafront promenade. From here a network of narrow, cobbled streets leads through the medieval quarter of tightly packed, terra-cotta-roof houses, and up to the ruins of a 16th-century hilltop fortress. The city has never been a real tourist destination. Before the Croatian war for independence, it was a relatively prosperous industrial center, but when the factories closed, Šibenik sank into an economic depression. However, the cathedral more than warrants a look.

GETTING HERE AND AROUND

The narrow cobblestone streets of this small city are most easily accessed on foot. Šibenik also makes for a decent base for visiting the nearby waterfalls of Krka National Park.

EXPLORING

Katedrala Sv. Jakova (*Cathedral of St. Jacob*). Šibenik's finest piece of architecture, the Katedrala Sv. Jakova, was built in several distinct stages and styles between 1431 and 1536, and today it is a UNESCO World Heritage Site. The lower level is the work of Venetian architects who contributed the finely carved Venetian-Gothic portals, whereas the rest of the building follows plans drawn up by local architect Juraj Dalmatinac, who proposed the Renaissance cupola. Note the frieze running around the outer wall, with 74 faces carved in stone, depicting the locals from that time. The cathedral's best-loved feature, the tiny baptistery with minutely chiseled stone decorations, was designed by Dalmatinac but executed by Andrija Aleši. ■ TIP→ **As you leave, take a look at the bronze statue just outside the main door: that's Dalmatinac himself, by Croatia's greatest 20th-century sculptor, Ivan Meštrović.** ✉ *Trg Republike Hrvatske* *Free.*

WHERE TO EAT

$$$$ MEDITERRANEAN Fodor's Choice ★

Pelegrini. In a carefully restored 14th-century palazzo opposite the historic St. James Cathedral in Šibenik, Konoba Pelegrini is consistently rated as one of the top restaurants in Croatia. The menu features traditional Dalmatian cuisine that is innovatively prepared, with exquisite flavor being the restaurant's guiding principle. **Known for:** excellent Dalmation cuisine; extensive wine list; five-course minimum for dinner. *$ Average main: 550 Kn* ✉ *Jurja Dalmatinca 1* ☎ *022/213–701* 🌐 *www.pelegrini.hr.*

$ MEDITERRANEAN

Vino&Ino. It's hard to pass the inviting Vino&Ino in the center of Šibenik and not stop in either for a coffee or a glass of wine and tapas. There's outdoor seating and always a balanced mix of locals and visitors enjoying the small-plates menu. **Known for:** live music in the summer; excellent coffee; tapas and small plates. *$ Average main: 20 Kn* ✉ *Fausta Vrančića BB* ☎ *091/250–6022* 🌐 *www.vinoiino.hr.*

WHERE TO STAY

$ B&B/INN FAMILY

Agroturizam Kalpic. Experience the peacefulness of the Croatian countryside at the Kalpic family estate while exploring both Šibenik and Krka National Park. **Pros:** shady garden for kids to play; nice break from the city *pršut* and cheese; traditional dishes from the restaurant. **Cons:** must have a car to reach it; too rural for city folk. *$ Rooms from: €90* ✉ *Kalpići 4, Lozovac* ☎ *091/584–5520* 🌐 *www.kalpic.com* *8 rooms* *All meals.*

$ B&B/INN

The Konoba. In the medieval, pedestrian-only Old Town, this B&B occupies two traditional stone buildings. **Pros:** in the Old Town; small (so guests receive individual attention from the owner); excellent breakfast (€7). **Cons:** access is difficult; no credit cards. *$ Rooms from: €95* ✉ *Andrije Kačića 8* ☎ *091/601–9789* 🌐 *www.bbdalmatia.com* *No credit cards* *5 rooms* *Breakfast.*

PRVIĆ

Prvić lies 4.5 nautical miles west of Šibenik by ferry.

Beyond Šibenik Bay lie the scattered islands of the Šibenik archipelago, four of which—Zlarin, Prvić, Kaprije, and Žirje—are accessible by ferry from Šibenik. For a quick taste of island life, the nearest, Zlarin and Prvić, can be visited as day trips, but if you intend to stay overnight, Prvić is the better equipped, with a lovely, small hotel, rooms to rent, and half a dozen rustic eateries. Tiny, car-free Prvić is just 3 km long (2 miles long) and has a year-round population of 540. Its two villages,

Prvić Luka and Šepurine, are made up of centuries-old traditional stone cottages and connected by a lovely footpath leading through a stand of pine trees that takes about 15 minutes to walk. Though some of the locals work in Šibenik, others still live by cultivating figs, olives, and vines and by fishing. There are no large beaches, but plenty of small, secluded pebble coves with crystal-clean water, perfect for swimming.

GETTING HERE AND AROUND

Through high season, there are four ferries per day from Šibenik, calling at Zlarin (30 minutes), Prvić Luka (45 minutes), Šepurine (1 hour), and Vodice (1 hour 10 minutes). All four then return to Šibenik, doing the same journey in reverse. Alternatively, you can take a water taxi from the Šibenik seafront to Prvić Luka (expect to pay a hefty 1,200 Kn, as opposed to the ferry, which charges 10 Kn).

WHERE TO EAT

$$$ PIZZA **Pizzeria Nanini.** This down-to-earth, family-run eatery occupying an old stone building furnished with heavy wooden tables offers a decent selection of Dalmatian dishes and pizzas, with an emphasis on fresh seafood. It stays open all year and is a popular spot for local wedding receptions. **Known for:** decent pizza; fresh seafood; popular with wedding parties. *Average main: €10 ✉ Prvić Luka BB ☎ 091/212–0684.*

WHERE TO STAY

$ HOTEL FAMILY **Hotel Maestral.** On the seafront in Prvić Luka, this 19th-century stone building was once the village school. **Pros:** delightful island location; small (so guests receive individual attention); good restaurant. **Cons:** if you miss the ferry, you could end up stranded; often fully booked; limited nightlife possibilities. *Rooms from: €104 ✉ Prvić Luka BB ☎ 022/448–300 www.hotelmaestral.com 11 rooms, 1 suite Breakfast.*

SPORTS AND THE OUTDOORS

SWIMMING

Swim Trek. Swim Trek is a Britain-based agency whose motto is "Ferries are for wimps—let's swim." The company offers a challenging and unusual one-week holiday, including swimming around the islands of the Šibenik archipelago. Participants cover an average of 4 km (2½ miles) per day, including the stretch between the islands of Zlarin and Prvić. Overnight accommodation is in the Hotel Maestral in Prvić Luka. ☎ *(+44) 1273/739–713 in U.K. www.swimtrek.com.*

KRKA NATIONAL PARK

Skradin is 16 km (10 miles) north of Šibenik.

The Krka River cuts its way through a gorge shaded by limestone cliffs and dense woodland, tumbling down toward the Adriatic in a series of spectacular pools and waterfalls. The most beautiful stretch has been designated as the Krka National Park.

GETTING HERE AND AROUND

Drive from Šibenik to the town of Skradin, then take a 25-minute boat ride up the Krka River on a national-park ferry.

EXPLORING

FAMILY Fodor's Choice ★ **Nacionalni Park Krka** (*Krka National Park*). There are several entrances into the park, but the easiest and most impressive route of arrival is to drive from Šibenik to the town of Skradin, then take a 25-minute boat ride up the Krka River on a national-park ferry (price is included in the entrance fee). The ferry will bring you to the park entrance close to Skradinski Buk and from there you can get off and go for a swim in the crystal-green waters or take a walk along the wooden bridges and explore the park further. There are a couple of snack bars, plus wooden tables and benches for picnics. However, for a full-blown meal, your best bet is to return to Skradin, a town that dates back to Roman times, which is itself well worth a look.

A series of seven waterfalls is the main attraction, the most spectacular being Skradinski Buk, where 17 cascades of water fall 40 meters into an emerald-green pool. Moving upriver, a trail of wooden walkways and bridges crisscrosses its way through the woods and along the river to Roški Slap, passing by the tiny island of Visovac, which is home to a Franciscan monastery that can be visited by boat. There is also an old mill with a museum that demonstrates the different ways the mill was used centuries ago. From here one can better understand how the power of these waters inspired Nikola Tesla, whose boyhood home is not far from the national park. In 1895 the first hydroelectric plant became operational here, only two days after Tesla's hydroelectric plant on Niagara Falls. This made the residents of Skradin the first European citizens to have electricity.

More than 860 species of plant life have been identified throughout the park and more than 200 bird species live there, making it one of the most valuable ornithological areas in Europe. Something many visitors miss is a hawk training center where you can observe birds of prey being trained by ornithological experts. For bird enthusiasts there is also Gudića Nature reserve where various species are closely studied and can be observed from boats. The Krka National Park office is located in Šibenik. ■ TIP→ **For the more active, there is a 8½-km-long (5-mile-long) hiking trail, Sitnice–Roški Slap–Ozidana Cave, that takes about 2½ hours and has educational panels along the way that explain plant and animal life, geological phenomena, and historic sites.** ✉ *Lozovac* ☎ *022/201–777* 🌐 *www.npkrka.hr* 🎫 *110 Kn (June–Sept.), 80 Kn (Oct. and Mar.–May), 30 Kn (Nov.–Feb.).*

7

WHERE TO EAT

$$$ MEDITERRANEAN FAMILY **Cantinetta.** Hidden away in the Skradin Bay, in a quiet location where the fresh waters from Krka National Park flow into the sea, Cantinetta is well recognized among local residents as the best place to eat in Skradin. From a humble family konoba to a serious culinary destination, this restaurant takes great pride in the well-preserved old recipes that have been passed on from generation to generation. **Known for:** best dining in Skradin; family recipes; reasonable prices. *Average main: €10 Aleja skradinskih svilara 7, Skradin 022/771–1024.*

$$$$ SEAFOOD FAMILY **Zlatne Školjke.** A favorite among the yachting crowd, due in part to its location near the ACI Marina, Zlatne Školjke occupies a natural stone building with a terrace overlooking the water. The restaurant is aptly named Zlatne Školjke, which means golden shell, because of the plethora of shellfish farms nearby. **Known for:** superfresh shellfish; terrace overlooking the water; lovely wine list. *Average main: 100 Kn Grgura Ninskog 9, Skradin 022/771–022 www.zlatne-skoljke.com.*

WHERE TO STAY

$ HOTEL FAMILY **Hotel Skradinski Buk.** A friendly, family-run hotel in a refurbished stone town house in the center of Skradin is also the only hotel in town. **Pros:** great location in pretty village close to the entrance of Krka National Park; friendly staff; good breakfast. **Cons:** only hotel in town and often fully booked; limited nightlife in Skradin. *Rooms from: €90 Burinovac, Skradin 022/771–771 www.skradinskibuk.hr 25 rooms, 4 suites Breakfast.*

SHOPPING

Vinarija Bedrica. While in Skradin, pay a visit to Vinarija Bedrica, an old-fashioned family-run wine cellar where you can taste and buy bottles of locally produced wine and *rakija* (fruit brandy). Try the famous Skradin rakija of rose petals. *Fra Luje Maruna 14, Skradin 022/771–270.*

TROGIR

27 km (17 miles) west of Split.

On a small island no more than a few city blocks in length, the beautifully preserved medieval town of Trogir is connected to the mainland by one bridge and tied to the outlying island of Čiovo by a second. The settlement dates back to the 3rd century BC, when it was colonized by the Greeks, who named it Tragurion. It later flourished as a Roman port. With the fall of the Western Roman Empire, it became part of Byzantium and then followed the shifting allegiances of the Adriatic. In 1420 the Venetians moved in and stayed until 1797. Today it is a UNESCO World Heritage Site, and survives principally from tourism. You can explore the city in about an hour. A labyrinth of narrow, cobbled streets centers on Narodni trg, the main square, where the most notable buildings are located: the 15th-century loggia and clock tower, the Venetian-Gothic Čipko Palace, and the splendid cathedral, with its elegant bell tower. The south-facing seafront promenade is lined with cafés, ice-cream parlors, and restaurants, and there are also several small, old-fashioned hotels that offer a reasonable alternative to accommodations in Split.

GETTING HERE AND AROUND

It is more convenient and affordable to take a short boat ride from Split to Trogir if visiting for a day, as parking is limited and expensive during high season.

EXPLORING

FAMILY
Fodor's Choice
★

Katedrala Sveti Lovrijenac (*Cathedral of St. Lawrence*). The remarkable Katedrala Sveti Lovrijenac, completed in 1250, is a perfect example of the massiveness and power of Romanesque architecture. The most striking detail is the main (west) portal, adorned with superb Romanesque sculpture by the Croatian master Radovan. The great door, flanked by a pair of imperious lions that form pedestals for figures of Adam and Eve, is framed by a fascinating series illustrating the daily life of peasants in a kind of Middle Ages comic strip. In the dimly lit Romanesque interior, the 15th-century chapel of Sveti Ivan Orsini (St. John Orsini) of Trogir features statues of saints and apostles in niches facing the sarcophagus, on which lies the figure of St. John. The bell tower, built in successive stages—the first two stories Gothic, the third Renaissance—offers stunning views across the ancient rooftops. Entrance ticket includes a visit to the cathedral, treasury, and the bell tower. ✉ *Trg Ivana Pavla II* ☎ *021/881–550* 🎫 *25 Kn.*

WHERE TO EAT

$$$$
MEDITERRANEAN
FAMILY

✕ **Calebotta.** Retreat to a quiet closed-in courtyard, where the Trogir cinema once sat, and allow the Calebotta family to take you away with their first-class service and menu of fresh ingredients expertly prepared like no other restaurant in Trogir. The sea-bream citrus carpaccio is a perfect way to start a meal on a hot summer afternoon. **Known for:** quiet courtyard location; fine dining; yummy desserts. [$] *Average main: €13* ✉ *Gradska 23* ☎ *021/796–413.*

$$$$
MEDITERRANEAN

✕ **Konoba Trs.** With a tremendous sense of style, Trs combines traditional food with some modern ingredients that are freshly sourced from their family farm in a nearby Trogir village. Chickpeas are tossed in with a traditional octopus salad, and grilled scampi is served up on grapefruit and sprinkled with pistachios. **Known for:** family farm to table; traditional dishes with twist; excellent rabbit stew. [$] *Average main: €20* ✉ *Ulica Matije Gupca 14* ☎ *021/796–956* 🌐 *www.konoba-trs.com.*

$$$
MEDITERRANEAN
FAMILY

✕ **Vanjaka.** In an elegant 17th-century stone building in the Old Town, close to the cathedral, this welcoming family-run restaurant serves Dalmatian specialties such as black risotto, gnocchi, and fresh fish, as well as a good choice of local wines. Sit outside on the open-air terrace, or take a table in the intimate air-conditioned dining room. **Known for:** Dalmatian cuisine; al fresco dining; local wines. [$] *Average main: 75 Kn* ✉ *Radovanov trg 9* ☎ *021/884–061* 🌐 *www.vanjaka.hr.*

7

WHERE TO STAY

$ HOTEL **Hotel Fontana.** Located in Old Town overlooking the Trogir Channel, Hotel Fontana is in an old stone building that's been been tastefully refurbished into a small family-run hotel above a popular restaurant. **Pros:** location on seafront promenade in the Old Town; breakfast served on the seafront terrace. **Cons:** some rooms rather small; basic furnishings; Wi-Fi does not work. *Rooms from: €50 Obrov 1 021/885–744 www.fontana-trogir.com 13 rooms, 1 suite Breakfast.*

KLAPA

When visiting towns and villages along the Dalmatian coast, you may be lucky enough to come across a group of locals giving an impromptu *klapa* (Dalmatian plainsong) performance. Traditionally, klapa groups are formed by men, who sing occasionally and for pleasure, about classic themes like love and family life, and local gossip. Each July the town of Omiš hosts a three-week Klapa Festival.

$$ B&B/INN **Hotel Pašike.** In a typical Dalmatian stone building in the heart of Old Town, this charming hotel is filled with inherited and restored antique furniture. **Pros:** great Old Town location; free airport transfers; friendly staff. **Cons:** some rooms are dark; no elevator. *Rooms from: €135 Sinjska BB 021/885–185 www.hotelpasike.com 13 rooms, 1 suite Breakfast.*

$ B&B/INN **Palace Domus Maritima.** This small family-run bed-and-breakfast is perfectly located a few minutes' walk from bustling Trogir and just across the street from the ACI Marina. **Pros:** relaxing garden; free parking close by. **Cons:** meals must be ordered in advance; noisy at night. *Rooms from: €85 Put Cumbrijana 10 091/513–7802 www.domus-maritima.com 8 rooms Breakfast.*

$ HOTEL **Tragos.** Occupying an 18th-century Baroque palace in the heart of the Old Town, two blocks from the cathedral, Tragos has 12 simply furnished, modern rooms, decorated in warm hues of cream, yellow, and orange, each with a modern, spacious tiled bathroom. **Pros:** located in Old Town; friendly and helpful staff; good restaurant. **Cons:** rooms can be noisy from downstairs restaurant; no elevator could be a problem for some visitors. *Rooms from: €110 Budislavićeva 3 021/884–729 www.tragos.hr 12 rooms Breakfast.*

$ B&B/INN **Villa Sikaa Hotel.** This 18th-century villa has been converted into a small, family-run hotel overlooking the Trogir Channel. **Pros:** seafront location offers great views of Trogir's Old Town; friendly and helpful staff; beautiful old building with modern facilities. **Cons:** front rooms can be noisy (loud music and motorbikes); two hotels are in the same building (which can be confusing); parking can be difficult. *Rooms from: 744 Kn Obala kralja Zvonimira 13 021/881–223 www.vila-sikaa-r.com 8 rooms, 2 suites Breakfast.*

OMIŠ AND THE CETINA VALLEY

28 km (17½ miles) southeast of Split.

An easy day trip from Split, Omiš is a pleasant seaside town with a colorful open-air market and a conglomeration of old stone houses backed by a small hilltop fortress. What makes it special is its location at the mouth of a dramatic gorge, where the Cetina River meets the sea. It is also the venue of the Dalmatian Klapa Festival, which attracts singers from all over Croatia. The Cetina River carves a spectacular gorge with the fertile, green **Cetina Valley** at the bottom, surrounded by sheer limestone cliffs. As the river tumbles its way down toward the sea over a series of rapids, it has become a popular and challenging site for rafting and rock climbing. An asphalt road follows the course of the river upstream from Omiš, leading to a couple of pleasant waterside restaurants.

GETTING HERE AND AROUND

Omiš is an easy day trip from Split by rental car.

WHERE TO EAT

$$$$ EASTERN EUROPEAN FAMILY

Radmanove Mlinice. This renovated water mill is well known for miles around for its fresh *pastrva* (trout) and *janjetina* (roast lamb) served at tables under the trees in a picturesque riverside garden. Throughout July and August, on Wednesday evenings, it also stages live folk music and dancing from 8 pm onward. *Average main: 90 Kn ✉ Cetina Valley regional road, in the direction of Zadvarje, Omiš ☎ 021/862–073 www.radmanove-mlinice.hr Closed Nov.–Mar.*

WHERE TO STAY

$ HOTEL FAMILY

Hotel Settlement Brzet. Overlooking a pebble beach and backed by a pine forest, Brzet's rooms are basic, but there is an on-site restaurant that's only a 10-minute walk from the Omiš town center. **Pros:** seafront location; all rooms have balconies and sea views; small beach. **Cons:** rooms rather basic; Omiš offers limited nightlife. *Rooms from: €58 ✉ Brzet 13, Omiš ☎ 021/756–880 www.brzet.hr 88 rooms Breakfast.*

$$ HOTEL FAMILY Fodor's Choice ★

Hotel Villa Dvor. Built into a sheer cliff face overlooking the River Cetina, the hotel is reached through a tunnel and then a glass elevator brings you to the reception. **Pros:** hillside location offers stunning view across river to Old Town and sea; elevator that must be first entered through a cave; rooftop Jacuzzi. **Cons:** the location/view outshines the hotel itself; Omiš offers limited nightlife. *Rooms from: €122 ✉ Mosorska Cesta 13, Omiš ☎ 021/863–444 www.hotel-villadvor.hr 23 rooms Breakfast.*

PERFORMING ARTS

FESTIVALS

Dalmatian Klapa Festival. Klapa singing, which is an integral part of the Dalmatian culture, is widely celebrated all summer long with festivals devoted specifically to this cherished tradition. The Dalmatian Klapa Festival celebrated in Omiš brings together the best Klapa from the region; it starts in late June and usually last three weeks. Performances are staged in the parish church and on the main square. ✉ *Ivana Katušića 5, Omiš* ☎ *021/861–015* 🌐 *fdk.hr/festival-in-omis.*

SPORTS AND THE OUTDOORS

The Cetina Valley has become a destination for both white-water rafters and rock climbers, who appreciate the sheer limestone cliffs of the canyon. Several small adventure-tour companies can arrange Cetina Valley trips. There's also a company in Split that organizes one-day rafting trips on the Cetina.

Active Holidays. Active Holidays offers rafting, canyoning, and rock climbing in the Cetina Valley, as well as windsurfing and sea kayaking off the coast at Omiš. ✉ *Knezova Kačić bb, Omiš* ☎ *021/861–829* 🌐 *www.activeholidays-croatia.com.*

Falco Tours. In addition to their Cetina river canoe safari, Falco Tours also offer bird-watching and sea kayaking. Their philosophy is to take it slow so that you can really enjoy the nature that surrounds you. ✉ *Omiš* ☎ *021/548–646* 🌐 *falco-tours.com.*

BRAČ

9 nautical miles south of Split by ferry.

Well-connected to Split by ferry and catamaran services, the island of Brač makes for the perfect island escape. It can be easily visited as a day trip from Split, but it is recommended to stay a few nights in order to uncover the true gifts the island has to offer. With much of the attention in recent years focusing on Hvar, Brač has been left to quietly develop as a solid, more sustainable tourist destination. Despite its proximity to the mainland, the slow pace of island life pervades the island's main attractions from the Blaca Monastery to the Dragon's cave to the Pučišća stone masonry school. Organizing a walking tour through the Dolce Vita trail to see, touch, and taste where the country's best olive oil comes from is a good place to start your explorations. Hooking up with one of the many outdoor adventure–sports companies for kayaking, climbing, windsurfing, or sailing is well worth it. Although a visit to the famous Zlatni Rat beach, which is also a prime windsurfing spot, can seem a bit overrated, exploring the waters on the more hidden sides of the island like Bobovisće or Sutivan will reveal the most crystal-clear water in the entire Adriatic. The top resort area is Bol.

GETTING HERE AND AROUND

Brač is accessible by ferry or boat. To get there, either catch an early-morning Jadrolinija ferry from Split to Supetar (9 nautical miles) and then take a bus across the island to the south coast, or catch the mid-afternoon Jadrolinija catamaran from Split to Bol (24 nautical miles), which then continues to Jelsa on the island of Hvar.

EXPLORING

Dominikanski Samostan (*Dominican Monastery*). With its beautiful gardens overlooking the sea, the Dominican Monastery on the western edge of Bol was founded in 1457. The monastery church is home to a valuable 16th-century painting by the Venetian Tintoretto, and the small museum displays ancient Greek coins and amphorae found on the nearby islands of Hvar and Vis. In addition to the museum and church, the Dominican monastery is an active community of priests studying and carrying out the Dominican mission in Croatia and Europe. ✉ *Andjelka Rabadana 4, Bol* ☎ *021/778–000* 🌐 *www.dominikanci.hr/index.php/samostani/bol* 🎫 *10 Kn.*

FAMILY **Galerija Branislav Dešković** (*Branislav Dešković Gallery*). In a fine Baroque building on Bol's seafront, the Galerija Branislav Dešković displays over 300 paintings and sculptures by 20th-century Croatian artists who have been inspired by the sea and landscapes of Dalmatia. ✉ *Porat bolskih pomoraca BB, Bol* ☎ *021/635–270* 🌐 *hvm.mdc.hr* 🎫 *15 Kn Adults, 5 kn Children.*

FAMILY Fodor's Choice ★ **Pustinja Blaca** (*Blaca Hermitage*). The Blaca Hermitage was built into a cliff face overlooking the sea by monks fleeing the Turks in the 16th century. From the bay below the complex, it's a 2-km (1-mile) hike uphill and well off the beaten path. The hike up is well worth the experience to understand the sacrifice the monks made in constructing the site without modern amenities. You can also arrive by car from Nerežišća over Vidova Gora to Dragovoda and then walk about 30 minutes up to the monastery. The monks who built the hermitage turned vast forests into rich vineyards and olive groves. Inside, visitors can see a fine collection of period furniture including a piano and telescope and old clocks. In its heyday, the hermitage had a printing press, a school, and an observatory. There are no longer any monks living there, but a guided tour is well worth the expense. It is now on the UNESCO World Heritage Site "tentative" list. Photographs of the monastery are not permitted—all the more reason to go and see it in person. ✉ *Blaca Bay* 🎫 *40 Kn.*

FAMILY **Sutivan Sports Rehabilitation Center.** After spending a few days swimming and lying on the beach, Sutivan Nature Park is a great place to make an afternoon picnic with kids. There is a small animal park that shelters a wide variety of domestic animals including ducks, pigs, goats, turtles, peacocks, parrots and cows. There are even donkeys and horses available for riding with a professional guide. The park is located about 3 km (2 miles) from Sutivan toward Mlin and has a large playground, a barbecue area, a botanical garden with a fountain, and also an amphitheater for performances and events. The restaurant only serves drinks and can prepare meals by reservation only. ✉ *Krtine BB,*

Sutivan ☎ *098/133–7345* 🌐 *www.park-prirode-sutivan.com* 🎟 *30 Kn.*

Vidova Gora. The village of Bol is backed by the highest peak on all the Croatian islands, Vidova Gora. From here, at a height of 2,552 feet above sea level, the Adriatic sea and the islands of Hvar and Vis spread out before you like a map. It's possible to reach the top following a clearly marked footpath from Bol, but be sure to wear good hiking boots, take plenty of water, and expect to walk at least two and a half hours to reach the summit. Alternatively, rent a mountain bike from Big Blue and cycle up—note that you need to be pretty fit to face the challenge. ■ **TIP→ If you have a head-lamp and are relatively fit, wake early and hike up before sunrise, or go in the late afternoon and watch the sun set from Croatia's highest island peak.** ✉ *4 km (2½ miles) north of the town center, Bol.*

BRAČ MARBLE

The island of Brač is well known for its fine white marble, quarried in the village of Pučišća, on the north coast. Through the centuries, it has been used for world-famous buildings, including Diocletian's Palace in Split, the U.S. White House, and the parliament building in Budapest. Today it is used by sculptors and for the reconstruction of historic monuments.

WHERE TO EAT

$ DELI

✕ **Arguola.** If you're looking for a quick bite for lunch on your way to the beach or after a late night out partying, this sandwich bar will do the trick. The salads and bread are made fresh and the portions are perfect. **Known for:** quick sandwiches; lunches to go; late night snacks. 💲 *Average main: €3* ✉ *Vladimir Nazora 6, Bol* ☎ *091/518–8295* 💳 *No credit cards* ⏲ *Closed Nov.–Apr.*

$$$$ MEDITERRANEAN

✕ **Kaštil Gospodnetic/Konoba Margera.** This 16th-century konoba tucked high up in the village of Dol (which means valley) not only offers an amazing view of the valley all the way to the sea, but also offers guests a chance to step back in time with a tour though the historic building before sitting down to a home-cooked meal. The meal price includes an appetizer, main dish, and dessert, and is recommended to be ordered in advance. **Known for:** Dalmatian farm fresh food; wine tours of the Venetian castle; amazing views. 💲 *Average main: 180 Kn* ✉ *Dol BB, Dol* ☎ *091/799–7182* 🌐 *www.konobadol.com.*

$$$ MEDITERRANEAN FAMILY

✕ **Konoba Kopacina.** It is hard to spend more than a day on the island of Brač and avoid the suggestion to try some roasted lamb; many people choose Konoba Kopacina as the place to enjoy this island delicacy. The sheep on Brač feed only on their mother's milk and wild herbs like the rosemary and sage that thrive on the island's rocky terrain. **Known for:** expertly grilled lamb; caramelized sheep cheese; good selection of local wines. 💲 *Average main: €10* ✉ *Vjaksić, Nerežišce* ☎ *021/647–707* 🌐 *www.konoba-kopacina.com.*

$$$ MEDITERRANEAN FAMILY Fodor's Choice ★ **Konoba Ranjak.** Lose track of time while sitting at one of Konoba Ranjak's large wooden tables set in the family's 500-year-old olive grove that transforms into a magical garden at night with lights decorating the olive trees. Nearly all the food, from the stuffed zucchini flowers to the olive spread and delectably roasted lamb and wine is produced on the farm with heart and soul. **Known for:** produces award winning olive oil; creative cooking; homegrown ingredients. *Average main: €10 Petra Jakšića 31, Gornji Ranjak, Supetar 091/631–6699 www.agroturizam-ranjak.hr Closed Nov.–Apr. except by special arrangement.*

$$$$ SEAFOOD **Ribarska Kučica.** On the waterside footpath near the Dominican monastery, with romantic nighttime views over the open sea, this friendly eatery serves seafood dishes, with pizza or pasta as a cheaper option. Look for the delicious gnocchi with Gorgonzola and prosciutto. **Known for:** beachside location; adjoining cocktail bar; slow service. *Average main: €20 Ante Starčević BB, Bol 021/635–033 www.ribarska-kucica.com Closed Oct.–May.*

WHERE TO STAY

$ HOTEL FAMILY **Bluesun Hotel Borak.** Set amid pine trees on the path to Zlatni Rat beach—and just a 10-minute walk from Bol's Old Town—this hotel occupies a modern, three-story white building with a restaurant terrace and a pool out front. **Pros:** proximity to Zlatni Rat beach; good sports facilities; family rooms available for those with kids. **Cons:** large and slightly impersonal; popular with large tour groups. *Rooms from: €110 Bračka Cesta 13 021/306–202 www.bluesunhotels.com Closed Nov.–Apr. 136 rooms, 48 suites Breakfast.*

$$$ RESORT **Hotel Bracka Perla.** This luxurious, adults-only hotel has only 11 rooms and is perfect for those seeking a quiet romantic getaway. **Pros:** walking distance from beach; knowledgeable and attentive staff; Jacuzzi, sauna, and fitness room. **Cons:** breakfast is small and not included; a little too quiet for some; no kids allowed. *Rooms from: €185 Put Vele Luke 53 021/755–530 www.agroturizam-brac.com 8 suites, 3 rooms Breakfast.*

$$ HOTEL **Hotel Osam.** This sleek adults-only new hotel with rooftop bar and swimming pool offers something not found elsewhere on Brač: an urban-style island retreat. **Pros:** excellent buffet breakfast; extremely convenient location; great restaurant. **Cons:** rooms are not soundproofed; swimming pool is small. *Rooms from: €125 Put Vele luke 4, Supetar 021/587–478 www.hotel-osam.com 26 rooms All meals.*

$ B&B/INN Fodor's Choice ★ **Villa Giardino.** Set in a quiet garden with Mediterranean plantings and an English lawn, this hotel is a five-minute walk from the harbor. **Pros:** attentive staff; peaceful yet centrally located; breakfast served in lovely garden. **Cons:** often fully booked; limited facilities. *Rooms from: €120 Novi Put 2 021/635–900 villa.giardino@st.t-com.hr Closed Nov.–Apr. 5 rooms Breakfast.*

SPORTS AND THE OUTDOORS

ADVENTURE TOURS

FAMILY **Aldora Sports.** If you want to explore the island of Brač with local outdoor enthusiasts committed to preserving the traditions and beauty of the island, the experts at Aldora Sports have you covered. From beginner to experienced, they offer unparalleled excursions and tours in walking, sailing, biking, kayaking, and hiking. ✉ *Porat BB, Sutivan* ☎ *021/638–512* 🌐 *www.aldura-sport.hr.*

BEACHES

FAMILY Fodor'sChoice ★ **Zlatni Rat.** The obvious spot for swimming and sunning is the glorious Zlatni Rat beach, complete with a café and snack bar, plus sun beds and parasols, and paddleboats and Jet Skis for rent through peak season. To the west of Zlatni Rat lies a small beach reserved for nudists. Regular taxi-boats run from the Old Town harbor to Zlatni Rat beach, if the 20-minute walk is too much. **Amenities:** food and drink; showers; toilets; water sports. **Best for:** nudists; snorkeling; sunrise; sunset; swimming; windsurfing. ✉ *Brac.*

WATER SPORTS

FAMILY **Big Blue.** For windsurfing and scuba-diving training, stand-up paddleboarding, and equipment rentals, this well-established local company also rents sea kayaks and mountain bikes. ✉ *Podan Glavice 2, Bol* ☎ *021/635–614* 🌐 *www.big-blue-sport.hr.*

HVAR

Hvar Town is 23 nautical miles south of Split by ferry.

The island of Hvar bills itself as the "sunniest island in the Adriatic." Not only does it have the figures to back up this claim—an annual average of 2,724 hours of sunshine with a maximum of two foggy days a year—but it also makes visitors a sporting proposition, offering them a money-back guarantee if there is ever a foggy day (which has been known to happen).

GETTING HERE AND AROUND

The easiest way to reach Hvar Town is to catch a mid-afternoon Jadrolinija catamaran from Split, which stops at Hvar Town (23 nautical miles) before continuing to the South Dalmatian islands of Korčula and Lastovo. Alternatively, take an early morning Jadrolinija ferry from Split to Stari Grad (23 nautical miles) and then catch a local bus across the island.

EXPLORING

Hvar is both the name of the island and the name of the capital, near the island's western tip. Little **Hvar Town** rises like an amphitheater from its harbor, backed by a hilltop fortress and protected from the open sea by a scattering of small islands known as Pakleni Otoci. Along the palm-lined quay, a string of cafés and restaurants is shaded by colorful awnings and umbrellas. A few steps away, the magnificent main square,

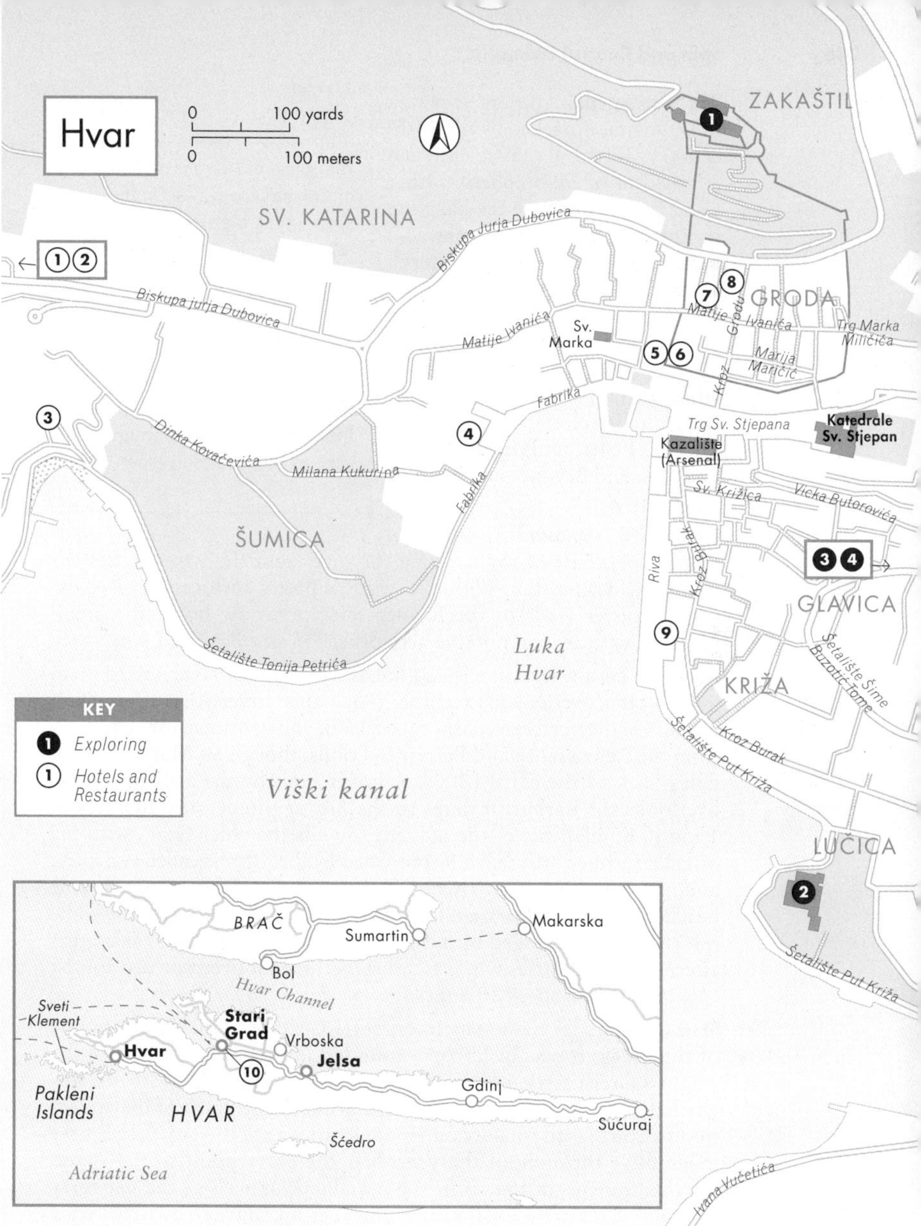

Exploring	Restaurants	Hotels
Franjevački samostan 2	Konoba Menego 5	Heritage Vila Apolon 10
Jelsa 3	Leporini 7	Hotel Adriana 4
Stari Grad 4	Macondo 1	Hotel Amfora 3
Tvrdalj 1	Passarola 6	Hotel Riva 9
	Restoran Palmižana Meneghello 8	Podstine 2

Trg Sveti Stjepan, the largest piazza in Dalmatia, is backed by the 16th-century **Katedrala Sveti Stjepan** (Cathedral of St. Stephen). Other notable sights include the kazalište (a theater) and the Franjevački Samostan (Franciscan Monastery). Hvar Town is currently a very "in" spot, so expect it to be crowded and expensive through peak season. Visitors have included King Abdullah of Jordan and his wife, Queen Rania, Italian clothing entrepreneur Luciano Benetton, Prince Harry of England, and Beyoncé and her husband, Jay Z.

A WORD ABOUT WINE

The island of Hvar makes some of Croatia's top wines. On the south coast, the steep, rugged, seaward-facing slopes between the villages of Sveti Nedelja and Ivan Dolac produce full-bodied reds, made predominantly from the Plavac Mali grape. In contrast, the vineyards in the flat valley between Stari Grad and Jelsa on the north side produce whites, such as the greenish-yellow Bogdanuša.

FAMILY **Franjevački samostan** (*Franciscan monastery*). East of town, along the quay past the Arsenal, lies the Franjevački samostan. Within its walls, a pretty 15th-century Renaissance cloister leads to the former refectory, now housing a small museum with several notable artworks. ✉ *Križa BB* 🎫 *25 Kn.*

FAMILY **Jelsa.** On Jelsa it feels like island life as it should be. Hvar's third main town is often overlooked except for the catamaran service it offers direct to Bol. On the northern coast of the island, you will see many structures from the Renaissance and Baroque periods, though **St. Mary's Church** dates back to the early 1300s. A **tower** built by the ancient Greeks overlooks the harbor; it dates to the 3rd or 4th century BC. About 1 km (0.6 mile) east of the modern town is the older **Grad,** with the original fortified area that was protected by the fortress called **Galešnik,** and now stands in ruins. This small town is surrounded by swimmable beaches—including the island's most popular nude beaches—and some resorts. It is surrounded by a thick forest of pine trees. Jelsa is a great alternative to Hvar Town, which has become an overcrowded tourist trap in high season. ✉ *20 km (13 miles) east of Hvar Town.*

FAMILY Fodor's Choice ★ **Stari Grad.** As its name suggests, Stari Grad, or Old Town, is one of the oldest towns in Europe, founded in 384 BC. The site of the original Greek settlement on Hvar, called Pharos by the Greeks, it is a conglomeration of smaller communities. While much of the attraction in Stari Grad focuses on its ancient history, the city is still very much alive throughout the year. It is the entry point to the island for bus transportation from the mainland, as well as the car ferry terminal. The town is 10 km (6 miles) east of Hvar Town. ✉ *Nova riva 3, Stari Grad* 🌐 *www.stari-grad.hr.*

Tvrdalj. The town's *trvdalj,* or fortress, is the palace of 16th-century poet Petar Hektorović. The villa was first renovated in 18th-century Baroque style, and a partial restoration was completed in the 19th century. Hektorović attempted to create a "model universe" to be embodied in his home. To that end, a large fish pond is stocked with gray mullet, as they were in the poet's own time, representing the sea; above the fish pond in a tower is a dovecote, representing the air. Ivy was allowed to cover the walls to tie the home to the land. Quotations from his poetry are inscribed on many walls. The home is not open to visitors, but the garden is worth a visit, and there is also a display of ancient agricultural equipment. *8 Ul. Molo Njiva 021/765–068 30 Kn.*

WHERE TO EAT

$$$ MEDITERRANEAN FAMILY **Konoba Menego.** On the steps between the main square and the castle, this authentic stone-walled konoba has candlelit tables and whole pršut hanging from the raftered ceiling. Come here to snack on small platters of locally produced, cold Dalmatian specialties such as *kožji sir* (goat cheese), *salata od hobotnice* (octopus salad), and *masline* (olives), accompanied by a carafe of homemade wine. **Known for:** small plates and brandy-marinated figs; no reservations; cash only. *Average main: 90 Kn Groda BB 021/742–036 www.menego.hr No credit cards Closed Dec.–Mar.*

$$$$ MEDITERRANEAN **Leporini.** A bit off the beaten path, this restaurant sits on a charming cobblestone street going up to the fortress and has cozy outdoor seating with a relaxed atmosphere that is perfect for enjoying classic fresh Dalmatian seafood. Classics like the Hvar *gregada* (fish stew with potatoes and olive oil) or *crni rižot* (black risotto) are highly recommended with the house red wine. **Known for:** superb semifreddo; outside seating in crowded pedestrian area; mouth-watering fish carpaccio. *Average main: €15 Groda 021/741–387.*

$$$$ SEAFOOD FAMILY **Macondo.** This superb fish restaurant lies hidden away on a narrow, cobbled street between the main square and the fortress—to find it, follow the signs from Trg Sv. Stjepana. **Known for:** superfresh seafood; well-versed waitstaff; simple furnishings. *Average main: 150 Kn 2 blocks north of Trg Sv Stjepana 021/742–850 No credit cards Closed Dec.–Mar.*

$$$$ MEDITERRANEAN Fodor's Choice ★ **Passarola.** Tucked away in a picturesque courtyard off the main square, Passarola has quickly risen to the list of top Hvar restaurants over the past few years. Great care is taken in selecting the best local, organic island ingredients, which are carefully prepared so that the focus stays always on those ingredients. **Known for:** top restaurant on the island; beautiful presentation and flavors; impressive wine list. *Average main: 225 Kn Dr. Mate Miličića 10 021/717–374 restaurant-passarola.eu Closed Nov.–Apr.*

$$$$ SEAFOOD **Restoran Palmižana Meneghello.** On the tiny island of Sveti Klement, a 20-minute taxi-boat ride from Hvar Town, this terrace restaurant is backed by a romantic wilderness of Mediterranean flora and offers stunning views over the open sea. Besides wonderfully fresh seafood, other dishes include *kožji sir sa rukolom* (goat cheese with arugula), and *pašticada* (beef stewed in sweet wine and prunes). **Known for:** being overpriced; exquisite view and heavenly surroundings. *Average main: 120 Kn Vinogradišće Uvala, Sveti Klement 021/717–270 No credit cards Closed Nov.–Mar.*

7

WHERE TO STAY

$ B&B/INN FAMILY **Heritage Vila Apolon.** Located in Hvar Stari Grad, this boutique villa offers sophisticated guests a taste of times past in an intimate island setting with a fine dining restaurant, which is sure to become one of the main dining attractions on the island. **Pros:** top Hvar restaurant; intimate and personal service; reasonable prices in comparison to similar style luxury accommodation on Hvar. **Cons:** still establishing solid clientele base; one room in back has no sea view. *Rooms from: €120 Šetalište Don Šime Ljubića 7, Stari Grad 021/778–320 apolon.hr Closed Nov.–Apr. 6 suites/rooms All meals.*

$$$$ HOTEL **Hotel Adriana.** This well-appointed hotel has a rooftop pool and sophisticated cocktail bar, affording stunning views onto the sea and Old Town, and a chic ground-floor restaurant serving Mediterranean cuisine on the harborfront. **Pros:** prime location on seafront promenade; beautifully designed interior; luxurious spa. **Cons:** very expensive; most bathrooms have a big shower but no tub; not always up to five-star standards. *Rooms from: €385 Fabrika bb 021/750–200 www.suncanihvar.hr 50 rooms, 9 suites Breakfast.*

$$$$ HOTEL FAMILY **Hotel Amfora.** This colossal white, modern structure sits in its own bay, is backed by pinewoods, and is a 10-minute walk along the coastal path from the center of town. **Pros:** location in newly landscaped grounds overlooking the sea; chic modern design; private beach cabins. **Cons:** vast 1970s building lacks charm; large and somewhat impersonal; overpriced; inconsistent service. *Rooms from: €250 Majerovića BB 021/750–300 www.suncanihvar.hr 246 rooms, 78 suites Breakfast.*

$ HOTEL FAMILY **Hotel Palace.** Commanding a prime site on the edge of the main square and overlooking the harbor, the Palace remains open most of the year, offering much lower prices during the off-season. **Pros:** centrally located; use of Hotel Amfora pool is free; very reasonable price given the location. **Cons:** rooms are dated; no a/c in rooms. *Rooms from: €120 Trg Sv. Stjepana 021/741–966 www.suncanihvar.com Closed Dec.–Mar. 62 rooms, 11 suites Breakfast.*

$$$ HOTEL **Hotel Riva.** Located on the palm-lined waterfront, opposite the ferry landing station, Hotel Riva is considered one of Hvar's hippest hotels. **Pros:** prime location on seafront promenade; urban, eclectic atmosphere; excellent bar and restaurant. **Cons:** expensive; rooms in front are very noisy night and day; small rooms. *Rooms from: €200 Obala Riva 27 021/750–100 www.suncanihvar.hr 46 rooms, 8 suites Breakfast.*

$$$$ HOTEL **Podstine.** With cool, peaceful rooms—most with sea views and balconies, and spacious marble bathrooms—this peaceful, family-run hotel lies on the coast, a 20-minute walk west of the town center. **Pros:** peaceful seafront location; beautiful gardens; small beach out front with sun beds and umbrellas. **Cons:** far from Old Town; no nightlife nearby (the hotel's bar shuts at 11 pm even in summer); standard rooms have no views. *Rooms from: €219 Podstine BB 021/740–400 www.podstine.com Closed Nov.–Mar. 40 rooms Breakfast.*

NIGHTLIFE AND PERFORMING ARTS

Croatia is generally not a hot spot for nightlife, but the island of Hvar is the exception. Over the past five years the island has initiated a renaissance of sorts by becoming a top party destination of the young and well-to-do. Unfortunately, this has more recently led to a less-than-desirable massive gathering of backpackers in search of the ultimate party and can be off-putting for those looking to enjoy the island's more natural attractions. Several stylish cocktail bars and clubs have opened in the past few years to cater to the annual influx of summer visitors, including the Ultra Music Festival that starts in Split and celebrates its last night with a beach party on Hvar. There is also a growing number of cultured evening events for the more discerning traveler.

NIGHTLIFE

BARS

Carpe Diem Bar. A harborside cocktail bar that's popular with twenty-somethings looking for a late-night extravaganza, Carpe Diem is the top party place and has certainly contributed to Hvar's reputation as the next Ibiza. ✉ *Riva* ☎ *021/742–369* 🌐 *www.carpe-diem-hvar.com.*

Hula Hula. This wooden beach bar, built into the rocks overlooking the sea, attracts bathers through daytime with its chill music, lounge chairs, VIP tables, and massages. Many stay for the sunset as the beach club transforms into a dance party with DJ music and cocktails. For celebrity-seekers, Beyoncé has been spotted here. ✉ *Coastal path, west of town* 🌐 *www.hulahulahvar.com.*

7

PERFORMING ARTS

FESTIVALS

Hvar Summer Festival. Classical-music recitals in the cloisters of the Franciscan monastery have long been the highlight of the Hvar Summer Festival. Also look out for theater, folklore, and jazz at various open-air locations around town. The annual festival runs for a month sometime between June and September. ✉ *Hvar.*

SPORTS AND THE OUTDOORS

BEACHES

Although there are several decent beaches within walking distance of town—the best-equipped being the Hotel Amfora's pebble beach, 10 minutes west of the main square—sun worshippers in the know head for the nearby Pakleni Otoci (Pakleni Islands), which can be reached by taxi-boats that depart regularly (in peak season, every hour, from 8 to 8) from in front of the Arsenal in the town harbor. The best known and best served are Sveti Jerolim (on the island of the same name, predominantly a nudist beach), Stipanska (on the island of Marinkovac, a clothing-optional beach), and Palmižana (on the island of Sveti Klement, also clothing-optional).

Carpe Diem Beach. Doubling as a daytime beach club and an after-dark party venue, Carpe Diem Beach lies on the tiny pine-scented island of Stipanska, a 10-minute taxi-boat ride from Hvar Town's harbor. It has two pebble beaches complete with wooden sun-beds and big parasols, an outdoor pool, and an open-air massage pavilion. There's also a lounge-bar and restaurant, and from mid-July to mid-August it hosts international DJs, playing till sunrise. **Amenities:** food and drink; showers; toilets. **Best for:** partiers; swimming. ✉ *Stipanska* 🌐 *www.carpe-diem-beach.com.*

DIVING

Diving Center Viking. Those with a taste for underwater adventure might have a go at scuba diving. The seabed is scattered with pieces of broken Greek amphorae, while the area's biggest underwater attraction is the Stambedar seawall, home to red and violet gorgonians (a type of coral), which is close to the Pakleni Islands. For courses at all levels, try Diving Center Viking. ✉ *Put Podstine 7* ☎ *021/742–529* 🌐 *www.viking-diving.com.*

SAILING

Hvar Town is a popular port of call for those sailing on the Adriatic; the town harbor is packed with flashy yachts through peak season.

ACI Palmižana. ACI Marina in Palmižana Bay on the island of Sveti Klement, one of the Pakleni Otoci, lies just 2.4 nautical miles from Hvar Town. This 211-berth marina is open from April through October, and is served by regular taxi boats from Hvar Town through peak season. ✉ *Palmižana Bay, Sveti Klement* ☎ *021/744–995* 🌐 *www.aci-marinas.com.*

FAMILY **Hvar Adventure.** Hvar Adventure arranges sea kayaking tours from Hvar Town to the Pakleni islets, as well as one-day sailing trips, hiking, cycling, and rock climbing. ✉ *Jurja Matijevića 20* 🌐 *www.hvar-adventure.com.*

Fodor's Choice ★ **Sunburst Sailing.** A 42-foot sailing yacht called Nera based in Split that is available for fully catered day charters and evening cruises. ✉ *Hrvatske mornarice 1* 🌐 *www.sunburstsailing.com.*

YOGA

Trendy Hvar even offers yoga.

Suncokret. Suncokret was founded by a New Yorker and her Dalmatia-born partner. Their holistic wellness retreats combine yoga, nature walks, Reiki, life-path workshops, and painting. Guests are accommodated in private cottages in the village, and typical Dalmatian meals are provided. Most courses last one week, but visitors are also welcome to drop in for a session. Dol lies 6 km (4 miles) from Starigrad and 26 km (16 miles) from Hvar Town. ✉ *Dol BB, Postira* ☎ *091/739–2526* 🌐 *www.suncokretdream.net.*

VIS

34 nautical miles southwest of Split by ferry.

Closed to foreigners until 1989, the distant island of Vis is relatively wild and unexploited. Built around a wide harbor, the town is popular among yachters, who appreciate its rugged nature, unpretentious fish restaurants, and excellent locally produced wine.

The pretty fishing village of Komiža is 11 km (7 miles) from Vis Town. Here you're just a 40-minute boat ride away from the Modra Spilja (Blue Cave), often compared to the Blue Grotto on Italy's Capri.

GETTING HERE AND AROUND

To get here from Split, you can either take the SEM Marina fast catamaran service, or a 2½-hour Jadrolinija ferry ride to arrive in Vis Town.

EXPLORING

FAMILY **Modra Spilja** (*Blue Cave*). Hidden away on the small island of Biševo (5 nautical miles southwest of Komiža), the Blue Cave is 78 feet long and 39 feet wide. Sunlight enters through the water, reflects off the seabed, and casts the interior in a fantastic shade of blue. Throughout the summer, local fishermen will take tourists (some coming from Split and Hvar by speedboat) into the Modra Spilja. It can be a long wait in summer when there's a line of small boats waiting to enter the cave. Ask at the marina or at the tourist-information office to see who is offering trips. ✉ *Biševo island* 🎫 *50 Kn cave entrance.*

WHERE TO EAT

$$ ECLECTIC ✕ **Fabrika.** The service may be a little slow but the cool atmosphere, like the tree painted on the inside wall and the bohemian furniture and original jewelry that are for sale, adds up to a funky little place to go for a burger and a drink. The owners—a brother and sister team—are a well-known Croatian singer and fashion blogger. **Known for:** great location; good breakfast menu; fashionable owners. 💲 *Average main: €5* ✉ *Riva Sv. Mikule 12, Komiža* ☎ *021/713–155* 💳 *No credit cards* ⏲ *Closed Oct.–Apr.*

$$$$ SEAFOOD FAMILY ✕ **Jastožera.** Originally built in 1883 as a lobster house, this cleverly converted restaurant has platforms with tables built out above the water, and small boat can drive right under the platforms and into the central dining room. The house specialty is *jastog sa spagetima* (lobster with spaghetti). **Known for:** access to main dining room via the water; slow service; grilled fish. 💲 *Average main: €25* ✉ *Gundulićeva 6, Komiža* ☎ *021/713–859* ⏲ *Closed Nov.–Mar.*

$$$$ SEAFOOD FAMILY ✕ **Konoba Bako.** Popular with locals and visitors alike, this excellent fish restaurant overlooks a tiny bay in Komiža. Outdoors, tables are set right up to the water's edge, and inside there's a small pool with lobsters and amphorae. **Known for:** good seafood; unbeatable view and location; sketchy service. 💲 *Average main: €25* ✉ *Gundulićeva 1, Komiža* ☎ *021/713–742* ⏲ *No lunch.*

$$$$ MEDITERRANEAN FAMILY Fodor's Choice ★ ✕ **Lola Konoba and Beer Garden.** A new garden restaurant, Konoba Lola offers something refreshingly different on the island of Vis. The atmosphere is relaxed, the food is fresh, and most of the vegetables come from Lola's own garden on the mainland. **Known for:** romantic garden setting; impressive cocktails and dessert; service with a smile. 💲 *Average main: €20* ✉ *Matije Gupca 12, Vis Town* ☎ *095/849–7932* 🌐 *www.lolavisisland.com* ⏲ *Closed Nov.–Mar.*

$$$$ SEAFOOD FAMILY **Pojoda.** A modern glass-and-wood conservatory that looks onto a courtyard garden of orange and lemon trees and accessed via an archway off a narrow side street—a popular spot among the sailing crowd that won't disappoint a food-savvy traveler. Pojoda dishes are named in local dialect: check out the *manistra na brudet* (bean and pasta soup) and *luc u verudi* (tuna stewed with vegetables), or try the *pojorski bronzinić*, a thick brodetto of squid with lentils and barley. **Known for:** grilled fresh fish; family-friendly atmosphere; brilliantly flavored lobster brudet. *Average main: €25 Don Cvjetka Marasovića 8, Vis Town 021/711–575 Closed for dinner in winter.*

$$$$ SEAFOOD **Villa Kaliopa.** With tables set under the trees in the romantic walled garden of a 16th-century villa, dinner at this restaurant in Vis Town is an unforgettable experience. The menu changes daily depending on what fresh fish and shellfish are available. **Known for:** excellent setting and location; not the best service; caters to the high-end crowd. *Average main: 100 Kn V Nazora 32, Vis Town 091/271–1755 No credit cards Closed Nov.–Mar.*

WHERE TO STAY

$$ HOTEL FAMILY **Hotel San Giorgio.** In Vis Town, east of the ferry quay, this chic little hotel is hidden away between stone cottages in a quiet, cobbled side street. **Pros:** yoga vacations offered; modern and comfortable rooms; good restaurant. **Cons:** a couple of blocks in from the seafront (only the top-floor suite has a sea view); often fully booked; 20-minute walk from ferry landing can be difficult for visitors with heavy luggage. *Rooms from: €152 Petra Hektorovića 2, Vis Town 021/711–362 www.hotelsangiorgiovis.com 4 rooms, 6 suites Breakfast.*

$ HOTEL FAMILY **Tamaris.** Overlooking the harbor and seafront promenade in Vis Town, Tamaris occupies a late-19th-century building. **Pros:** on seafront promenade in center of town; most rooms have sea views; cheerful café terrace out front. **Cons:** rooms very basic; service rather indifferent. *Rooms from: €116 Šetalište Apolonija Zanelle 5, Vis Town 021/711–350 25 rooms Breakfast.*

SPORTS AND THE OUTDOORS

DIVING

Issa Diving Centre. Scuba-diving enthusiasts will find underwater attractions including several underwater caves, at least half a dozen shipwrecks, and some spectacular coral reefs. Beginners and those with previous experience should contact Issa Diving Centre for organized diving trips and training at all levels. They have four dive instructors and three dive masters, a very experienced team. *Ribarska 91, Komiža 021/713–651 www.scubadiving.hr.*

MAKARSKA

67 km (42 miles) southeast of Split.

The seafront promenade, lined with palm trees and cheerful open-air cafés, looks onto a protected bay dotted with wooden fishing boats. From here one enters the Old Town, a warren of stone buildings and cobbled streets surrounding the main square, which is backed by the parish church and a small open-air market off to one side. The atmosphere is relaxed and easygoing. The only drama you'll likely see is created by the limestone heights of Biokovo Mountain, which seems to alternate between protecting and threatening the town, depending on the color of the sky and the cloud formations that ride over its rugged peaks.

Makarska has developed an unpretentious, affordable brand of tourism that is popular with East Europeans.

GETTING HERE AND AROUND

The cobblestone streets of this small bayside town are most easily accessed on foot.

EXPLORING

FAMILY **Park Prirode Biokovo** (*Biokovo Nature Park*). Behind Makarska, a large area of the rocky heights that form the majestic Biokovo Mountain have been designated as a nature park. Part of the Dinaric Alps, which run from Slovenia down to Montenegro, Biokovo abounds in rare indigenous plant species, and is primarily limestone with little green coverage. It's possible to reach the highest peak, Sveti Jure (5,781 feet) in five and a half hours from Makarska. However, this is a strenuous hike, especially in summer, for which you will need good boots and plenty of water. It is not recommended to hike it alone. It is best to organize an excursion through Biokovo Active Holidays, a company that offers organized trips up the mountain, traveling part of the way by jeep. ✉ *Marineta, Mala Obala 16* ☎ *021/616–924* 🌐 *www.biokovo.com.*

WHERE TO EAT

$$$$ MODERN EUROPEAN Fodor's Choice ★ **Jeny.** Jeny is one of the only serious fine dining restaurants on the Makarska Riviera, and the time and care that have gone into creating the wine pairing menu and the expertise of the food preparation stand head and shoulders above anything else for miles. The scallops are tenderly cooked and the filet mignon has a garlic crust that leaves you wanting more. **Known for:** delectable scallops; sophisticated wine pairing menu; wonderful overall dining experience. $ *Average main: €25* ✉ *Čovići 1, Tucepi* ☎ *021/623–704* 🌐 *www.restaurant-jeny.hr.*

$$$$ MEDITERRANEAN FAMILY **Konoba Ranc.** Surrounded on all four sides by the shade of an olive grove, this restaurant is the perfect place to wind down a day of sun and sightseeing. It's known for the steak and lamb from the *peka* (covered iron pot over an open fire) and fish prepared on the grill. **Known for:** outdoor area for kids to run around; hearty food; al fresco dining. $ *Average main: €20* ✉ *Kamena 62, Tucepi* ☎ *021/623–563* 🌐 *www.ranc-tucepi.hr.*

$$$$ ECLECTIC **Stari Mlin.** Ethnic music, incense, and colorful canvases set the mood inside this old stone building, where the interior garden is draped with vines and decorated with pots of herbs and cherry tomatoes. Barbecued seafood tops the menu, but there's also a select choice of authentic Thai dishes. **Known for:** quality Croatian fare; excellent mojitos; waitstaff try to up-sell. *Average main: €25 Prvosvibanska 43 021/611–509.*

WHERE TO STAY

$$ B&B/INN Fodor's Choice ★ **Boutique Hotel Marco Polo.** Boutique Hotel Marco Polo is more than just a hotel, it is an entire experience. **Pros:** excellent restaurant; pool/spa and beach chairs; rooftop terrace to escape the beachfront crowds. **Cons:** can get crowded; hard to find a spot on the beach. *Rooms from: €155 Obala 15, Gradac 021/695–060 www.hotel-marcopolo.com Closed Nov.–Mar. 25 rooms.*

$ HOTEL **Hotel Biokovo.** In the center of Makarska, on the palm-lined seafront promenade, this old-fashioned hotel was renovated in 2004. **Pros:** centrally located; handicap access; friendly and helpful staff; pleasant café and decent restaurant. **Cons:** limited facilities; parking can be a problem. *Rooms from: €57 Obala Kralja Tomislava 021/615–244 www.hotelbiokovo.hr 55 rooms, 1 suite Breakfast.*

$$ HOTEL **Hotel Porin.** This 19th-century building stands on the seafront promenade and was refurbished to form a small hotel, which opened in 2002. **Pros:** location on seafront promenade in the Old Town; front rooms have lovely views onto the bay; small, so guests receive individual attention from the staff; parking available if you make reservation. **Cons:** often fully booked; limited facilities. *Rooms from: €160 Marineta 2 021/613–688 www.hotel-porin.hr 7 rooms, 1 suite Breakfast.*

SPORTS AND THE OUTDOORS

BEACHES

The main town beach, a 1½-km (1-mile) stretch of pebbles backed by pine woods, lies northwest of the center and close to a string of big modern hotels. Alternatively, walk along the narrow coastal path southeast of town to find rocks and a series of secluded coves. Farther afield, the Makarska Riviera is a 40-km (25-mile) stretch of coast running from Brela to Gradac. And although the Makarska Riviera is not the French Riviera, it offers the stunningly beautiful backdrop of the Biokovo Mountain, several easily accessed islands at its doorstep, and an assortment of small coved private beaches and villages that are each islands unto themselves. Be sure to check out the free app from iTunes, "Makarska Riviera," which, once downloaded, will help you find all the secluded private beaches along the riviera.

DIVING

Local underwater attractions include a nearby reef, known as **Kraljev Gaj,** which is populated by sponges, coral, octopi, and scorpion fish, while farther out from the coast you can visit the *Dubrovnik,* an old steam boat that sank in 1917.

FAMILY **More Sub.** Scuba-diving enthusiasts, as well as complete beginners, can try More Sub for organized diving trips and training at all levels. ✉ *Krešimira 43* ☎ *021/611–727* 🌐 *www.more-sub-makarska.hr.*

LASTOVO

Lastovo Island is 80 km (50 nautical miles) west of Dubrovnik (no direct ferry) and 80 km (50 nautical miles) southeast of Split (daily direct ferry connection).

Very few Croatians have visited Lastovo, though they will all tell you that it's beautiful. Like Vis, Lastovo was a Yugoslav military naval base during the Tito years, and was therefore closed to foreigners, so commercial tourism never developed. Today, there is still just one hotel.

Lying far out to sea, Lastovo is an island of green, fertile valleys and is practically self-sufficient: locally caught seafood—not least the delicious lobster—and homegrown vegetables are the staple diet. The main settlement, Lastovo Town, is made up of stone houses built amphitheater-style into a hillside, crisscrossed by cobbled alleys and flights of steps; they're renowned for tall chimneys resembling minarets. The only other settlement on the island is the small port of Ubli, which is 10 km (6 miles) from Lastovo Town.

GETTING HERE AND AROUND

Although it is officially in Southern Dalmatia, locals chose to have direct transport links with Split in Central Dalmatia rather than Dubrovnik. To get there, take the Jadrolinija daily ferry service from Split to Ubli, stopping at Hvar Town and Vela Luka en route. Jadrolinija also runs a daily catamaran from Split covering the same route; it's faster but a little more expensive.

7

WHERE TO EAT

$$$ SEAFOOD **Konoba Bačvara.** Traditional home-cooked Dalmatian fare is served at this family-run eatery in an old stone building in Lastovo Town. Barbecued seafood predominates, and you'll also have the chance to try homegrown vegetables and local wine. **Known for:** affordable; refreshing escape; homegrown veggies. *Average main: 70 Kn* ✉ *Počuvalo* ☎ *020/801–131* *No credit cards* *Closed Nov.–May.*

$$$$ SEAFOOD **Konoba Triton.** Triton is widely acknowledged to be the best restaurant on the island, and it's particularly popular with those traveling by sailboat, who can moor up on a small quay out front. The owner catches and cooks the fish himself; he also produces the wine, olive oil, and vegetables. **Known for:** good antipasto; free mooring for those arriving by boat; fresh-caught fish. *Average main: 250 Kn* ✉ *Zaklopatica* ☎ *020/801–161* 🌐 *www.triton.hr* *No credit cards* *Closed Nov.–Mar.*

WHERE TO STAY

$ HOTEL FAMILY **Hotel Solitudo.** The only hotel on the island, Hotel Solitudo (confusingly sometimes referred to as Hotel Ladesta) is a modern white building on a peaceful bay backed by pines, 3 km (2 miles) north of Ubli. **Pros:** recently renovated; peaceful off-the-beaten-path island; on-site dive shop. **Cons:** basic breakfast; spotty service. *Rooms from: €103* ✉ *Pasadur, 3 km (2 miles) from Ubli* ☎ *020/802–100* 🌐 *www.hotel-solitudo.com* *60 rooms, 12 suites* *Breakfast.*

SPORTS AND THE OUTDOORS

BEACHES

The best beaches lie on **Saplun,** one of the tiny unpopulated **Lastovnjaci Islands,** which are a short distance northeast of Lastovo and are served by taxi-boats through high season.

DIVING

FAMILY **Paradise Diving Center.** Paradise Diving Center is a scuba-diving center based in the Hotel Solitudo. Just a five-minute boat ride from the diving center and at a depth of 49 feet lies a reef of red, yellow, and violet gorgonias. Farther afield, experienced divers can expect to explore sea caves and sunken ships. ✉ *Pasadur, 3 km (2 miles) from Ubli* ☎ *020/802–100* 🌐 *www.diving-lastovo.com.*

SAILING

Marina Lastovo. This 50-berth marina is attached to Hotel Solitudo. ✉ *Pasadur, 3 km (2 miles) from Ubli* ☎ *020/802–100* 🌐 *www.marina-lastovo.com.*

8

DUBROVNIK AND SOUTHERN DALMATIA

Updated by Andrea MacDonald

A region would be lucky to have just one sight as majestic as Dubrovnik. In Southern Dalmatia, the walled city is only the beginning. Head south to pine-scented hiking trails in Cavtat, or up the coast to a garden full of exotic trees in Trsteno. Tour an ancient salt factory, feast on world-class oysters and superb red wine from the Pelješac Peninsula, then head out to sea to explore Marco Polo's birthplace on Korčula and Odysseus's mythical cave on Mljet. Along the way you'll find some of the best windsurfing and sailing in Europe, kayak trips to citrus and sage-covered islands, centuries-old houses, millennia-old caves, fresh seafood, and always, everywhere, that big blue sea.

The highlight of Southern Dalmatia is undoubtedly the majestic walled city of Dubrovnik, from 1358 to 1808 a rich and powerful independent republic that exerted its economic and cultural influence over almost the entire region. Jutting out to sea and backed by rugged mountains, it's an unforgettable sight and now Croatia's most upmarket and glamorous destination.

There are regular local ferry and catamaran services from Dubrovnik to outlying islands. The nearest and most accessible of these are the tiny Elafitis, ideal as a day trip for someone on a short stay who still wants a brief taste of island life.

Moving down the mainland coast you come to the bucolic Konavle region, the breadbasket of the area. Full of family farms, folk festivals, and wineries, it provides a wonderful glimpse into rural life. The gateway to Konavle is Cavtat, a town founded by the ancient Greeks as Epidaurum. It was the residents from here who founded Dubrovnik after their town was destroyed in the early 7th century. Today's Cavtat is a cheerful holiday resort with a palm-lined seaside promenade, several sights of cultural note, and a laid-back vibe.

Back up the coast, northwest of Dubrovnik, lies the village of Trsteno, with its delightful Renaissance arboretum stepping down toward the sea in a series of terraces. Proceeding northwest one arrives at Ston, known for its oysters and salt pans, and its 14th-century walls forming the gateway to Pelješac Peninsula. Pelješac is of particular note for its excellent red wines: several families open their vineyards and cellars to the public for wine tastings. The main destination here is Orebić, a low-key resort with a good beach and water-sports facilities, backed by a majestic hillside monastery. From Orebić there are regular ferry crossings to Korčula Town, on the island of Korčula, one of the most sophisticated settlements on the Croatian islands, with its fine

Gothic and Renaissance stone buildings bearing witness to almost 800 years of Venetian rule. In contrast to Korčula, the sparsely populated island of Mljet offers little in the way of architectural beauty but has preserved its indigenous coniferous forests, which rim the shores of two emerald-green saltwater lakes. They are contained within the borders of Mljet National Park, a haven for hiking, mountain biking, swimming, and kayaking.

ORIENTATION AND PLANNING

GETTING ORIENTED

Occupying the tail end of Croatia before it trails off into Montenegro and the Gulf of Kotor, Southern Dalmatia is bordered to the east by Bosnia-Herzegovina and to the west by the Adriatic Sea. Heading out across the water you will hit Korčula, Mljet, and the Elafiti Islands. On the other side is Italy.

GREAT ITINERARIES

IF YOU HAVE 3 DAYS

Devote Day 1 to **Dubrovnik,** walking a full circuit of the city walls, exploring the historic monuments in the Old Town, and riding the cable car to the top of Mt. Srđ at sunset. On Day 2 head to **Lokrum Island** for Dubrovnik's most peaceful beaches, then drive down to **Cavtat** (stopping to admire the view along the way) for dinner along the promenade, or even farther south to **Konavle** for a traditional cooking class. On Day 3, take the midday ferry to **Lopud,** one of the car-free Elafiti Islands, to enjoy the sandy beach and some romantic escapism. If you're after some peace and quiet, spend your final night here; otherwise, return to Dubrovnik for the bright lights.

IF YOU HAVE 5 DAYS

Spend your first three days as outlined above. On Day 4, take a morning ferry to **Korčula Town** and spend the day exploring the Old Town; if you're lucky, catch an evening performance of the Moreška sword dance. On Day 5, take a day trip to **Mljet** or the **Pelješac Peninsula** or rent a motorboat and visit the tiny islets of the Korčula archipelago. Spend your final night soaking up Korčula's lively evening atmosphere in one of its fine restaurants or cocktail bars.

IF YOU HAVE 7 DAYS

Spend your first five days as on the itinerary above, but save **Pelješac Peninsula** for Day 6 when you'll head to **Orebić**. Organize a wine-tasting tour of the peninsula, or go windsurfing. On Day 7, leave Orebić in the morning and spend the afternoon in **Ston**, walking the city walls, visiting the salt pans, and feasting on oysters. Make a stop in **Trsteno** before heading back to Dubrovnik for your final evening.

PLANNING

WHEN TO GO

Southern Dalmatia works for half the year and sleeps for the other: most of the region shuts down through the winter. Dubrovnik is the exception; sightseeing is just as important as swimming here, so even in winter you will find many restaurants and attractions still open, plus bargain-priced accommodation and a chance to tune into the local way of life.

The best time to visit the region is the shoulder season: May through June and September through October. The days are still warm enough to swim but not too hot for sightseeing, there are many local festivals to enjoy, and the locals are more relaxed.

July and August is when everything happens at full speed; the prices are high, the hotels fully booked, the harbors are full of boats, and the small streets full of people. In Dubrovnik, everyone from backpackers to international performers in town for the Summer Festival scramble to find a room, and the prices rise accordingly. The payoff of a summer visit is that you're guaranteed hot, sunny weather and plenty of entertainment. If you plan to visit during this period, make sure to book accommodation well in advance and make dinner reservations a day or two ahead for restaurants you particularly want to visit.

TOP REASONS TO GO

Wall walking: Walk the entire circuit of Dubrovnik's medieval city walls—which date back to the 13th century—for splendid views. Then take the cable car up Mt. Srđ for the postcard-perfect views of the walls, the city, and the sea together in all their glory.

Mussel up: Feast on fresh oysters straight out of the sea and local wine at a waterside restaurant in the Pelješac Peninsula's Mali Ston. The oysters are justifiably famous and served year-round.

Sword dancing: Watch an incredibly entertaining, centuries-old sword dance in Korčula Town, the stunning city where Marco Polo was born.

Secluded swimming: Swim in Mljet's pristine Veliko Jezero surrounded by dense pine forests, then take a kayak to the Benedictine monastery on an island in the middle of the lake.

Chilling out: Spend a day hiking, biking, or just lounging on the relaxed, sun-drenched Elafiti Islands.

GETTING HERE AND AROUND

AIR TRAVEL

Southern Dalmatia is served by Dubrovnik Airport (DBV) at Čilipi, 18 km (11 miles) southeast of the city.

The national carrier, Croatia Airlines, operates internal flights between Dubrovnik, Zagreb, Pula, and Osijek. Through summer, it also flies regularly between Dubrovnik and Athens, Amsterdam, Berlin, Düsseldorf, Frankfurt, Rome, Venice, and Zurich. British Airways operates flights year-round between Dubrovnik and London. It is also possible to fly direct to Rome, Barcelona, Istanbul, and Frankfurt through the winter. Many other airlines offer seasonal or charter service to Dubrovnik from destinations all around Europe and the U.K.; check Sky Scanner for your best options.

Atlas organizes an airport shuttle bus, which leaves on the half hour between 4:30 am and 9 pm and also meets all incoming flights. It picks up from the main bus station in Dubrovnik and the bus stop near the cable car, and drops off at the main bus station and the Pile Gate. A one-way ticket costs 40 Kn and can be purchased from the driver. Journey time is approximately 30 minutes.

Airline Contacts **British Airways.** 🌐 *www.britishairways.com.* **Croatia Airlines.** ✉ *Dubrovnik Airport, Cilipi* ☎ *020/773–232* 🌐 *www.croatiaairlines.com.*

Airport Contacts **Dubrovnik Airport.** ✉ *Čilipi, Cilipi* ☎ *020/773–100 general info* 🌐 *www.airport-dubrovnik.hr.*

Airport Transfer Contacts **Atlas Shuttle Bus.** ☎ *012/415–611* 🌐 *www.atlas-croatia.com.*

BOAT AND FERRY TRAVEL

Jadrolinija runs a regular ferry service between Dubrovnik and Bari (Italy), departing from Bari late in the evening and arriving in Dubrovnik early the next morning, with a similar schedule in the other direction. Through the summer, Jadrolinija runs four ferries a day from

8

Dubrovnik to the Elafiti Islands (Koločep, Lopud, and Šipan) and a once-daily service to Mljet and Korčula before carrying on to Split.

Krilo's faster, more comfortable catamaran, *Kapetan Luka,* also travels twice daily between Split and Dubrovnik, stopping in Korčula and Mljet en route. You can also take a high-speed catamaran operated by G&V Line, running daily from Dubrovnik to Šipan, Sobra, and Polače on Mljet, Korčula, and Lastovo. There are five daily Jadrolinija ferries between Mljet and Prapratno on the Pelješac Peninsula.

Tickets can be purchased at the individual ferry companies' offices in the harbor, or head to Avansa Travel for information and tickets. They have a very comprehensive website and an office in Travel Corner across the street from the ferry terminal in Gruž. The staff are very friendly and will simplify everything for you.

Contacts **Avansa Travel.** ✉ *Obala Stjepana Radića 40, Gruž* ☎ *020/492–313* 🌐 *www.avansa-travel.com.* **G&V Line.** ✉ *Vukovarska 34, Gruž* ☎ *020/313–119* 🌐 *www.gv-line.hr.* **Jadrolinija.** ✉ *Stjepana Radića 40, Dubrovnik* ☎ *020/418–000* 🌐 *www.jadrolinija.hr.* **Krilo (Kapetan Luka).** ✉ *Obala Stjepana Radića 40, Gruž* ☎ *020/492–313* 🌐 *www.krilo.hr.*

BUS TRAVEL

There are regular bus routes between Dubrovnik and destinations all over mainland Croatia, with hourly buses to Split, 14 daily to Zagreb, and 4 to Rijeka (Kvarner). Within the Southern Dalmatia region, there are a couple of buses daily to Ston and onward to Orebić on the Pelješac Peninsula, which continue to Korčula. Regular local buses run up the coast to Trstenik and down the coast to Cavtat (you can also catch the bus to Cavtat at the bus stop near the cable car). Remember that if you're traveling between Central and Southern Dalmatia by road, you'll pass through a narrow coastal strip called Neum, which belongs to Bosnia-Herzegovina, so have your passport at hand for the border checkpoint. Most Croatian buses have a 20-minute stop here so people can jump off and shop, since many things are much cheaper in Bosnia.

Contacts **Dubrovnik Bus Station.** ✉ *Obala Pape Ivana Pavla II 44A, Gruž* ☎ *060/305–070* 🌐 *libertasdubrovnik.hr.*

CAR TRAVEL

While visiting Dubrovnik and the islands, you are certainly better off without a car; parking is hard to find and very expensive, and the bus system is great. If you must bring a car into Dubrovnik, there is a public parking garage at Ilijina Glavica on Zagrebačka street leading to the Old Town, where you'll find the most reasonable prices and space. You may want to rent a car for a day or two if you are traveling up the coast to the Pelješac Peninsula or down the coast to Konavle, as these areas are not well served by public transport.

TAXI TRAVEL

In Dubrovnik, there are taxi ranks at the main bus station and the airport, just outside the city walls at Pile Gate and Ploče Gate, in front of Gruž harbor, and in Lapad. It isn't possible to hail a taxi in Dubrovnik; you must go to the rank or call ☎ *080–0970* to arrange a pickup. Most taxi stands post authorized prices.

TOURS

Atlas. Atlas organizes one-day excursions from Dubrovnik to neighboring countries (passports required). In Bosnia-Herzegovina, you can visit the pilgrimage site of Medjugorje, where the Virgin Mary is said to have appeared in 1981, or Mostar with its Turkish-inspired Old Town and reconstructed bridge. Or take a day-trip to Budva and the Bay of Kotor in Montenegro. Tours can be booked directly with Atlas, at the main tourist information center near Pile Gate, or at Travel Corner in Gruž. ☎ *012/415–611* 🌐 *www.atlas-croatia.com.*

Secret Dalmatia. One of the pioneers in custom-made tours in the region, Secret Dalmatia organizes upmarket itineraries around Southern Dalmatia and Montenegro with a focus on local experiences, food and wine tastings, and off-the-beaten-track destinations. Their superhelpful and friendly team can organize private or small-group tours. ☎ *091/567–1604* 🌐 *www.secretdalmatia.com.*

Fodor's Choice ★ **Tureta Travel.** This boutique travel agency offers personalized day trips and multiday itineraries around Southern Dalmatia and other parts of Croatia. These tours are particularly useful for reaching off-the-beaten-track areas and organizing local experiences, such as cooking classes in Konavle and wine tours of the Pelješac Peninsula, with a bit of sailing or sea kayaking thrown in. This should be your first call if you want a bit of help planning your trip. ✉ *Odranska 1, Zagreb* ☎ *095/252–1992* 🌐 *www.tureta-travel.com.*

ABOUT THE RESTAURANTS

Seafood-lovers rejoice: the fresh catch predominates throughout Southern Dalmatia. Look for squid, prawn, salmon, and everything from tuna steaks to octopus to the popular mussels *buzara* (tomato and white wine sauce). Restaurants in Dubrovnik are the most expensive, but also the most sophisticated, where excellent produce is accentuated by sophisticated new flavors, herbs, and recipes still unheard-of in many other towns. The region's top venue for shellfish is the village of Mali Ston on the Pelješac Peninsula, where locally grown *ostrige* (oysters) and *dagnje* (mussels) attract diners from far and wide. Similarly, the island of Mljet is noted for its *jastog* (lobster), a culinary luxury highly appreciated by the sailing crowd. Be sure to find a restaurant that serves food prepared *ispod peke* ("under the bell"): a terra-cotta casserole dish, usually containing either lamb or octopus, is buried in white embers over which the *peka* (metal dome) is placed to ensure a long, slow cooking process—it usually needs to be ordered a day in advance but it's worth the wait. Another must-try for meat lovers is *pašticada,* a sweet and rich, slow-cooked beef dish typically served with gnocchi. For dessert, the region's specialty is *rožata,* an egg-based pudding similar to French crème caramel. Of course, all meals should be accompanied by a glass of excellent local wine; Plavac Mali, Pošip, Malvazija, and Dingač are names you'll get to know.

ABOUT THE HOTELS

Southern Dalmatia's most luxurious hotels are in Dubrovnik, and while prices there are higher than elsewhere, it is possible to find accommodation to suit lower budgets, particularly in private apartments. There are a number of large, 1970s socialist-era hotels scattered around the area; many are disappointingly impersonal, full of tour groups, and in desperate need of sprucing up. Opt for boutique hotels or apartments wherever possible, where the service is more personal and you have a great chance to live as the locals do. For most of the region, the season runs from Easter through late October, peaking during July and August, when prices rise significantly.

Hotel reviews have been shortened. For full information, visit Fodors.com.

Fodor's Choice ★ **Dominium Travel.** With so many private apartments throughout the region, deciding which one to choose can be overwhelming, not to mention a little risky. Do yourself a favor and contact Dominium Travel, a young, enthusiastic company that manages more than 500 private apartments in 20 destinations along the coast, including Dubrovnik, Pelješac, Mljet, and Konavle. They don't charge a fee, they'll work with you to find the perfect apartment to suit your budget and style, and they'll even give you a glass of wine and walk you straight to your front door when you arrive. ✉ *Trogirska 2a, Pile* ☎ *020/420–059* 🌐 *www.book-dubrovnik.com.*

	WHAT IT COSTS IN EUROS (€) AND CROATIAN KUNA (KN)			
	$	**$$**	**$$$**	**$$$$**
Restaurants	under 70 Kn	70 Kn–110 Kn	111 Kn–140 Kn	over 140 Kn
	under €10	€10–€14	€15–€20	over €20
Hotels	under 925 Kn	925 Kn–1,300 Kn	1,301 Kn–1,650 Kn	over 1,650 Kn
	under €125	€125–€175	€176–€220	over €220

Restaurant prices are the average cost of a main course at dinner or, if dinner is not served, at lunch. Hotel prices are the lowest cost of a standard double room in high season.

VISITOR INFORMATION

Contacts Cavtat Tourist Office. ✉ *Zidine 6, Cavtat* ☎ *020/479–025* 🌐 *visit.cavtat-konavle.com.* **Dubrovnik Tourist Office.** ✉ *Brsalje 5, Pile* ☎ *020/312–011* 🌐 *www.tzdubrovnik.hr* ✉ *Obala Ivana Pavla II, Gruž* ☎ *020/417–983* 🌐 *www.tzdubrovnik.hr.* **Korčula Tourist Office.** ✉ *Obala Dr Franje Tuđmana 4, Korcula* ☎ *020/715–701* 🌐 *www.visitkorcula.eu.* **Lopud Tourist Office.** ✉ *Obala Iva Kuljevana 12, Lopud* ☎ *020/322–322.* **Mljet Tourist Office.** ✉ *Sobra BB, around the side of the café at the ferry pier, Sobra* ☎ *020/746–025* 🌐 *www.mljet.hr.* **Orebić Tourist Office.** ✉ *Zrinsko-frankopanska 2, Orebic* ☎ *020/713–718* 🌐 *www.visitorebic-croatia.com.* **Šipan Tourist Office.** ✉ *Šipanska Luka* ☎ *020/758–084.* **Ston Tourist Office.** ✉ *Pelješki put 1, Ston* ☎ *020/754–452* 🌐 *www.ston.hr.*

DUBROVNIK

Nothing can prepare you for your first sight of Dubrovnik. Lying 216 km (135 miles) southeast of Split and commanding a jaw-dropping coastal location, it is one of the world's most beautiful fortified cities. Its massive stone ramparts and fortress towers curve around a tiny harbor, enclosing graduated ridges of sun-bleached orange-tiled roofs, copper domes, and elegant bell towers. And it never gets old; whether you're looking at it from the cable car, a kayak out at sea, or from the road leading out of town, your imagination will run wild picturing what it looked like seven centuries ago when the walls were built, without any suburbs or highways around it, just this magnificent stone city rising out of the sea.

In the 7th century AD, residents of the Roman city Epidaurum (now Cavtat) fled the Avars and Slavs of the north and founded a new settlement on a small rocky island, which they named Laus, and later Ragusa. On the mainland hillside opposite the island, the Slav settlement called Dubrovnik grew up. In the 12th century, the narrow channel separating the two settlements was filled in (now the main street through the Old Town, called Stradun), and Ragusa and Dubrovnik became one. The city was surrounded by defensive walls during the 13th century, and these were reinforced with towers and bastions in the late 15th century.

From 1358 to 1808, the city thrived as a powerful and remarkably sophisticated independent republic, reaching its golden age during the 16th century. In 1667 many of its splendid Gothic and Renaissance buildings were destroyed by an earthquake. The defensive walls survived the disaster, and the city was rebuilt in Baroque style.

Dubrovnik lost its independence to Napoléon in 1808, and in 1815 passed to Austria-Hungary. During the 20th century, as part of Yugoslavia, the city became a popular tourist destination, and in 1979 it was listed as a UNESCO World Heritage Site. During the war for independence, it came under heavy siege. Thanks to careful restoration, few traces of damage remain. It's only when you experience Dubrovnik yourself that you can understand what a treasure the world nearly lost.

8

GETTING HERE AND AROUND

Dubrovnik is best explored on foot, as parking is extremely expensive and the Old Town is car-free. The city is not linked to the rest of the country by train, but there are regular bus routes to destinations all over mainland Croatia and beyond. The main bus station is located near the ferry terminal in Gruž, 20 minutes outside the Old Town.

EXPLORING

All of the main sites lie in Stari Grad (Old Town) within the city walls, a compact, car-free area. You can buy a one-, three- or seven-day Dubrovnik Card, which allows free entrance to several sights around town, including the city walls, plus free bus transportation.

TOP ATTRACTIONS

FAMILY
Fodor's Choice ★

Dubrovnik Cable Car. Reopened in July 2010 after being destroyed in the siege of Dubrovnik, the ultramodern cable car whisks you to the top of Mt. Srđ for the best view of the city and the islands. At the top, you can join an hour-long buggy tour of the area or have a cocktail at the smart Panorama Restaurant. The Imperial Fort, built between 1806 and 1812 by Napoléon Bonaparte during his short rule of the city, now hosts the Homeland War Museum, where you can learn about the siege. To reach the cable car from the walled city, go up the stairs from the Stradun

Dubrovnik
TO LAPAD
Brsalje ul.
Pile
Ul. Između Vrta
Ul. uz Posat
Ul. Srednji Kono
Ul. Iza Grada
Zagrebačka ul.
Ul. Iza Grada
Peline ul.
Ul. Celestina Medovića
Ul. od Sigurate
Palmotićeva ul.
Antuninska ul.
Nalješkovićeva ul.
Kunićeva ul.
Hanibala Lucića
Prijeko ul.
Petrilovrijenci ul.
Vetranićeva ul.
Zamanjina ul.
Dropčeva ul.
Boškovićeva ul.
Žudioska ul.
Kovačka ul.
Poljana Paska Miličevića
Garište ul.
Zlatarićeva ul.
Getaldićeva ul.
Čubranovićeva ul.
Đorđićeva ul.
Placa
Široka ul.
Vara
Ul. za Rokom
Ul. od Puča
Faričeva ul.
Puzljiva ul.
Ul. od Šorte
Domina
Ul. Svetog Josipa
Ul. Nikole Božidarevića
OLD CITY
Miha Pracata
Ul. Između Polača
Cvijete
Zuzorić
Lučarica
Luža
Ul. Od Puča
Ul. od Kaštela
Ul. od
Ul. Svete Marije
Zvijezdićeva
Ul. Josipa Jurja Strossmayera
Uska ul.
Ul. Marojice Kaboge
Ul. Dinka Ranjine
Ul. uz Jezuite
Gundulićeva Poljana
Bunijeva Poljana
Pred Dvorom
Poljana Mrtvo Zvono
Ul. od Margarite
Crijevićeva ul.
Grbava
Ul. od Kaštela
Ul. Kneza Hrvaša
Stulina
Ilije Sarake
Pobijana
Ispod
Adriatic Sea
1 2 3 4 5 7 9 13 14
1 2 3 4 5 8 9 10 11 12

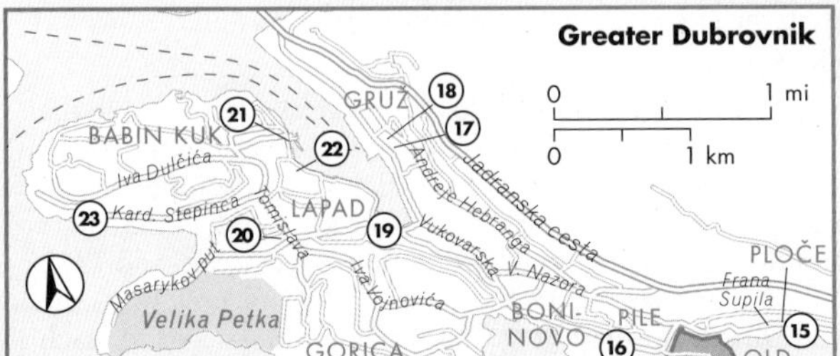
Greater Dubrovnik
0 1 mi
0 1 km
GRUŽ
BABIN KUK
LAPAD
Iva Dulčića
Kard. Stepinca
Tomislava
Masarykov put
Velika Petka
GORICA
Adriatic Sea
Andreje Hebranga
Jadranska cesta
Vukovarska
V. Nazora
Iva Vojnovića
BONINOVO
PILE
PLOČE
Frana Supila
OLD CITY
15 16 17 18 19 20 21 22 23

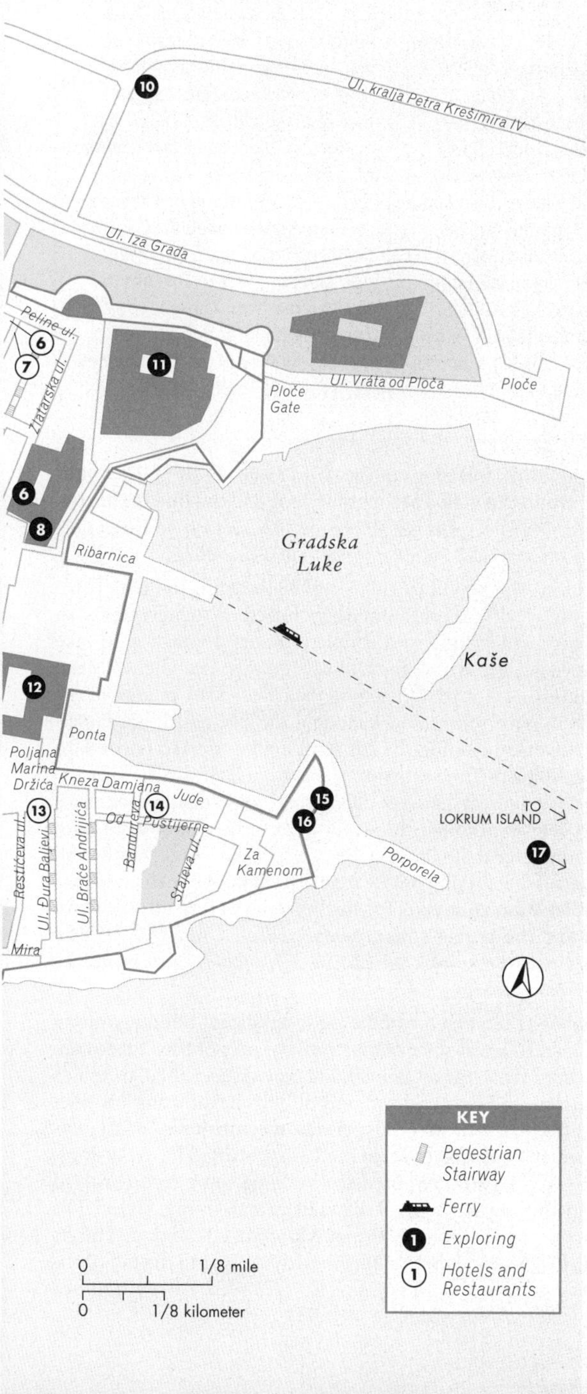

Exploring

Akvarij 16
Bell Tower 9
Crkva Svetog Vlaha 6
Dominikanski samostan 11
Dubrovnik Cable Car 10
Franjevačka samostan 3
Gradske Zidine 2
Jesuit Steps 13
Katedrala Velika Gospa 14
Knežev Dvor 12
Lokrum Island 17
Onofrio Fountain 1
Orlando's Column 7
Placa 4
Pomorski Muzej 15
Sponza Palace 8
War Photo Limited 5

Restaurants

Amfora 17
Azur 12
Bota Šare Oyster & Sushi Bar 13
Konoba Amoret 11
Lady Pi-Pi 1
Nishta 2
Orsan 21
Pantarul 20
Proto 4
Taverna Otto 19
Tovjerna Sesame 16

Hotels

Amoret Apartments 9
Apartments Paviša 7
Fresh* Sheets Kathedral 10
Hotel Berkeley 18
Hotel Excelsior 15
Hotel Kazbek 22
Hotel More 23
Karmen Apartments 14
Prijeko Palace 3
Pucić Palace 8
St. Joseph's 5
Villa Ragusa 6

GAME OF THRONES

WELCOME TO KING'S LANDING

Perhaps no film setting is as evocative as Dubrovnik, or as *Game of Thrones* fans know it better, King's Landing. The popular HBO show has been filmed in the walled city, on Lokrum Island (where you'll find a small museum and the original Iron Throne) and in Trsteno since season one. There are many *Game of Thrones* tours to choose from, most interesting only to avid fans of the show and all following a similar structure: a walking tour of the main filming spots where the guide holds up a still shot of the scene so you can compare the set to reality. More broadly appealing are tours that combine details of Dubrovnik history with the stories and legends of King's Landing. We can recommend **Tour the Game of Thrones** (🌐 *www.tourthegameofthrones.com*), pioneers of GoT tours. ■ TIP→ **If you can't make it to Lokrum to see the real Iron Throne, you can pose on a replica at the Dubrovnik City Shop (Boškovićeva 7) in the Old Town.**

(toward the mountain) and exit via the Buža Gate. ■ TIP→ **Plan your visit for sunset, when the views are magnificent and the line is shorter.** ✉ *Lower station, Petra Krešimira IV, Ploce* ☎ *020/414–355* 🌐 *www.dubrovnikcablecar.com* 🎫 *85 Kn one-way, 140 Kn return.*

Fodor's Choice ★ **Gradske Zidine** (*City Walls*). Dubrovnik's city walls define the Old Town and are one of the world's most stunning architectural achievements. A walk along the top, which can last a couple of hours if you stop to take in the incredible views, is the ultimate Dubrovnik must-do. The walls run for 2 km (1¼ miles), completely encircling the town. They're part of the fortification system with four gates, including the Pile and Ploče Gates, as well as four towers, including the freestanding Lovrijenac Fortress to the west and the Minčeta Tower toward the land, which was built at the height of the Ottoman threat. Most of the original construction took place during the 13th century, though the walls were further reinforced with towers and bastions over the following 400 years. On average they are 80 feet high and up to 10 feet thick on the seaward side, 20 feet thick on the inland side. ■ TIP→ **Plan your walk for the morning or late afternoon to avoid the heat and the cruise-ship crowds.** ✉ *Stari Grad* ☎ *020/638–800* 🌐 *www.citywallsdubrovnik.hr* 🎫 *150 Kn, including entrance to Lovrijenac Fortress.*

Knežev Dvor (*Rector's Palace*). One of the most significant buildings along the Croatian Coast, this was the administrative center of the Dubrovnik Republic. It's where the Grand Council and Senate held their meetings and the chief citizen, the Rector, lived and did business during his one-month term. It also held a courtroom, prisons, meeting halls, and a gunpowder room, which exploded twice in the 15th century. The explosions, plus the earthquake of 1667, required the building to be reconstructed over the years in varying Baroque, Renaissance, and Gothic styles. The palace is now home to the Cultural History Museum, containing exhibits that give a picture of life in Dubrovnik from early days until the fall of the republic. ✉ *Pred Dvorom 3, Stari Grad* ☎ *020/321–422* 🌐 *www.dumus.hr* 🎫 *120 Kn* ⏲ *Closed Nov.–Mar.*

Placa (*Stradun*). This was once the shallow sea channel separating the island of Laus from the mainland. Although it was filled in during the 12th century, it continued to divide the city socially for several centuries, the nobility living in the area south of Placa and the commoners living on the hillside to the north. The Placa, commonly known as the Stradun, is 300 meters long and cuts straight through the Old Town from the Pile to the Ploče Gate; it is the best people-watching promenade and shopping street in town. It is paved with limestone and is polished by use; in the middle of summer, when the street is being walked upon by thousands of people, it shines like glass, particularly impressive at night when it reflects the light from the street lamps. ✉ *Stari Grad.*

Fodor's Choice ★ **Pomorski Muzej** (*Maritime Museum*). Above the aquarium, located on the first and second floors of St. John's Fortress, this museum's exhibits illustrate how rich and powerful Dubrovnik became one of the world's most important seafaring cities. On display are intricately detailed models of ships as well as engine-room equipment, sailors' uniforms, paintings, and maps. ✉ *St. John's Fort, Damjana Jude 2, Stari Grad* ☎ *020/323–904* 🌐 *www.dumus.hr* 🎫 *120 Kn* ⏲ *Closed Mon.*

Fodor's Choice ★ **War Photo Limited.** Shocking and impressive, this modern gallery devotes two entire floors to war photojournalism. The permanent exhibition showcases photos and video from former Yugoslavia, while recent exhibitions have included images from conflicts in Syria, Afghanistan, and Iraq. Refreshingly impartial, the message—that war is physically and emotionally destructive whichever side you are on—comes through loud and clear. ✉ *Antuninska 6, Stari Grad* ☎ *020/322–166* 🌐 *www.warphotoltd.com* 🎫 *50 Kn* ⏲ *Closed Nov.–Mar. Closed Tues.*

8

WORTH NOTING

Akvarij (*Aquarium*). This dark, cavernous space in the St. John's Fortress houses several small pools and 27 well-lit tanks containing a variety of fish from rays to small sharks, as well as other underwater denizens such as sponges, sea horses, sea urchins, and an octopus. ✉ *Damjana Jude 2, Stari Grad* ☎ *020/323–978* 🎫 *60 Kn.*

Bell Tower. All walks down the Stradun lead to one point: the bell tower, the centerpiece of Luža Square. It was erected in 1444, but growing instability led to its closure at the start of the 20th century. After nearly 30 years, it was reopened in 1929, using the original designs. The bright white structure, one of the main symbols of the city, reaches 31 meters high and features a moon dial and the original bell from 1506. Look a little closer to see Dubrovnik's two favorite mascots tolling the hours on either side of the bell; known as Maro and Baro, the current figures are made of bronze, while the original wooden men now live in the Rector's Palace. ✉ *Luža, Stari Grad.*

Crkva Svetog Vlaha (*Church of St. Blaise*). This 18th-century Baroque church replaced an earlier one destroyed by fire. Of particular note is the silver statue on the high altar of St. Blaise holding a model of Dubrovnik, which was the only thing that survived the fire. It is paraded around town each year on February 3, the Day of St. Blaise. ✉ *Luža 3, Stari Grad* 🎫 *Free.*

Dominikanski samostan (*Dominican monastery*). With a splendid, late-15th-century floral Gothic cloister as its centerpiece, the monastery is best known for its museum, which houses a rich collection of religious paintings by the Dubrovnik School from the 15th and 16th centuries. Look out for works by Titian, Božidarević, Hamzić, and Dobričević, as well as gold and silver ecclesiastical artifacts crafted by local goldsmiths. ✉ *Sv. Dominika 4, Stari Grad* ☎ *020/321–423* 🎫 *30 Kn.*

Franjevačka samostan (*Franciscan monastery*). The monastery's chief claim to fame is its pharmacy, which was founded in 1318 and is still in existence today; it's said to be the oldest in Europe. There's also a delightful cloistered garden, framed by Romanesque arcades supported by double columns, each crowned with a set of grotesque figures. In the Treasury a painting shows what Dubrovnik looked like before the disastrous earthquake of 1667. ✉ *Placa 2, Stari Grad* ☎ *020/321–410* 🎫 *30 Kn.*

Jesuit Steps. Find this monumental Baroque staircase, Dubrovnik's very own version of the Spanish Steps, at the south side of Gundulićeva Poljana. At the top is the lovely Jesuit Church of St. Ignatius of Loyola, built 1699–1725. This staircase will be particularly familiar to *Game of Thrones* fans for a certain "shameful" scene. ✉ *Poljana Ruđera Boškovića 6, Stari Grad.*

Katedrala Velika Gospa (*Assumption of the Virgin Mary Cathedral*). The present structure was completed in 1713 in Baroque style after the original was destroyed in the 1667 earthquake. Legend says that Richard the Lionheart was shipwrecked on Lokrum Island, and vowed to show his thanks to God for saving his life by building a cathedral on the spot; locals convinced him to move his plans to Dubrovnik instead. The interior contains a number of notable paintings, including a large polyptych above the main altar depicting the *Assumption of Our Lady,* attributed to Titian. The treasury displays 138 gold and silver reliquaries, including the skull of St. Blaise in the form of a bejeweled Byzantine crown and also an arm and leg of the saint, likewise encased in decorated gold plating. ✉ *Držićeva Poljana, Stari Grad* 🎫 *Cathedral free, Treasury 20 Kn.*

OFF THE BEATEN PATH

Lokrum Island. Some of Dubrovnik's most natural and peaceful beaches lie on the tiny island of Lokrum, a short distance southeast of the Old Town. Lush and fertile, this tiny island is home to the ruins of an abandoned 11th-century monastery, set in exotic botanical gardens. Lokrum has swirled with legend and mystery ever since Richard the Lionheart was supposedly cast ashore there in 1191 when returning from the Crusades. The story goes that when the Benedictine Monks were expelled from the island to make room for aristocrats in the 19th century, they left behind a curse on any future owners of the land, including Habsburg Emperor Maximilian, who turned the monastery into his summer residence eight years before he was executed in Mexico. To this day it is considered bad luck to stay overnight on the island, though many a pair of romantics have tried. At the top of the island is a star-shape fortress built by Napoléon's troops during French occupation, later used by the Austrian army. A network of footpaths lead down to the rocky shoreline, past the "dead sea" lake, where it's possible to swim. There are cliffs to jump from, coves to bathe in, and a small stretch of coast reserved for nudists. One of the most popular day trips from Dubrovnik, it's a wonderful place to spend a day spotting the peacocks (a Habsburg legacy) or feeding the wild rabbits. To reach Lokrum, take a taxi-boat from the old harbor; they run every half hour during the summer. ✉ *15-min boat ride from Dubrovnik's old harbor* 🌐 *www.lokrum.hr.*

Onofrio Fountain. Built from 1438 to 1440, the Onofrio Fountain is the first sight you see upon entering the Pile Gate. The 16-sided stone fountain is topped by a large dome and was designed by architect Onofrio Giordano della Cava. Along with the Small Onofrio Fountain at the other end of the Stradun, it was part of a complex water-supply system designed to bring water into the Old Town from a well 12 km (7½ miles) away. The water is still cold and drinkable, and the fountain is a nice place to rest and refuel. ✉ *Pred Dvorom, Stari Grad.*

Orlando's Column. Dating back to 1418, Orlando's Column, located at the end of the Stradun and serving as a popular meeting point, is dedicated to legendary 8th-century knight Roland, who is said to have saved Dubrovnik from a Saracen attack near Lokrum. The white stone column has become a symbol of freedom for the city, and the white Libertas flag is traditionally flown from the top during important events, such as the opening ceremony of the Dubrovnik Summer Festival. ✉ *Luža, Stari Grad.*

NEED A BREAK

Buža. Walk through an 800-year-old wall to find a secret swimming spot across the sea from a cursed island. Sounds like a fairy tale, but in Dubrovnik such places actually exist, and there are two of them. One of the *Buža* (hole-in-the-wall) bars is marked by a wooden sign pointing toward "cold drinks." The other has no signage at all; you just walk through a doorway in the city walls. With tables arranged on a series of terraces built into the rocks and jazzy soundtracks to go along with stunning vistas, both bars make a great place to stop for a drink or a swim; you can jump right off the rocks in front of the bar into the sea. ✉ *Stari Grad* ✥ *The only bars on the seaside of the city walls—look for "cold drinks" sign.*

Sponza Palace. Originally the location where all trade goods coming into Dubrovnik went to be taxed, this 16th-century Gothic Renaissance palace served as the mint, an arsenal, and eventually a place for the most educated citizens, called the "Academy of the Learned," to discuss cultural matters. It now contains the archives from the Republic, some of the most important documents in the city's history. There's not much to see inside except the occasional art exhibition, but the shady, arcaded interior is a lovely spot to escape the heat and crowds. Turn left as you enter to find the "Memorial Room for the Defenders of Dubrovnik," a small gallery with photographs of those who died defending the city, as well as the harbor under attack, and remnants of the flag that once flew atop Mount Srdj. Even if you're not interested in the palace itself, this heart-wrenching little gallery is worthwhile. ✉ *Placa BB, Stari Grad* ☎ *020/321–032* 🎫 *25 Kn, Memorial Room free.*

8

CLOSE UP

Dubrovnik Under Siege

From November 1991 to May 1992, Dubrovnik was intermittently shelled by the Yugoslav army and Serb and Montenegrin irregulars, who were stationed on the rugged hills behind the city. Electricity and water supplies were cut off, and the local population took refuge in basements, surviving on a slowly diminishing quantity of foodstuffs, fuel, and medical supplies. The city's massive medieval fortifications stood up well to the assault, though none of Dubrovnik's main monuments was targeted—apparently the Yugoslav army wanted to capture the city intact. Extensive media coverage whipped up a storm of international criticism over the wanton bombing of this historic city, which effectively turned world opinion against Belgrade and in favor of granting Croatia diplomatic recognition. Once hostilities ceased, the cleanup and rebuilding began. During the second half of the 1990s, money poured in from all over the world for the restoration and today, thanks to the work of highly skilled craftspeople, barely any traces of war damage remain. But there is still a subtle reminder of the damage wrought upon 68% of the buildings in the Old Town. Look closer at the clay roof tiles when you're walking the city walls; the brighter orange tiles are new, the faded tiles are the originals.

WHERE TO EAT

As elsewhere along the coast, seafood dominates Dubrovnik's menus, but here it is being turned into sophisticated sushi, sashimi, and stir-fry. Yes, restaurants in Dubrovnik are more expensive than elsewhere in Croatia, and the Old Town is packed with touristy restaurants and waiters trolling for customers (particularly the narrow street Prijeko, which runs parallel to the Stradun). But go to the right places, where the quality matches the prices, and you won't mind paying a little extra.

$$$$ SEAFOOD Fodor's Choice ★

Amfora. Located on a noisy road near the port and nothing special from the outside, Amfora is the best restaurant in Dubrovnik and one of the best in the country. Dishes burst with flavor from herbs grown right on the premises, the fresh produce comes straight from the market across the road, the fish and meat are locally sourced, and the sesame-encrusted bluefin tuna steak will change your life. **Known for:** local, high-quality produce; excellent seafood; hands-on, friendly owner. *Average main: 170 Kn* *Obala Stjepana Radica 26, Gruž* *020/419–419* *amforadubrovnik.com.*

$$ ASIAN FUSION Fodor's Choice ★

Azur. Run by local brothers who own a Mediterranean-inspired restaurant of the same name in China, Azur is an Asian-inspired restaurant right under the city walls, near one of the Buža Bars. Spread over two shady terraces with fresh green linens, it has a hip soundtrack, friendly staff, and fantastic prices for food that you don't find elsewhere in Dubrovnik, such as cashew nut prawns, salmon ceviche, and baba ghanoush. *Average main: 110 Kn* *Pobijana 10, Stari Grad* *020/324–806* *www.azurvision.com/#!dubrovnik/crrl.*

$$ JAPANESE

✕ **Bota Šare Oyster & Sushi Bar.** Tucked away on a small terrace near the cathedral, Bota Šare takes the best local produce and turns it into beautifully presented sushi, sashimi, carpaccio, and tartare. If Japanese isn't your thing, you can also feast on fresh or tempura oysters from nearby Ston; it's safe to say the Šare family, who also runs one of the best restaurants in Mali Ston, does them best. **Known for:** Dalmatian ingredients meet Japanese cuisine; excellent oysters from Ston. Ⓢ *Average main: 80 Kn* ✉ *Od Pustijerne bb, Stari Grad* ☎ *020/324–034* 🌐 *www.bota-sare.hr* ⏲ *Closed Jan.–Feb.*

$$ SEAFOOD

✕ **Konoba Amoret.** A great choice for traditional food in the Old Town, this restaurant right beside the cathedral serves quality meals with an unbeatable ambience: it's open late, it's great for people-watching under the stars, and live musicians often set up on the cathedral steps. It isn't on the menu, but ask nicely if you can order the *gregada,* a typical, mouthwatering fish stew big enough for two. **Known for:** traditional Dalmatian food; great Old Town location. Ⓢ *Average main: 110 Kn* ✉ *Od Pustijerne, Stari Grad* ☎ *020/323–739* 🌐 *www.amoret-dubrovnik.com* ⏲ *Closed Nov.–Apr.*

$$ EASTERN EUROPEAN

✕ **Lady Pi-Pi.** This family-run *konoba* (traditional restaurant) set high up in the Old Town, with a shady terrace and impressive views, was named after the unusual stone statue at the entrance, built years ago by the family father. Today the statue, plus the cozy atmosphere and simple but delicious menu, draws a nightly crowd. **Known for:** no reservations; grilled dishes; fabulous views. Ⓢ *Average main: 100 Kn* ✉ *Antuninska 23, Stari Grad* ☎ *020/321–154* ⏲ *Closed Oct.–May.*

$$ VEGETARIAN
Fodor's Choice ★

✕ **Nishta.** Specializing in vegan fare, this playful eatery on Prijeko has just a dozen tables and is deservedly popular; for years it was the only veggie option in town. Their menu features everything from gazpacho to burritos to falafel, plus they do a nice meat-free version of *pašticada* so vegetarians can finally try a traditional Dalmatian dish. **Known for:** some of the best—and only—vegan food in the region; international flavors. Ⓢ *Average main: 80 Kn* ✉ *Prijeko BB, Stari Grad* ☎ *020/322–088* 🌐 *www.nishtarestaurant.com* ⏲ *Closed Sun.*

$$$ SEAFOOD

✕ **Orsan.** This long-standing restaurant has a pretty leafy terrace overlooking the Yacht Club Orsan marina, opposite Gruž Harbor, on the edge of the Lapad Peninsula. One of the better restaurants in Lapad, it serves excellent fresh seafood and has a smart ambience and lovely view. **Known for:** popularity with locals; seafood. Ⓢ *Average main: 130 Kn* ✉ *Ivana Zajca 2, Lapad* ☎ *020/436–822* 🌐 *www.restaurant-orsan-dubrovnik.com.*

$$$ EASTERN EUROPEAN
Fodor's Choice ★

✕ **Pantarul.** A local favorite, a little off the beaten track but worth the trek, Pantarul is a fun bistro with a uniquely Dubrovnik feel—even the name means "fork" in local dialect. A love of traditional dishes comes through here; try the rock-samphire and cuttlefish risotto, and for an unusually delicious treat, try the *komiža* bread, flatbread stuffed with marinated anchovies. **Known for:** Dubrovnik comfort food; local favorite; friendly service. Ⓢ *Average main: 120 Kn* ✉ *Kralja Tomislava 1, Lapad* ☎ *020/333–486* 🌐 *www.pantarul.com.*

OFF THE BEATEN PATH

✕ **Piknik.** For a totally different foodie experience, order a Piknik. You'll get an insulated backpack thoughtfully stocked with gourmet Croatian goodies—ham, cheese, fresh fruit, homemade baked treats, and lemonade, plus chilled wine or craft beer and everything you need to get set up: blankets, utensils, and a map to the best secret beach or panoramic viewpoint to enjoy it. **Known for:** organic gourmet delicacies; unique meals prepared with heart. ✉ *Dubrovnik* ☎ *098/175–1103* 🌐 *www.piknikdubrovnik.com.*

$$$$ SEAFOOD ✕ **Proto.** This restaurant dates back to 1886, and most locals will respectfully acknowledge that it's still one of the best in town. The menu features an excellent selection of traditional Dalmatian dishes, reliably prepared, with solid seafood dishes and notable steaks. **Known for:** more than a century in Dubrovnik; reliably high-standard food. $ *Average main: 160 Kn* ✉ *Široka 1, Stari Grad* ☎ *020/323–234* 🌐 *www.esculaprestaurants.com.*

$$ MEDITERRANEAN ✕ **Taverna Otto.** Located in a cavernous 450-year-old stone building once used as a boathouse, Otto's has a short, Mediterranean-inspired menu that changes often, ensuring all dishes are consistently fresh. The vibe is cool, the service laid-back and friendly, and it's worth venturing out of the Old Town to check it out. **Known for:** consistently fresh food; intimate space. $ *Average main: 110 Kn* ✉ *Nikole Tesle 8, Gruž* ☎ *020/358–633* 🌐 *www.tavernaotto.com.*

$$$ MEDITERRANEAN ✕ **Tovjerna Sesame.** Just a short distance outside the Pile Gate, this romantic restaurant occupies a vaulted indoor space as well as a breezy, vine-covered terrace. Its jazzy soundtrack and bohemian decor are second only to the fine menu, prepared by a Cordon Bleu–trained chef. **Known for:** great chef; confident, homemade dishes. $ *Average main: 120 Kn* ✉ *Dante Alighierija bb, Pile* ☎ *020/412–910* 🌐 *www.sesame.hr.*

ST. BLAISE

The bearded figure of St. Blaise, Dubrovnik's patron saint, was featured on the Republic's coins and flags. The former Bishop of Sebaste in Turkey, Blaise lost his life in AD 316 during a Roman-led anti-Christian campaign. Also a doctor, he once miraculously saved a child who was choking on a fish bone, and today those ailing from throat problems still pray to him for healing. He was made Dubrovnik's protector in 972, having appeared to the Rector in a dream warning of an imminent Venetian attack and thus saving the city.

WHERE TO STAY

There are a few different areas to consider when looking for accommodation in Dubrovnik. The Old Town, with an abundance of historical charm, is central and expensive, and the boutique hotels and apartments within its walls are small and extremely desirable. The most exclusive establishments line the coastal road east of the center, offering stunning views of the Old Town and the sea. More modern and slightly cheaper hotels are found in Lapad, 3 km (2 miles) west of the center. It has a summer resort feel, with live music by night, a busy bar-lined promenade, and a recently renovated beach. The most affordable, and often the most unique accommodation is to be found in private apartments all over the city.

$$$ RENTAL Fodor's Choice ★ **Amoret Apartments.** In the heart of the Old Town, these tastefully furnished studios, with heavy antiques and traditional Dubrovnik decor, are an excellent value. **Pros:** Old Town location; homey and atmospheric rooms with antique furniture; inexpensive by Dubrovnik standards. **Cons:** rooms can be noisy at night. $ *Rooms from: €180* ✉ *Stari*

Grad ✥ Various locations throughout the Old Town ☎ 020/323–739 🌐 www.dubrovnik-amoret.com ⇆ 15 apartments 🍴 No meals.

$ RENTAL **Apartments Paviša.** These five fabulously located and well-equipped apartments represent some of the best value you'll find in Dubrovnik. **Pros:** spacious apartments; excellent value for money; friendly service from owners. **Cons:** often fully booked. [$] *Rooms from: €120 ✉ Zudioska 19, Stari Grad ☎ 098/427–399 🌐 www.apartmentspavisa.com ⇆ 5 apartments 🍴 No meals.*

$$$$ B&B/INN **Fresh* Sheets Kathedral.** Jon and Sanja, the charming Canadian/Croatian couple who own the quirky Life According to Kawa shop and a retro laundrette, also run this impeccable, lusciously modern boutique hotel smack in the Old Town. **Pros:** good location in the Old Town; friendly and personal service; lovely rooms. **Cons:** no elevator; no breakfast. [$] *Rooms from: €248 ✉ Bunićeva poljana 6, Stari Grad ☎ 091/799–2086 🌐 freshsheetsbedandbreakfast.com ⇆ 6 rooms 🍴 No meals.*

$$ HOTEL Fodor's Choice ★ **Hotel Berkeley.** One block back from Gruž harbor, this welcoming three-star hotel run by a Croatian-Australian family provides excellent value in what you might call the "real Dubrovnik"; there's a small outdoor pool and Jacuzzi, a deck lined with sun beds, and an on-site spa. **Pros:** excellent cooked-to-order breakfast; proximity to port; well-priced spa on-site. **Cons:** distance from Old Town. [$] *Rooms from: €150 ✉ Andrije Hebranga 116A, Gruž ☎ 020/494–160 🌐 www.berkeleyhotel.hr ⏲ Closed Jan. and Feb. ⇆ 24 rooms 🍴 Breakfast.*

$$$$ HOTEL **Hotel Excelsior.** On the coastal road east of the center, this prestigious hotel was the first five-star property in Dubrovnik, dating back to 1913—everyone from Queen Elizabeth II to Francis Ford Coppola has come to stay. **Pros:** seafront location with great views of the Old Town; spacious rooms; luxurious spa. **Cons:** big, with somewhat impersonal service; modern, but slightly lacking in charm; poor sound insulation between neighboring rooms. [$] *Rooms from: €350 ✉ Put Frane Supila 12, Ploce ☎ 020/353–300 🌐 www.alh.hr ⇆ 158 rooms 🍴 Breakfast.*

8

$$$$ HOTEL Fodor's Choice ★ **Hotel Kazbek.** This boutique five-star property was built as a 16th-century villa and also served as a WWII prison and a schoolhouse before becoming the refined Hotel Kazbek. **Pros:** friendly, personal service; richly decorated rooms; restaurant and bar on-site. **Cons:** distance from the Old Town; quite expensive. [$] *Rooms from: €390 ✉ Lapadska Obala 25, Lapad ☎ 020/362–999 🌐 www.kazbekdubrovnik.com ⏲ Closed Nov.–Apr. ⇆ 13 rooms 🍴 Breakfast.*

$$$$ HOTEL **Hotel More.** Rising from a seaside walkway up a forested cliff on Lapad Peninsula, this five-star hotel boasts one of the most peaceful locations in Dubrovnik, one of the best places for a swim, and the city's most unique place for a cocktail. **Pros:** friendly service; nicely decorated rooms and views; excellent restaurants and cave bar. **Cons:** distance from town; layout can get confusing. [$] *Rooms from: €230 ✉ Kardinala Stepinca 33, Lapad ☎ 020/494–200 🌐 hotel-more.hr ⇆ 82 rooms 🍴 Breakfast.*

$ RENTAL Fodor's Choice ★ **Karmen Apartments.** An excellent budget choice in the Old Town, these apartments are more like a time machine back to old Dubrovnik, '60s London, or wherever else the brilliant Van Bloemen family, who founded the Troubadour in London, feel like taking you with their fascinating stories. **Pros:** location in Old Town; homey and atmospheric rooms with bohemian decor; fascinating, friendly owners. **Cons:** often fully booked; can be noisy at night. *Rooms from: €75 Bandureva 1, Stari Grad 020/323–433 www.karmendu.tk 4 apartments.*

$$ HOTEL Fodor's Choice ★ **Prijeko Palace.** This 15th-century noble palace in the Old Town has been reconstructed into a fantastical half hotel, half art gallery, with each room a unique creation by a different artist. **Pros:** perfect location in the Old Town; unique choice for art and history lovers; rooftop restaurant on-site. **Cons:** often fully booked. *Rooms from: €170 Prijeko 22, Stari Grad 020/321–145 www.prijekopalace.com 9 rooms Breakfast.*

$$$$ HOTEL **Pucić Palace.** Occupying a beautifully restored 18th-century Baroque palace beside Gundulić Square and its morning market, this boutique hotel offers the sort of aristocratic delights that its location suggests: rooms with dark wood parquet floors and wood-beam ceilings, antique furnishings, and Italian mosaic-tile bathrooms supplied with Bulgari toiletries. **Pros:** prime location in Old Town; beautifully furnished interior; peaceful ambience. **Cons:** very expensive; no parking nearby. *Rooms from: €465 Ul od Puča 1, Stari Grad 020/326–222 www.thepucicpalace.com 19 rooms Breakfast.*

$$$$ HOTEL **St. Joseph's.** Lovingly restored into a luscious boutique hotel in the middle of the Old Town, this 16th-century house has six spacious rooms, each uniquely designed with features such as exposed beams, original stone walls, plush furniture and carpets, and deep, inviting bathtubs. **Pros:** peaceful and luxurious Old Town retreat; breakfast, including a green smoothie, served in your room. **Cons:** very expensive; no hotel facilities outside the room. *Rooms from: €450 Sv. Josipa 3, Stari Grad 020/432–089 www.stjosephs.hr 6 rooms Breakfast.*

$ RENTAL **Villa Ragusa.** An excellent budget option in the Old Town, these five quiet, nicely furnished apartments are spacious, comfortable, and well equipped, with televisions, kitchenettes, and great views. **Pros:** Old Town location; reasonable prices. **Cons:** no breakfast; located several flights of steps up from the Stradun. *Rooms from: €90 Zudioska 15, Stari Grad 098/765–634 villaragusadubrovnik.com 5 apartments No meals.*

NIGHTLIFE AND PERFORMING ARTS

Throughout the summer, there's no better place to be than Dubrovnik's Old Town at night. From wine bars to jazz cafés, English pubs to beach clubs, there is something for every nocturnal taste. Terraces spill onto the streets, musicians set up in squares, and you can grab a seat anywhere, or even just a cushion, to have a drink or an ice cream and enjoy the show. In July and August, the world-renowned Dubrovnik Summer Festival offers quality theatrical performances in venues across town.

CLOSE UP

The Republic of Dubrovnik

As an independent republic from 1358 to 1808, Dubrovnik kept its freedom not through military power, but thanks to diplomatic cunning. Would-be aggressors, including Hungary and the Ottoman Turks, were paid an annual fee in return for peaceful relations, and Dubrovnik avoided involvement in international conflicts between Christians and Muslims, preferring to remain neutral.

The republic's economy was based on shipping and trading goods between Europe and the Middle East, and by the 16th century the republic had consulates in some 50 foreign ports, along with a merchant fleet of 200 ships on the Mediterranean. By this time its territory had also extended to include 120 km (75 miles) of mainland coast (from Neum to the Bay of Kotor) plus the islands of Lastovo and Mljet.

The chief citizen was the Rector, who had to be over 50; he was elected for only a month at a time to share management of the republic's business with the Great Council (composed of members of the local nobility) and the Senate (a consultative body made up of 45 "wise men," all over the age of 40). Most of the military and naval commands were held by members of the nobility, while lower-ranking soldiers were mercenaries from the regions that are now Germany and the Czech Republic. The increasingly prosperous middle class carried on trade. The Archbishop of Dubrovnik had to be a foreigner (usually an Italian), a law intended to keep politics and religion apart.

Outstandingly sophisticated for its time, Dubrovnik was very socially conscious: the first pharmacy opened in 1317; the first nursing home was founded in 1347; slave trading was abolished in 1418; and the first orphanage opened in 1432.

NIGHTLIFE

BARS

Art Cafe. If you're looking for the student population of Dubrovnik, they're on the terrace of this quirky little bar just outside the Old Town, drinking smoothies by day and cocktails by night, all while sitting in brightly colored bathtubs. Kitschy decor, funky music, and lots of locals equal an authentic Dubrovnik experience. ✉ *Branitelja Dubrovnika 25, 435 yards northwest of the Pile Gate, Pile* ☎ *020/311–097.*

Bar by Azur. From the brothers who run Azur Restaurant comes this chic cocktail bar on the other side of the Old Town. With a cool mix of locals and tourists, it's a great place to pull up a cushion on the narrow steps, try a new cocktail, and snack on delicious prosciutto and cheese with truffle oil. ✉ *Kunićeva 5, Stari Grad* ☎ *020/324–806* 🌐 *www.azurvision.com.*

Fodor's Choice ★ **Cave Bar More.** When the Hotel More was being built, a piece of machinery fell through the ground; it was only then that an 8,000-year-old cave was discovered underneath. It has been carefully converted into a three-story bar, with twinkling lights and stalactites, making it a great place to cool down during the day and an unforgettable setting for a cocktail by night. ✉ *Kardinala Stepinca 33, Lapad* ☎ *020/494–200* 🌐 *hotel-more.hr/4cave_bar_more.php*.

Fodor's Choice ★ **D'Vino Wine Bar.** A cozy, candlelit wine bar with a cheeky vibe, D'Vino is a great place to spend an evening, chatting and people-watching with the fun, knowledgeable staff. They have an impressive selection of Croatian wine by the glass and bottle, plus tasting menus and wine flights accompanied by gourmet cheese and antipasto platters. ✉ *Palmotićeva 4a, Stari Grad* ☎ *020/321–130* 🌐 *www.dvino.net*.

Soul Caffe. This small, velvet-draped bar with stone walls and a bluesy ambience is where to find the hip locals and other travelers who want to hide from the crowds. They serve excellent coffee in the daytime, dark beers and a wide selection of *rakija* (fruit brandy) in the evening, and the service is very friendly. ✉ *Uska ulica 5, Stari Grad* ☎ *095/199–8507*.

Troubadour Hard Jazz Cafe. Everyone has spent at least one great night watching live jazz under the stars at this Dubrovnik institution. Well-worn antiques and memorabilia fill the cozy, candlelit interior, while in summer, tables spill onto the piazza. It's not cheap, but it's a cool way to finish a night. ✉ *Bunićeva poljana 2, Stari Grad* ☎ *020/323–476*.

DANCE CLUBS

Fodor's Choice ★ **Culture Club Revelin.** Surely one of the most unique places in the world to party, Culture Club Revelin is the best nightclub in Dubrovnik, with big-name DJs and theme nights throughout the summer. Find it located in the 500-year-old Revelin Fort, part of the Old Town's fortification system, near the Ploče Gate. ■ TIP→ **Admission is often free before midnight; look for staff handing out flyers around town.** ✉ *Svetog Dominika 3, 100 meters from the Ploče Gate, Ploce* ☎ *020/436–010* 🌐 *www.clubrevelin.com*.

PERFORMING ARTS

FESTIVALS

Fodor's Choice ★ **Dubrovnik Summer Festival.** The city's cultural highlight is the annual Dubrovnik Summer Festival, which runs from mid-July to late August and attracts thousands of artists from around the world. A variety of open-air classical concerts, ballet, and theatrical performances are held at various venues within the walls, and the city becomes a riot of folklore, traditional dresses, midnight performances, and music. Tickets, ranging from 30 Kn to 500 Kn, can be purchased online or at the festival box office. ✉ *Od Sigurate 1, Stari Grad* ☎ *020/326–100* 🌐 *www.dubrovnik-festival.hr*.

FILM

Fodor's Choice ★ **Kino Slavica.** Watch a movie outdoors with either the city walls or the Adriatic Sea as your backdrop at Dubrovnik's two open-air cinemas, which show predominantly English-language films in their original version nightly throughout the summer. Kino Slavica is located in a walled garden on the main road between the Old Town and Lapad, while Kino Jadran is right in the Old Town, completely hidden from sight. ■ TIP→ **They sell drinks on-site but you are welcome to bring your own.** ✉ *Branitelja Dubrovnika 42, Pile* ☎ *020/638–640* 🌐 *www.kinematografi.org* 🎫 *25 Kn*.

SPORTS AND THE OUTDOORS

BEACHES

Closest to the Old Town, **Banje Beach** has the Banje Beach club, where you can party into the early hours. For more family-friendly beaches, head to **Lapad,** where you and the kids can enjoy water sports and inflatable toys. The upmarket hotels east of the Ploče Gate have their own beaches; walk past them along the coast to find a private spot for a dip, or keep walking about 20 minutes to **Sveti Jakov** beach, a sandy sliver with a spectacular view of the Old Town. The most natural and peaceful beaches lie on the tiny island of **Lokrum,** popular with rock-jumpers and naturists. For the most unique Dubrovnik experience, head to either of the Buža bars to swim directly under the city walls, or to local favorite **Šulić** beach, in the shadow of the Lovrijenac Fortress.

SEA KAYAKING

Fodor's Choice ★ **Adriatic Kayak Tours.** There are literally a sea full of kayaking companies in Dubrovnik, but the best is Adriatic Kayak Tours. Besides introductory half-day sea-kayaking tours around Zaton Bay, they run day trips to the Elafiti Islands and even farther to the Konavle region and Montenegro. ✉ *Zrinsko Frankopanska 6, Ploce* ☎ *020/312–770* 🌐 *www.adriatickayaktours.com.*

SHOPPING

It's getting harder to find quality souvenirs in Dubrovnik as more and more shops cater to the cruise ship crowds looking for candy and *Game of Thrones* paraphernalia. Here are a few places where you can pick up souvenirs and authentic products, including olive oil, Dalmatian wine, and rakija.

Croata. In the 17th-century, Croatian military uniforms featured patterned scarves knotted around the neck. French soldiers appreciated the style, introduced them to Parisian society with the name "cravat," a play on the word Croat, and the rest is sartorial history. You can pick up an "original Croatian tie" from this chain boutique near the Rector's Palace. ✉ *Pred dvorom 2, Stari Grad* ☎ *020/638–330* 🌐 *www.croata.hr.*

Dubrovačka Kuća. This tastefully decorated shop near the Ploče Gate stocks a fine selection of regional Croatian wines and sweets, rakija, olive oil, and handmade jewelry, plus works of art by contemporary local artists on the upper two levels. ✉ *Svetog Dominika BB, Stari Grad* ☎ *020/322–092.*

Dubrovnik Treasures. You'll find this lovely oasis of a shop just steps from the bustling Pile Gate (and a second location farther down the Stradun). The jewlery is handmade by local artists who use sterling silver, coral, and semiprecious stones to turn traditional designs into beautiful modern pieces. ✉ *Celestina Medovića 2, Stari Grad* ☎ *020/321–098* 🌐 *www.dubrovniktreasures.com.*

Life According to Kawa. From purses to T-shirts to jewelry, everything in this quirky shop just outside the Ploče Gate is unique, local, artisanal, and fun. Pop in for some shopping or just hang out on the couch with a hand-roasted coffee or craft beer. ✉ *Hvarska 2, Ploce* ☎ *099/668–0145.*

ELAFITI ISLANDS

Lopud is 7 nautical miles northwest of Dubrovnik by ferry.

Sometimes you need a break from the city crowds, and the lush, laid-back Elafiti Islands are happy to provide a retreat. Historically, the 13 tiny islets have always been under Dubrovnik's control; the local aristocracy kept summer villas here (which are now scattered in various states of ruin around the islands). Today only the three larger ones—Koločep, Lopud, and Šipan—are inhabited, with a total population of around 1,000.

Lopud is best equipped to deal with visitors, with one main settlement made up of old stone houses built around a sheltered bay, plus a handful of lovely restaurants and hotels. The main sights are a 15th-century Franciscan monastery (currently closed for renovation), the remains of 30 chapels built during the golden age of the Republic, and 16th-century Sutvrac Fortress on the highest point of the island. So much more than its famous sliver of sandy beach (the family-friendly Šunj, one of the region's rare sandy beaches), Lopud is a wonderful place for hiking along herb-scented paths that crisscross the island to the roaring sound of cicadas.

Even more peaceful is the island of Šipan. Famous for holding the world record for most olive trees, it's a great place to rent a bike and explore hidden beaches and forgotten churches. If it's a slower pace of life that you're after, Šipan is most likely to be your favorite.

GETTING HERE AND AROUND

Many companies run daily, full-day, three-island cruises that stop at Lopud, Koločep, and Šipan and include lunch onboard. Lopud is accessible from Dubrovnik by ferry. Only the island of Šipan has cars, and Lopud is best explored on foot or by golf cart.

OFF THE BEATEN PATH

Your Black Horizon Art Pavilion. Francesca von Habsburg isn't your typical noble; famous as a London "It Girl" from the 1980s and today an art patron, her organization sponsored this light installation on Lopud, inaugurated at the 2005 Venice Biennale. A play on light and perspective, you'll find it hidden away in the middle of the island. ✉ *Lopud* 🌐 *www.TBA21.org/lopud* ⏲ *Closed Oct.–May.*

WHERE TO EAT

$$ SEAFOOD — ✕ **Konoba Kod Marka.** With its prime location overlooking the harbor in Šipanska Luka, opposite the bay from the ferry pier, this Šipan seafood restaurant is one of the most renowned in the area, popular with sailors who spend the night here. Be sure to make a reservation, grab a seat on the terrace, order a glass of wine, and ask for the catch of the day. **Known for:** fresh catch of the day; seaside location. [$] *Average main: 100 Kn* ✉ *Šipanska Luka* ☎ *020/758–007* ⏲ *Closed Oct.–May.*

$$ EASTERN EUROPEAN — ✕ **Konoba Peggy.** With a pretty terrace and a wonderful view over the bay, Konoba Peggy has a menu featuring typical Dalmatian fare, including fresh fish cooked over an open fire in front of you, plus succulent steaks. You'll find this family-run konoba on a narrow side street above the ferry

landing. **Known for:** traditional cuisine; friendly staff; lovely views. *Average main: 85 Kn* *Narikla 22* *098/301–389* *Closed Nov.–Apr.*

$$$ SEAFOOD Fodor's Choice ★ **Restoran Obala.** This smart restaurant offers fine dining on the seafront promenade, with idyllic sunset views across the bay and wonderfully formal waiters. The house specialty is *školjke na buzaru* (mixed shellfish cooked in wine and garlic), and they also do an excellent prawn and truffle risotto. **Known for:** local seafood; seaside location; excellent service. *Average main: 140 Kn* *Obala Iva Kuljevana 18* *020/759–170* *www.obalalopud.com* *Closed Nov.–Apr.*

$$$ EASTERN EUROPEAN FAMILY **RobiNzooN.** It takes a special place to attract visitors away from the shore on an island and dine inland at a restaurant that specializes in meat dishes rather than seafood. Located in a big garden, this restaurant exudes local charm, with all members of the family pitching in to cook and serve your meal. **Known for:** good place to try lamb peka; family vibe. *Average main: 120 Kn* *Od polja 7* *099/757–4057* *No credit cards* *Closed Oct.–June. No lunch.*

WHERE TO STAY

$ HOTEL **Hotel Glavović.** With a prime location on the seafront promenade, Lopud's first hotel, opened in 1927, may need spruced-up furnishings and a bit of refurbishment, but have a glass of wine, chat with owner Vlasta about its history, and look closer at the old photographs on the walls and you'll understand that this hotel is something more than just its faded decor. **Pros:** short walk to ferry terminal; location overlooking the harbor. **Cons:** very basic rooms and common area; no elevator. *Rooms from: €100* *Obala Iva Kuljevana* *020/759–340* *www.hotel-glavovic.hr* *Closed Nov.–Apr.* *12 rooms* *Breakfast.*

$ HOTEL Fodor's Choice ★ **Hotel Šipan.** Located in an old olive oil factory right on the waterfront in peaceful Šipanska Luka, this is one of the most welcoming and relaxing hotels in the region, with cozy, warmly decorated rooms and excellent facilities. **Pros:** waterfront location; friendly staff; good on-site restaurant. **Cons:** often fully booked. *Rooms from: €100* *Šipanska Luka* *020/361–700* *www.hotel-sipan.com* *Closed Oct.–Apr.* *73 rooms* *Breakfast.*

$$$$ HOTEL **Hotel Villa Vilina.** This old stone villa, with palms out front overlooking the sea, has been carefully restored as a boutique hotel with a small pool. **Pros:** traffic-free island with regular ferries to Dubrovnik; location in a raised garden overlooking the harbor; breakfast and dinner served on lovely outdoor terrace. **Cons:** often fully booked; far from urban glamour (no nightlife, shopping). *Rooms from: €250* *Obala Iva Kuljevana 5* *020/759–333* *www.villa-vilina.hr* *Closed Nov.–May.* *15 rooms* *Breakfast.*

$$$ HOTEL Fodor's Choice ★ **Lafodia Sea Resort.** The luxurious Lafodia rises up a hillside overlooking the harbor and bay with sleek rooms and terraces, five restaurants, a bakery, and a gorgeous infinity pool. **Pros:** seafront location with views over the bay; wonderful spa; new and modern amenities. **Cons:** big and rather impersonal; distance from the ferry. *Rooms from: €200* *Obala Iva Kuljevana 35* *020/450–300* *www.lafodiahotel.com* *Closed Oct.–Apr.* *182 rooms* *Breakfast.*

CAVTAT

17 km (10½ miles) southeast of Dubrovnik.

While Dubrovnik's streets are being polished under the shoes of thousands of visitors per day, Cavtat's pine-covered trails seem comparatively tourist-free. There are secluded swimming spots, quiet walking paths, and park benches waiting for you to sit and enjoy the beauty and tranquillity that you came to Croatia to find.

Founded by the ancient Greeks as Epidauros, then taken by the Romans and renamed Epidaurum, the original settlement on the site of Cavtat was subsequently destroyed by tribes of Avars and Slavs in the early 7th century. The Romans fleeing Epidaurum founded Dubrovnik.

Today's Cavtat, which developed during the 15th century under the Republic of Dubrovnik, is an easygoing seaside resort. The medieval stone buildings of the Old Town occupy a small peninsula with a natural bay to each side. A palm-lined seaside promenade with open-air cafés and restaurants curves around the main bay, while the second bay is overlooked by a beach backed by several socialist-era hotels.

GETTING HERE AND AROUND

The drive to Cavtat, whether by car or bus from Dubrovnik (departing half-hourly from the main bus station and the cable car), offers some of the best views over the Old Town and the Župa Dubrovačka. Another option is a taxi boat along the coast from Dubrovnik's Old Harbor (1 hour; 60 Kn one-way).

EXPLORING

Kuća Bukovac (*Vlaho Bukovac Home*). The former home of local son Vlaho Bukovac (1855–1922), one of Croatia's greatest artists, has been beautifully converted into a gallery of his life and work. The two floors feature family and self-portraits and oil paintings from the periods he spent in Paris, Zagreb, Prague, and Cavtat. The house—with walls covered in murals Bukovac painted as a young man, period furniture, and personal items, plus the gardens surrounding it—is a lovely place to spend a quiet afternoon. ✉ *Bukovćeva 5* ☎ *020/478–646* 🌐 *www.kuca-bukovac.hr* 🎫 *30 Kn.*

Mauzolej Obitelji Račić (*Račić Mausoleum*). In the cemetery, on the highest point of the peninsula, this mausoleum was created by beloved Croatian sculptor Ivan Meštrović for the Račić family in 1921. Made from white marble and capped with a cupola, it is octagonal in plan, and the main entrance is guarded by two art nouveau caryatids. It is a peaceful site, and the views from the top are fantastic. ✉ *Rat* ☎ *020/478–646* 🎫 *10 Kn* 🕐 *Closed Nov.–Mar.*

OFF THE BEATEN PATH

Kameni Dvori. Konavle, the southernmost tip of Croatia before it trails off into Montenegro, is a bucolic region known for its rural agriculture, traditional embroidery, folk dress, and dance. The highlights of this region aren't along the coast, but rather inland in vineyards and farms. The best place to get a sense of Konavle life is this wonderfully rustic villa and konoba in the settlement of Lovorno, 14 kms

(9 miles) south of Cavtat. Take a traditional cooking class with the exceptionally friendly family who own the house and you'll try their homemade wine and rakija, get your hands dirty in the garden choosing vegetables for the soup, and make fresh bread and their specialty, Livorno skewers. You might even find yourself milking a goat. It's a great excursion from Dubrovnik. ✉ *Lovorno 11* ☎ *020/797–056* 🌐 *www.holiday-village-konavle.com.*

WHERE TO EAT

$$$$ SEAFOOD Fodor's Choice ★ **Bugenvila.** Bugenvila is vibrant in every sense, from the flowers climbing the sides of the terrace to the happy patrons tucking into sophisticated dishes such as butter-poached lobster, green lettuce gazpacho, bluefin tuna sashimi, and mojito sorbet. The menu changes regularly but is always fresh and exciting. **Known for:** sophisticated, top-quality food; haute cuisine in a casual setting. [$] *Average main: 170 Kn* ✉ *Obala A. Starcevica 9* ☎ *020/479–949* 🌐 *bugenvila.eu* ⏲ *Closed Nov.–Mar.*

$$ SEAFOOD **Konoba Kolona.** Located one street behind Tiha Bay, Konoba Kolona is a firm favorite among locals; when the owner is the same person who catches the fish and serves it to you, you can't go wrong. It has two large covered terraces plus indoor seating and reasonable prices for popular dishes such as lobster by the kilo, mussels *buzara* (tomato and white wine sauce) , and octopus carpaccio. **Known for:** fresh seafood; popularity with locals; friendly service. [$] *Average main: 110 Kn* ✉ *Put Tihe 2* ☎ *020/478–787.*

WHERE TO STAY

$ HOTEL Fodor's Choice ★ **Castelletto.** With bougainvillea-strewn terraces, cheerful rooms, a small pool, and wonderful staff, family-run Castelletto is a perfect place to unwind and peacefully enjoy the view. **Pros:** very friendly owners; excellent buffet breakfast; private bar on-site. **Cons:** 10-minute uphill walk from center; often fully booked. [$] *Rooms from: €99* ✉ *Frana Laureana 22* ☎ *020/479–547* 🌐 *www.dubrovnikexperience.com* *13 rooms* *Breakfast.*

$$ HOTEL **Hotel Cavtat.** Hotel Cavtat represents a nice middle ground between the big resorts in Cavtat and the smaller villas. **Pros:** beachfront location; modern facilities; good restaurant and spa options; beautiful infinity pool. **Cons:** slightly impersonal service; rooms in older building somewhat outdated with no view. [$] *Rooms from: €140* ✉ *Tiha 8* ☎ *020/202–000* 🌐 *www.hotel-cavtat.hr* ⏲ *Closed Nov.–Apr.* *91 rooms, 1 suite* *Breakfast.*

$$$ HOTEL **Hotel Croatia.** Sprawling across its own rocky, pine-studded peninsula, with quiet walking trails through the property, this vast hotel offers guests the chance to find their own place in the sun or shade, seemingly miles away from the rest of the world. **Pros:** two private beaches; five restaurants on-site; lovely indoor saltwater pool. **Cons:** large property with an impersonal atmosphere; distance from center of town. [$] *Rooms from: €190* ✉ *Frankopanska 10* ☎ *020/475–555* 🌐 *www.adriaticluxuryhotels.com* ⏲ *Closed Nov.–Mar.* *487 rooms* *Breakfast.*

$$$$ HOTEL **Villa Pattiera.** This family-run boutique hotel is perfectly positioned on the seafront promenade in the center of Cavtat; the beach, the best restaurants, and the harbor are steps away. **Pros:** centrally located; friendly staff; excellent breakfast on pleasant terrace. **Cons:** often full; some noise in front rooms. *Rooms from: €230* ✉ *Trumbićev Put 9* ☎ *020/478–800* 🌐 *www.villa-pattiera.hr* ⏲ *Closed Nov.–Mar.* *12 rooms* *Breakfast.*

EN ROUTE **Trsteno Arboretum.** The area around Dubrovnik has many fine examples of summer villas built by noble families, but the one in Trsteno is something special. Within the grounds of a small Renaissance villa is an arboretum set up during the 16th century by the Gučetić family. Laid out on a geometric plan, the garden is filled with hundreds of exotic species of trees and shrubs, most of which were brought home from distant voyages by local sailors. An original aqueduct is still in use, and a Baroque fountain of Neptune and two nymphs dates from 1736. The site has been continuously developed for five centuries, acquiring Renaissance, Baroque, and Romantic forms along the way. The surroundings are breathtaking, with the grounds running down toward a cliff overlooking the sea. Buses run regularly to Trsteno from Dubrovnik, and it makes a great stopover on the way to the Pelješac Peninsula. ✉ *Potok 20, Trsteno* ☎ *020/751–019* *40 Kn.*

SPORTS AND THE OUTDOORS

The beaches east of the center, near **Uvala Tiha** (Tiha Bay), are where you'll find the large modern hotels and family-friendly beaches. Walk around the peninsula to find smaller beaches and a more peaceful spot to swim.

DIVING

Epidaurum Diving and Water Sports Center. There are some excellent underwater sights around Cavtat, including shipwrecks and amforas. Epidaurum Diving and Water Center organizes certification and dive trips, as well as Jet-Skiing, parasailing, and other types of water fun. ✉ *Šetalište Žal* ☎ *020/471–386* 🌐 *www.epidaurum.com.*

STON

54 km (34 miles) northwest of Dubrovnik; 67 km (42 miles) plus 2 nautical miles from Korčula.

On the surface, they are sleepy little fishing villages. But Ston (on the main Dubrovnik-Orebić road) and Mali Ston (Little Ston, just off the main road) have three unique properties that make them an excellent stopover between Dubrovnik and Korčula: walls, salt, and oysters.

GETTING HERE AND AROUND

Driving from Dubrovnik, Mali Ston is the first main village you come to on the Pelješac Peninsula, followed by Ston. Several buses ply this route daily in both directions.

PELJEŠAC PLEASURES

The Pelješac Peninsula is vacation at its best. You know that red wine you've been drinking since you got to Croatia? It comes from the vineyards here. Those secret beaches you've been trying to find? The peninsula is surrounded by them. And those famous oysters you've been eating in Dubrovnik? They pull them out of the channel right in front of you here and serve them to you with a slice of lemon. A wild, untouched region full of secluded coves, stone villages, and breathtaking views, it is best known for its red wines made from the Plavac Mali grape: **Postup Dingač.** Everything about the latter variety is hearty, including its alcohol percentage; the best place to try it is either in Dubrovnik restaurants or at the wineries themselves. Vinarija Miloš, near Ston, is renowned for its unique stagnum wines and family atmosphere (🌐 *www.milos.hr*), while California wine lovers might recognize the name Mike Grgich, who was born in Dalmatia but gained fame in Napa Valley; the Grgić winery in the village of Trstenik is one of the most sophisticated on the peninsula. You need to have private transport to reach the best parts of the peninsula, so if you don't, join an organized tour; **Tureta Travel** and **Secret Dalmatia** are two of the best operators.

EXPLORING

Solana Ston (*Salt Pans*). The Republic of Dubrovnik, interested in the ancient salt flats here as a revenue source, founded the town in 1333. You can take a fascinating tour of the massive salt pans, the oldest in Europe, to learn about the old processes, many of which are still used today. If the salt pans are closed, ask at Vila Koruna (which also owns the salt pans) about organizing a tour. ✉ *Pelješki put 1* ☎ *020/754–027* 🌐 *www.solanaston.hr* 🎫 *15 Kn* 🕙 *Closed Oct.–Apr.*

Ston Walls. In order to protect the early settlement, a 7-km (4½-mile) fortified wall was built connecting Ston and Mali Ston and effectively controlling land access to the peninsula. Today the fortified wall stretches 5½ km (3 miles) and is one of the best-preserved walls in the world. Locals will tell you it's second in length only to the Great Wall of China; a disputable claim, but nevertheless it is an impressive sight. There is a Ston Wall marathon every September; through the year you can take a slightly strenuous walk atop a section between Ston and Mali Ston (40 minutes) for incredible views of the channel and the salt pans. ✉ *Ston* ✣ *Follow signs to the entrance from Vila Koruna in Mali Ston (approx. 500 meters away).*

WHERE TO EAT AND STAY

$$$ SEAFOOD Fodor's Choice ★ ✕ **Bota.** Occupying a 14th-century salt warehouse, Bota (part of the Šare family empire) is known for its menu of outstanding, locally caught seafood—it's the best place to try Ston's famous oysters. If raw oysters make you squeamish, try the *pohane oštrige* (oysters deep-fried in bread crumbs), and don't leave without trying the unusual *stonski makaruli,*

MALI STON OYSTERS

Ston is renowned throughout Croatia, and increasingly internationally, for the oysters grown in Mali Ston Bay. Their high quality is due to the perfect brackish conditions of the bay; salty sea water mixed with the fresh, mineral-laden water that flows in from the nearby Neretva River. They have been farmed since Roman times, appreciated by nobles from the Dubrovnik Republic right up to the Habsburgs. But as famous as these oysters are, oyster farming in Ston is still a small-scale operation; only a handful of local families have permits. While you can try them in the best restaurants in the country, nothing beats an oyster straight out of the bay with just a slice of lemon and a glass of wine to wash it down. Mali Ston has several great restaurants, foremost among them Bota, plus a handful of oyster stands along the road for a quick bite.

a cake made from pasta, nuts, sugar, and cinnamon, unique to Ston. **Known for:** superb oysters; great seafood. *$ Average main: 140 Kn ✉ Mali Ston ☎ 020/754–482 🌐 www.bota-sare.hr.*

$ HOTEL **Vila Koruna.** The prime location right beside the city walls in the center of town makes up for the slightly outdated rooms at this cheap and cheerful family-run hotel. **Pros:** close to the Dubrovnic–Orebić road; friendly staff; good restaurant. **Cons:** rooms very hot in summer; some beds slightly uncomfortable. *$ Rooms from: €60 ✉ Mali Ston ☎ 020/754–999 🌐 www.vila-koruna.hr ⏲ Closed Dec.–Mar. 6 rooms 🍽 Breakfast.*

OREBIĆ

Orebić is 110 km (69 miles) northwest of Dubrovnik and 2 nautical miles northeast of Korčula.

Backed by the rocky heights of Sveti Ilija (3,153 feet), Orebić straggles along the coast, facing across a narrow sea channel to the island of Korčula. Historically, the town spent several centuries under the Republic of Dubrovnik, supplying many able seamen to the republic's merchant navy. From 1865 to 1887 the town even had its own shipping company: today you can see a string of villas and their gardens overlooking the coastal promenade, built by wealthy local sea captains. Learn more about the seafaring history at the charming Maritime Museum on Orebić's main street, complete with naval instruments, maps, old documents, and photos. Today Orebić is best known for its sandy beach, delightful hillside monastery, and as the gateway to the Pelješac Peninsula and its highly esteemed red wines.

GETTING HERE AND AROUND

Hourly car and passenger ferries link Orebić to Korčula through peak season; journey time is 20 minutes. There are also daily buses to and from Dubrovnik, which start or finish in Korčula and also pass through Ston.

EXPLORING

Franjevački samostan (*Franciscan Monastery of Our Lady of the Angels*). A 20-minute walk up the hill above Orebić brings you to the 15th-century Franciscan monastery, perched 492 feet above sea level. The view across the channel to Korčula is spectacular; the view, in fact, explains the monastery's prime location. During the days of the Republic of Dubrovnik, Pelješac was under Dubrovnik's control, while Korčula was ruled by her archrival, Venice. From this privileged vantage point, the Franciscan monks would spy upon their island neighbors, under strict orders to send a messenger to Dubrovnik if trouble looked likely. Today the monastery is a most welcoming retreat, with a lovely cloister and a small museum, displaying scale models of the ships that local sea captains sailed across the oceans and an array of votive pictures dedicated to the Virgin, commissioned and donated by sailors who had been saved from trouble on the high seas. Before leaving, check out the cemetery, where gray marble tombstones shaded by cypress trees mark the final resting places of many a local seafarer. ✉ *Orebic* ☎ *020/713–075* 🎫 *20 Kn.*

Korta Katarina Winery. Perched on a hill overlooking Trstenica Beach, the award-winning Korta Katarina winery is a beautiful place to try Pelješac wines and the most accessible from Orebić. *Korta* is the name for the typical courtyards outside sea captains' homes around town, while *Katarina* is a family name of the American couple who came to Croatia on a rebuilding mission, fell in love with it, and opened the winery. Call ahead to arrange a visit, which typically includes a one-hour tour of the state-of-the-art winery plus three tastings (dinner can also be arranged), or just show up and enjoy a glass of *Pošip,* a Dalmatian white wine, or *Plavac Mali,* a red, on the sweeping terrace. ✉ *Bana J. Jelacica 3* ☎ *020/713–817* 🌐 *www.kortakatarinawinery.com* 🕙 *Closed Oct.–Apr.*

Vinarija Bartulović. The Bartulović family has been making wine on Pelješac for some 480 years, and today it's the young, energetic winemaker Mario who will tell you all about the wine-making process, his experiences on the Dingač slopes, and his family's traditions. Vinarija Bartulović is especially popular with visitors thanks to its authentic Dalmatian konoba, located in the former wine cellar, with exposed stone walls and rustic wooden tables. It's the best choice if you want to combine wine tasting with a full-blown meal (call one day in advance). ✉ *Prizdrina Pelješac, 13 km (8 miles) southeast of Orebić, Prizdrina* ☎ *020/742–506* 🌐 *www.vinarijabartulovic.hr.*

WHERE TO EAT AND STAY

$$ SEAFOOD ✕ **Karako.** When a restaurant has views this great and a location this prime, it could be forgiven if the food weren't the best. Such is not the case with Karako; located steps away from the sea, it offers up some of the tastiest seafood around—try their tuna steak—perfectly cooked at a large outdoor grill with friendly service to boot. **Known for:** freshest seafood; lovely seaside location. 💲 *Average main: 90 Kn* ✉ *Šetalište kneza Domagoja 32* ☎ *098/976–8371* 💳 *No credit cards* 🕙 *Closed Oct.–May.*

8

$$ SEAFOOD **Stari Kapetan.** Designed to look like an actual ship with a life-size captain at the helm, what at first glance might seem like a tourist trap is actually one of the best restaurants in town. Try the seafood platter for two, with tuna steak, grilled squid, mussels, scampi, and extraordinary sea bream, plus a glass of homemade Plavac, and salute the old captain for me. **Known for:** unusual maritime-inspired design; excellent seafood; al fresco seaside dining. *Average main: 80 Kn* *Boutique Hotel Adriatic, Šetalište Kneza Domagoja 8* *020/714–488* *www.hoteladriaticorebic.com/en/restaurant.php.*

$$ HOTEL FAMILY **Aminess Grand Azur Hotel.** Set on a pebbly beach 10 minutes from the center of Orebić, where the peninsula trails off into the sea with Korčula on the other side, this is a great base for the whole family. **Pros:** perfect for families with children; beachfront location; generous buffet and all-inclusive service. **Cons:** can be hectic in the high season; not enough beach chairs; distance from center of town. *Rooms from: €170* *Petra Kresimira IV 107* *052/858–600* *www.aminess.com* *Closed Nov.–Apr.* *185 rooms* *All-inclusive.*

$$ HOTEL Fodor's Choice ★ **Boutique Hotel Adriatic.** Locals are proud of their sea history in Orebić, but the Mikulić family has gone the extra mile and turned their hotel—easily one of the most elegant, charming, and classy hotels in Southern Dalmatia—into an unofficial seafaring museum. **Pros:** beautifully restored rooms with stone walls; close to center and beach; excellent restaurant. **Cons:** often fully booked; no elevator. *Rooms from: €165* *Šetalište Kneza Domagoja 8* *020/714–488* *www.hoteladriaticorebic.com* *6 rooms* *Breakfast.*

SPORTS AND THE OUTDOORS

BEACHES

Orebić's best beach, **Trstenica,** is a 1½-km (1-mile) stretch of sand and pebble on the east side of the island.

WINDSURFING

Water Donkey Windsurfing and Kitesurfing Center. Just a few kilometers up the road from Orebić, Viganj is regarded as one of the top windsurfing locations in Croatia and beyond. It hosts the Croatian surfing championship annually and has held both the European and world championships as well. You can rent equipment and take lessons from the friendly staff. They also rent kayaks, bikes, and stand-up paddle boards. *Ponta Beach, Viganj* *091/152–0258* *www.windsurfing-kitesurfing-viganj.com.*

KORČULA

Korčula island is 49 nautical miles northwest of Dubrovnik and 57 nautical miles southeast of Split by ferry.

Southern Dalmatia's largest island, Korčula was named Kerkyra Melaina, , or "Black Corfu," by the ancient Greeks for the dark Aleppo pine trees that cover the island. Between the 10th and 18th centuries it spent several periods under Venetian rule, much to the frustration of Dubrovnik, which considered the Italian city-state its archrival. Today it's known for its traditional sword dances, excellent white wines, and its main, though disputed, claim to fame as the birthplace of Marco Polo. **Korčula** is also the name of the capital near the island's eastern tip, which at first sight seems like a smaller version of Dubrovnik—the same high walls, the circular corner fortresses, and the church tower projecting from within an expanse of red roofs. The main difference lies in the town plan, as narrow side streets run off the main thoroughfare at odd angles to form a herringbone pattern, preventing cold winter winds from whistling unimpeded through town. Eight centuries under Venetian rule bequeathed the town a treasure trove of Gothic and Renaissance churches, palaces, and piazzas, all built from fine local stone, on which the island's early wealth was based. Today, as some other destinations along the coast succumb to mass tourism, Korčula, with its miles of mountainous roads perfect for biking, increasingly exciting hotel and restaurant scene, and its proud, welcoming locals, is quietly emerging as the most sophisticated and alluring island in the region.

GETTING HERE AND AROUND

The Krilo Jet fast catamaran travels twice daily between Dubrovnik and Split, stopping at Korčula Town en route, while Jadrolinija offers a similar once-daily service. Bus service between Dubrovnik and Korčula Town follows the regional road along Pelješac Peninsula, stopping in Ston before boarding a ferry at Orebić for a short crossing to Korčula.

EXPLORING

8

TOP ATTRACTIONS

Gradski Muzej Korčula (*Town Museum*). Located in a 16th-century stone palace on the main square, this charming museum contains items from all eras of the island's history, from neolithic stone knives to vessels excavated from Greek and Roman shipwrecks to models of wooden ships built in the 1960s. Check out the quirky objects in the original kitchen in the attic, such as gadgets for making macaroni or kneading bread. ✉ *Trg Sv. Marka* ☎ *020/715–786* 🌐 *www.gm-korcula.com* 🎫 *20 Kn.*

Katedrala (*Cathedral*). On the main square, the splendid Gothic-Renaissance cathedral is built from a wheat-colored stone that turns pale gold in sunlight, amber at sunset. Enter through the beautifully carved Romanesque main portal, which is guarded by Adam and Eve standing underneath twin lions. ■ **TIP→ Make sure to climb the bell tower for the best view in town—it's steep and a bit awkward, but worth it.** ✉ *Trg Sv. Marka* 🎫 *10 Kn, bell tower 25 Kn.*

Kuća Marca Pola (*Marco Polo House*). A couple of blocks east of the main square is the place where the legendary 13th-century discoverer is said to have been born, when Korčula was part of the Venetian Empire. The house itself is nearly in ruins but the tower next door is open, with a very modest exhibition on the first floor about Polo's life and a belvedere up top offering panoramic views. ✉ *Ul. Depolo* ☎ *020/716–529* 🎫 *20 Kn* ⏲ *Closed Nov.–Mar.*

Exploring

Gradski Muzej Korčula **3**

Katedrala **1**

Kopnena Vrata .. **4**

Kuća Marca Pola **2**

Marco Polo Museum **5**

Restaurants

Aterina **2**

Eko Škoj **5**

Konoba Belin **8**

Konoba Feral **3**

Maksimilijan Garden **7**

Zure **4**

Hotels

Aminess Lume ... **9**

Korčula Waterfront Accommodation . **6**

Lešić Dimitri Palace **1**

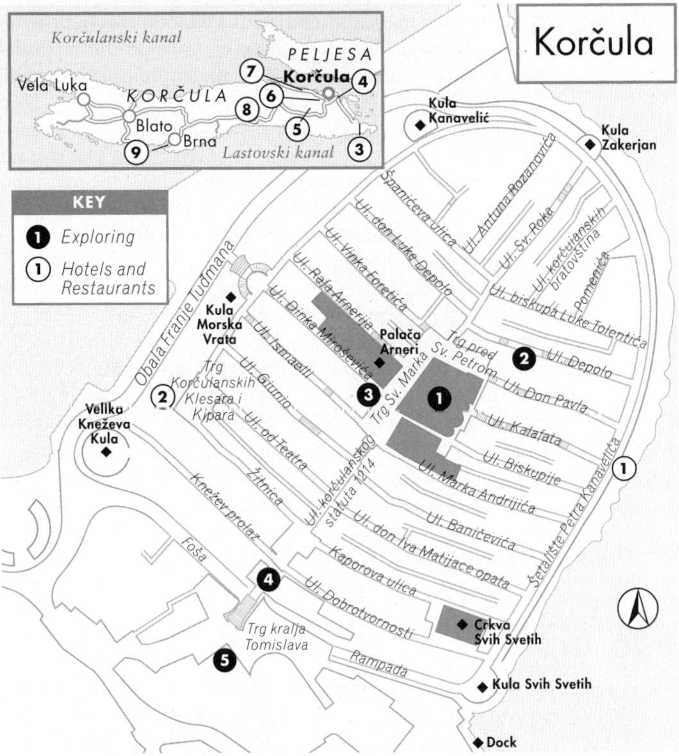

WORTH NOTING

Kopnena Vrata (*Land Gate*). This gate, the main entrance into the Old Town, is topped by the 15th-century Revelin Tower, housing an exhibition connected with the Moreška sword dance and offering panoramic views over the Old Town. Like the other towers around town, it features a winged lion—the symbol of Venice—and the seal of the Rector of Korčula. ✉ *Kopnena Vrata* 🎫 *20 Kn* 🕙 *Closed Nov.–Apr.*

NEED A BREAK

✕ Kavana No 1. For the best view of Korčula Town from above, take the road leading uphill from the main bus station until you see the large shopping center (15 minutes' walk). You'll find a Tommy supermarket, a few other shops, and the Kavana No 1 restaurant, where you can enjoy a coffee or a quick meal on their large terrace with a perfect panorama of the Old Town below. **Known for:** brilliant view of Korčula Town; casual dining. ✉ *Ulica Ante Starčevića 6* ☎ *091/621–4864* 🌐 *www.domino-korcula.com.*

Marco Polo Museum. Meticulously researched, a little cheesy, but undeniably charming, this multimedia, multistory exhibition, complete with life-size figures in medieval costumes, leads visitors through seven stages of the explorer's life, from setting sail from Korčula for the first time, through serving the Kublai Khan, and back home again. The kids will love it, and you will learn a thing or two as well. ✉ *Plokata 19. travnja 33* ☎ *098/970–5334* 🎟 *60 Kn* ⏲ *Closed Oct.–May.*

WHERE TO EAT

$$ MEDITERRANEAN Fodor's Choice ★ **Aterina.** Follow the scent of fresh basil—Chef Maja's favorite herb—to Aterina, a playful restaurant occupying a square on the periphery of the Old Town, with views to the palm-lined promenade and sea below. It offers a refreshing change from typically heavy Dalmatian dishes, with ingredients such as chickpeas, goat cheese, and pesto gracing the menu, along with a seemingly impossible accomplishment: desserts that sound like they could be healthy. **Known for:** fresh, local flavors; excellent vegetarian options. 💲 *Average main: 90 Kn* ✉ *Trg korčulanskih klesara i kipara 2* ☎ *091/986–1856* ⏲ *Closed Oct.–June.*

$$$ ECLECTIC Fodor's Choice ★ **Eko Škoj.** For one of the most authentic and delicious agritourism experiences in the region, head to the hills around Žrnovo. Inside their tiny stone konoba, rustically strung with lavender and bouquets of elderflower, the Marović family has set up a tasting room where you can try their homemade liqueurs, marmalades, and award-winning olive oil. **Known for:** organic food; exquisite homemade ice cream; charming, beautifully decorated house. 💲 *Average main: €20* ✉ *225 Žrnovo, Prvo Selo* ☎ *099/683–4749* 🌐 *www.ekoskoj.com* ⏲ *Closed Sun. No dinner.*

$$ EASTERN EUROPEAN FAMILY **Konoba Belin.** On the road high above Korčula Town lies Žrnovo, a village full of centuries-old stone houses and the folks whose families built them. Konoba Belin is one such house, and a visit there will give you a glimpse into the local way of life. **Known for:** traditional macaroni cooking class; family atmosphere. 💲 *Average main: 80 Kn* ✉ *Žrnovo 50* ☎ *091/503–9258* ⏲ *Closed Sept.–May. No lunch.*

$$ SEAFOOD **Konoba Feral.** The village of Lumbarda is known for two things: beaches and Grk wine, a dry white made exclusively on this part of the island by a handful of families. You can enjoy them both at this beachside konoba, where you'll tuck into über-fresh octopus while sipping homemade Grk made by the charming local brothers who own the restaurant. **Known for:** fresh seafood; family atmosphere. 💲 *Average main: 85 Kn* ✉ *Lumbarda 63, 7 km (4 miles) southeast of Korčula Town, Lumbarda* ☎ *020/712–090* ⏲ *Closed Oct.–May.*

$$ BARBECUE Fodor's Choice ★ **Maksimilijan Garden.** With comfy seats scattered around the shady garden of Croatian-American Maxo Vanka's memorial art gallery, a jazzy soundtrack, and an unrivaled view of Korčula Town ahead, Maksimilijan Garden is a lovely place to relax at the end of a hot afternoon. The menu features grilled meats, steaks, risotto, and a fabulous cocktail menu. **Known for:** great outdoor space; light meals and cocktails. 💲 *Average main: 100 Kn* ✉ *Sv. Nikola* ☎ *091/170–2567.*

$$ SEAFOOD **Zure.** The family behind this friendly restaurant in Lumbarda is one of the biggest Grk producers on the island, and everything here—from the olive oil to the pomegranate rakija—is grown, caught, or raised by them and local cooperatives. What's on offer depends on the day's catch, which father and sons will proudly bring to your

table before you order. **Known for:** family-run agritourism; one of the biggest wine producers in the region. *Average main: 100 Kn* *Podstrana 239, Lumbarda* *020/712–334* *Closed Jan.–Mar. No lunch.*

WHERE TO STAY

$$ RESORT **Aminess Lume.** When you're ready to enjoy the more natural side of the island, this resort hotel 32 km (20 miles) southwest of Korčula Town is a perfect base for mountain biking to pristine beaches and viewpoints, visiting wineries in nearby Smokvica, or just lying on a lounger and staring at the sea. **Pros:** light, attractive rooms with sea views; excellent buffet breakfast and dinner; great beach and facilities; friendly staff. **Cons:** far from the Old Town. *Rooms from: €130* *Brna BB* *052/858–600* *Closed Oct.–Apr.* *76 rooms* *Breakfast; Some meals.*

$ RENTAL Fodor's Choice ★ **Korčula Waterfront Accommodation.** Located in a quiet bay a 10-minute walk from Korčula Town, on a large private dock perfect for sunbathing and impromptu barbecues, these homey, spacious rooms are run by Paulina and Antonio, the most helpful couple you could hope to meet on holiday. **Pros:** helpful and very friendly hosts; quiet location with private dock; breezy, well-equipped rooms. **Cons:** no breakfast; not many restaurants or shops nearby. *Rooms from: €70* *Šetalište Tina Ujevića 33* *098/937–0463* *korcula-waterfront-accommodation.com* *No credit cards* *5 rooms* *No meals.*

$$$$ HOTEL Fodor's Choice ★ **Lešić Dimitri Palace.** A cluster of stone buildings woven into the fabric of the Old Town, Lešić Dimitri Palace is more than a hotel; it's a night in an Arabian desert, a bath surrounded by the grandeur of old Venice, a night sleeping amid the soft textiles of South Asia. **Pros:** excellent restaurant; stunning interior design; personalized service; Old Town location. **Cons:** very expensive; no pool; no extra facilities for children. *Rooms from: €495* *Don Pavla Poše 1-6* *020/715–560* *www.ldpalace.com* *Closed Nov.–Apr.* *5 apartments* *Breakfast.*

NIGHTLIFE AND PERFORMING ARTS

NIGHTLIFE

BARS

Fodor's Choice ★ **Cocktail Bar Massimo.** Surely among the world's most impressive venues, Cocktail Bar Massimo is located inside one of the turrets of the fortified town walls and offers wonderful sunset views over the peninsula. Drinks are raised up the turret on a pulley, and you have to climb a steep ladder to get to the top (ladies wearing dresses, you have been warned!). *Šetalište Petra Kanavelića* *020/715–073* *Closed Oct.–May.*

PERFORMING ARTS

DANCE

Fodor's Choice ★ **Moreška.** For one of the most entertaining cultural performances you'll see in Croatia, catch a performance of the Moreška, a colorful medieval sword dance—with real swords—that has been performed in Korčula for more than 400 years. The word Moreška means "Moorish" and is said to celebrate the victory of the Christians over the Moors in Spain, told through the story of a clash between the Black King and the White King over a young maiden. The dance itself is not native to Croatia and was once performed in many Mediterranean countries, but the tradition has disappeared elsewhere and nowadays remains only here. The hour-long performance involves traditional a cappella singing, a live brass band, and the energetic sword dance, performed only by males from local families. Performances take place throughout the summer on an open-air stage just outside the city walls next to the Land Gate, with a spectacular performance held on July 29, the feast day of Korčula's protector, St. Theodore. ✉ *Kopnena Vrata* 🌐 *www.moreska.hr* 🎫 *100 Kn.*

FESTIVALS

Korkyra Baroque Festival. This 10-day Baroque music festival takes place in September in venues across Korčula Town, including the cathedral and the atrium of City Hall. Established in 2012, it has become one of the most important festivals on the island, attracting musicians and visitors from around the world. ✉ *Korcula* ☎ *099/319–5427* 🌐 *www.korkyrabaroque.com.*

SPORTS AND THE OUTDOORS

BEACHES

The sea around Korčula is so clean and clear you can swim anywhere (and the locals do), including right outside the Old Town walls and beside the harbor. But with some of the best swimming spots in the entire country, you can afford to be choosy. The closest spot for a quick swim is **Banje,** a small pebble beach about 10 minutes on foot east of the town walls. The best beaches near Korčula Town are 6 km (4 miles) away in the village of **Lumbarda**: sandy **Przina,** 2 km (1 mile) south of Lumbarda, and smooth-white-stoned **Bili Žal,** a short distance east. Farther away are many beaches that can be discovered only by boat or bike. **Pupnatska Luka,** 15 km (9.3 miles) southwest of Korčula Town, is a perfect wedge of shingle beach backed by steep hills. **Vaja Beach,** near the village of **Račišće** 13 km (8 miles) away, is a secret bay that involves a steep downhill hike, but you're rewarded with an isolated, perfect white pebble beach.

Korčula Outdoor. For more active tours around the island, contact this bohemian company that will take you mountain biking, kayaking, rock climbing, and sailing to secret beaches, wineries, and the more hidden corners of Korčula. ✉ *Korcula* ☎ *091/622–4566* 🌐 *www.korcula-outdoor.com.*

NEED A BREAK

Moro Beach Stupe. Once upon a time, a venue as chic as this could only have opened on Hvar. A short taxi boat ride from Korčula Town, this is a perfect place to spend a lazy afternoon sipping cocktails by the sea, swinging on an Instagram-worthy swing set in the water, and listening to the DJ spinning records from a spot in the rocks. By sunset, it turns into a fine dining restaurant serving up organic food by two of Zagreb's top chefs. With the opening of Moro Beach Club, Korčula officially claims the title of Ibiza of the Adriatic. ✉ *Stupe Beach* ✣ *Taxi-boat transfer from Korčula Old Town* ☎ *099/490–9606* 🌐 *www.stupe.hr.*

8

SHOPPING

Korčula Town is renowned for its shopping, particularly its handmade jewelry. It's the best place in the region to stock up on unique souvenirs and quality gifts.

Bags by Kristina. This lovely boutique sells handmade leather bags embellished with abstract photos of Dalmatia, typically with a sea or stone motif, by designer-photographer Kristina Fazinić. They make wonderful and uniquely Croatian gifts. ✉ *Ul. Baničevića 4A* ☎ *091/271–1887* 🌐 *bagsbykristina.com.*

Cukarin. This family-run store is renowned for its five different types of delicious handmade biscuits, as well as roasted almonds and homemade rakija flavored with local herbs. ✉ *Hrvatska Bratske Zajednice BB* ☎ *020/711–055* 🌐 *www.cukarin.hr.*

Galerija Vapor. Funky jewelry, colorful sculptures, and paintings with pop-art twists by contemporary Croatian artists adorn the walls of this cavernous gallery inside the Sea Gate. ✉ *Kula morska vrata* ☎ *020/715–258* 🌐 *www.vapor-gallery.com.*

MLJET

Polače is 18 nautical miles west of Dubrovnik by ferry.

Mljet is a long, thin island of steep, rocky slopes and dense pine forests, more than a third of which is contained within Mljet National Park. The kings of Bosnia, who ruled the island during medieval times, gave it to Benedictine monks from Puglia in Italy during the 12th century, who in turn passed it on to the Republic of Dubrovnik in 1410. No great towns ever grew up here, and today it is home to half a dozen small villages, with a total population of about 1,100 people. Most people come for the National Park, but it's worth checking out the other parts of the island as well, including the Odysseus Cave and one of Croatia's few sandy beaches, Saplunara, at the southeastern tip of the island.

GETTING HERE AND AROUND

Mljet National Park is a popular excursion from Dubrovnik and Korčula. G&V Line sails here from Dubrovnik, and Krilo Jet travels from Dubrovnik and Korčula. Sobra is the main port on the island, while Polače and Pomena are the most convenient ports for the national park. Buses connect points across the island, including Saplunara beach.

EXPLORING

Fodor's Choice ★ **Nacionalni Park Mljeta** (*Mljet National Park*). Within the densely forested park lie two interconnected saltwater lakes—Malo Jezero (Little Lake) and Veliko Jezero (Big Lake)—ideal for swimming from spring to autumn. Boats run to the charming 12th-century Benedictine monastery on Otočić Svete Marije (St. Mary's Islet), in the middle of Veliko Jezero (30 Kn return); or you can rent a little blue kayak from Mali Most (80 Kn per hour), the bridge between the two lakes, and paddle out there. A series of footpaths and bike paths traverse the park; mountain bikes are also available for hire at Mali Most and at Hotel Odisej in Pomena. A local bus runs from the port of Sobra to the national park at the west end of the island. If you arrive on Mljet through Polače, you are within walking distance of the park. Upon arrival, pay the entrance fee at one of several wooden kiosks (if you stay overnight, this fee is included in the price of your accommodation). ✉ *Pristanište 2, Govedari* ☎ *020/744–041* 🌐 *www.np-mljet.hr* 🎟 *June–Sept., 125 Kn; Oct.–May, 70 Kn.*

Odysseus Cave. There are wonderful swimming spots all around Mljet, but the village of Babino Polje, in the center of the island, might be home to the most magical spot of all. Greek legend has it that when the hero Odysseus was shipwrecked off the island, known as Ogygia, he swam into a cave where he was met by a nymph called Calypso; he was so bewitched by her that he stayed for the next seven years. The cave isn't easy to reach, which adds to its mystique. Get there directly by boat, or take a car or scooter; park at the Tommy market and follow the signs on foot (the walk includes a steep downhill section). The cave is a great place for a swim, particularly at noon when the sun is high and the water looks aquamarine. There are a few cafés along the way to stop for refreshments. ✉ *Babino Polje.*

WHERE TO EAT AND STAY

$$$$ SEAFOOD

✕ **Stermasi.** This organic, traditional konoba is pricey, but the views are incredible and the food is of excellent quality; try octopus or goat under the bell, wild boar with homemade gnocchi, or Mljet-style fish stew. Most of the dishes take time to prepare, but with such pleasant service and delicious wines to choose from, you won't mind the wait. **Known for:** organic, local food; excellent seafood. $ *Average main: 300 Kn* ✉ *Maranovici, Saplunara 2* ☎ *098/939–0362* 🌐 *www.stermasi.hr.*

$$$ RENTAL

Boutique Pine Tree Resort. All of Mljet is peaceful, but Saplunara is where you go to really get away from it all, and this boutique property represents relaxation at its best. **Pros:** wonderful owners; peaceful location. **Cons:** difficult to reach; far from the national park. $ *Rooms from: €178* ✉ *Saplunara 17* ☎ *098/266–007* 🌐 *www.boutiquepinetree.com* *6 rooms* *Breakfast.*

$ HOTEL

Hotel Odisej. Located within the national park in the village of Pomena, just 15 minutes' walk away from the lakes, the Odisej's main appeal is that it's the only hotel on the island. **Pros:** seafront location near the national park; restaurant on-site. **Cons:** large and rather impersonal; food disappointing. $ *Rooms from: €108* ✉ *Pomena BB, Pomena* ☎ *020/362–111* 🌐 *www.adriaticluxuryhotels.com* ⏲ *Closed Nov.–Mar.* *157 rooms* *Breakfast.*

8

SPORTS AND THE OUTDOORS

BEACHES

One of Croatia's few sandy beaches, **Saplunara** lies at the southeastern tip of the island, outside the national park. Happily, it remains relatively wild and untended, and you will find several seasonal restaurants in the tiny nearby settlement of the same name. Within the park, the water in **Malo Jezero** (Little Lake) and **Veliko Jezero** (Big Lake) tends to be several degrees warmer than the sea and makes a perfect place for a swim and kayak.

9

MONTENEGRO

Updated by Elizabeth Gowing

An independent country since 2006, tiny Montenegro (about the size of Connecticut) lies on the Adriatic coast and is bordered by Croatia, Bosnia-Herzegovina, Serbia, Kosovo, and Albania. The 650,000 people who live here call it Crna Gora, which, like "Montenegro," means "black mountain"—a reminder of the pine-forested alpine terrain of most of the country.

Montenegro's main draw is its beautiful coastline, dotted with delightful Venetian-era fortified towns, home to excellent seafood restaurants, and set against the dramatic mountains of the interior.

Montenegro's first known inhabitants were the Illyrians, who were farmers and hunters, and also worked iron and traded with the ancient Greeks. Urbanization began in the 4th century BC when the Greeks founded Budva, on the coast. In AD 9, the Romans annexed the region into the province of Illyricum (which ran down the Adriatic coast from the Istrian peninsula to Albania), calling it Doclea after the dominant local Illyrian tribe. When the Roman Empire was divided between east and west in AD 395, the fault line passed right through Montenegro. Later, this was to be the dividing line between Eastern Orthodox and Roman Catholic lands.

In the 7th century, the Slavs arrived from the region that is now Poland. They mixed with the descendants of the Romanized Illyrians and lived in the mountains, in clans, each ruled by a *župan* (chieftain). Originally pagan, they soon adopted Christianity. In 1077, their independent state of Duklja (the Slavicized version of the Roman name, Doclea) was recognized as a kingdom by the pope. Later, Duklja became known as Zeta (derived from the old Slavic word for harvest) and kept its freedom through paying off the Byzantine Empire, and fighting off the Ottoman Turks. Because of the constant threat of Ottoman invasion and fear of rival clans, courage in combat was emphasized as a major virtue in Zeta.

Meanwhile, most of the Montenegrin coast was under Venetian rule from 1420 to 1797, though independent Montenegro had its capital at Cetinje, home of the first printing press in southern Europe in 1494.

Due to ties with Italy, Roman Catholicism was the dominant faith along the coast, whereas the Eastern Orthodox Church prevailed in Zeta. In fact, politics and religion became so intertwined in Zeta that from 1550 to 1696 it was governed by bishops. In 1697, the Petrović-Njegoš family took the helm as prince-bishops. The greatest of their rulers, still loved and revered in Montenegro today, was Petar II Petrović-Njegoš who organized a 32-man band of traveling magistrates as well as a police force, paid for from a system of taxation that he organized. He was also an epic poet, and his work, *The Mountain Wreath*, is considered Montenegro's national poem.

King Nikola Petrović, who ruled from 1860, was another notable ruler, and father; six of his nine daughters married royal or aristocratic

Europeans (including a grand duke of Russia and King Victor Emmanuel of Italy), which earned him the nickname "the father-in-law of Europe." King Nikola introduced free elementary education, an agricultural college, post and telegraph offices, and freedom of the press.

During both world wars, Montenegro sided with the Allies. In 1945, it became one of the six constituent republics that made up Yugoslavia, governed along communist lines by President Tito. Yugoslavia was not part of the Soviet Bloc, however, as Tito broke off relations with Stalin in 1948. The country was ruled under Tito's own form of communism—far more liberal than that in the former USSR.

During the breakup of Yugoslavia in the 1990s, no fighting took place on Montenegrin soil, though the region did suffer economic hardship and a degree of political isolation; a small number of civilians were killed by NATO bombing. When Croatia and Slovenia claimed independence from Yugoslavia in 1991, Montenegro remained loyal to Belgrade. However, by May 2006, when all that was left of Yugoslavia was the so-called Union of Serbia and Montenegro, Montenegro held a referendum and voted for independence (though it was close run, with only 55.5% of the votes in favor) and became its own democratic republic. Today, tourism is the main force behind the economy, and foreign investors (particularly Russian and British) keen to be in on the potential boom are buying up properties fast.

ORIENTATION AND PLANNING

GETTING ORIENTED

Of the small diamond-shape stretch of mountainous terrain that makes up Montenegro, only the southwestern face is usually visited by tourists as is the coastal strip. The most charming sites of this stretch of 100 km (60 miles)—as the crow flies—are at the northern end, though because of the short distances involved, more adventurous visitors can use any of the towns along the coast as a base to visit the inland towns and mountains. The coastline borders Croatia at its northern end and Albania to the south. Onward travel to the better-known towns and islands of Croatia is easily arranged by public transport or hired car, and the less discovered beaches and ancient sites of Albania are also accessible by regular buses across Montenegro's southern border. The UNESCO World Heritage Sites and legendary hospitality of Kosovo and Serbia are also only a bus journey away.

WHEN TO GO

May is a lovely time to visit coastal Montenegro, with temperatures running 14°C–22°C (56°F–72°F) but before the busiest crowds of summer. After that, temperatures rise to reach a peak in August with an average daily maximum of 29°C (84°F). These are fine days for sun worshippers or anyone willing and able to laze under sunshades and admire the sparkle on the water, but if you are wanting to explore the towns where sun glare bounces off the white stone, you may prefer to choose a different time of year (or at least plan your sightseeing for

Montenegro
Budva Riviera
E80
2-3
Bečići
Rafailovici
Budva
Jaz
Trsteno
Sveti Stefan
Ostrvo
Sv Nikola
E65
Budva
Gradska
Plaža
Petrovac
ADRIATIC SEA
BOSNIA-
HERZEGOVINA
SERBIA
KOSOVO
ALBANIA
CROATIA
Šula
Pljevlja
Tara
Durmitor
National
Park
Plužine
Žabljak
Grab
Bijelo
Polje
Golija
Sinjajevina
18
Šavnik
Mojkovac
Biogradska Gora
National Park
Budimlja
Njegoš
Kolašin
Berane
Rozaje
Nikšić
Morača
6
9
Vilusi
Andrijevica
Grahovo
E762
2
Plav
Gusinje
Prokletije
National Park
Cuce
Zijova
Danilovgrad
Risan
Perast
Kosić
Morinj
Dobrota
Bijela
PODGORICA
Herzeg
Novi
Prčanj
Tivat
Kotor
see detail
map
Lovćen
National
Park
Bay of
Kotor
Tuzi
Golubovci
Sveti
Stefan
Budva
Riviera
see inset
Lake
Skadar
National
Park
Petrovac
Lake
Skadar
Sutomore
Šušanj
TO
ANCONA
Bar
Rashtish
E851
ADRIATIC
SEA
Ulcinj
TO BARI
0
30 miles
0
30 kilometers

TOP REASONS TO GO TO MONTENEGRO

Beautiful views: In Kotor, climb to St. John's Fortress, following the medieval walls for postcard views.

Luxurious getaways: Indulge in a night (or if you can't afford it, a meal or a spa day pass) at the luxurious Sveti Stefan Aman resort. Once a village of old stone cottages, it's now a private island.

The yachting life: Charter a yacht for a private sailing trip round the Bay of Kotor.

Floating churches: Visit Gospa od Skrjelo (Our Lady of the Rock), a lovely church perched on a tiny islet, opposite Perast, just outside Kotor.

Mediterranean villages: Zigzag down the mountain road above Kotor to get a full view of the bay including Kotor, Perast, and the other villages clustered around the sapphire water of the Mediterranean's only fjord.

early in the days). By September, temperatures are cooling (17°C–26°C [62°F–78°F])—and the crowds in the most popular sites (notably Kotor) are thinning—while the sea is still as warm as in June or July (24°C [75°F]) so this is also a great time to visit. After this the season is properly over, and winter on the coast is a little bleak (temperatures in January run 5°C–12°C [40°F–53°F]) and many businesses shut down.

PLANNING

GETTING HERE AND AROUND

AIR TRAVEL

Montenegro Airlines has service from both Tivat and Podgorica Airports to London and various other European capitals. Well served by international airlines, Dubrovnik Airport, in Croatia, is a popular alternative gateway to Montenegro, but it's important to note that car-rental agencies may charge extra for taking the vehicle across borders.

9

Airport Contacts Dubrovnik Airport. ✉ *Čilipi BB, Dubrovnik* ☎ *20/773–171 passenger services* 🌐 *www.airport-dubrovnik.hr.* **Podgorica Airport.** ✉ *Podgorica Airport, Podgorica* ☎ *020/444–244* 🌐 *www.montenegroairports.com.* **Tivat Airport.** ✉ *Tivat Airport* ☎ *032/671–337* 🌐 *www.montenegroairports.com.*

BOAT TRAVEL

Montenegro Lines operates regular overnight car ferries year-round to the Montenegrin port of Bar, 38 km (24 miles) south of Budva, from Bari in Italy. The crossing takes 10 hours and costs about €100 per person one-way (in a two-berth cabin with bathroom).

BUS TRAVEL

Buses are cheap (e.g., €7.50 for the two-hour journey from Kotor to Podgorica) and cover practically the entire country. They are generally clean and reliable. Numerous small bus lines operate regularly along the coast between Herzeg Novi (in the north) and Ulcinj (in the south), stopping at most towns along the way. For other routes, inquire at the bus station of departure.

Contacts **Kotor Bus Station.** ✉ *Ul. Put prvoboraca BB, Kotor* ☎ *032/325–809* 🌐 *www.autobuskastanicakotor.me.*

CAR TRAVEL

Although Montenegro's buses have good service along the coast and can get you to most points in the country, renting a car gives you much more flexibility and makes life easier especially when visiting the mountains.

Since the Old Town is compact and pedestrian-friendly, you do not need to rent a car in Kotor. It's easy to reach nearby Perast by bus or taxi.

CRUISE SHIP TRAVEL

Arriving at Kotor from the water is an impressive experience in itself, so be sure to be up on the deck in advance. Your ship will sail up a 28-km-long (18-mile-long) bay (often referred to as a fjord), with rugged mountains rising in the background. Cruise ships dock on the quay, immediately in front of Kotor's medieval walled Old Town.

TOUR OPTIONS

Many private travel agencies offer tours, including hiking in the mountains, rafting on the Tara River and visits to the towns of the interior, including the "toytown" former capital, Cetinje and nearby Lovćen, and the other national parks, including Lake Skadar (good for birdwatching), Biogradska Gora, and Durmitor. Other companies will offer tours from Montenegro to other countries in the region, including through the Prokletije national park into Kosovo and Albania, or to Dubrovnik or other destinations in Croatia.

ABOUT THE RESTAURANTS

Along the Montenegrin coast, seafood predominates, with starters including *salata od hobotnice* (octopus salad) and *riblja čorba* (fish soup), followed by risotto dishes—most notably *crni rižot* (black risotto prepared with cuttlefish)—*lignje* (squid), or fresh fish from the Adriatic prepared on a barbecue. The quality is generally excellent, and the prices are slightly lower than in neighboring Croatia. Note that on restaurant menus, fresh fish is priced by the kilogram. Inland, cheeses and meat dishes are more common. Cheeses to try include *sir iz ulje* (cheese preserved in olive oil) and *kožji sir* (goat's cheese), which are generally eaten at the beginning of the meal rather than at the end. Popular meat specialties are *pršut* (prosciutto), *Njeguški stek* (steak stuffed with prosciutto and cheese), and *jagnjece pečenje sa ražnja* (whole lamb roasted on a spit).

Montenegrins are also fond of the ubiquitous Balkan *Šopska salata* (a chopped salad of tomato, green peppers, cucumber, onion, olives, and strong white cheese grated over the top). When it comes to local wines, Vranac is the most highly esteemed red, and Krstac a reliable white.

ABOUT THE HOTELS

The main delight of Montenegro's accommodation are the small, family-run establishments, many of which are centuries-old stone villas that have been converted into delightful little boutique hotels full of character, and with great hospitality. However, many visitors still prefer to rent a private room or apartment, which can be arranged through local tourist information offices and travel agencies. The tourist season runs from Easter to late October and peaks in July and August, when prices rise significantly and it may be difficult to find a place to sleep if you have not booked in advance. *Hotel reviews have been shortened. For full information, visit Fodors.com.*

WHAT IT COSTS IN EUROS (€)				
	$	$$	$$$	$$$$
Restaurants	under €10	€10–€16	€17–€20	over €20
Hotels	under €85	€85–€150	€151–€200	over €200

Restaurant prices are the average cost of a main course at dinner or, if dinner is not served, at lunch. Hotel prices are the lowest cost of a standard double room in high season.

VISITOR INFORMATION

Contacts National Tourism Organization of Montenegro. ✉ *Marka Miljanova 17, Podgorica* ☎ *077/100–001* 🌐 *www.montenegro.travel.*

KOTOR

44 km (28 miles) from the border crossing between Croatia and Montenegro.

Backed by imposing mountains, tiny Kotor lies hidden from the open sea, tucked into the deepest channel of the Bokor Kotorska (Kotor Bay), which is Europe's most southerly fjord. To many, this town is more charming than its sister UNESCO World Heritage Site, Dubrovnik, retaining more authenticity but with fewer tourists, and spared the war damage and subsequent rebuilding that has given Dubrovnik something of a Disney feel.

Kotor's medieval Stari Grad (Old Town) is enclosed within well-preserved defensive walls built between the 9th and 18th centuries and is presided over by a proud hilltop fortress. Within the walls, a labyrinth of winding cobbled streets leads through a series of splendid paved piazzas, rimmed by centuries-old stone buildings. The squares are now haunted by strains from buskers, but although many now house trendy cafés and chic boutiques, directions are still given medieval-style by reference to the town's landmark churches.

In the Middle Ages, as Serbia's chief port, Kotor was an important economic and cultural center with its own highly regarded schools of stonemasonry and iconography. From 1391 to 1420 it was an independent city-republic, and later it spent periods under Venetian, Austrian, and French rule, though it was undoubtedly the Venetians who left the strongest impression on the city's architecture. Since the breakup of Yugoslavia, some 70% of the stone buildings in the romantic Old Town have been snapped up by foreigners, mostly Brits and Russians. Porto Montenegro, a new marina designed to accommodate some of the world's largest superyachts, opened in nearby Tivat in 2011, and along the bay are other charming seaside villages, all with better views of the bay than the vista from Kotor itself, where the waterside is congested with cruise ships and yachts. Try sleepy Muo or the settlement of Prčanj in one direction around the bay, or Perast and the Roman mosaics of Risan in the other direction.

GETTING HERE AND AROUND

AIR TRAVEL

Tivat Airport is 8 km (5 miles) from Kotor. Less convenient is the capital's Podgorica Airport, 90 km (56 miles) inland. Alternatively, some visitors fly in to Dubrovnik (Croatia) and drive 60 km (38 miles) down the coast to Kotor.

AIRPORTS AND TRANSFERS

Buses run regularly between Tivat Airport and Kotor; inquire at the airport information desks for schedule and fare information. There are frequent buses from Podgorica to Kotor, but you will need to take a taxi from Podgorica airport to the bus station (approximately €8). You can catch a taxi year-round from both Tivat and Podgorica airports.

BOAT TRAVEL

During the summer, private taxi boats operate from Kotor's harbor, taking passengers up the coast to the village of Perast.

BUS TRAVEL

Regular buses run along the coast, stopping in Kotor en route. There's also a special service between Kotor and Budva.

CAR TRAVEL

Having a car in Kotor is not recommended, as the Old Town is pedestrian-only and parking spots can be hard to find, especially in high season.

VISITOR INFORMATION

Kotor's tourist information office gives out free maps and information and can help find private accommodation. You'll find the office in a kiosk just outside the Main Town Gate.

Contacts Kotor Tourist Board (*Turistička Organizacija Kotora*). ✉ *Stari Grad 315* ☎ *032/322–886* 🌐 *www.tokotor.me.* **Tourist Info Biro–Kotor.** ✉ *Stari Grad* ☎ *032/325–950* 🌐 *www.tokotor.com.*

EXPLORING

Kotor's Old Town takes approximately half a day to explore. Plan your visit for the morning, when the main sights are open to the public and the afternoon sun has yet to reach peak force.

TOP ATTRACTIONS

Crkva Sv. Luke (*St. Luke's Church*). Built in 1195, this delightful Romanesque church is the only building in the Old Town to have withstood all five major earthquakes that affected Kotor. Originally a Catholic church, the building later became an Orthodox place of worship. The church is open every day from 9 to 9. ✉ *Trg bratstvo i jedinstva.*

Crkva Sv. Nikole (*St. Nicholas' Church*). Designed by a Russian architect and built in pseudo-Byzantine style between 1902 and 1909, this is Kotor's most important Orthodox church (the Cathedral, by definition, is Catholic). The gold used to gild the spires was a gift from Russia. ✉ *Trg bratstvo i jedinstva.*

Exploring
Crkva Sv. Luke ... 8
Crkva Sv. Nikole .. 7
Glavna Gradska Vrata 4
Gradske Zidine ... 1
Katedrala Sv. Tripuna 10
Kneževa palata ... 3
Pomorski Muzej Crne Gore 9
Toranj za sat 5
Trg od Oržja 6
Tvrdjava Sv Ivana 11
Zgrada Napoleonovog pozorišta 2

Restaurants
Galion 10
Hotel Astoria Restaurant 8
Konoba Scala Santa 9
Luna Rossa 6

Hotels
Hotel Astoria 7
Hotel Cattaro 3
Hotel Monte Cristo 5
Hotel Splendido .. 2
Hotel Vardar 4
Palazzo Radomiri 1

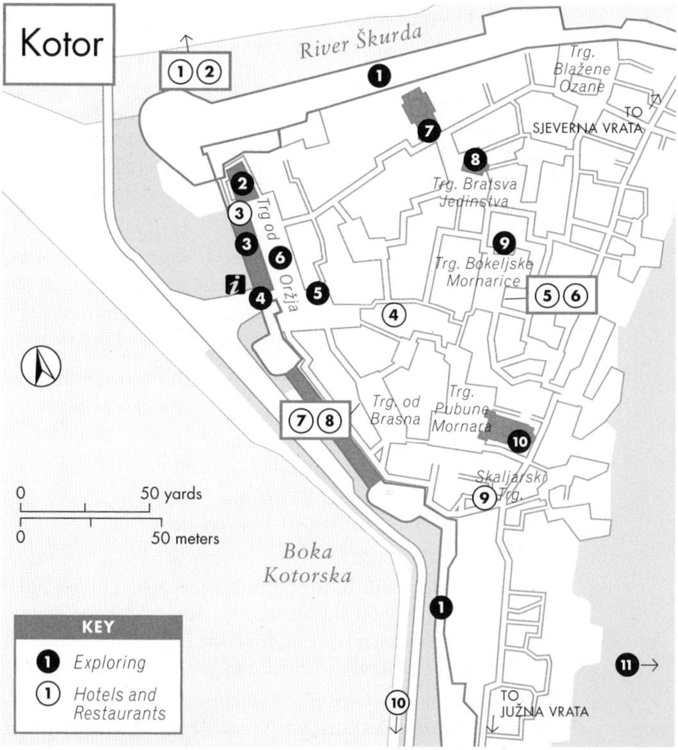

Glavna Gradska Vrata. The Main Town Gate (also known as the Sea Gate because of its position on the coast), which accesses the Stari Grad (Old Town) via the western facade of the city walls, dates back to the 16th century, and comprises Renaissance and Baroque details. Originally, the outer gate bore a relief of the Venetian Lion, but in Tito's time this was replaced by the socialist star and dates recording the liberation of Kotor on November 21, 1944, at the end of WWII. There are two other entrances to the Stari Grad: the Južna Vrata (South Gate) and the Sjeverna Vrata (North Gate). ⊠ *Jadranski put.*

Gradske Zidine. Especially beautiful at night when they are illuminated, the well-preserved town walls were built between the 9th and 18th centuries. They measure almost 5 km (3 miles) in length, and reach up to 66 feet in height and 52 feet in width. They form a triangular defense system around the Old Town, then rise up the hill behind it to Tvrdjava Sv. Ivana (St. John's Fortress), 853 feet above sea level. You can walk up to the fortress along the walls, but allow at least one hour to get up and back down. Wear good hiking shoes—and don't forget to bring some water. ⊠ *Stari Grad* 🎫 *€3.*

Katedrala Sv. Tripuna (*St. Tryphon's Cathedral*). Undoubtedly Kotor's finest building, the Romanesque cathedral dates back to 1166, though excavation work shows that there was already a smaller church here in the 9th century. Due to damage caused by a succession of disastrous earthquakes, the cathedral has been rebuilt several times—the twin Baroque bell towers were added in the late 17th century. Inside, the most important feature is the 14th-century Romanesque Gothic ciborium above the main altar. Also look out for fragments of 14th-century frescoes, which would once have covered the entire interior. A collection of gold and silver reliquaries, encasing body parts of various saints and crafted by local masters between the 14th and 18th century, is on display in the treasury. ✉ *Trg Ustanka Mornara* ☎ *032/322–315* 🎟 *€2.50 for combined ticket to cathedral and treasury.*

BEST BETS FOR CRUISE PASSENGERS

Kotor Old Town. Roam the car-free streets of this centuries-old fortified town, now a UNESCO World Heritage Site.

St. John's Fortress. Follow Kotor's medieval walls uphill to arrive at this small fort, affording magnificent views of the Old Town and the bay below.

Our Lady of the Rock. Take a boat ride across the bay from Perast to visit a tiny islet capped by a church.

WORTH NOTING

Kneževa palata. Built in the 18th century, the Duke's Palace comprises almost the entire west side of the Old Town. Originally it was the official seat of the Venetian governor. Like the Napoléon Theatre, it is now part of the Hotel Cattaro. ✉ *Stari Grad.*

Pomorski Muzej Crne Gore (*Montenegrin Naval Museum*). Housed within the 18th-century Baroque Grgurina Palace, this museum traces Montenegro's cultural and economic ties to the sea. In the 18th century, tiny Kotor had some 400 ships sailing the world's oceans. The exhibition extends over three floors and includes model ships; paintings of ships, ship owners, and local naval commanders; navigation equipment; and uniforms worn by Montenegrin admirals and captains. ✉ *Trg Grgurina, Stari Grad* ☎ *032/304–720* 🌐 *www.museummaritimum.com* 🎟 *€4.*

Toranj za sat (*Clock Tower*). Built in the 17th century and considered a symbol of Kotor, the Clock Tower stands directly opposite the Main City Gate. In front of the Clock Tower, the "Pillar of Shame" was used to subject local criminals to public humiliation. ✉ *Trg od Oružja, Stari Grad.*

Trg od Oružja (*Square of Arms*). The Main Town Gate leads directly into the Square of Arms, Kotor's main square, today a large paved space animated by popular open-air cafés. Under Venice, arms were repaired and stored here, hence the name. Notable buildings on the square include the 17th-century Toranj za Sat (Clock Tower), the 19th-century Napoleonovog Pozorišta (Napoléon Theatre), and the 18th-century Kneževa Palata (Duke's Palace), the latter two now forming part of the upmarket Hotel Cattaro. ✉ *Trg od Oružja, Stari Grad.*

Tvrdjava Sv Ivana (*St. John's Fortress*). On the hill behind Kotor, 853 feet above sea level, this fortress is approached via a series of bends and some 1,300 steps. The fantastic view from the top makes the climb worthwhile: the terra-cotta rooftops of the Old Town, the meandering fjord, and the pine-clad mountains beyond. On the way up, you will pass the tiny Crkva Gospe od Zdravlja (Church of Our Lady of Health), built in the 16th century to protect Kotor against the plague. Be sure to wear good walking shoes and take plenty of water. The route up starts from behind the east side of the city walls. ✉ *Above Old Town.*

Zgrada Napoleonovog pozorišta (*Napoléon Theatre Building*). Standing in the north corner of the Square of Arms, this building was turned into a public theater, one of the first of its kind in the Balkans, by the French in 1810. Today, following extensive renovation work, it is part of the upmarket Hotel Cattaro. ✉ *Trg od Oružja, Stari Grad.*

WHERE TO EAT

$$ SEAFOOD

✕ **Galion.** Serving creative twists on local food, such as beetroot risotto with sheep cheese or tuna ceviche, this sophisticated restaurant occupies an old stone building with a glass-and-steel winter terrace extension. It's a five-minute walk along the coast from the Old Town. **Known for:** great locale with views of both the Old Town and the sea; the signature mille-feuille cakes; creative takes on traditional dishes. [$] *Average main: €13* ✉ *Šuranj BB* ☎ *032/325–054.*

$$ ECLECTIC

✕ **Hotel Astoria Restaurant.** The restaurant and bar housed in this 13th-century town house fuse ancient and modern, Montenegrin and international, in a setting dominated by a tree set within the main room, its branches spreading out across the ceiling. A light menu offers both Mediterranean and Asian dishes, and—a welcome opportunity for diners in Kotor who don't eat fish—some vegetarian and meat dishes. **Known for:** exuberant eclecticism in decor and menu; great location; Mediterranean and Asian menu with veggie and meat options. [$] *Average main: €13* ✉ *322, Stari Grad* 🌐 *www.astoriamontenegro.com.*

$$ SEAFOOD

✕ **Konoba Scala Santa.** The look at this Old Town eatery is rustic, but this is one of the best places in town for lobster, excellent mussels, and fresh fish, such as simple barbecued *zubatac* (dentex) drizzled with olive oil and served with a wedge of lemon. The candlelit dining room has exposed stone walls, a wood-beam ceiling hung with fishing equipment, and a big open fireplace. **Known for:** oldest tavern in the Old Town; great Montenegrin seafood dishes; big open fireplace and outdoor dining in the summer. [$] *Average main: €12* ✉ *Trg od Salate* ☎ *067/393–458.*

$$$ MEDITERRANEAN

✕ **Luna Rossa.** Choosing one of the al fresco dining opportunities in Kotor's charming squares is tricky, but the Luna Rossa restaurant, housed in an attractive 13th-century stone building, offers a spectacular location and tastily prepared fish dishes. Choose between the rooftop café offering a bird's-eye view of the town or seating in the square. **Known for:** fresh fish; great location; rooftop café with bird's-eye views. [$] *Average main: €18* ✉ *423, Stari Grad.*

WHERE TO STAY

$$$ HOTEL

Hotel Astoria. In the heart of the Old Town the quirky Hotel Astoria and its restaurant, housed in a 13th-century town house, are a breath of fresh air amid the blander options available elsewhere in the center of Kotor. **Pros:** creative design; central location. **Cons:** expensive for its category; the huge fleshy murals of Adam and Eve in the public restaurant may not be to everyone's taste. *Rooms from: €195 ✉ Kotor 322, Stari Grad 🌐 www.astoriamontenegro.com 9 rooms 🍽 Breakfast.*

$$ HOTEL **Hotel Cattaro.** This solid old hotel is as magically central as it gets, occupying the 19th-century Napoléon Theatre, the 18th-century Duke's Palace, and other historic buildings on the Old Town's main square. **Pros:** located in Old Town; historic building. **Cons:** expensive; slightly lacking in charm; tends to book up. *Rooms from: €139 ✉ Trg od Oružja BB, Stari Grad ☎ 032/311–000 🌐 www.cattarohotel.com 19 rooms 🍽 Breakfast.*

$$ HOTEL **Hotel Monte Cristo.** The family-run Hotel Monte Cristo, housed in a 13th-century building once the home of the first Bishop of Kotor, offers reasonably priced accommodation in the heart of the Old Town. **Pros:** location; on-site restaurant. **Cons:** its position in the midst of Old Town café life can make it noisy at night; no elevator or step-free access. *Rooms from: €120 ✉ 423-424, Stari Grad 12 rooms 🍽 Breakfast; Some meals.*

$$ HOTEL **Hotel Splendido.** With splendid views over the fjord, this white stone, 200-year-old villa sits amid oleander on the waterfront in Prčanj, 3 km (2 miles) from Kotor. **Pros:** lovely old building; away from the hustle of Kotor Old Town; pool area, private beach, seaside terrace dining. **Cons:** outside Kotor; stark decor; private beach is small. *Rooms from: €117 ✉ Glavati BB, Prcanj ☎ 032/301–700, 032/336–246 🌐 www.splendido-hotel.com 43 rooms 🍽 Breakfast.*

$$ HOTEL **Hotel Vardar.** Described as the only soundproofed place to stay in the Old Town, the Hotel Vardar is centrally located, some rooms having a view of the lovely main square where the hotel's restaurant offers a chance for people-watching in the shade of sun umbrellas. **Pros:** Old Town location; soundproofing; stylish bathrooms. **Cons:** even full soundproofing can't guarantee a night free of local bars' music; no twin rooms; breakfast area is in a dark separate restaurant from the terrace. *Rooms from: €139 ✉ Stari Grad 476 🌐 www.hotelvardar.com 25 rooms 🍽 Breakfast.*

$$$ HOTEL Fodor's Choice ★ **Palazzo Radomiri.** The owners of this family-run boutique hotel were inspired by local sea captains bringing back treasure from around the world and the rooms; suites in the hotel's three 18th-century stone buildings are named after ships in the fleet belonging to the original owners, and are furnished with antiques. **Pros:** lovely old building; tastefully furnished; good sports facilities. **Cons:** outside Kotor; stairs and steps throughout make access difficult; often full in summer. *Rooms from: €180 ✉ Dobrota 221, 4 km (2 miles) from Kotor ☎ 032/333–172 🌐 www.palazzoradomiri.com ⊗ Closed mid-Oct.–mid-Apr. 10 rooms 🍽 Breakfast.*

SHOPPING

Market. This market that sells fruit and vegetables is just outside the city walls (on the main coastal road) and is filled with colorful, local, seasonal produce laid out on marble slabs: artichokes, asparagus, and cherries in spring; tomatoes, eggplants, and peaches in summer, alongside pots of the tiny local mountain strawberries. It's also a great place to buy the local dried porcini mushrooms. It takes place every day. ✉ *Kotor* ✥ *E65 runs all the way down the coast. The market is on the roadside, immediately outside the Old Town walls.*

SPORTS AND THE OUTDOORS

BEACHES

The small pebble Gradska Plaža (Town Beach), just outside the town walls, is fine for a quick dip after a hot day of sightseeing.

SAILING

Several charter companies are based in the protected waters of Kotor Bay. For a one-week trip in August, expect to pay €2,500 for a 40-foot sailboat sleeping six, plus €130 per day for a skipper; prices do not include food, fuel, or mooring fees. Early booking (e.g., by February for the summer) will offer worthwhile discounts. Montenegro Charter Company offers one-day sailing trips (with skipper) on a private yacht around Kotor Bay.

The former military shipyard in Tivat, 5 km (3 miles) away, has been totally renovated and reopened as Porto Montenegro, a luxury marina, able to accommodate some of the world's largest super-yachts.

Montenegro Charter Company. ✉ *Bulevar Sv. Petra Cetinjskog 92, Podgorica* ☎ *067/201–655 (mobile)* 🌐 *www.montenegrocharter.com.*

PERAST

15 km (9 miles) from Kotor.

Tiny Perast is a peaceful bayfront village of stone villas set in gardens filled with fig trees and oleander. It was built by wealthy local sea captains during the 17th and 18th centuries, at a time when it was prosperous enough to have some 100 merchant ships navigating the oceans. In fact, Perast's naval skills were so respected that in the early 18th century, the Russian czar, Peter the Great, sent his young officers to study at the Perast Maritime Academy.

In the bay in front of Perast lie its main attractions: Sveti Djordje (St. George) and Gospa od Skrpjela (Our Lady of the Rock), a pair of tiny, charming islets, each topped with a church. Perast has no beach to speak of, though swimming and sunbathing are possible from the jetties along the waterfront.

Each year on July 22, Perast celebrates the *fasinada,* a local festival honoring the folkloric origins of Our Lady of the Rock, with a ritual procession of boats carrying stones out to the island at sunset. The stones are dropped into the water around the island, protecting it from erosion by the sea for the coming year. The Fasinada Cup sailing regatta is held on the same day.

GETTING HERE AND AROUND

Perast can be reached by car or bus and can also be visited on an organized half-day boat trip from Kotor's harbor. ■ TIP→ **There are no ATMs in Perast, so get cash out in Kotor or elsewhere before you arrive.**

EXPLORING

Begin your exploration with a look in the Perast Town Museum, then take a taxi-boat from the quayside to visit the island church, Our Lady of the Rock. Head back to town for lunch at one of the area's charming rustic eateries.

The islands of Gospa od Škrpjela (Our Lady of the Rock) and Sveti Djordje (St. George). St. George's is a natural island but its sibling, Our Lady of the Rock, is man-made. Folklore has it that in 1452, local sailors found an icon depicting the Virgin and Child cast upon a rock jutting up from the water. Taking this as a sign from God, they began placing stones on and around the rock, slowly building an island over it. By 1630 they had erected a church upon the new island. The original icon, which has been attributed to the 15th-century local artist Lovro Dobričević, is displayed on the altar. Over the centuries, locals have paid their respects to it by donating silver votive offerings, some 2,500 of which are now on display.

The other island, home to the Monastery of St. George and dating back to the 12th century, is still inhabited by monks and closed to the public. In the 18th century the island became a favorite burial place for local sea captains, whose crypts remain today. **TIP→ Though closed to the public, you can snap photos from shore or neighboring Our Lady of the Rock to your heart's content.**

To visit Our Lady of the Rock, hop on a taxi-boat from the waterfront (a five-minute trip that costs €5 round-trip. The Ship Travel Dado boats run there April to October. (☎ *069/045–262* 🌐 *www.shiptravel-dado.co.me*, *shiptravel-dado@t-com.me*). ✉ *Kotor Bay* ☎ *069/045–262 for Kotor tourist office.*

Muzej Grad Perasta. In the 17th-century Renaissance-Baroque Bujović Palace, on the water's edge, Muzej Grad Perasta (Perast Town Museum) displays paintings of local sea captains and their ships, plus a horde of objects connected to Perast's maritime past. ✉ *Obala Marka Martinovića BB* ☎ *032/373–519* 🌐 *www.muzejperast.me* 🎫 *€2.50.*

Roman Mosaics at Risan. These beautiful mosaics are from a 2nd-century house in a small excavation site that is worth a brief stop if you are in the area. Particularly charming is the mosaic depicting Hypnos, the Roman god of sleep. Tour guides are available, as well as detailed information panels in many languages. ✉ *Risan BB, Risan* ☎ *032/371–233* 🌐 *www.risanmosaics.me* 🎫 *€3* ⏲ *Closed after 3 pm Dec.–Apr.*

WHERE TO EAT

$$$$ ✕ **Ćatovića Mlini.** For 20 years, this charming, family-run and child-friendly restaurant has occupied a former water-driven flour mill and has long been a favorite with locals. With the millstream and lots of shade, this is the perfect place to cool off on hot days, and kids love the miniature bridges over the water. **Known for:** family-friendly; historic building; excellent menu. 💲 *Average main: €25* ✉ *Morinj BB* ☎ *032/373–030* 🌐 *www.catovicamlini.com.*

SEAFOOD
FAMILY

$$ MEDITERRANEAN **Stari Mlini.** This rustic old mill on the Ljuta River, 7 km (4 miles) down the coastal road from Perast, dates back to 1670 and has been run by the current family for 40 years. The restaurant offers excellent food with an emphasis on fish (you can visit the restaurant's own trout ponds set in the attractive grounds). **Known for:** spectacular sea views; excellent local almond cake specialty; located in a historic mill. *Average main: €16 Ljuta BB, Kotor 032/333–555 www.starimlini.com.*

WHERE TO STAY

$$ HOTEL **Restaurant and Hotel Conte.** These four stone buildings dating from the 15th and 16th centuries have been tastefully converted into well-appointed apartments, some with kitchens and one with a Jacuzzi. **Pros:** lovely old building; tastefully furnished; good restaurant. **Cons:** Muzak in the restaurant. *Rooms from: €125 Obala Kapitana Martka Martinovica 067/257–387 www.hotel-conte.me 18 rooms.*

SVETI STEFAN

Often referred to as the "jewel of the Montenegrin coast," Sveti Stefan is a tiny island protected by 600-year-old defensive walls inside of which nestle several dozen limestone cottages and a small church. The island is actually joined to the mainland by a causeway, with a gravel beach on each side. Originally a fishing village, it was fortified with sturdy walls in the 15th century to protect it from the Turks and marauding pirates. By the late 19th century, however, many residents had emigrated abroad, due to the poor local economy. In 1955, the few remaining inhabitants were relocated so that the entire village could be renovated and turned into a unique luxury hotel. The resort opened with a splash in 1960, attracting over the years international jet-setters and celebrities, from Richard Burton and Elizabeth Taylor to Claudia Schiffer and Sylvester Stallone. But when the war hit in the 1990s, tourists stopped coming and the economy took a nosedive, leading Sveti Stefan to fall into total disrepair. Now, after years of exhaustive renovation, it has reopened as the Aman Sveti Stefan, an exclusive resort of luxury suites.

GETTING HERE AND AROUND

Sveti Stefan is only about 9 km (5 miles) from Budva so accessible by taxi if Budva is your base. Buses between Petrovac and Budva run along the main road above the resort. A scramble down the steps that lead past the houses and private land owned by families in the village takes you—more directly than the winding road for cars—to the public beach with the picture-postcard view of the island.

WHERE TO EAT

$$ MEDITERRANEAN **Restaurant Drago.** This small family-run restaurant has been specializing in seafood since 1967. Set on the mainland hillside overlooking the sea, Restaurant Drago has a large terrace at the front, wonderful ocean views, and perfect sight lines to the fairy-tale island hotel, Aman Sveti Stefan. **Known for:** wonderful views; delicious local seafood; warm staff. *Average main: €10 Slobode 32 069/032–050 viladrago.com/restaurant Closed Nov.–Mar.*

WHERE TO STAY

$$$$ HOTEL Fodor's Choice ★ **Aman Sveti Stefan.** Connected to the mainland by a narrow causeway, the glamorous Aman Sveti Stefan, is a small village of cobblestone lanes, quaint courtyards, and hand-restored medieval stone cottages with terra-cotta tile roofs, all within 15th-century defensive walls. **Pros:** historic buildings; stunning island location; modern interior design. **Cons:** some rooms have small windows and can be rather dark; very expensive; beaches are gravel. *Rooms from: €971 Sveti Stefan Island, Budva 033/420–000 www.amanresorts.com/aman-sveti-stefan Island closed mid-Oct.–Apr.; Vila Miločer remains open. 58 rooms Breakfast; All meals.*

$ HOTEL **Vila Drago.** This friendly family-run hotel has an unbeatable location and thoughtful touches (a free bottle of wine in your room and beach towels), but the real draw here are the unbeatable views of the magical Sveti Stefan. **Pros:** great location; all but two rooms have views of Sveti Stefan; nice extra touches. **Cons:** gravel beaches; Aman Sveti Stefan dominates the cultural landscape. *Rooms from: €40 Slobode 32 068/514–874 viladrago.com 8 rooms Breakfast.*

UNDERSTANDING CROATIA

A SHORT HISTORY OF CROATIA

CROATIAN VOCABULARY

A SHORT HISTORY OF CROATIA

The Early History of the Croatian Lands

The three main regions that form Croatia today are known as Slavonia, Dalmatia, and Croatia proper (the inland region also known as Civil Croatia). These have also been called the "Triune Kingdom." In addition, the ethnically mixed Istrian peninsula is now considered Croatian territory. Bosnia-Herzegovina has a mixed population and once had a pronounced regional identity, but some Croat nationalists consider it their territory.

Even before the influx of the Slavs between AD 500 and 800, the region of Croatia had a long history. The Illyrians and Thracians were originally at home there, and traces of Hellenistic and Celtic influences can also be seen. From the 3rd century BC to the 1st century AD, Rome controlled the Balkans; indeed, at times Croatian history was closely tied to Roman politics, even though it was hardly a central province of the far-flung empire. For instance, the well-known Emperor Diocletian (AD 284–305) was from Dalmatia, as were four other emperors. After his reign, Diocletian returned to his native Split, where he built a large palace. The city of Pula also contains many important Roman sites dating from this time.

Rome's influence on the Croatian lands has been far-reaching. The Romans developed the region's basic infrastructure and industries related to mining and metallurgy. The Croatian coast was established as an outpost of European high culture; this connection was soon strengthened by the Croats' conversion to Christianity and later by ties to the Renaissance city-states of Italy, especially Venice. The Italian influence can be felt even today, particularly in the Istrian peninsula and on some of the islands.

As the Empire was divided into its eastern and western halves, the internal frontier came to symbolize for many the "fault line" between Latin culture and Roman Catholicism, on the one hand, and Greek culture and Orthodox Christianity, on the other. The division was actually always quite porous and inexact, but its nature changed during the Ottoman Turkish invasions starting in the 14th century. Islam again became one of the major religions of Europe, and new ethnic groups arrived or were created in the former Byzantine lands.

Despite the fact that the Croatian lands clearly belonged to Rome's sphere of influence, the Croatian culture went through some complicated developments after the fall of the western portion of the Roman Empire in AD 476. First, many Croats—like their neighbors, the Slovenes—had been converted to Christianity by Frankish (or "German") missionaries from Charlemagne's Holy Roman Empire. Second, Croatian monks working in Dalmatia developed a unique alphabet, known as Glagolitic, from contact with Orthodox missionaries. Croatia remained Catholic after the official religious break between Rome and Constantinople in 1054, but the Glagolitic alphabet was used in some places into the 19th century, serving to reinforce Croatian identity amidst various political and ethnic rivalries. Finally, the Ottoman occupation of the Balkans made much of Croatia into a contested region of population flux and the new cultural norms associated with being a "bulwark of Christendom."

The first independent Croatian state was formed by the leader Tomislav. In 924 he was crowned king of Croatia and recognized by the pope. Although historians disagree over the exact extent of his territory, Tomislav did set another important precedent as well: he united many regions of the former Roman provinces of Dalmatia and Pannonia (central Croatia and Slavonia). The national symbols of the kuna (currency denomination) and šahovnica (red-and-white checkerboard coat of arms) originated at this time.

Croatia in the High Middle Ages

By 1102 the royal line had died out, and the Sabor (assembly of nobles) accepted Hungarian rule. Croatia preserved its own laws and customs through the Pacta Conventa, which seems to have been essentially a personal union between the countries, not an annexation. Medieval Croatia also achieved considerable cultural heights. The first known writing in Croatian dates from around 1100, on a stone tablet from the island of Krk, known as the Baščanska Ploča. In the 16th century, Dubrovnik dramatist and poet Ivan Gundulić (1555–1638) wrote *Osman* in the Croatian language to inspire resistance to the Turks. Croatia's unique literary history had begun. Dubrovnik also boasted major scientists and composers. Soon there were three major outside forces contending for Croatian territory: the Ottoman Empire, the Kingdom of Hungary, and the Venetian Republic. The Venetians quickly displaced rivals such as the Byzantine Empire and the kingdoms of Serbia and Bosnia. A major blow came in 1202, when Venice directed the Fourth Crusade to sack the important port of Zadar.

The Ottoman expansion into Europe reached Hungary in 1526; Sultan Suleiman defeated Hungary's King Lajos at Mohacs. The Croatian nobles had already been defeated at Udbina in 1493. Ottoman rule would last for 150 years, but the Hungarian and Croatian nobility quickly opted for personal union with the royal Habsburg family in Vienna. In 1593 the Croats stemmed the tide of Turkish invasion by the successful defense of the fortress-city of Sisak, but intense fighting in the area continued until the Treaty of Karlowitz in 1699. That momentous agreement removed most of Croatia and Hungary from Ottoman sovereignty, and Habsburg rule continued.

The wealthy city-state of Dubrovnik retained its independence until Napoléon's invasion of 1797. Bosnia-Herzegovina, home to many Croats and other groups, would remain under Ottoman rule until 1878. As central Croatia was liberated by the crusading Habsburgs, they created a military frontier zone that is often known by its Croatian (and Serbian) name of Vojna Krajina. The frontier included the Lika region south of Zagreb and stretched all along the southern periphery of the Empire from Italy to Romania. The Austrians recruited Serbs and other groups into the area, adding new minority groups to the Croatian lands.

The nobility, or landowning class, of Croatia played the key role in developments over the next several centuries. Croatia's basic feudal structure was preserved by the Habsburgs, although some nobles from the Zrinski and Frankapan families were executed for plotting against Vienna. The country also remained overwhelmingly Catholic; Catholic scholars working in Venice and Rome also produced the earliest dictionaries and grammars of the Croatian language. These trends stand in sharp contrast to the neighboring Serb lands, where Ottoman rule removed nearly all traces of the traditional elites. The Croat nobles resented Vienna for its attempts at centralization and its territorial compromises with the Ottomans. At times the Croats gravitated, culturally and politically, toward outside powers that could provide leverage in their struggle against Vienna: Russia, France, and even at times their own erstwhile foes the Venetians and the Ottomans.

The Croatian National Revival

The remaining Croatian nobility was revived as a political "nation" by the enlightened despotism of one of the most iconoclastic of the Habsburg emperors, Joseph II (r. 1780–90). Joseph's modernizing vision involved centralization of power in Vienna and, to some extent, Germanization. Both of these processes elicited strong negative reactions around the Empire, where traditional autonomy existed in many areas. In Croatia it was the nobility who responded with alarm both to Joseph and to the excesses of the French Revolution. Many in the Croatian elite chose to strengthen ties with Hungary, forming a political party known as the Unionists, or Magyarones, a term corresponding basically to "Hungarophiles."

In 1809 the invading Napoléon created a short-lived satellite state out of conquered Habsburg lands called the Illyrian Provinces. This state abolished feudalism and turned local administration, including language policy, over to the Croats and Slovenes. These actions increased popular awareness of Croatian nationality. It was from these two starting points—both of them reactions to external events—that the tortured development of modern, mass nationalism in Croatia began.

The Magyarone solution soon became problematic as Hungary gradually increased its control over the Croatian lands decade by decade. Croats, now alienated from both Vienna and Budapest, began to react in various new ways. Of considerable importance was the Illyrian Movement, which was at once a Croatian national movement and a kind of supra-national forerunner of Yugoslavism. Its chief exponent was the writer and editor Ljudevit Gaj, who helped establish the basis for the modern Croatian language. The Illyrians espoused political cooperation among the Slovenes, Serbs, and Croats within the framework of the Habsburg Empire; they were basically federalists and did not seek an independent nation-state just for Croats. The National Party, led by Bishop Josip Strossmayer, revived Illyrianism in the form of Yugoslavism and also greatly enriched Croatian cultural life by founding the Yugoslav Academy of Sciences and the modern University of Zagreb.

In 1848, nationalism and liberalism brought major insurrections across Europe. Although Hungary rebelled, the Croats remained loyal to Vienna. In the middle of the 19th century, the Croatian political scene was dominated by an important figure named Josip Jelačić (1801–59), an Austrian military officer and a convinced Illyrianist. In 1848 the Habsburgs turned to him to help defeat the nationalist uprising in Hungary. He succeeded and managed to unite nearly all Croatian territory under Austrian rule. He also abolished feudalism and promoted Croatian interests on major cultural issues. Although Jelačić is a Croatian hero today, he also propounded a progressive version of nationality based on regional rather than ethnic identity. The long-reigning Emperor Franz Josef tried to placate the Hungarians by issuing the Ausgleich (Compromise) in 1867, breaking the empire in two and renaming it "Austria-Hungary." The Croats wisely negotiated their own version of the Ausgleich, known as the Nagodba, in 1868.

Into the Great War: From Habsburgs to Yugoslavs

This arrangement gave the Croats, at last, a considerable degree of internal autonomy, and Croatia even had representatives in the Hungarian parliament and cabinet and also in Vienna. But it also provided for the Croatian territories to be split up again, with control over Dalmatia and Istria going to Vienna while Slavonia and central Croatia were under the Hungarian crown. In addition, the major port of Rijeka was run as a separate entity by Budapest.

These final Habsburg decades were turbulent. Territorial divisions wounded Croatian pride and hindered economic development. Hungarian manipulation of the political scene and attempts at Magyarization continued. Count Károly Khuen-Hédervàry ruled from 1883 to 1903 and became notorious for setting Croatia's Serbian and ethnic Croatian populations against each other. Despite his tactics and the turmoil of World War I, the Serbs and Croats of Croatia actually achieved a considerable level of political cooperation. They succeeded in forming coalitions to push for reunification of the Croatian lands and to oppose misrule from both Budapest and Vienna.

In 1918, with the Habsburg Empire vanquished, a combination of factors induced Croatian politicians to lead their country into the new Kingdom of Serbs, Croats, and Slovenes (called Yugoslavia after 1929). By 1921 many Croats grew suspicious of the new state, run from Belgrade by the Serbian king. Many political parties, as well as the *ban* (viceroys) and the Sabor, were suppressed. Royal legitimacy was shaky: Serbs dominated the police, military, and economy; agriculture, the mainstay of the economy, languished; and Italy retained possession of large amounts of Croatian territory in Istria and Dalmatia. Stjepan Radić, the leader of the powerful Croatian Peasant Party, alternately boycotted and negotiated with the central government; his murder in 1928 fueled radicalism in Croatia.

As World War II approached, Belgrade grew more willing to compromise with Croatia. A 1939 arrangement known as the Sporazum restored the ban and Sabor and combined many Croatian lands into one autonomous unit. But war broke out just weeks later.

World War II and the Second Yugoslavia

The darkest chapter in Croatian history took place amidst the chaos of World War II. An interwar political agitator on the fascist right, Ante Pavelić (1889–1959) rose to power and ruled the "Independent State of Croatia" for 49 bloody months.

Pavelić, who founded the Ustaša (insurrectionist) movement in 1929, originally developed his ideas within the tradition of the Croatian Party of Right. This group, founded by Ante Starčević (1823–96) in 1861, advocated the creation of a greater Croatia, including Bosnia-Herzegovina. They believed that Bosnian Muslims (today's Bosniaks) and Serbs were ethnic Croats who had been forced to adopt other faiths. Pavelić developed ties with similar movements in Nazi Germany, Bulgaria, Hungary, and especially Mussolini's Italy. The Ustaša helped assassinate King Aleksandar in 1934. The most revolutionary aspects of the Ustaša movement were their willingness to use terror and genocide against minorities in order to form an ethnically "pure" Croatian state and their desire to create a mass political movement that displaced the established elites in the country. Mussolini's army installed Pavelić's government in Zagreb after the Axis invasion of 1941, and the Nazis agreed to let Pavelić rule. Croatia was immediately split into two spheres of influence. The Ustaša were unpopular, but they ruled by terror over a population that included vast numbers of non-Croatians, especially Serbs. The Germans were increasingly disconcerted by the Ustaša's murderous policies, which spawned significant resistance movements. The main German goal in the region was simply the extraction of mineral and agricultural wealth. In all, the Ustaša government killed more than 300,000 Serbs, along with tens of thousands of Jews and Roma (Gypsies). In addition to a number of concentration camps like the notorious Jasenovac east of Zagreb—where about 85,000 people, mostly Serbs, were killed—many horrific rural massacres occurred. Pavelić's state was a failure; the communist Partisans and the Chetniks (Serbian royalists) actually controlled much of its territory.

Yugoslavia was reconstituted after World War II, this time under the rule of Josip Broz Tito (1892–1980), a communist born in Croatia. The trauma of World War II was the main reason for decades of "Croatian silence" in Yugoslavia. In 1967, leading cultural and academic figures broke ranks with the party and publicly asserted the distinctiveness and legitimacy of the Croatian language. This was divisive, because it ran counter to the official embrace of a common "Croato-Serbian" or "Serbo-Croatian" language and culture.

A period of dissent and crackdown known as the "Croatian Spring" followed. There were demonstrations, strikes, and many debates in print about Yugoslavia's political discrimination and economic exploitation. This lasted until 1972, and resulted in Tito's sidelining numerous prominent Croatian communists, including many who could have provided cosmopolitan, intelligent alternatives to both communism and what came after. This repression belies the fact that Tito's regime became, after 1952, the most liberal socialist state in Eastern Europe; in addition, the LCY (League of Communists of Yugoslavia) was not averse to using the nationalism of some Yugoslav peoples (such as the Bosnians, the Macedonians, and the Albanians of Kosovo) to further its agenda—just not Croatian nationalism.

Famous political figures in Croatia in the postwar period included Tito, of course, but also his close ally Vladimir Bakarić, who held a number of important governmental posts. Franjo Tuđman, a communist Partisan officer during World War II and then a historian, was jailed several times for questioning centralist orthodoxy on national issues. The poet Vlado Gotovac, who again became a pro-democracy dissident under President Tuđman in the 1990s, was purged in the Croatian Spring, and the philosophers Milan Kangrga and Rudi Supek of the countrywide Praxis movement attracted attention and official disfavor with their alternative analyses of Marx.

Despite significant grievances, Croatia underwent considerable modernization under communist rule. There were increases in industrialization, urbanization, life expectancy, standard of living, and literacy. New universities were founded in Split, Rijeka, and Osijek. Croatia's beaches became famous across Europe. The economy was also helped by the large numbers of Croats who worked abroad as *Gastarbeiter* (guest workers), but heavy emmigration and low birth rates left many worried about the country's demographic future.

Both Serbia and Croatia felt the heavy hand of Tito's rule; as the most powerful traditional nations in Yugoslavia, Tito neutralized their ability to rock the federal boat. The LCY encouraged nation-building, however, in Bosnia, Macedonia, Montenegro, and among the Albanians of Kosovo both as a counterweight to Croatian and Serbian ambitions and as a developmental strategy.

From Tito to Tuđman and Beyond: Sovereign Croatia

Historians disagree over when Yugoslavia passed the point of no return. At some point in the decade between Tito's death in 1980 and the momentous political changes in Slovenia and Croatia by 1991, the breakup actually began. In 1990, Slovenia and Croatia held free, multiparty elections, declared their sovereignty, and held referenda in which they overwhelmingly approved the idea of independence. But even then the eventual violence was not inevitable. Two highly regarded Croatian reformist politicians, Ante Marković and Stjepan Mesić, were stymied in their efforts to place the Yugoslav federation on a new foundation. What soon exploded were not the so-called ancient ethnic hatreds but rather the aggressive and conflicting aims of various political factions competing in a superheated environment. This violence was furthered by the egoism of conniving politicians, sensationalism in the media, and mixed signals from Western Europe and the United States.

The 1980s had been extremely tense across the country. Serbs and Albanians clashed in Kosovo; hyperinflation, unemployment, public debt, and strikes characterized a ruined economy; and the fall of the Berlin Wall marked the end of other European socialist states. The rise of the dictator Slobodan Milošević in Serbia brought new levels of confrontation to politics and revealed gross Serbian manipulation of the economy. Croats and Slovenes gradually realized that Yugoslavia was unworkable as a country. The Serbian population, incited by ambitious politicians, lashed out at Croat police in the spring of 1991. Thus, even before Croatia's declaration of independence on June 25, 1991, the villages of Pakrac and Borovo Selo became scenes of bitter bloodshed, as did the famed Plitvice Lakes National Park and other areas in central Croatia. There were about 600,000 Serbs living in Croatia, over 12% of the population. The new Croatian government, led by the now-nationalist Tuđman, was brash in its treatment of minorities and irresponsible in its handling of the legacy of World War II, and these approaches greatly increased Serbs' anxiety.

After secession, full-scale fighting broke out. The autumn of 1991 saw two shocking sieges: the bloody street-fighting and massacres at Vukovar in Slavonia and the weeks-long shelling of venerable Dubrovnik for no legitimate military purpose. The contemporary Croatian poet Slavko Mihalić described this era as one in which the Serbian leader—"the one who sends the bombs"—grimly and accurately promised to turn Croatia into a "national park of death." In fact Milošević was willing to let Croatia secede but without its Serb-inhabited regions; later, he and Tuđman agreed on how to partition Bosnia-Herzegovina as well. In May 1992 the war spread to independence-minded Bosnia, where 200,000 people died, many of them civilians, and 2 million were made homeless. In Croatia, 10,000 people were killed and over a fourth of the country fell to the Serbs. Large numbers of Croats and Bosnians were driven from their homes with terror campaigns of "ethnic cleansing." With American aid, Croatian forces rallied in the summer of 1995 and recaptured Slavonia and the Krajina region. Many thousands of Serbs fled and property issues remain unresolved. Croatian forces also committed atrocities in Bosnia-Herzegovina, but most of the international community finally recognized that the lion's share of guilt for the wars themselves belonged to the Serbian government. The Dayton Peace Agreement of late 1995, backed by NATO's military might, paved the way for Serbian withdrawal from Croatia and Bosnia.

President Tuđman was roundly criticized internationally for his authoritarian tendencies and overzealous nationalism. Internal opposition grew as well, especially over his censorship and policies in Bosnia. Tuđman allowed political parties other than the HDZ (Croatian Democratic Union), but they were weak until his death in December 1999. Since then, Mesić has been president, and the prime ministership has been held by both the Social Democrats of Ivica Račan and the revived HDZ of Ivo Šanader. Since Tuđman's death, Croatia has begun serious cooperation with The Hague war-crimes tribunal. Many other reforms have also succeeded, but open questions include the quest for autonomy by the ethnically and historically distinct region of Istria and Croatia's ability to cooperate on a variety of issues with its neighbors. Most Croats still look forward to joining the European Union in the next several years. *—John K. Cox, Associate Professor of History, Wheeling Jesuit University*

CROATIAN VOCABULARY

BASICS

ENGLISH	CROATIAN	PRONUNCIATION
Yes/no	Da/ne	dah/neh
Please	Molim (vas)	**moh**-leem (vahs)
Thank you (very much)	Hvala (lijepo)	**hvah**-lah (lyeh-poh)
Excuse me	Oprostite	oh-proh-stee-teh
Hello	Zdravo	**zdrah**-voh
I'm sorry.	Žao mi je.	**zhah**-oh mee yeh
Do you speak English?	Da li govorite engleski?	Dah lee **goh**-voh-ree-teh **ehn**-glehs-kee?
I don't understand.	Ne razumijem.	neh rah- **zoo**-myehm
Please show me ...	Molim vas pokažite mi ...	moh-leem vahs **poh**-kah-zhee-teh mee
I am American (m/f).	Ja sam yah sahm Amerikanac/ Amerikanka	**ah**-meh-ree-kah-nahts/ **ah**-meh-ree-kahn-kah
My name is ...	Zovem se ...	**zoh**-vehm seh
Right/left	Desno/Lijevo	**dehs**-noh/ **lyeh**-voh
Open/closed	Otvoreno/zatvoreno	**oh**-tvoh-reh-noh/ **zah**-tvoh-reh-noh
Where is ... ?	Gdje je ... ?	gdyeh yeh
... the train station?	... željeznička?	**zheh**-lehz-neech-kah
... the bus stop?	... autobusna?	**ahoo**-toh-boos-nah
... the airport?	... aerodrom?	**ah**-eh-roh-drohm
... the post office?	... pošta?	**posh**-tah
... the bank?	... banka?	**bahn**-kah
Here/there	Ovdje/tamo	**ohv**-dyeh/ **tah**-moh
I would like... (m/f)	Molim (vas) htio/ htjela bih...	hteeoh/htyeh-lah beeh
How much does it cost?	Koliko košta?	**koh**-lee-koh **kosh**-tah
Postcard	Razglednica	**rahz**-gleh-dnee-tsah
Help!	Upomoć!	**oo**-poh-moch

	ENGLISH	CROATIAN	PRONUNCIATION
NUMBERS			
	One	Jedan	**yeh**-dahn
	Two	Dvad	vah
	Three	Tri	tree
	Four	Četiri	**cheh**-tee-ree
	Five	Pet	peht
	Six	Šest	shest
	Seven	Sedam	**seh**-dahm
	Eight	Osam	**oh**-sahm
	Nine	Devet	**deh**-veht
	Ten	Deset	**deh**-seht
	One hundred	Sto	stoh
	One thousand	Tisuća	**tee**-soo-chah
DAYS OF THE WEEK			
	Sunday	Nedjelja	**neh**-dyeh-lyah
	Monday	Ponedjeljak	**poh**-neh-dyeh-lyahk
	Tuesday	Utorak	**oo**-toh-rahk
	Wednesday	Srijeda	**sryeh**-dah
	Thursday	Četvrtak	**cheht**-vruh-tahk
	Friday	Petak	**peh**-tahk
	Saturday	Subota	**soo**-boh-tah
WHERE TO SLEEP			
	A room	Soba	**soh**-bah
	The key	Ključ	klyooch
	With bath/shower	S kupaonicom/tušem	suh koo-pah- **oh**-nee-tsohm/ **too**-shehm
FOOD			
	A restaurant	Restoran	rehs- **toh**-rahn
	The menu	Jelovnik	yeh- **lohv**-neek
	The check, please.	Molim, račun.	**moh**-leem, **rah**-choon
	Can I order, please?	Mogu li naručiti, molim vas?	**moh**-goo lee nah- **roo**-chee tee, **moh**-leem vahs

ENGLISH	CROATIAN	PRONUNCIATION
Breakfast	Doručak	**doh**-roo-chahk
Lunch	Ručak	**roo**-chahk
Dinner	Večera	**veh**-cheh-rah
Bread	Kruh	krooh
Butter	Putar/maslac	**poo**-tahr/mahs-lahts
Salt/pepper	Sol/papar	sohl/ **pah**-pahr
Wine	Vino	**vee**-noh
Beer	Pivo	**pee**-voh
Water/mineral water	Voda/mineralna voda	**voh**-dah/ **mee** neh rahl-nah **voh**-dah
Milk	Mlijeko	**mlyeh**-koh
Coffee	Kava	**kah**-vah
Tea	Čaj	chay

TRAVEL SMART CROATIA

GETTING HERE AND AROUND

AIR TRAVEL

Flying time from London to Zagreb is 2 hours 30 minutes, from Prague to Zagreb it is 90 minutes, and from Warsaw it is 1 hour 40 minutes.

Flying time from Bratislava to Dubrovnik is 85 minutes and from Budapest to Dubrovnik is 75 minutes.

Domestic air tickets in Croatia are best purchased online. Airports in both countries have offices for the national airlines (Croatian Airlines in Croatia), but their opening hours are unreliable, and attempting to purchase a ticket at the airport may backfire. The national airline also has a usable website where e-tickets can be purchased.

Skyscanner. A flight comparison website that searches all airlines, destinations, and dates. 🌐 *www.skyscanner.com.*

AIRPORTS

There are airports in Dubrovnik (DBV), Osijek (OSI), Pula (PUY), Rijeka (RJK), Split (SPU), Zadar (ZAD), and Zagreb (ZAG). You can fly direct to all of them year-round from international destinations, although in winter most international flights go to Zagreb.

Information Dubrovnik Airport. ☎ *020/773–100* 🌐 *www.airport-dubrovnik.hr.* **Osijek Airport.** ☎ *031/284–611* 🌐 *www.osijek-airport.hr.* **Pula Airport.** ☎ *060/308–308* 🌐 *www.airport-pula.hr.* **Rijeka Airport.** ☎ *051/841–222* 🌐 *www.rijeka-airport.hr.* **Split Airport.** ☎ *021/203–555* 🌐 *www.split-airport.hr.* **Zadar Airport.** ☎ *023/205–800* 🌐 *www.zadar-airport.hr.* **Zagreb Airport.** ☎ *060/320–320* 🌐 *www.zagreb-airport.hr.*

GROUND TRANSPORTATION

Ground transportation to major cities from airports in Croatia is well organized and user-friendly; shuttle buses and taxis operate at most airports all year long.

Contacts Atlas. ☎ *12/415–611* 🌐 *www.atlas-croatia.com.*

FLIGHTS

There are no direct air connections between the United States and Croatia, though some U.S.-based airlines offer code-share flights through their European travel partners. Travelers from the United States must fly into a major European hub such as Amsterdam, London, Frankfurt, Budapest, Prague, Vienna, or Warsaw and then transfer to a flight to Zagreb, Split, or Dubrovnik. Several European airlines, in addition to the national carrier, offer connections to Croatia.

Traveling to Croatia using a combination of a major airline and a low-cost European airline is a good idea. If you are traveling to Istria or Kvarner, a budget flight to nearby Venice (2½ hours by car) or Trieste (1½ hours to Rijeka by car) is a sound option. Most of these discount airlines sell tickets only on the Internet. Just be aware that so-called London-based discount airlines rarely fly from Heathrow (more often it's Gatwick or Stansted). All these airlines have stringent baggage limits and offer few free in-flight services, if any. And if you transfer from a major airline to a discounter, you will have to reclaim your bags and recheck them, so make sure you leave plenty of time between your flights.

BOAT AND FERRY TRAVEL

Several companies run ferries between Italy and Croatia, the largest being the national carrier, Jadrolinija. The most popular route is Ancona to Split (9–10 hours) or Zadar (6 hours), with up to 10 crossings weekly through the summer from Jadrolinija and Italian-based company SNAV. Farther south, a Jadrolinija ferry travels four times weekly between Bari and Dubrovnik (7–10 hours). Up the coast, Trieste Lines operates a high-speed ferry between Trieste and ports in Istria including Rovinj (1 hour 30 minutes), Pula (2 hours 45 minutes), and Porec (1 hour), while Venezia Lines and Atlas

Kompas connect those same Istrian ports with Venice (3–4 hours). Trieste Lines also connects Piran in Slovenia with Porec, Pula, and Rovinj (1–2 hours).

If you're planning to travel to the islands, it's worth noting that local ferries are quick and cheap for foot passengers, whereas car passengers might end up waiting hours for a spot in high season while paying quadruple the price.

Information Direct Ferries. *www.directferries.co.uk.* **Jadrolinija.** *051/666–111* *www.jadrolinija.hr.* **SNAV.** *081/428–5555 in Italy* *www.snav.it.* **Trieste Lines.** *0923/873–813* *www.triestelines.it.* **Venezia Lines.** *052/422–896* *www.venezialines.com.*

BUS TRAVEL

Bus travel in Croatia is inexpensive, efficient, and the best way to travel long distances. You can generally reach even the smallest towns by public bus, while larger cities are connected by regular, comfortable, and usually air-conditioned coaches. Many companies travel similar routes, meaning there are often a couple of options a day to most places you want to go. You can usually just show up and buy a ticket at the station or from the driver, but during the summer it's best to buy tickets at least a couple of days in advance for the major routes (between Zagreb and the coast, or Dubrovnik and Split, for example). On some routes you have to pay for each piece of luggage you put in the hold (typically about 7 Kn per bag), so make sure to carry some small change (you usually have to pay a few kunas for the toilets in the station as well). Be aware that seating is assigned if you book in advance, but not if you buy your ticket on the spot; however, other than busy buses, seat reservations are not usually adhered to.

GetByBus is an excellent resource for checking routes and timetables and buying tickets in advance.

FlixBus. Flixbus is a German bus company that operates many routes around Croatia that can be booked online and combined with international bus passes. Their buses are generally comfortable, air-conditioned, and have free Wi-Fi onboard. *030/300–137–300* *www.flixbus.com.*

GetByBus. *www.getbybus.com.*

CAR TRAVEL

GASOLINE

Most gas stations are open daily from 6 am to 8 pm; from June through September, many stations are open until 10 pm. In the bigger cities and on main international roads, stations offer 24-hour service. All pumps sell Eurosuper 95, Eurosuper 98, and Eurodiesel.

PARKING

In Croatia the historic centers of walled medieval towns along the coast (Split, Trogir, Hvar, Korčula, and Dubrovnik) are completely closed to traffic, putting heavy pressure on the number of parking spaces outside the fortifications. Most towns mark parking spaces with a blue line and a sign denoting time restrictions. Buy a ticket at the closest parking machine and leave it in the front window; make sure to have change on you because not all parking machines take bills or cards. Because parking is limited, it can also be expensive (particularly in Dubrovnik).

ROAD CONDITIONS

The A1 highway that links Zagreb with Rijeka, Zadar, and Split is fast and has frequent, well-maintained rest stops. Construction is still underway to connect Dubrovnik to the highway, but for now it stretches only to Ploče, and the remaining 100 km (62 miles) to Dubrovnik is done by winding coastal road. Roads in Slavonia are typically flat, well marked, and well maintained. During winter, driving through the inland regions of Gorski Kotar and Lika is occasionally made hazardous by heavy snow. It's advisable not to take a car to the islands, but if you do decide to drive, remember that the

TRAVEL TIMES FROM ZAGREB BY CAR		
Zadar	3 hours	285 km (177 miles)
Pula	3½ hours	264 km (164 miles)
Rijeka	2 hours	160 km (99 miles)
Split	4 hours	408 km (253 miles)
Dubrovnik	7½ hours	550 km (341 miles)
Osijek	2½ hours	283 km (175 miles)
Kotor	8 hours	690 km (428 miles)

roads are narrow, twisty, and unevenly maintained.

ROADSIDE EMERGENCIES

In case of a breakdown, contact your rental agency or the Croatian Automobile Club, which offers 24/7 roadside assistance.

Emergency Services Croatia. ☎ *987* 🌐 *www.hak.hr.*

RULES OF THE ROAD

Croatians drive on the right and follow rules similar to those in other European countries. Speed limits are 50 kph (30 mph) in urban areas, 90 kph (55 mph) in the outskirts, 110 kph (68 mph) on main roads, and 130 kph (80 mph) on motorways. Seatbelts are compulsory. The permitted blood-alcohol limit is 0.05%; drunk driving is punishable and can lead to severe fines. Talking on the phone while driving is prohibited unless the driver is using a hands-free device.

DRIVING TIMES

The A1 Highway connecting Zagreb to Rijeka, Zadar, and Split is the fastest route to Kvarner and Central Dalmatia. If traveling farther south to Dubrovnik, you will switch to the coastal road that passes through a 22 km (13 miles) section of Bosnia and Herzegovina, which can mean delays at the border.

CAR RENTAL

It is possible to rent a car very cheaply in Croatia, for as little as €5 a day (excluding insurance). Most major car rental companies are represented in the main tourist areas and airports, but you'll find the best rates online; check the website Auto Europe for the best deals.

In Croatia an International Driver's Permit is desirable but not necessary to rent a car from a major agency; a valid driver's license is all you'll need. The minimum age required for renting is usually 23 or older, and some companies also have maximum ages; be sure to inquire when making your arrangements.

If you intend to drive across a border, ask about restrictions on driving into other countries. Also, when you reserve a car, ask about cancellation penalties, taxes, drop-off charges (if you're planning to pick up the car in one city and leave it in another), and surcharges (for being under or over a certain age, for additional drivers, or for driving across state or country borders or beyond a specific distance from your point of rental). All these things can add substantially to your costs. Request car seats and extras such as GPS when you book.

Finally, make sure that a confirmed reservation guarantees you a car; agencies sometimes overbook, particularly for busy weekends and holiday periods.

CAR-RENTAL INSURANCE

If you own a car, your personal auto insurance may cover a rental to some degree, though not all policies protect you abroad; always read the fine print. If you don't have auto insurance, then seriously consider buying Collision Damage Waiver (CDW), which eliminates your liability for damage to the car. Some credit cards offer CDW coverage, but it's usually supplemental to your own insurance and rarely covers SUVs, minivans, luxury models, and the like. If your coverage is secondary, you may still be liable for loss-of-use costs from the car-rental company. But no credit-card insurance is valid unless you use that card for *all* transactions, from reserving to paying the final bill.

Some rental agencies require you to purchase CDW coverage; many will even include it in quoted rates. All will strongly encourage you to buy CDW—possibly implying that it's required—so be sure to ask about such things before renting. In most cases it's cheaper to add a supplemental CDW plan to your comprehensive travel-insurance policy *(see Trip Insurance under Essentials)* than to purchase it from a rental company.

CRUISE TRAVEL

Dubrovnik, Split, Hvar, and Korčula are common port calls for Eastern Mediterranean cruises. Small ships cruise up and down the country's coastline. *For more information on cruising in Croatia, see "Sailing and Cruising in Croatia" in Chapter 1, Experience Croatia.*

TRAIN TRAVEL

The train is a great option for getting to and from Croatia, with direct international connections with Austria, Germany, Hungary, Slovenia and Switzerland. However, within Croatia trains are typically slower than buses and there are far fewer of them. Many routes operate intermittently, particularly through the summer when fewer locals use the service, and less-used stations have fallen into disrepair. The bus is a better option along the coast, but if you're travelling around the mainland it's worthwhile to compare both options, just in case the train timetable suits you better.

ESSENTIALS

ACCOMMODATIONS

You can find any type of accommodation you like in Croatia, from five-star hotels to hostels, private villas to Airbnb. In Zagreb, Istria, and Dalmatia, standards (and sometimes prices) are as high as those in Western Europe, while in less busy regions, such as Slavonia, you might not be spoiled for choice but you can always find something suitable (and the prices are far lower).

On the coast, prices are at their highest in July and August, and apart from the large hotels, often fully booked. On the other hand, outside of the high season, you can usually find a real bargain for places that might be totally out of your budget through the summer; another great reason to consider traveling to Croatia in the shoulder months. Booking.com is the most popular website for booking hotels in Croatia, although you'll often get a better price if you book directly with the hotel.

The lodgings we list are the cream of the crop in each price category. Properties are assigned price categories based on the range from their least expensive standard double room at high season (excluding holidays) to the most expensive.

All foreign guests have to pay a tourist tax for each night they stay in a hotel or private accommodation. It's a negligible amount, between 2 Kn and 7 Kn per night depending on the hotel category and the season, and it's most often just added to your bill.

Be sure you understand the hotel's cancellation policy. Some places allow you to cancel without any kind of penalty—even if you prepaid to secure a discounted rate—if you cancel at least 24 hours in advance. Others require you to cancel a week in advance or penalize you the cost of one night. Small inns and B&Bs are most likely to require you to cancel far in advance. Most hotels allow children under a certain age to stay in their parents' room at no extra charge, but others charge for them as extra adults; find out the cutoff age for discounts.

APARTMENT AND VILLA RENTALS

Private accommodation has always been popular, especially along the coast, when grandmothers used to wait at the bus station with faded photos of their room for rent. In recent years the number of private beds has skyrocketed in places like Dubrovnik, and you can now find everything from a single bed in a family home to a fully renovated five-star apartment. Private villas are also very popular in Istria and Dalmatia and a great option if you are traveling in a group or as a family; these restored stone houses usually have private swimming pools and kitchens, and are a wonderful chance to stay off the beaten track and interact with locals. There are many websites where you can book private accommodation; start with Booking.com, HomeAway, Airbnb, and Croatian Villas.

Croatia Specialists Airbnb. 🌐 *www.airbnb.com.* **Booking.com.** 🌐 *www.booking.com.* **Croatian Villas.** 🌐 *www.croatianvillas.com.* **HomeAway.** 🌐 *www.homeaway.com.*

COMMUNICATIONS

INTERNET

Wi-Fi service has become indispensable in Croatia, and you will have to be on an island pretty far out or way in the hinterlands of Lika or Slavonia not to find some signal. Most of the bigger cities (Zagreb, Rijeka, Split, Dubrovnik) offer free Wi-Fi in the busiest city zones, and most coffee shops, restaurants, and hotels will offer complimentary reception to their guests and patrons.

PHONES

It's getting less and less easy to make plans without access to a smartphone; even the most local of apartment owners might ask you to WhatsApp them when you arrive into town. Roaming costs can be enormous if you use your phone from home; the good news is that roaming fees have recently been abolished throughout the EU, so if you have a SIM card from another European country you can use it in Croatia too. If you don't have a European SIM, you can either buy an international SIM card before leaving home, or bring an unlocked mobile phone with you (ask your provider to unlock it for you) and pick up a cheap local SIM card in Croatia. You'll then have a local number and can make local calls at local rates, as well as having some data allowance. The largest local networks in Croatia are VIPnet, Tele2, and T-Mobile; just pop into one of their shops to pick up a SIM. If you run out of credit, you can top up at any local newsstand.

CALLING WITHIN CROATIA

To make a local call in Croatia, dial the area code (if you are not already in that area) followed by the number you wish to reach.

Area and country codes are as follows: Croatia (385), Dubrovnik (20), Split (21), Zagreb (1), Rijeka (51), Pula and Istria (52), Osijek (31).

CALLING OUTSIDE CROATIA

To make an international call out of Croatia, dial "00," then the appropriate country code (Australia 61; Canada 1; United States 1; and United Kingdom 44).

CUSTOMS AND DUTIES

You're always allowed to bring goods of a certain value back home without having to pay any duty or import tax. But there's a limit on the amount of tobacco and liquor you can bring back duty-free, and some countries have separate limits for perfumes; for exact figures, check with your customs department. The values of so-called duty-free goods are included in these amounts. When you shop abroad, save all your receipts, as customs inspectors may ask to see them as well as the items you purchased. If the total value of your goods is more than the duty-free limit, you'll have to pay a tax (most often a flat percentage) on the value of everything beyond that limit.

As with most European countries, you can import duty-free 200 cigarettes, one liter of spirits, and two liters of wine into Croatia. Foreign citizens can bring personal items into the country without paying customs taxes.

EATING OUT

Food in Croatia varies by region. In general, fish dominates along the coast and meat rules the interior; that said, one of the most popular dishes in Dalmatia is veal *peka* while the must-try dish in Slavonia is fish *paprikaš*. *For information on food-related health issues, see Health below*

MEALS AND MEALTIMES

As the working day begins early here (with some offices opening as early as 7:30 am on weekdays), you'll find cafés open early as well. Lunch is usually served between noon and 3 in restaurants, and dinner is most often served after 7. In the height of the tourist season at the coast, restaurants may stay open later (after 10pm) to handle the volume. *Bifes* (stand-up take-out places) are open most of the day and serve both hot and cold food.

Unless otherwise noted, the restaurants listed in this guide are open daily for lunch and dinner.

PAYING

Credit cards are becoming more and more accepted, but it's a good idea to ask before you order, just in case. ATMs are found in abundance on the Croatian coast, as well as in Zagreb, so you can usually ensure that dinner goes on as planned. The tip should not be included in the bill, so scrutinize any bill that appears to add one. If service has been good, a 10% to 15% gratuity will be appreciated by the waitstaff.

RESERVATIONS AND DRESS

Regardless of where you are, it's a good idea to make a reservation if you really want to eat at a particular restaurant. We mention them specifically only when reservations are essential or when they are not accepted. Large parties should always call ahead to check the reservations policy. We mention dress only when men are required to wear a jacket or a jacket and tie.

WINE, BEER AND SPIRITS

Wine is produced in Croatia and enjoyed regularly with meals. Most Croatian wineries don't export their wines, so tasting here is a good idea, since you're unlikely to find them at home. Croatia produces wine in Istria, Slavonia, and most of the Dalmatian coast, especially the Pelješac peninsula. The traditional aperitif in this part of the world is *rakija,* a fruit or herbal spirit made in abundance. It's quite cheap to buy and varies greatly in quality. The fruit varieties (pear, blueberry, plum) are drinkable enough as an aperitif; the herbals are a bit rough going down. Many establishments brew their own with great pride. If you're staying in a family-run pension, trying some of the home brew is an instant icebreaker.

ELECTRICITY

CROATIA ELECTRICITY

Electricity in Croatia is 220 volts; the country uses standard European plugs with two round prongs. Consider making a small investment in a universal adapter, which has several types of plugs in one lightweight, compact unit. Most laptops and mobile phone chargers are dual voltage (i.e., they operate equally well on 110 and 220 volts), so require only an adapter. These days the same is true of small appliances such as hair dryers. Always check labels and manufacturer instructions to be sure. Don't use 110-volt outlets marked "for shavers only" for high-wattage appliances such as hair dryers.

EMERGENCIES

Embassy in Croatia **U.S. Embassy.** ✉ *Ulica Thomasa Jeffersona 2, Zagreb* ☎ *01/661–2300* 🌐 *www.usembassy.hr.*

HEALTH

Water is safe for drinking throughout Croatia. EU countries have reciprocal health-care agreements with Croatia, entitling those nationals to medical consultation for a basic minimum fee. Citizens from outside the EU have to pay in accordance with listed prices. Most doctors speak some English.

OVER-THE-COUNTER REMEDIES

In Croatia, over-the-counter medications are sold in pharmacies, which are open until 6 or 7 pm on weekdays and 1 or 2 pm on Saturday. In each town there is usually a 24-hour pharmacy for emergencies. Most European pharmacists speak a word or two of English or German, but you're better off asking for a remedy by its medical name (e.g., ibuprofen) than its brand name (e.g., Advil). Pharmacies don't have a lot of open shelf space for goods, so you will have to ask the pharmacist for what you want. In both countries paracetemol (and its brand name Panadol) is more recognized than acetaminophen (and the brand name Tylenol) for basic pain relief. Claritin, the allergy relief medication, is sold in Croatia by that name at the pharmacy. Many products that Americans would normally find in their local drugstore—cough syrup, diaper cream, cough drops, muscle cream, and vitamins, to name a few—must be bought in the pharmacy in Croatia. While this system is inconvenient, if you get an allergy attack in the middle of the night, the upside is that prices are kept down by the government, so many things will be a fraction of the cost at home. The word for pharmacy in Croatia is *ljekarna,* but stick to the equally understood *apoteka.*

SHOTS AND MEDICATIONS

If you travel a lot internationally—particularly to developing nations—refer to the CDC's *Health Information for International Travel* (aka Traveler's Health Yellow Book). Info from it is posted on the CDC website (*www.cdc.gov/travel/yb*), or you can buy a copy from your local bookstore for $24.95.

Health Warnings World Health Organization (*WHO*). *www.who.int.*

HOURS OF OPERATION

In Croatia business hours are from 8:30 to 4. Banks are open in all the main cities weekdays from 8 to 7, and on Saturday from 8 to noon; in smaller towns banks have shorter hours and are often closed during lunchtime. Post offices are open weekdays 7 to 7, and on Saturday from 7 to noon; in smaller towns post offices are open shorter hours, sometimes only in the morning. During the high tourist season (June through September), post offices are generally open until 8 pm, including Saturday. In Zagreb, shops and department stores are open weekdays 8 to 8, and on Saturday from 8 to 1. Malls and shopping centers are typically open 9 to 8, seven days a week. Along the coast most shops are open weekdays from 8 to 1 and 5 to 8, Saturday from 8 to 1. On the islands hours vary greatly from place to place, but usually at least one general store will be open Monday through Saturday for essentials.

HOLIDAYS

In Croatia, national holidays include the following: January 1 (New Year's Day); January 6 (Epiphany); Easter Sunday and Monday; May 1 (May Day); Corpus Christi (40 days after Easter); June 22 (Anti-fascist Day); June 25 (Statehood Day); August 5 (National Thanksgiving Day); August 15 (Assumption), October 8 (Independence Day), November 1 (All Saints' Day), December 25 and 26 (Christmas).

MONEY

Costs for goods and services are slightly cheaper than those of Western Europe, mostly because Croatia is not on the euro. Zagreb and the coastal areas are substantially more expensive than areas inland such as Slavonia. Groceries can be expensive at shops on the islands, so if you've rented an apartment for a week or more, consider buying some staples at one of the hypermarkets in a bigger city.

ITEM	AVERAGE COST
Cup of coffee	$2.25
Glass of wine	$5
Glass of beer	$3
Sandwich	$3
1-mile taxi ride in capital city	$4
Museum admission	$3–$5
Based on an exchange rate of 6.2 Kn to US$1, effective at the time of writing.	

Prices throughout this guide are given for adults. Substantially reduced fees are almost always available for children, students, and senior citizens.

U.S. banks seldom have Croatian currency on hand, and it may take as long as a week to order. If you're planning to exchange funds before leaving home, don't wait till the last minute.

ATMS AND BANKS

Your own bank will probably charge a fee for using ATMs abroad; the foreign bank you use may also charge a fee. Nevertheless, you'll usually get a better rate of exchange at an ATM than you will at a currency-exchange office or even when changing money in a bank. And extracting funds as you need them is a safer option than carrying around a large amount of cash.

ATMs are found throughout Croatia, islands included. PINs with more than four digits are not recognized at ATMs in many countries. If yours has five or more, try to change it before you leave.

CREDIT CARDS

It's a good idea to inform your credit-card company before you travel, especially if you're going abroad and don't travel internationally very often. Otherwise, the credit-card company might put a hold on your card owing to unusual activity—not a good thing halfway through your trip. Record all your credit-card numbers—as well as the phone numbers to call if your cards are lost or stolen—in a safe place, so you're prepared should something go wrong. Both MasterCard and Visa have general numbers you can call (collect if you're abroad) if your card is lost, but you're better off calling the number of your issuing bank, because MasterCard and Visa usually just transfer you to your bank; your bank's number is usually printed on your card.

If you plan to use your credit card for cash advances, you'll need to apply for a PIN at least two weeks before your trip. Although it's usually cheaper (and safer) to use a credit card abroad for large purchases (so you can cancel payments or be reimbursed if there's a problem), note that some credit-card companies *and* the banks that issue them add substantial percentages to all foreign transactions, whether they're in a foreign currency or not. Check on these fees before leaving home, so there won't be any surprises when you get the bill.

Before you charge something, ask the merchant whether he or she plans to do a dynamic currency conversion (DCC). In such a transaction the credit-card *processor* (shop, restaurant, or hotel, not Visa or MasterCard) converts the currency and charges you in dollars. In most cases you'll pay the merchant a 3% fee for this service in addition to any credit-card company and issuing-bank foreign-transaction surcharges.

Dynamic currency conversion programs are becoming increasingly widespread. Merchants who participate in them are supposed to ask whether you want to be charged in dollars or the local currency, but they don't always do so. And even if they do offer you a choice, they may well avoid mentioning the additional surcharges. The good news is that you *do* have a choice. And if this practice really gets your goat, you can avoid it entirely thanks to American Express; with its cards, DCC simply isn't an option.

Major credit cards are accepted in most hotels, shops, and restaurants, but make sure to have some cash on you for smaller groceries, toilet stops if you're traveling, and ice cream breaks. Some private accommodations will accept credit cards, although cash payments will likely get you a little discount.

CURRENCY AND EXCHANGE

The Croatian currency is called the kuna (Kn), which is made up of 100 lipa. The kuna is not yet fully convertible, so you cannot expect to readily buy the currency outside of Croatia or exchange it once outside the country.

Most hotels in Croatia are also priced in euros and some will accept euros as payment.

For the most favorable rates, change money through banks. Although ATM transaction fees may be higher abroad than at home, ATM rates are excellent because they are based on wholesale rates offered only by major banks. You won't do as well at exchange booths in airports or rail and bus stations, in hotels, in restaurants, or in stores.

Even if a currency-exchange booth has a sign promising no commission, rest assured that there's some kind of huge, hidden fee. (Oh ... that's right. The sign didn't say no *fee.*). And as for rates, you're almost always better off getting foreign currency at an ATM or exchanging money at a bank.

PASSPORTS AND VISAS

U.S. citizens do not need visas to enter Croatia for a typical vacation visit.

RESTROOMS

Public restrooms can be found in most cities in Croatia, usually near high traffic areas like markets, bus or train stations, and beaches. Where there are permanent facilities, a price is usually posted outside (between 3 to 6 Kn), and an attendant is on hand to accept payment. At some places by the seaside, coin-operated portable toilets are common, especially in the busy summer season. Make sure you have small coins handy.

SAFETY

Croatia is relatively safe by Western standards, and there are no particular local scams that visitors should be aware of. Violent crime is rare. Be on guard for pickpockets in crowded markets, and don't wander alone down dark streets at night.

Distribute your cash, credit cards, IDs, and other valuables between a deep front pocket, an inside jacket or vest pocket, and a hidden money pouch.

TAXES

In Croatia foreigners who spend over 740 Kn in one store on a single day can reclaim the V.A.T. (value added tax) upon leaving the country. To do this, you need to present the receipts and the goods bought at the *carina* (customs) desk at the airport, ferry port, or border crossing on your way out of the country.

When making a purchase, ask for a V.A.T. refund form and find out whether the merchant gives refunds—not all stores do, nor are they required to. Have the form stamped like any customs form by customs officials when you leave the country or, if you're visiting several European Union countries, when you leave the EU. After you're through passport control, take the form to a refund-service counter for an on-the-spot refund (which is usually the quickest and easiest option), or mail it to the address on the form (or the envelope with it) after you arrive home. You receive the total refund stated on the form, but the processing time can be long, especially if you request a credit-card adjustment.

Global Blue is a Europe-wide service with 225,000 affiliated stores and more than 700 refund counters at major airports and border crossings. Its refund form, called a Tax Free Check, is the most common across the European continent. The service issues refunds in the form of cash, check, or credit-card adjustment.

V.A.T. Refunds Global Blue. *www.global-blue.com.*

TIME

Croatia is on Central European Time (CET), one hour ahead of Greenwich Mean Time and six hours ahead of the Eastern time zone of the United States.

TIPPING

When eating out in Croatia, if you have enjoyed your meal and are satisfied with the service, it is customary to leave a 10% to 15% tip. It is not usual to tip in cafés or bars. Maids and taxi drivers are not usually tipped. Tour guides do receive a tip, especially if they are particularly good. For porters on trains and bellhops at hotels, 5 Kn to 10 Kn per bag will be appreciated.

TOURS

Guided tours are a great option when you don't want to do it all yourself. You travel with a group (sometimes large, sometimes small), stay in prebooked hotels, eat with your fellow travelers (the cost of meals is sometimes included in the price of your tour, sometimes not), and follow a schedule. These days you can find a tour to suit whatever your interests may be, whether you're in Croatia for the food, wine, biking, sea, or history. The companies listed here are reliable and fun and cover a wide range of destinations and travel styles across Croatia.

Backroads. Cycling tours are extremely popular in Croatia, and this company for active travelers is one of the best. 🌐 *www.backroads.com.*

Intrepid Travel. Intrepid Travel is a well-respected company with a strong emphasis on sustainable travel. They specialize in small-group tours and cover a wide range of activities in Croatia, from sailing and cycling the islands to visiting the national parks inland. They use 100% local guides and focus on authentic, off-the-beaten-track experiences. 🌐 *www.intrepidtravel.com.*

Peregrine Adventures. A premium adventure company with small group sizes, local guides, and a wide range of tours across Croatia, including sailing and overland trips. 🌐 *www.peregrineadventures.com.*

Trafalgar Travel. A longstanding company known for its knowledgeable guides with itineraries across Croatia, Slovenia, and the Balkans. 🌐 *www.trafalgar.com.*

Tureta Travel. A boutique Zagreb-based company specializing in tailor-made tours to all corners of Croatia. 🌐 *www.tureta-travel.com.*

TRIP INSURANCE

We believe that comprehensive trip insurance is especially valuable if you're booking a very expensive or complicated trip (particularly to an isolated region) or if you're booking far in advance. Comprehensive travel policies typically cover trip cancellation and interruption, letting you cancel or cut your trip short because of a personal emergency, illness, or, in some cases, acts of terrorism in your destination. Such policies also cover evacuation and medical care. Some also cover you for trip delays because of bad weather or mechanical problems as well as for lost or delayed baggage. Another type of coverage to look for is financial default—that is, when your trip is disrupted because a tour operator, airline, or cruise line goes out of business. Generally you must buy this when you book your trip or shortly thereafter, and it's available to you only if your operator isn't on a list of excluded companies.

When making your choice, consider what you're already covered for back home. You might have some auto insurance through your credit card or regular car insurance. Credit cards also occasionally provide a level of emergency medical coverage. Similarly, your homeowner's insurance may cover your belongings overseas. When it comes to health care, EU citizens are covered for emergency health treatment in Croatia. For non-Europeans, Medicare and most private health insurance plans don't cover you in Croatia; check if there is a reciprocal agreement between your country and Croatia for emergency medical care.

Consider buying medical-only coverage at the very least. EU citizens are covered for emergency health care in Croatia, but neither Medicare nor some private insurers cover medical expenses abroad; check if there is a reciprocal agreement between your country and Croatia. Medical-only policies typically reimburse you for medical care (excluding that related to preexisting conditions) and hospitalization abroad, and provide for evacuation. However, you still have to pay the bills and await reimbursement from the insurer.

VISITOR INFORMATION

ONLINE RESOURCES

The first place to start to plan a trip to Croatia is the Croatian National Tourist Board's website. In addition to a general overview of the culture and history of the country, it has lots of practical information on accommodations, travel agencies, and events. Then consult Regional Tourist Board sites to narrow the focus even further.

Contacts Croatia National Tourist Board. 🌐 *www.croatia.hr.* **Dalmatia Region.** 🌐 *www.dalmatia.hr.* **Istria Region.** 🌐 *www.istra.hr.* **Kvarner Region.** 🌐 *www.kvarner.hr.*

INDEX

PHOTO CREDITS

Front cover: xbrchx/iStockphoto [Description: Hvar waterfront, Croatia]. **Back cover,** from left to right: Sergey Novikov / Shutterstock; ailenn/Shutterstock; Dziewul I Dreamstime.com. **Spine:** Zocchi Roberto / Shutterstock. **Top Experiences:** 1, Ivica Drusany / Shutterstock. 2, anshar / Shutterstock. 4, Anton_Ivanov / Shutterstock. 5, Anton_Ivanov / Shutterstock. 5 (top), Alexey Stiop / Shutterstock. 5 (bottom), Dziewul I Dreamstime.com. 6 (top left), K13 ART / Shutterstock. 6 (bottom left), stjepann / Shutterstock. 6 (top right), Ken Gillham / age fotostock. 6 (bottom), Ivica Drusany / Shutterstock. 7 (top), Liane Matrisch / age fotostock. 7 (bottom), Funkystock / age fotostock. 8 (top left), DavorLovincic/iStockphoto. 8 (top right), parkerphotography / Alamy. 8 (bottom), Florin Stana / Shutterstock. **Chapter 1: Experience Croatia:** 13, Alexey Stiop / Shutterstock. 20, Tatiana Popova / Shutterstock. 21, Rudolf Abraham / Alamy. **Chapter 2: Zagreb and Environs:** 35, funkyfood London - Paul Williams / Alamy. **Chapter 3: Slavonia:** 79, Attila JANDI / Shutterstock. **Chapter 4: Istria:** 105, Hemis / Alamy. **Chapter 5: Kvarner:** 143, Funkystock / age fotostock. **Chapter 6: Zadar and Northern Dalmatia:** 179, Tibor Bognár. **Chapter 7: Split and Central Dalmatia:** 211, xbrchx / Shutterstock. **Chapter 8: Dubrovnik and Southern Dalmatia:** 257, Jan Wlodarczyk / age fotostock. **Chapter 9: Montenegro:** 297, Florin Stana / Shutterstock. **About Our Writers:** All photos are courtesy of the writers except for the following: Frank Galparsoro & Vera Brljevic, courtesy of Siniša Gulić; Elizabeth Gowing, courtesy of Jonada Jashari; Jadranka and Armando Rodriguez, courtesy of Matija Elena Rodriguez.

Fodor's ESSENTIAL CROATIA

Editorial: Douglas Stallings, *Editorial Director*; Margaret Kelly, Jacinta O'Halloran, *Senior Editors*; Kayla Becker, Alexis Kelly, and Amanda Sadlowski, *Editors*; Teddy Minford, *Content Editor*; Rachael Roth, *Content Manager*

Design: Tina Malaney, *Design and Production Director;* Jessica Gonzalez, *Production Designer*

Photography: Jennifer Arnow, *Senior Photo Editor*

Maps: Rebecca Baer, *Senior Map Editor*; David Lindroth, Mark Stroud, *Cartographers*

Production: Jennifer DePrima, *Editorial Production Manager*; Carrie Parker, *Senior Production Editor*; Elyse Rozelle, *Production Editor*; David Satz, *Director of Content Production*

Business & Operations: Chuck Hoover, *Chief Marketing Officer*; Joy Lai, *Vice President and General Manager*; Stephen Horowitz, *Director of Business Development and Revenue Operations;* Tara McCrillis, *Director of Publishing Operations;* Eliza D. Aceves, *Content Operations Manager and Strategist*

Public Relations and Marketing: Joe Ewaskiw, *Manager;* Esther Su, *Marketing Manager*

Writers: Vera Brljevic, Sierra Christianson, Francois Galparsoro, Elizabeth Gowing, Elizabeth Hughes, Robert Komljen, Andrea MacDonald, Ivan Verunica

Editor: Margaret Kelly

Production Editor: Jennifer DePrima

1st Edition

ISBN 978-1-64097-016-8

ISSN 2574–352X

PRINTED IN THE UNITED STATES OF AMERICA

10 9 8 7 6 5 4 3 2 1

ABOUT OUR WRITERS

Frank Galparsoro and Vera Brljevic are founders of the FrankAboutCroatia Blog, a leading Croatian travel blog. Navigation officer by vocation, and travel writer by profession, Frank traveled to all corners of the world before settling down in Croatia. After she graduated from the University, Vera sailed the high seas, and lived in Canada before returning to her native Croatia where she now works in the hotel industry. They are travelers, writers, polyglots, avid cyclists, coffee addicts, and food and wine enthusiasts.

Elizabeth Gowing worked as a teacher in inner-city London before moving to Kosovo in 2006, and from there to Albania in 2013. She is co-founder of Kosovan charity The Ideas Partnership which harnesses the power of volunteers to tackle challenges in the environment, the promotion of cultural heritage, and support to Roma communities. She is the translator of three books from Albanian to English and author of *Travels in Blood and Honey: Becoming a Beekeeper in Kosovo,* and *Edith and I: On the Trail of an Edwardian Traveller in Kosovo,* about inspiring Balkan traveler Edith Durham.

After meeting in Bosnia in the aftermath of the Yugoslav wars, **Elizabeth Hughes and Robert Komljen** eventually decided to make their home in Croatia. Born and raised in central Bosnia, Robert is a metallurgic engineer. He finds it ironic that he is the one in the family whose bags are most often packed, as he traverses the deserts of the Middle East and the hills of Europe visiting aluminum factories. And although Elizabeth long ago retired her army combat boots, she often draws on her military experience to raise two boys while living in a former communist country that challenges her independent spirit.

Within ten minutes of her first arrival in Croatia **Andrea MacDonald**, mesmerized by the stunning old architecture and gorgeous locals, decided to rip up her return ticket and stay. She has since worked at a hostel in Istria learning the proper way to fold bed sheets, spent two summers guiding boat tours around the Dalmatian islands, and wrote a master's thesis about her travels around this wonderfully surprising country. These days, she divides her time between Croatia and her native Canada, leading tour groups around Europe and searching the rest of the world for a sea as beautiful as the Adriatic.

Sierra and Ivan Verunica are a Seattleite-Croatian couple who met, as passionate travel professionals would, at the border of Chile and Bolivia. They run INCroatia, an education and sports travel company that shows thousands of young people that Croatia is not just the sun and the sea. Understanding the important balance of work and play they can often be found outdoors, at local festivals, or planning an adventure.